Pro JSF and Ajax

Building Rich Internet Components

Jonas Jacobi and John R. Fallows

Apress®

Pro JSF and Ajax: Building Rich Internet Components

ISBN-13: 978-1-59059-580-0

ISBN-10: 1-59059-580-7

Printed and bound in the United States of America 9 8 7 6 5 4 3 2

Lead Editor: Tony Davis
Technical Reviewers: Peter Lubbers, Kito D. Mann, Matthias Wessendorf
Editorial Board: Steve Anglin, Dan Appleman, Ewan Buckingham, Gary Cornell, Jason Gilmore, Jonathan Hassell, James Huddleston, Chris Mills, Matthew Moodie, Dominic Shakeshaft, Jim Sumser, Matt Wade
Project Managers: Beckie Stones, Elizabeth Seymour
Copy Edit Manager: Nicole LeClerc
Copy Editor: Kim Wimpsett
Assistant Production Director: Kari Brooks-Copony
Production Editor: Laura Cheu
Compositor: Molly Sharp, ContentWorks
Proofreader: Elizabeth Berry
Indexer: Carol Burbo
Artist: Kinetic Publishing Services, LLC
Cover Designer: Kurt Krames
Manufacturing Director: Tom Debolski

Distributed to the book trade worldwide by Springer-Verlag New York, Inc., 233 Spring Street, 6th Floor, New York, NY 10013. Phone 1-800-SPRINGER, fax 201-348-4505, e-mail `orders-ny@springer-sbm.com`, or visit `http://www.springeronline.com`.

For information on translations, please contact Apress directly at 2560 Ninth Street, Suite 219, Berkeley, CA 94710. Phone 510-549-5930, fax 510-549-5939, e-mail `info@apress.com`, or visit `http://www.apress.com`.

The source code for this book is available to readers at `http://www.apress.com` in the Source Code Section.

To the love of my life, Marianne,
and our princesses, Emma and Isabelle,
for keeping my spirit up.
—Jonas Jacobi

To my wife, Nan, for her love, support, and patience,
and our son, Jack, for his natural inspiration.
—John R. Fallows

Contents at a Glance

Contents

PART 1 ■■■ Developing Smarter with JavaServer™ Faces

Foreword

Does the world really and truly need another JavaServer Faces book?

I was fairly well convinced the answer could only be a resounding "no!" After all, there are a good half-dozen books out in stores today, by a whole host of Web luminaries, and I've even personally helped as a technical reviewer on half of those. So what more could really be said on the subject?

But when I thought about this a bit more, it became clear that all of these books go only so far. They'll show you how to use what JSF gives you out of the box, throw you a bone for writing your own components and renderers, and give you maybe even a bit more. But none that I've seen get to the heart of why JSF is really and truly a cool and important technology; they make JSF look like YAMVCF (Yet Another Model-View-Controller Framework) for HTML—more powerful here and there, easier to use in many places, a bit harder to use in others, but really nothing major. And certainly nothing that takes us beyond the dull basics of building ordinary-looking Web applications.

This book goes a lot further. It covers the basics, of course, and shows you how to build components, but then it keeps going: on to Ajax, on to HTC, on to XUL—and how you can wrap up this alphabet soup underneath the heart of JSF, its component model, and how you can leverage it to finally develop Web applications that don't need radical rearchitecting every time the winds of client technologies blow in a different direction. Along the way, you'll learn a wide array of open source toolkits that make Web magic practical even when you're not a JavaScript guru.

So, heck, I'm convinced. The world *does* need another JSF book.

Adam Winer
JSF Expert Group Member and Java Champion

About the Authors

JONAS JACOBI is a J2EE and open source evangelist at Oracle.

A native of Sweden, Jonas has worked in the software industry for more than 15 years. Prior to joining Oracle, Jonas worked at several major Swedish software companies in management, consulting, development, and project management roles.

For the past three years, Jonas has been responsible for the product management of JavaServer Faces, Oracle ADF Faces, and Oracle ADF Faces Rich Client in the Oracle JDeveloper team.

Jonas is a popular speaker at international conferences such as Oracle OpenWorld, EclipseWorld, and JavaPolis, and he has written numerous articles for leading IT magazines such as *Java Developer's Journal, JavaPro,* and *Oracle Magazine*. Jonas has also contributed to the online appendix of *JavaServer Faces in Action*, by Kito D. Mann (Manning, 2005), and was a technical reviewer of *Oracle JDeveloper 10g Handbook*, by Avrom Roy-Faderman, Peter Koletzke, and Paul Dorsey (McGraw-Hill Osborne, 2004).

Apart from spending his spare time working on open source projects such as Weblets, Mabon, and D^2, he likes golf, sailing, and fast cars (preferably driving them); he also enjoys spending time with his wife, Marianne, and his daughters, Emma and Isabelle.

JOHN R. FALLOWS is a JavaServer Faces technology architect at Oracle.

Originally from Northern Ireland, John graduated from Cambridge University in the United Kingdom and has worked in the software industry for more than ten years. Prior to joining Oracle, John worked as a research scientist for British Telecommunications Plc.

For the past four years, John has played a leading role in the Oracle ADF Faces team to influence the architecture of the JavaServer Faces standard and to extend the standard to provide Ajax functionality in the ADF Faces project.

John is an active participant in the open source community, contributing to both the Apache MyFaces project and the Apache Maven project. John is also leading three new open source projects on Java.net—Weblets, Mabon, and D^2—all of which evolved while researching the foundational technologies for this book.

Apart from spending his spare time writing articles about new and exciting technologies, John likes to play soccer with his friends and likes to spend time with his beautiful wife, Nan, and their wonderful son, Jack.

About the Technical Reviewers

PETER LUBBERS is an information architect at Oracle. A native of the Netherlands, Peter served as a Special Forces commando in the Royal Dutch Green Berets. Prior to joining Oracle, Peter architected and developed the internationalized Microsoft Office User Specialist (MOUS) testing framework. At Oracle, Peter develops automated help-authoring solutions. Three of these solutions are currently patent pending. He is also the author of the award-winning *Oracle Application Server Portal Configuration Guide* (Oracle, 2005).

KITO D. MANN is the editor-in-chief of JSF Central (`http://www.jsfcentral.com`) and the author of *JavaServer Faces in Action* (Manning, 2005). He is also a member of the JSF 1.2 and JSP 2.1 expert groups and principal consultant at Virtua, specializing in enterprise application architecture, development, mentoring, and JSF product strategy. Kito has consulted with several Fortune 500 clients, including Prudential Financial and J.P. Morgan Chase & Company, and he was recently the chief architect of an educational application service provider. He has a bachelor's degree in computer science from Johns Hopkins University.

MATTHIAS WESSENDORF is a PMC member of the Apache MyFaces project, a well-known JavaServer Faces implementation. Matthias is currently working as a Java Web developer in Germany, focusing on Web technologies such as JSF, Struts, Ajax, and XUL.

Matthias is the author of two developer handbooks, *Struts: Websites mit Struts 1.2 & 1.3 und Ajax effizient entwickeln* and *Web Services und mobile Clients: SOAP, WSDL, UDDI, J2ME, MIDlet, WAP & JSF*, and he has written numerous articles about JavaServer Faces for leading IT magazines in Germany.

Matthias is a frequent speaker at international conferences such as ApacheCon and JAX and also lectures in the Department of Computer Science at the University of Applied Sciences in Dortmund, Germany. During his limited spare time, he enjoys listening to electronic dance music and reading a good book.

Acknowledgments

After completing this book, we found ourselves wondering if we would do it again, and sure, we would! However, anyone who believes a book project is a simple single-author or small-team effort has never written a book. No first-time author, or authors, would be anything without guidance and tremendous support from family, friends, and colleagues.

Peter Zadrozny, thank you, thank you, and thank you! You introduced us to Apress, convinced Apress that this would be the book of the year, and then guided us through everything that newbie authors, like ourselves, needed to know. Without you and your guidance, we would never have taken the first steps toward becoming full-feathered authors.

We thank Apress and Tony Davis for giving us the opportunity to write this book and trusting Peter Zadrozny's instincts.

Peter Lubbers worked tirelessly to help us make this a better book. We owe you *big* time! Kito D. Mann, although he has an extremely busy schedule, took time from his family to provide us with his technical knowledge. Matthias Wessendorf was there from the very first draft to the final product, educating us about MyFaces and providing encouragement when it felt like we would never reach the end. Adam Winer, our ADF Faces colleague and a Java Champion, answered our questions on JSF 1.2 and made sure we kept our edge.

Elizabeth Seymour patiently answered all our questions about book-related and non-book-related issues. Kim Wimpsett helped us with grammar, spelling, and consistency throughout the book, and for this we are forever grateful. Laura Cheu patiently let us do last-, last-, and last-minute edits to text, code, and figures and patiently educated and guided us through the Apress process of finalizing our book. Without you, we would probably still be working on Chapter 4.

We would also like to thank our colleagues at Oracle Server Technologies for supporting us during this year and encouraging us to do our very best.

Jonas Jacobi and John R. Fallows

I have a list as long as any Oscar-winning actor or actress, but I only have so much space; if I've missed someone, you have my heartfelt apologies. I would first like to thank my good friend Peter Z'd for letting me in on the "how-to-make-your-family-happy-when-writing-a-book" secret and for always being there whenever I had doubts about this project.

To a true friend—John R. Fallows. I don't think my vocabulary has enough superlatives to describe my coauthor and colleague. I will be forever in his debt for all the knowledge I pulled out of him during long hours and for the patience and dedication he brought to this project; without John this would not have been possible.

To the most important person in my life, my wonderful wife, Marianne, without whom I wouldn't have been able to complete this book! To my beautiful daughters, Emma and Isabelle, for patiently waiting for me to come home and play.

Jonas Jacobi

I would first like to thank my very good friend and coauthor, Jonas Jacobi, for proposing that we work on this book together. Jonas has my deepest respect for his ability to consume highly detailed architectural knowledge and simplify it for the reader in a practical and entertaining way. There is no doubt that without Jonas this book would simply not have been possible.

To my amazing wife, Nan, whose endless patience and support made it possible for me to work on this book while she was pregnant with our son, Jack, and for the first six months of his life.

To my son, Jack, for those lovable deep laughs that made me smile no matter how tired I was.

To my dad, for always encouraging me to reach for the stars.

John R. Fallows

Introduction

Since JavaServer Faces first arrived on the Internet technology stage as the new standard for building Java-based Web applications, it has gained significant attention from the Java EE Web development community. Many developers are excited that they can use the standard JavaServer Faces HTML Basic `RenderKit` to create HTML-based Web applications, much as they did in the past with other technologies, such as Apache Struts. However, this is only the tip of the iceberg—the true power of JavaServer Faces lies in its extensible component model, which allows you to go far beyond those humble HTML beginnings.

Based on the recent surge in demand for improved usability in Web applications, it is understandable that the hottest topic at the moment is Rich Internet Applications (RIAs) and how they offer distributed, server-based Web applications with a rich interface and the interaction capabilities of desktop applications. Although RIAs hold significant promise, they still have issues with compatibility, portability, usability, and reusability. Many Web application developers are struggling to keep up with new RIA frameworks, both open source and vendor specific, as they appear on the market. What is needed is a standard way of defining an RIA regardless of what RIA framework is being used.

The debate over the best way to develop and deploy RIAs will not end with this book, but looking at the software industry today more and more developers are using the Web to deploy their applications.

User interfaces for these Web applications are often built with technologies such as HTML, CSS, JavaScript, and the DOM. These technologies were not developed with enterprise applications in mind, and with an increasing pressure from consumers to provide applications with features not fully described or supported by these technologies, developers are looking for alternative solutions or to extend the standards.

JSF does not just let you pick a single RIA technology such as Ajax, Mozilla XUL, Microsoft HTC, Macromedia Flash, and so on; it lets you pick and combine any RIA technologies you want and use them where they make the most sense. As with any technology, each RIA technology has its own advantages and disadvantages, but as a JSF component writer, you have the opportunity to leverage the best functionality of each RIA technology to provide the application developer with an extremely powerful RIA solution.

We have been very much involved in the development and the use of component-based frameworks over the past five years, starting with Oracle's own UI component framework, ADF UIX, and lately with Oracle's JSF component library, ADF Faces.

One day a very good friend asked us, "Why don't you guys share some of your experience and write a book about it?" What surprised us was that nobody had actually written a book targeting developers who are interested in the same thing we are—how to develop reusable standards-based JSF components for RIAs.

So, here we are, hoping that you will enjoy reading this book as much as we enjoyed writing it.

An Overview of This Book

Pro JSF and Ajax: Building Rich Internet Components is written to give you all the means to provide your Web application developers with easy-to-use Rich Internet Components (RICs). We decided early on that we would focus on establishing a clear blueprint that you as a developer could follow to be successful in your own JSF component development. We also decided that we would not limit this book to "just" JSF components and that we would incorporate everything you would need to know to be successful in developing, packaging, and deploying your own RICs.

This book is not, and we would like to emphasize this, *not* an introductory level book about JSF or about writing simple JSF components. Sure, this book introduces JSF and covers the basics of writing JSF components, but if you have not acquainted yourself with JSF before reading this book, we strongly encourage you to refer to a few excellent books that will introduce you to JSF and give you the foundation needed to fully appreciate this book. We recommend *JSF in Action*, by Kito D. Mann (Manning, 2005), which is an excellent and very complete book on JSF, and *Core JavaServer Faces*, by David Geary and Cay Horstmann (Prentice, 2004). We are also looking forward to seeing *Java Server Faces: The Complete Reference*, by Ed Burns and Chris Schalk (McGraw-Hill Osborne, 2006), in stores.

Pro JSF and Ajax: Building Rich Internet Components contains ten chapters that focus on writing JSF components. The book's examples are fairly extensive, so we recommend you download the example source code from the Apress Web site to give you a better overview of the examples discussed (see the next section for more information). We assume that, as an experienced Web developer and JSF developer, you can extrapolate the demonstrated topic into your own environment; thus, we avoid cluttering the text and examples with information that is of little use.

Chapter 1 gives a fast-paced and in-depth introduction to JSF, its component model, and its lifecycle. You might have followed our recommendation to read up on JSF before buying this book or you are already experienced working with JSF; either way, this chapter contains crucial information about JSF and its lifecycle that is needed in order to successfully build scalable and reusable JSF components.

Chapter 2 introduces the first JSF component: the date field component. We played with the idea of having a component comprised of three input fields representing *day*, *month*, and *year*, but this did not provide us with enough material to work with when moving forward through the book. So instead, we focused this chapter on the essentials of building a component, such as creating prototypes, managing resources, creating renderers, controlling rendering of children, handling conversion, and figuring out what's going on during postback. To be able to keep track of all the tasks associated with creating JSF components, this chapter introduces the first steps in a JSF component design blueprint. The date field component created in this chapter also introduces you to some new concepts and open source projects when you improve its user interactivity in Chapter 7.

Chapter 3 introduces the second component: the deck component. The deck component works like an accordion to show and hide information. This chapter discusses the JSF event model and teaches you how to create new behavioral superclasses and new event types with corresponding listener interfaces. By the time you finish Chapter 3, you will have enough knowledge to start writing your own basic HTML components. During the course of this book, you will be enhancing the deck and date field components, and you will be providing them with extremely rich user interactivity that leverages RITs.

Chapter 4 introduces you to three RITs (Ajax, Mozilla XUL, and Microsoft HTC) and gives you a high-level overview of these technologies. You will use these technologies in Chapters 6, 7, 8, and 9 to build rich interactivity into the date field and deck components. Of course, some simple applications in this chapter will highlight the core features of each technology.

As promised, to be able to successfully build and package JSF components, and especially RICs, you need a solution that can easily package resources, such as JavaScript libraries, CSS, and images, into the same component library as your JSF infrastructure (renderers, behavioral superclasses, and so on) and then serve them out from the same JAR. Chapter 5 introduces a new open source project—Weblets—that makes resource file management and versioning as easy for Web development as it already is for desktop-based Java development.

Chapters 6, 7, 8, and 9 address the need for a smoother and richer user experience when users interact with your components in a JSF Web application. These four chapters leverage everything you have learned so far and guide you through the gotchas of building Ajax-enabled JSF components with HTML, XUL, and HTC. These chapters also introduce you to one established and two new open source projects: the Dojo toolkit, Mabon, and D^2.

Finally, Chapter 10 pulls it all together. In this chapter, you will learn how to leverage all of the aforementioned techniques to provide your Web application developers (and users) with enterprise-class JSF components that support multiple clients.

Obtaining This Book's Source Code

All the examples in this book are freely available from the Source Code section of the Apress Web site. Point your browser to `http://www.apress.com`, click the Source Code link, and find the *Pro JSF and Ajax: Building Rich Internet Components* book. You can download the source as a zip file from this book's home page. All source code is organized by chapter. The zip file contains an application workspace, built with Oracle JDeveloper 10.1.3, and contains one project per chapter. Each project includes a WAR file that is ready to deploy to any J2EE 1.3–compliant application server. For more information about Oracle JDeveloper, please refer to the Oracle Web site at `http://otn.oracle.com/products/jdev/`.

Obtaining Updates for This Book

There are no errors in this book. Just kidding! Despite our best efforts to avoid any errors, you may find one or two scattered throughout the book. We apologize for those potential errors that may be present in the text or source code. A current errata list is available from this book's home page on the Apress Web site (`http://www.apress.com`), along with information about how to notify us of any errors you may encounter.

Contacting Us

Any feedback, questions, and comments regarding this book's content and source examples are extremely appreciated. You can direct your questions and comments to `projsf@gmail.com`. We will try to reply to your questions and comments as soon as we can, but please remember, we (like you!) may not be able to respond immediately.

Lastly, we would like to thank you for buying this book! We hope you will find this book to be a valuable source of information and inspiration and that you enjoy reading it.

PART 1

■ ■ ■

Developing Smarter with JavaServer™ Faces

JavaServer Faces (JSF) is a user interface (UI) component framework for Java 2 Enterprise Edition (J2EE) Web applications that, once adopted, allows organizations to migrate from old technologies, such as character-based platforms for virtual terminals (VTs), to more up-to-date standard-based platforms and technologies, such as JSF and Java. Over the past 15 years, the software industry has seen many technologies and platforms rise and fall. Usually, the use of a particular technology declines for several reasons, including fashion and competition. Another common reason for the fall of certain technologies is that if they are designed and maintained by one company, then the consumers of these technologies are forced to rely on support provided solely by the creators. Whenever a creator decides to deprecate a technology in favor of a more advanced solution, the consumer is left with an outdated, unsupported platform. JSF allows organizations and consumers to leverage the latest technology as it emerges, with minimal impact on existing JSF applications. JSF also brings extreme reuse of functionality and visual appearance to the software industry. Part 1 of this book will teach you what JSF is all about, describe how to leverage JSF by developing your own components, and open your eyes to a new horizon.

CHAPTER 1

The Foundation of JSF: Components

JavaServer Faces (JSF) is a user interface (UI) framework for Java Web applications. It is designed to significantly ease the burden of writing and maintaining applications that run on a Java application server and render their UIs back to a target client.

—JavaServer Faces specification

For those of you who have not had a chance to get acquainted with JSF before reading this book, this chapter will give you a fast-paced introduction to its core functionality. If you are already familiar with JSF, you may still find some of the discussion of component and lifecycle architecture to be of interest, because these topics are fundamental to your understanding of the rest of this book. This chapter will cover application development, give an overview of JSF and how it relates to other similar frameworks, and provide an in-depth examination of the JSF architecture and its component model. By the end of this chapter, you should understand the JSF architecture, its building blocks, and its request lifecycle.

Before jumping into the architecture of JSF, we'll define the audience for JSF (and ultimately for this book). The JSF specification defines the types of developers who make up the core audience: page authors, application developers, component writers, tools providers, and JSF implementers, as shown in Table 1-1.

Table 1-1. *JSF Developer Types**

Type	Description
Page author	A page author is responsible for creating the UI and has knowledge about markup and scripting languages, as well as the rendering technology such as JavaServer Pages (JSP). According to the JSF specification, this developer type is generally not familiar with programming languages such as Java or Visual Basic.
Application developer	An application developer is, according to the JSF specification, in charge of the server-side functionality of an application that may or may not be related to the UI. The technical skills of an application developer generally include Java, Enterprise JavaBeans (EJBs), or other server technologies.

Continued

Table 1-1. *Continued*

Type	Description
Component writer	A component writer is the main provider of reusable components. This developer is responsible for creating component libraries that can be consumed by others, such as the page author.
Tools provider	A tools provider, as implied by the name, provides tools that can support developers who are building applications with JSF.
JSF implementers	A JSF implementer is a developer who provides the runtime (or implementation of the JSF specification) for all the previously defined developers. Examples of available implementations are the Sun Reference Implementation (RI) (`http://java.sun.com/j2ee/javaserverfaces/`) and Apache MyFaces (`http://myfaces.apache.org`).

** Source: The JavaServer Faces 1.1 specification*

In our experience, page authors and application developers are usually the same person, so they are knowledgeable in both UI design and programming languages, such as Java or Visual Basic. We will focus most of our attention on component writers in this book.

Overview of Application Development Technologies

During the relatively short history of computers and software, application development has undergone several major evolutionary steps, all promising increased developer productivity and flexibility. These technology improvements have progressed exponentially since the computer was first introduced, and it looks like computer and software technologies will continue to evolve at the same tremendous pace well into the future.

> *No exponential is forever . . . but we can delay "forever."*
>
> —Gordon Moore (famous for Moore's law),
> Fairchild Camera and Instrument Corporation

During these evolutionary years, the deployment profile for an application, as well as the computer and software technology used to develop such an application, has changed.

One-Tier

At the end of the 1970s and beginning of the 1980s, a fundamental shift occurred from large and centralized computers to personal computers (PCs), which moved the power of control from a few to many (anyone with a PC). Though most of the applications released during this period were more powerful than anything so far developed, they were developed and designed for single-user tasks and lacked collaboration over common data; at this point, no central databases or email systems existed. Applications deployed or installed this way are referred to as *one-tier* applications.

From a maintenance point of view, this one-tier solution is an application that resides on an individual's machine and that controls interaction with business logic. These one-tier applications all integrate three application layers (presentation, business logic, and data), making it hard to maintain and almost impossible to share and scale information.

Two-Tier: Client-Server

Two-tier, or *client-server*, solutions took center stage in the 1980s and pushed one-tier solutions into the history archives. A two-tier architecture, which enables sharing data, changed the way applications were developed and deployed. Two-tier applications directly interact with the end user; business and presentation logic are stored on the client, and data resides on a remote server. This architecture allows multiple users to access centralized data with applications such as desktop email clients (such as Microsoft Outlook or Mozilla Thunderbird). Although the two-tier solution solves the issue of having multiple users accessing the same data source, it also has its limitations, such as the lack of flexibility of the design to later modification or porting, which in turn increases maintenance costs.

Multitier: Web Applications

The next phase in application development arrived with the Internet and the Web browser and introduced the *three-tier*, or *multitier*, architecture. In the one-tier solution, presentation, business logic, and data are all integrated in one monolithic application. The multitier architecture breaks this type of application into three layers, allowing developers to focus on specific domain areas—model (data access), view (presentation), and controller (logic). This programming paradigm, representing the split between these layers, is known as the Model-View-Controller (MVC) architecture and was first introduced in SmallTalk and spread to the developer community in the 1980s.

Splitting the one-tier application into layers—in combination with a standard client (for example, the Web browser) and a standard communication protocol (for example, Hypertext Transfer Protocol [HTTP])—suddenly gave users ubiquitous access to centralized and familiar applications such as email via a browser (for example, Google's browser-based Gmail). Applications are no longer something that only come on a CD or are downloaded. A multitier solution gives the application owner centralized maintenance and administration, which allows the application owner to provide instantaneous upgrades for everyone using the application.

Exploring Application Development Today

In this new world of multitier applications, developers need to keep up-to-date with emerging technologies and standards provided through such organizations as the World Wide Web Consortium (W3C) and the Java Community Process (JCP). The industry is evolving, which is good, but this also adds pressure on the application developer to always be building competitive multitier applications. If you look at a typical multitier software solution—serving a retail company, for example—it might include support for multiple agents such as Web browsers, mobile devices, and character-based Video Terminals (VT, for example, VT100). Figure 1-1 shows a simplistic schema over the architecture for such a multitier application.

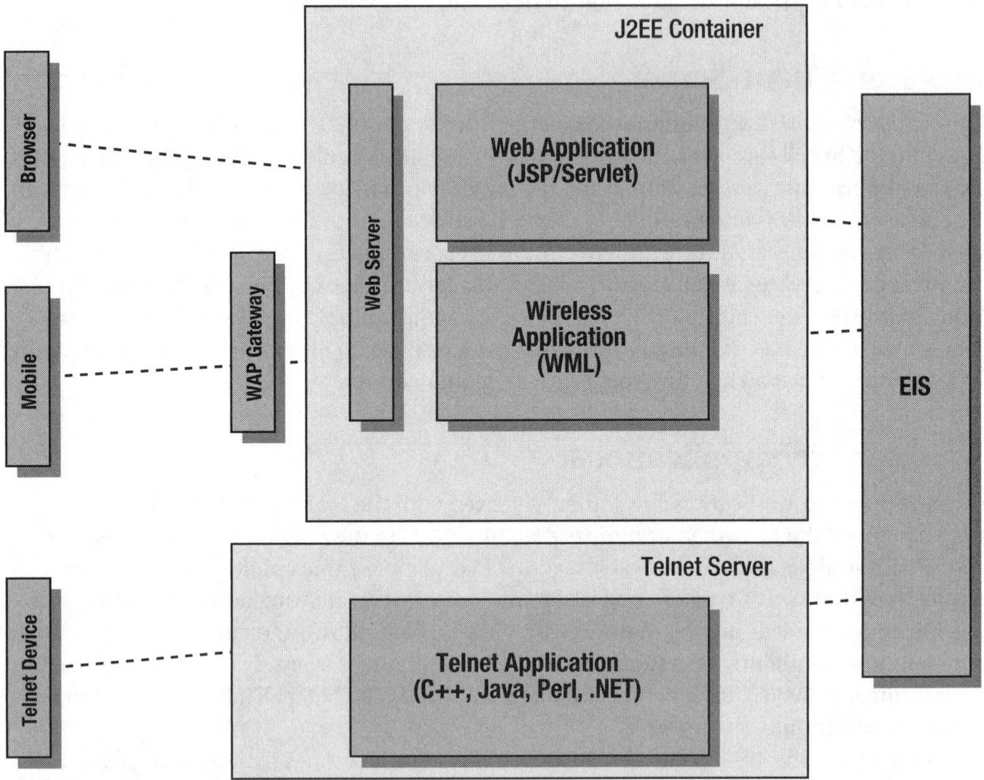

Figure 1-1. *Common J2EE architecture for a typical multitier software solution, serving a retail company*

In this scenario, the application developer is forced to provide not one application but three. This architecture contains one application for the Web interface, one for the mobile device, and finally one for the Telnet device (such as a VT terminal or handheld character-based device). All three applications use their own technology stack, which for the administrator or application developer will be a maintenance nightmare, and may cause issues with security and scalability. For the application developer, it all boils down to one question: "How many technologies do I have to learn in order to successfully build a complete solution for my project?"

Frameworks

Compared to ten years ago, customers today have much higher demands and more specific requirements for new Web application projects. They require richer and more user-friendly Web applications with built-in security, accessibility, internationalization, portability, and so on. Multitier applications must successfully deliver all these features, despite the increased complexity of additional failure scenarios and increased scalability and security requirements.

The growing complexity of building applications creates a need for simplicity. So far, in the J2EE realm, there has not been a clear choice of technology for Web applications. The traditional application programming interfaces (APIs), such as JSP and servlets, do not really provide enough abstraction from the underlying grunt work of implementing a multitier application. To fulfill these requirements and to provide some level of simplicity, the industry has evolved in a direction whereby open source communities and software companies are providing application developers with frameworks to protect them from the complexity introduced by multitier applications.

Tapestry, Struts, Tiles, TopLink, Hibernate, ADF UIX...

Many frameworks have the same underlying ideas but solve a problem a little differently and in different layers of a multitier application (the view layer, the controller layer, and the model layer). Examples of frameworks are Struts (an open source controller framework); TopLink and Hibernate (model frameworks); and Tiles, Tapestry, XUL, and ADF UIX (so-called view frameworks).

The benefits of application frameworks are the modularity, reusability, and inversion of control (IoC) they provide to developers. By encapsulating implementation details, frameworks enhance modularity and improve software quality by centralizing the impact of design and implementation details. Thanks to the stable environment provided by frameworks, they also enhance reusability by allowing developers to create generic components that can be reused in new applications. This reuse of framework components improves application developer productivity and the quality of application software. By leveraging IoC, the framework manages which application-specific methods are called in response to user events.

■ **Note** IoC means you have registered some part of your code with the framework, and the framework will call this code when the client requests it. This is also referred to as the *Hollywood principle*. ("Don't call us. We'll call you.")

In the previous retail software scenario (refer to Figure 1-1), frameworks can help increase developer productivity and ease of maintenance, but the frameworks are also incompatible with each other, which makes integration hard to handle. In contrast, JSF is a standard framework that aims to solve incompatibility.

Introducing JSF

In short, JSF is a UI component framework for J2EE applications. Before we start covering UI components (and by *UI components* we mean building blocks for application developers, not components of the framework itself), it is worthwhile to elaborate on why you need yet another framework. JSF is, after all, attempting to solve the same problems as the aforementioned Apache Tapestry or Oracle ADF UIX, frameworks that have been around for quite some time and have proved to be successful.

The differentiator that JSF brings, which other similar frameworks do not have, is the backing of a standard specification (JSR-127). Because JSF is part of the J2EE standard specification, it is a top priority for every major J2EE tools vendor in the market (including Oracle, IBM, Borland, and Sun) to support it, which in turn will guarantee a wide adoption and good tools support.

Most Web applications are stuck in the 1990s where too much effort was put into basic plumbing and not into high-level components. Basically, when there is limited abstraction or no abstraction over the markup, the development of Web applications becomes cumbersome and hard to maintain. You can invest a lot of time into the application to make it rich and interactive using various technologies from applets, plug-ins (Flex), Dynamic HTML (DHTML), and JavaScript. Used together, these technologies can make up an interactive and powerful Web application, but how do you maintain such an application? How do you reuse what you have built?

Component Model

JSF brings to the table a best-of-breed J2EE framework. JSF is here to simplify life for application developers, making it possible for them to focus on the view without needing to know the underlying markup or scripts. They will see an improvement in productivity with JSF using UI components that hide most of the grunt work of integrating richer functionality into Web applications. The goal is to provide an easy way to construct UIs from a set of reusable UI components.

These reusable components come in various shapes with different functionality, from layout components (such as the layout of an entire page) to simple buttons. Application developers can use these components to construct a page and nest UI components within each other to get the desired effect; for example, nesting text fields and buttons within a row layout component will render the nested UI components in a single row on the client. This structure of nested components is often referred to as a *parent-to-child* relationship and visualized as a UI component hierarchy. This UI component hierarchy represents a JSF page description at runtime.

Navigation Model

JSF provides a declarative navigation model, which allows application developers to set navigation rules to define the navigation from one view to another in a Web application. Navigation rules in JSF are defined inside the JSF configuration file, `faces-config.xml`, and are page-based. Code Sample 1-1 shows a navigation rule configured in `faces-config.xml`.

Code Sample 1-1. *Navigation Rule Configured in* `faces-config.xml`

```
<navigation-rule>
  <from-view-id>/login.jspx</from-view-id>
  <navigation-case>
    <from-outcome>success</from-outcome>
    <to-view-id>/result.jspx</to-view-id>
  </navigation-case>
</navigation-rule>
```

In Code Sample 1-1, a navigation rule is set so that from a view, `login.jspx`, on an outcome of `success`, the user will be sent to a page called `result.jspx`. The outcome is the return value from an action performed in the application such as a button being clicked. In JSF, an action is attached to the `UIComponent`, which allows for fine-grained control on the page. These actions can either have their own navigation rule or share the same navigation rule.

Application Lifecycle

Another benefit that application developers will discover when using JSF is that the framework helps manage UI state across server requests. Instead of having to take care of user selections and passing these selections from page to page, the framework will handle this for you. The JSF framework also has built-in processes in the lifecycle to assist with validation, conversion, and model updates. As a side bonus, JSF provides a simple model for delivering client-generated events to server-side application code.

Application Development with JSF

One of the key differentiators with JSF is that its architecture is designed to be independent of specific protocols and markup, and as such it allows developers to attach any rendering technology to the JSF application. In JSF it is the `RenderKit` that is responsible for the presentation of the JSF application by rendering the markup to the client. You can define a `RenderKit` for any type of markup (HTML, DHTML, Telnet/character mode, and eventually SVG, Flash, XUL, and so on) and use it to display a JSF page.

This separation between the page description (UI component hierarchy) and the rendering of markup is a key differentiator that provides flexibility to the component developer while protecting the application developer from changes isolated at the rendering layer. Instead of having to learn and implement different rendering technologies to solve a common problem, such as portability between different browsers (such as Netscape vs. Internet Explorer), application developers can use custom JSF components to build applications targeted for different browsers, personal digital assistants (PDAs), and so on, with a common programming model—JSF and Java.

Applying this new knowledge about JSF to the previous sample in Figure 1-1, the retail solution, the architecture could look similar to Figure 1-2.

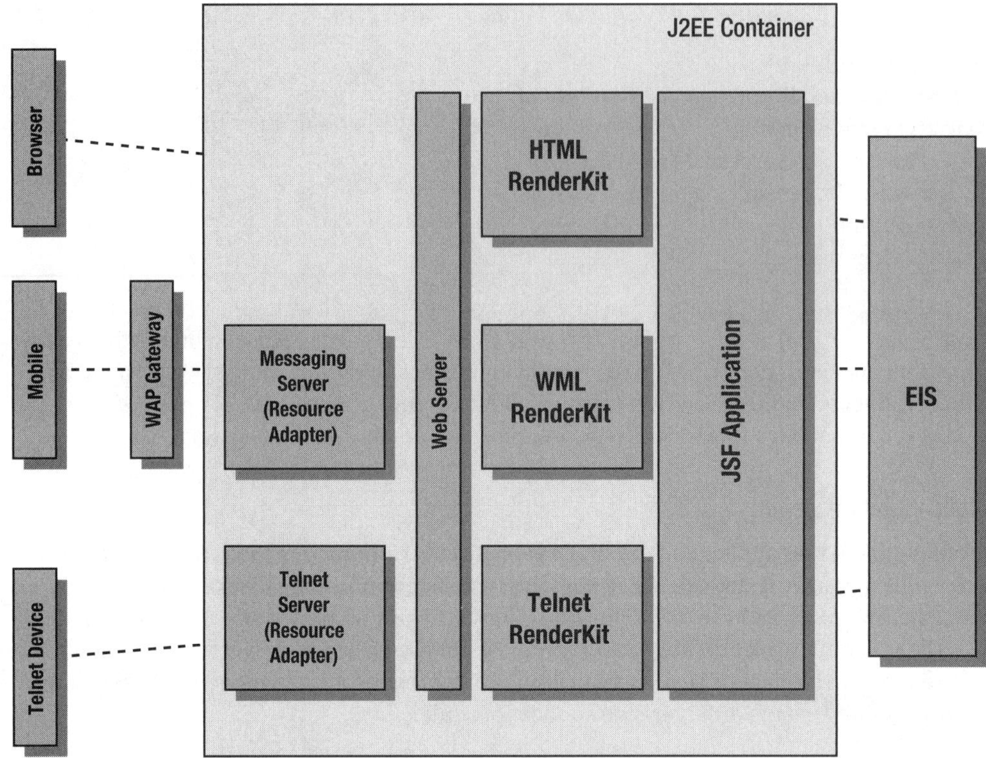

Figure 1-2. *J2EE architecture using JSF for a typical multitier software solution, serving a retail company*

In this architecture, only one application is serving three different agents using three different `RenderKits`—Hypertext Markup Language (HTML), Wireless Markup Language (WML), and Telnet. In practice, the application would probably still be three different pages but with a main difference; they will all be built on the same technology—JSF and Java. This will both save development time and reduce maintenance. Furthermore, and perhaps most important, JSF establishes standards, which are designed to be leveraged by tools (such as Oracle JDeveloper, Sun Studio Creator, and Eclipse plug-ins such as Exadel Studio) to provide developers with the ease of use that has long been sought in the J2EE developer community.

JSF Architecture

From a satellite view, JSF implements what is known as the Model 2 pattern, which is based on the MVC architecture. If you look at how the Model 2 pattern is applied in a JSF application, you can see it consists of three elements—the view, the navigation model, and the application logic, as shown in Figure 1-3.

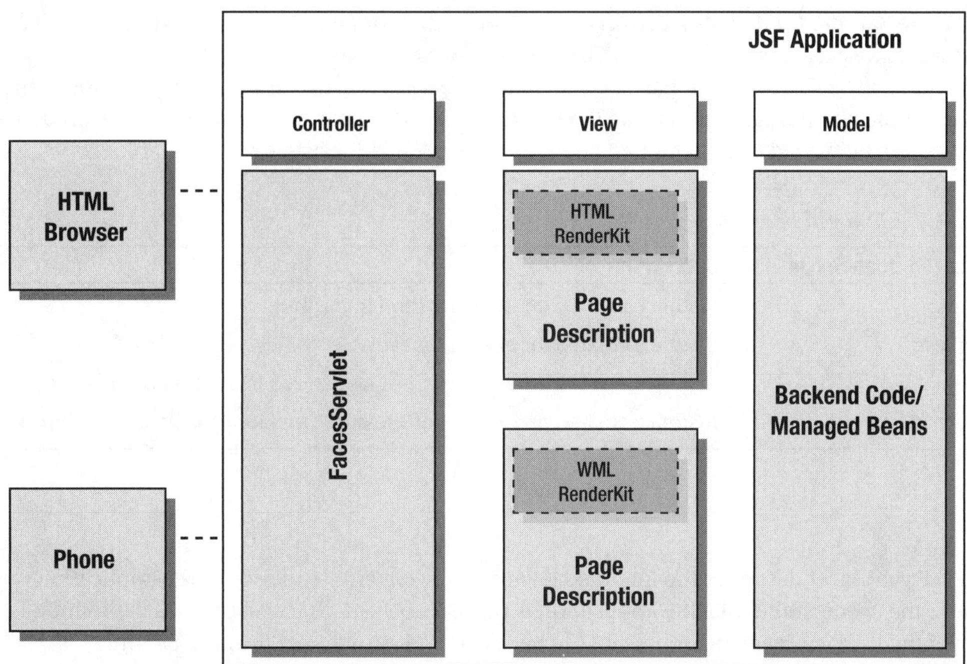

Figure 1-3. *MVC architecture with JSF (Model 2)*

Model

With JSF, the concept of a managed bean has been introduced. The managed bean is the glue to the application logic—backing code or backing bean. Managed beans are defined in the `faces-config.xml` file and give the application developer full access to all the mapped backing bean's methods. This concept of IoC is successfully used in frameworks such as Spring, HiveMind, and Oracle ADF model binding (JSR-227). The managed bean facility is responsible for creating the backing beans or other beans such as Data Access Objects (DAO). In JSF, a backing bean is a plain old Java object (POJO) with no dependency on implementation-specific interfaces or classes. The aforementioned JSF controller—the `FacesServlet`—is not aware of what action has been taken; it is aware only of the outcome of a particular action and will use that outcome to decide where to navigate. In JSF it is the component that is aware of which action, or method, to call on a particular user event. Code Sample 1-2 shows a managed bean defined in the `faces-config.xml` file.

Code Sample 1-2. *Managed Bean Defined in the* `faces-config.xml` *File*

```
<managed-bean>
  <managed-bean-name>sample</managed-bean-name>
  <managed-bean-class>
    com.apress.projsf.ch1.application.SampleBean
  </managed-bean-class>
  <managed-bean-scope>session</managed-bean-scope>
</managed-bean>
```

Code Sample 1-2 defines a backing bean, `sample`, that points to a class called `com.apress.projsf.ch1.applictaion.SampleBean`. The `<managed-bean-scope>` indicates where an instance of this bean will be stored after it has been created—`request`, `session`, or `application` scope. The code sample also has an option to set the scope to `none` for a bean that should not be stored in any scope but instead be instantiated on every access. Table 1-2 lists all the available scopes.

Table 1-2. *Managed Bean Scopes*

Managed Bean Scope	Description
None	Instance created for every method invocation
Request	Instance created for every request
Session	Instance created on initial request and stored in the session
Application	Instance created on initial request and stored in the Web application

View

The JSF view layer describes the intended layout, behavior, and rendering of the application. One of the cornerstones of a JSF application is the `UIComponent`. `UIComponents` are the foundation of the JSF view layer and represent the behavior and structure of the application. A developer would use these `UIComponents` to construct an application by nesting components within each other. This nested structure will at runtime be represented as a component hierarchy, as shown in Figure 1-4, which in turn represents the view or UI, much like developing a Swing-based application.

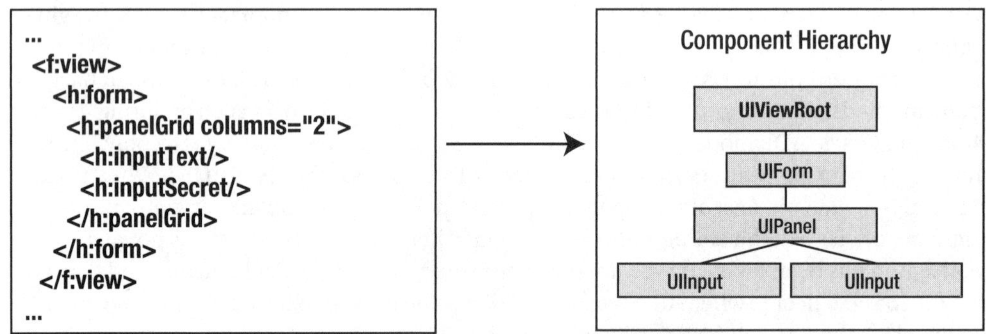

Figure 1-4. *From page description to a JSF component hierarchy*

The default page description defined by the JSF specification is JSP, but there is nothing in the JSF specification preventing an implementer from providing an alternative page description, such as an Extensible Markup Language (XML)–based, WML-based, or plain HTML-based page description. Using JSP as the page description has its good and bad sides. On the plus side, it is a well-known and widespread solution; as such, learning how to build applications with JSF and JSP presents a fairly shallow learning curve for most J2EE developers. In addition, as a bonus, the adoption of JSF as the view technology of choice for new Web applications is good. The consequence is that JSF has a dependency on JSP, and as such, it needs to work around the different lifecycles of an application that is partially JSP and partially JSF. Later in this chapter (refer to the section "JSF and JSP"), we will cover these differences and the impact they have on applications built with JSP syntax and JSF components.

Controller

JSF comes with a simple controller—the `FacesServlet`. The `FacesServlet` acts as a gatekeeper, controlling navigation flow and dispatching requests to the appropriate JSF page.

A Component-Based UI Framework

We have set the stage for the book, so it is now time to focus on the pieces that are differentiating JSF from other technologies: `UIComponents`. JSF is a component-based UI framework where components, such as `HtmlDataTable` and `HtmlPanelGrid`, can be viewed as prefabricated blocks that allow application developers to productively build complex applications with reusable components. It also allows application developers to focus on the application logic rather than on building the dynamic/rich functionality themselves.

■ **Note** JSF is all about components—and reusable components at that! JSF was first released in March 2004 with a subsequent point release, 1.1, in August 2004. The initial JSR (JSR-127) has been replaced by JSR-252, which delivers the JSF 1.2 release.

A JSF component consists of five building blocks:

- *`UIComponent`*: The `UIComponent` is responsible for the behavior and for accessing the data model.
- *`Renderer`*: The `Renderer` is in charge of the markup rendered to the client for a specific component family.
- *`RenderKit`*: This is a library of `Renderers` with a common rendering technology (for example, HTML).
- *Renderer-specific component subclass*: The renderer-specific component subclass is a convenience class and represents renderer-specific facets and attributes.
- *JSP tag*: The default page description language is JSP, so JSF needs to follow the contract of JSP and provide JSP tags representing each JSF component.

JSF addresses the idea of a clear separation between the application logic and the visual presentation by strongly separating the UI from the underlying data model. The `Renderer` is in charge of the markup rendered to the client, and the `UIComponent` is responsible for the behavior and accessing data model. Figure 1-5 shows the separation of UI, behavior, and data model.

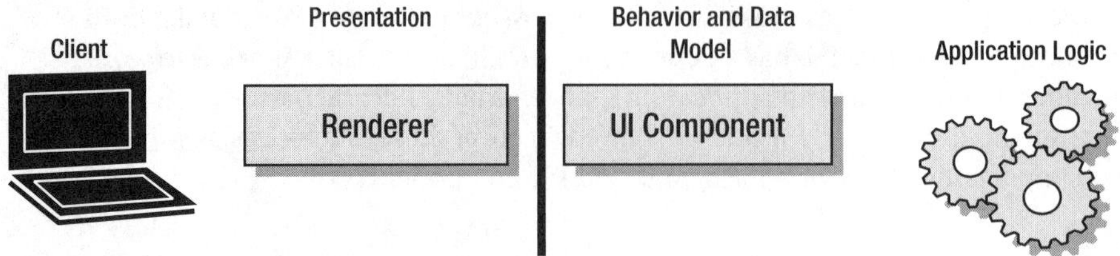

Figure 1-5. *Separation of UI from behavior and data model*

To illustrate the benefit of separating the UI and data models, let's look at an example of the common HTML form element `<select>`. This list element has a `multiple` attribute that changes the behavior from allowing a single-select option to multiple-select options. This model has no separation of rendering and behavior. For an application developer to change the behavior of the element from single select to multiple select, it requires just a minor adjustment—simply setting the attribute `multiple`. However, this will have a bigger impact on the underlying application logic since the values passed from the client are now structured as a list of key-value pairs instead of just a single key-value pair.

The `UISelectOne` and `UISelectMany` UI components provide a good example of clear separation between behavior and appearance. For example, the `UISelectOne` component has a distinct behavior to select a single value from many available options, and the `UISelectMany` component has the behavior of selecting many values from a list of available options. The `UISelectOne` component has three renderer types—`Listbox`, `Radio`, and `Menu`. Changing the appearance from `Radio` to `Menu` will not affect the underlying behavior.

However, if application developers want to change the behavior to a multiple-select component, they have to replace the entire `UISelectOne` JSF component with a `UISelectMany` JSF component, rather than just setting an attribute in the page markup, as they would do when using the `<select>` element directly. This clear separation between changing the behavior of a JSF component and changing its appearance gives application developers a better understanding of the impact of their changes when modifying the page definition. Figure 1-6 illustrates the `UIComponent` and three `Renderers` with different appearances.

Figure 1-6 illustrates a component—`UISelectOne`—from the JSF specification that has three different renderers attached—`Listbox`, `Menu`, and `Radio`. In some cases it might be necessary to create new `UIComponents` or `Renderers`.

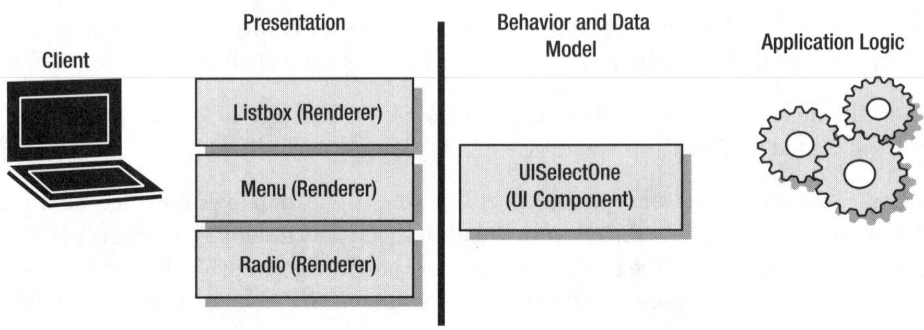

Figure 1-6. `UISelectOne` *and its renderers*

A good rule to follow is before starting a component project, search the Web for already created components. In most cases, you can probably get away with writing a new Renderer for an already existing component, and a fair number of components already exist. If you can't find the component you are looking for, then it is time to build your own. To build a new component, you should make sure it introduces a new behavior, functionality, or definition and that the component has a distinct server-side behavior. If the component exists and you just need a new appearance, then you need to create a new Renderer (for example, to enable Ajax or an existing input component).

Let's now look at the different pieces making up a JSF component.

UIComponent

The foundations of all JSF components are the abstract UIComponent and UIComponentBase classes. The UIComponent class (javax.faces.component.UIComponent) defines the behavioral agreement and state information for all components, and the UIComponentBase class (javax.faces.component.UIComponentBase) is a convenience subclass that implements almost all methods of the UIComponent class. A simplified description of a UIComponent is that it is a regular JavaBean with properties, events, and listeners.

The JSF specification defines a set of standard UIComponent subclasses, or behavioral *superclasses* (for example, UISelectOne and UISelectMany), which all extend the UIComponentBase class. In most cases, component writers will extend these standard UIComponent subclasses. However, they can subclass the UIComponentBase class as well. A JSF component consists of a UIComponent and one or more Renderers. It is important to understand that the standard UIComponent subclasses define only non-renderer-specific behaviors, such as UISelectOne. Table 1-3 gives an overview of the available standard behavioral UIComponents and lists their associated convenience subclasses, renderer types, and JSP tags.

Table 1-3. *Components Provided by the JSF Implementation**

UI Component	Renderer-Specific Class	Renderer Type	Syntax/JSP Tag
UIColumn	null**		<h:column>
UICommand	HtmlCommandButton	Button	<h:commandButton>
	HtmlCommandLink	Link	<h:commandLink>
UIData	HtmlDataTable	Table	<h:dataTable>
UIForm	HtmlForm	Form	<h:form>
UIGraphic	HtmlGraphicImage	Image	<h:graphicImage>
UIInput	HtmlInputHidden	Hidden	<h:inputHidden>
	HtmlInputSecret	Secret	<h:inputSecret>
	HtmlInputText	Text	<h:inputText>
	HtmlInputTextArea	Textarea	<h:inputTextarea>
UIMessage	HtmlMessage	Message	<h:message>
UIMessages	HtmlMessages	Messages	<h:messages>
UIOutput	HtmlOutputFormat	Format	<h:outputFormat>
	HtmlOutputLabel	Label	<h:outputLabel>

Continued

Table 1-3. *Continued*

UI Component	Renderer-Specific Class	Renderer Type	Syntax/JSP Tag
	HtmlOutputLink	Link	<h:outputLink>
	HtmlOutputText	Text	<h:outputText>
UIPanel	HtmlPanelGrid	Grid	<h:panelGrid>
	HtmlPanelGroup	Group	<h:panelGroup>
UIParameter	null*		<h:parameter>
UISelectOneBoolean	HtmlSelectBooleanCheckbox	Checkbox	<h:selectBooleanCheckbox>
UISelectItem	null		<h:selectItem>
UISelectItems	null		<h:selectItems>
UISelectMany	HtmlSelectManyCheckbox	Checkbox	<h:selectManyCheckbox>
	HtmlSelectManyListbox	Listbox	<h:selectManyListbox>
	HtmlSelectManyMenu	Menu	<h:selectManyMenu>
UISelectOne	HtmlSelectOneListbox	Listbox	<h:selectOneListbox>
	HtmlSelectOneMenu	Menu	<h:selectOneMenu>
	HtmlSelectOneRadio	Radio	<h:selectOneRadio>
UIViewRoot	null		<f.view>

** Source: The JavaServer Faces specification 1.1*
*** This component has no associated renderer.*

For each combination of `UIComponent` and `Renderer`, there is a renderer-specific subclass, or convenience class. A standard JSF implementation, such as the Sun RI or the MyFaces runtime, comes with a set of HTML renderers (provided through the standard HTML `RenderKit`) and a set of HTML renderer-specific subclasses, such as `HtmlSelectOneRadio`.

Renderer-Specific Component Subclass

In most cases, this subclass creates an instance of the component at runtime. As defined by its name, this subclass provides access to renderer-specific attributes on a JSF component such as `style`, `disabled`, `tooltip`, and so on—providing property getters and setters for all of these component attributes. In conjunction with the binding attribute on the JSF JSP tag, this subclass allows application developers to use JavaBean property setters to change renderer-specific attributes on the component at runtime.

Although this does work and is a useful tool for prototyping, we recommend that, where possible, application developers avoid modifying the renderer-specific attributes directly from the backing bean application logic and instead use the behavioral superclass of the component. If application developers use the parent class instead of the convenience subclass, they have no need to modify the backing bean code when the JSF component changes to use a different renderer-specific component in the page definition, such as from `HtmlSelectOneRadio` to `HtmlSelectOneListbox`. The backing bean code needs to change only when the behavioral superclass also changes, such as changing from `HtmlSelectOneRadio` to `HtmlSelectManyList`.

This subclass is optional, but it is good practice to provide this subclass with the JSF component, since sometimes application developers may like to use it for convenience, and for component writers it is hard to know whether application developers will try to use this.

Since this convenience class extends the `UIComponent` and the behavioral subclass (for example, `UISelectOne`) at runtime, the component instance will not only contain information available in this convenience class but also contain information from the extended `UIComponent` classes. If you look at the inheritance model that is used by JSF to create an instance of a component, it will look something like Figure 1-7.

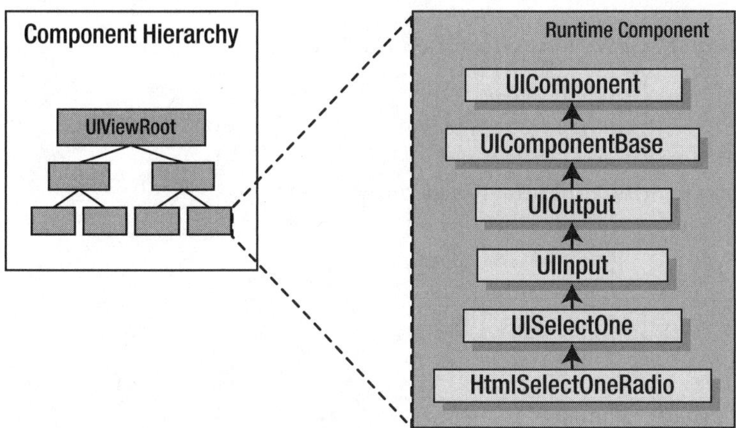

Figure 1-7. `UIComponent` *inheritance*

This model allows programmatic access to all properties and attributes defined by the different classes that build up the component. As mentioned earlier, the `UIComponentBase` class contains behavioral agreements for all components, the `UISelectOne` subclass contains properties and methods specific to its behavior (for example, select one), and the renderer-specific subclass (for example, `HtmlSelectOneListbox`) contains getters and setters for all renderer-specific attributes as well as the `rendererType` for that particular component.

Using a Renderer-Specific Component Subclass

Code Sample 1-3 illustrates the benefit of using the behavioral superclass instead of the convenience class to manipulate the page at runtime. The first bit of code illustrates a page with a simple `selectOneRadio` component with three options and a `commandButton`.

Code Sample 1-3. *JSF* `selectOneRadio` *Bound to a Renderer-Specific Subclass*

```
<h:form>
  <h:selectOneRadio binding="#{sample.selectOneRadio}" >
    <f:selectItem itemLabel="Jonas" itemValue="jonas.jacobi" />
    <f:selectItem itemLabel="John" itemValue="john.fallows" />
    <f:selectItem itemLabel="Duke" itemValue="java.dude" />
  </h:selectOneRadio>
  <h:commandButton value="Select Duke"
                   actionListener="#{sample.onAction}" />
</h:form>
```

In the selectOneRadio JSP tag, or custom action, the binding attribute is set to a value-binding expression—#{sample.selectOneRadio}. This expression points to a backend JavaBean property—selectOneRadio—that in turn is wired to the component instance for the UIComponent created by this JSP tag. Code Sample 1-4 shows the backend JavaBean, or the managed bean, that contains the page logic that at runtime will set the default option on the selectOneRadio component to java.dude at runtime, whenever the user clicks the command button.

Code Sample 1-4. *Backing Bean Using the* HtmlSelectOneRadio *Subclass*

```
package com.apress.projsf.ch1.application;

import javax.faces.event.ActionEvent;
import javax.faces.component.html.HtmlSelectOneRadio;

public class SampleBean
{
  public void onAction(
    ActionEvent event)
  {
    _selectOneRadio.setValue("java.dude");
  }

  public void setSelectOneRadio(
    HtmlSelectOneRadio selectOneRadio)
  {
    _selectOneRadio = selectOneRadio;
  }

  public HtmlSelectOneRadio getSelectOneRadio()
  {
    return _selectOneRadio;
  }

  private HtmlSelectOneRadio _selectOneRadio;
}
```

In Code Sample 1-4, the managed bean is using the renderer-specific subclass HtmlSelectOneRadio. If application developers want to change the UI and replace the selectOneRadio component with a selectOneMenu component in the page, a class cast exception is thrown at runtime. The application developer can avoid this by instead using the parent class of the selectOneRadio component—UISelectOne. Code Sample 1-5 shows how the page and the managed bean source look with the recommended approach.

Code Sample 1-5. *JSF* `selectOneRadio` *Bound to a Behavioral Superclass*

```
<body>
  <h:form>
     <h:selectOneRadio binding="#{sample.selectOne}" >
       <f:selectItem itemLabel="Jonas" itemValue="jonas.jacobi" />
       <f:selectItem itemLabel="John" itemValue="john.fallows" />
       <f:selectItem itemLabel="Duke" itemValue="java.dude" />
     </h:selectOneRadio>
     <h:commandButton value="Select Duke"
                      actionListener="#{sample.onAction}" />
  </h:form>
 </body>
```

Code Sample 1-5 contains the same page description except for one minor adjustment to the value-binding expression. To be more generic, the method name in the managed bean has been changed to `selectOne` instead of `selectOneRadio`, so the expression in the page description has to change to reference the more generic backing bean property name, as shown in Code Sample 1-6.

Code Sample 1-6. *New Backing Bean Using the UISelectOne Class*

```
package com.apress.projsf.ch1.application;

import javax.faces.event.ActionEvent;
import javax.faces.component.UISelectOne;

public class SampleBean
{

  public void onAction(
    ActionEvent event)
  {
    _selectOne.setValue("java.dude");
  }

  public void setSelectOne(
    UISelectOne selectOne)
  {
    _selectOne = selectOne;
  }

  public UISelectOne getSelectOne()
  {
    return _selectOne;
  }

  private UISelectOne _selectOne;
}
```

The new managed bean is now leveraging the inheritance of the components to make it more agnostic to changes in the UI. Instead of the convenience class `HtmlSelectOneRadio`, the behavioral superclass `UISelectOne` is used. Application developers can now change to another component within the same component family without fear of breaking the application logic.

Accessing Renderer-Specific Attributes

In the previous example, we programmatically set the `value` property on the `UISelectOne` component, which is a property defined by the behavioral superclass. But how does an application developer get access to the renderer-specific attributes if a renderer-specific subclass is not provided or (as in Code Sample 1-6) is not used? All attributes and properties are accessed via a centralized `Map` that can be accessible from any of the `UIComponent` classes and subclasses through a property called `attributes`, as shown in Code Sample 1-7.

Code Sample 1-7. *Using the Component Attributes Map to Update a Render-Specific Attribute*

```
// Renderer-specific attribute example
Map attrs = selectOne.getAttributes();
attrs.put("style", "font-face:bold");
```

Code Sample 1-7 shows how a developer can access attributes without using a renderer-specific subclass. Component writers can also introduce an interface for renderer-specific attribute methods, implemented by each renderer-specific subclass.

Saving and Restoring State

One crucial part of building Web applications is state saving. Take the traditional HTML-based shopping cart as an example. Here the application developer has to store the user product selections and persist this information until the user finishes shopping. In most cases, a shopping cart application is built up with multiple pages so the state of each page has to be saved until the buyer has finished shopping. The state is stored in hidden form fields, stored in the session, or passed on as a request to the next page. Those who have dealt with this know this is not a trivial task to accomplish.

State management is one of the primary benefits of using JSF to build applications. JSF provides automatic UI state handling through a class called `StateManager`, which saves and restores state for a particular view (hierarchy of `UIComponents`) between requests on the server. Each `UIComponent` saves and restores its own internal state when requested by the `StateManager`; the `StateManager` itself saves and restores the state associated with the structure of the `UIComponent` hierarchy. If a `UIComponent` is marked as being `transient`, then it is omitted from the structure by the `StateManager`, causing it to be removed from the `UIComponent` tree at the end of the request.

Two alternatives exist for storing the state of a view—on the client side and server side. By default state is saved on the server. The server-side implementation is supported by the JSP and Servlet specifications, but JSF conceals all the details of how this works. A class called `ResponseStateManager`, which is created and managed by a `RenderKit`, manages the client-side state saving. Client-side state saving depends not only on the JSF implementation but also heavily on the markup language rendered to the client and on how state can be managed by that client. With HTML as markup, the state is typically stored in a hidden form field.

Note Although JSF 1.1 kept the name of the view state in a hidden form field as a private implementation detail, JSF 1.2 now standardizes the name as `javax.faces.ViewState` so that alternative postback mechanisms, such as Ajax, can more easily be integrated with the JSF lifecycle.

One of the drawbacks of saving state in the user session on the server is memory consumption. If scalability is an issue for application developers, the client-side implementation will prevent memory consumption from shooting through the roof and will have an advantage in clustered environments. But, since state will now have to be sent back and forth between the client and the server, response time might increase. You can configure the state-saving method, as shown in Code Sample 1-8, in the application deployment descriptor file—`WEB-INF/web.xml`—by setting the parameter `STATE_SAVING_METHOD` to `client` or `server`.

Code Sample 1-8. *Setting the Method of Saving State to the Server Side in the Deployment Descriptor*

```
<context param>
  <param-name>javax.faces.STATE_SAVING_METHOD</param-name>
  <param-value>server</param-value>
</context param>
```

Component Family and Component Type

The component family is a string that represents the behavior of the component (for example, an input component or command component). The component family is declared in the JSF configuration file—`faces-config.xml`—and used to select a `Renderer` for a particular component. Code Sample 1-9 shows how you associate a `Renderer` with a particular component family.

Code Sample 1-9. *Associating a Renderer to a Particular Component Family*

```
<render-kit>
  <renderer>
    <component-family>
      javax.faces.Input
    </component-family>
    <renderer-type>
      com.apress.projsf.Date
    </renderer-type>
    <renderer-class>
      com.apress.projsf.ch2.render.html.basic.HtmlInputDateRenderer
    </renderer-class>
```

Note The prefix javax.faces is reserved for use by component families defined in the JSF specification. All samples in this book use the com.apress.projsf prefix for custom component families.

The component type is a string that is used as an identifier for the UIComponent subclass. You can find information about the relationship between the component type and UIComponent subclass in the JSF configuration file, as shown in Code Sample 1-10.

Code Sample 1-10. *Mapping of Component Type and* UIComponent *Subclass*

```
<component>
  <component-type>
    com.apress.projsf.ProInputDate
  </component-type>
  <component-class>
    com.apress.projsf.ch2.component.pro.ProInputDate
  </component-class>
```

In Code Sample 1-10, a UIComponent subclass—com.apress.projsf.component.pro.ProInputDate—has been assigned com.projsf.ProInputDate as the component type. By convention, the component type is also declared in the UIComponent subclass as a constant—COMPONENT_TYPE. This simplifies life for developers so they don't need to remember the component type for every component.

Note The prefix javax.faces is reserved for use by component types defined in the JSF specification. All samples in this book use the com.apress.projsf prefix for custom component types.

Converters, Validators, Events, and Listeners

Apart from providing UIComponents, a JSF implementation also provides helper classes for these UIComponents. These helper classes are divided into converters, validators, and an event and listener model. The converters provide a bidirectional type conversion between the submitted value of a component and the corresponding strongly typed object in the model tier. The validators perform validation on the strongly typed object; for example, they can ensure that a date is not in the past. Code Sample 1-11 shows an inputText component with attached date converter.

Code Sample 1-11. inputText *Component with Attached Date Converter*

```
<h:inputText value="#{sample.date}" >
  <f:convertDateTime pattern="yyyy-MMM-dd" />
</h:inputText>
```

JSF also provides a way to attach listeners to components and broadcast events to those listeners, much the same way it works in AWT and Swing. For example, a `commandButton` is a source of `ActionEvents`. When a `commandButton` is clicked, a postback occurs, and a new `ActionEvent` is stored in an event queue. Any event listeners registered with the `commandButton` are notified of this event. Code Sample 1-12 shows a `commandButton` with an attached `Listener`.

Note The JSF specification for registering listeners and broadcasting events is based on the design patterns of the JavaBean specification, version 1.0.1.

Code Sample 1-12. `commandButton` *with Attached Listener*

```
<h:commandButton value="Login"
                 action="success"
                 actionListener="#{sample.onLogin}" />
```

In Code Sample 1-12, a `commandButton` component has two properties—`action` and `actionListener`. Both attributes take method-binding expressions, and the differences are that the `action` attribute requires a method that returns a `String` object and the `actionListener` attribute requires a method that accepts an `ActionEvent` that has a `void` return type. The `action` attribute's string value is used for navigation purposes.

When the queued `ActionEvent` is processed, these method-binding expressions will be used to execute the backing bean methods referenced by `action` and `actionListener`.

Facets

A JSF view is comprised of a component hierarchy, providing access to each parent component's children by index. Sometimes it is also necessary to provide an alternative way of adding subordinate components that are not part of this ordered list.

One example is the `dataTable` component, where the children represent the columns to be rendered in the table. In some cases it might be useful to identify a component that represents the header and/or footer of the entire table, separate from the usual child collection that represents the individual columns. These `header` and `footer` child components are called *facets*, referenced only by name, with no specific order. The name of a facet represents the role that the nested component will play in the parent component. It is important to note that a parent component can contain only one child component per named facet, but the same parent component can contain many indexed child components.

Code Sample 1-13 shows how to add a `header` facet to both the `dataTable` component and the `column` component.

Code Sample 1-13. *Facets Within a* `dataTable` *Component*

```
<h:dataTable value="#{sample.tableList}" var="rows" >
  <f:facet name="header" >
    <h:outputText value="Contact Information" />
  </f:facet>
```

```
  <h:column>
    <f:facet name="header" >
      <h:outputText value="Firstname" />
    </f:facet>
    <h:outputText value="#{rows.firstname}" />
  </h:column>
  ...
</h:dataTable>
```

Renderers

The JSF specification outlines two models for how a JSF component can handle values from incoming requests (*decode*) and outgoing response (*encode*). These two models—direct implementation and delegated implementation—have two distinct approaches; the direct implementation relies on the `UIComponent` instance to handle decode and encode, and the delegate implementation delegates these responsibilities to a `Renderer`. As you have seen in Figure 1-5, the delegate approach allows application developers to work with the `UIComponent` independently from what will be rendered on the client. In this book, we will discuss only the delegate implementation approach, since our goal is to provide multiple `Renderers` for each behavioral component. This approach is also what makes JSF such a powerful UI framework.

■ **Note** The direct implementation approach provides slightly better performance since there is no need to delegate to a `Renderer`, but it also severely limits extensibility and portability across clients.

`Renderers` are responsible for the presentation of a JSF component and must generate the appropriate client-side markup, such as HTML and JavaScript, or XUL. `Renderers` are also in charge of converting information coming from the client to something understandable for the component (for example, a string value from an HTML form `POST` converted to a strongly typed `Date` object).

Although a `Renderer` introduces client-side attributes such as `style`, `disabled`, `tooltip`, and so on, these attributes are actually exposed in the renderer-specific component subclass (for example, `HtmlSelectOneRadio`).

One major difference between `UIComponents` and `Renderers` is the way they are defined at runtime. `Renderers` are defined as singletons, so there is only one `Renderer` for all instances of a `UIComponent` for each particular renderer type.

■ **Caution** Since individual `Renderer` instances will be instantiated as requested during the rendering process and used throughout the life of a Web application, it is important to understand that each instance may be invoked from more than one request-processing thread simultaneously. This requires that `Renderers` are programmed in a thread-safe manner.

Renderer Types

The renderer type is an identifier that is defined by the component, and in combination with the component family, it uniquely identifies which Renderer class to use with the component. Combining the renderer type and the component family is extremely powerful since it allows the reuse of the renderer type for multiple behavioral components.

Code Sample 1-14 illustrates how a component family is associated with a specific Renderer and renderer type.

Code Sample 1-14. *Renderer Type As Defined in the JSF Configuration File*

```
<render-kit>
  <renderer>
    <component-family>
      javax.faces.Input
    </component-family>
    <renderer-type>
      com.apress.projsf.Date
    </renderer-type>
    <renderer-class>
      com.apress.projsf.ch2.renderer.html.HtmlInputDateRenderer
    </renderer-class>
```

Table 1-4 contains a subset of the standard component families with their associated components and component and renderer types.

Table 1-4. *A Subset of All Standard Component Families and Their Components, Component Types, and Renderer Types*

Component Family*	Component	Component Type	Renderer Type**
Command	UICommand	Command	
	HtmlCommandButton	HtmlCommandButton	Button
	HtmlCommandLink	HtmlCommandLink	Link
Data	UIData	Data	
	HtmlDataTable	HtmlDataTable	Table
Form	UIForm	Form	
	HtmlForm	Form	Form
Graphic	UIGraphic	Graphic	
	HtmlGraphicImage	HtmlGraphicImage	Image
Input	UIInput	Input	
	HtmlInputHidden	HtmlInputHidden	Hidden
	HtmlInputSecret	HtmlInputSecret	Secret
	HtmlInputText	HtmlInputText	Text
	HtmlInputTextArea	HtmlInputTextArea	Textarea

Continued

Table 1-4. *Continued*

Component Family*	Component	Component Type	Renderer Type**
Output	UIOutput	Output	
	HtmlOutputFormat	HtmlOutputFormat	Format
	HtmlOutputLabel	HtmlOutputLabel	Label
	HtmlOutputLink	HtmlOutputLink	Link
	HtmlOutputText	HtmlOutputText	Text
Panel	UIPanel	Panel	
	HtmlPanelGrid	HtmlPanelGrid	Grid
	HtmlPanelGroup	HtmlPanelGroup	Group

* *The fully qualified name of the component family is* javax.faces.<name in table>.
** *The fully qualified name for renderer type is* javax.faces.<name in table>.

Table 1-4 shows that the renderer type Text is used in several places—for both the HtmlInputText component and the HtmlOutputText component. The combination of the component family Output and the renderer type Link uses the Renderer class that would generate a regular HTML link element—<a href="...">some text</a>—to the client.

RenderKits

The functionality of a RenderKit is to support UIComponents that use the delegate implementation approach with the delegation of Renderers to the UIComponent. RenderKits group instances of Renderers with similar markup types, and the default RenderKit provided by all JSF implementations is the HTML Basic RenderKit containing Renderers that output HTML 4.0.1. Other possible RenderKits can have Renderers supporting view technologies such as SVG, WML, Ajax, XUL, and so on. In this book, you'll look at additional RenderKits for Microsoft's DHTML/HTML Components (HTC) and Mozilla's XUL/XML Binding Language (XBL) technologies.

The RenderKit is not responsible for creating the Renderer because it will store only a single instance of each renderer type. Each RenderKit is associated to a view (component hierarchy) at runtime as a UIViewRoot property. If no RenderKit has been set, the default RenderKit will be used. When it comes to RenderKits, many times you have no need to create a new RenderKit. Adding a custom Renderer to an already existing RenderKit is just a configuration operation. If a RenderKit identifier is omitted, the custom Renderer is automatically added to the default HTML Basic RenderKit. If you would like to add a RenderKit with custom Renderers, you can do the same thing—update the JSF configuration file. Code Sample 1-15 shows how you can add a new Renderer to the JSF configuration file.

Code Sample 1-15. *New Renderer Added to the Default HTML Basic RenderKit*

```
<render-kit>
  <!-- no render-kit-id, so add this Renderer to the HTML_BASIC RenderKit -->
  <renderer>
```

```
    <component-family>
      javax.faces.Input
    </component-family>
    <renderer-type>
      com.apress..projsf.Date
    </renderer-type>
    <renderer-class>
      com.apress.projsf.ch2.renderer.html.HtmlInputDateRenderer
    </renderer-class>
    ...
</render-kit>
```

By not adding a `RenderKit` identifier to the `RenderKit` configuration, the `Renderer` sample in Code Sample 1-15—`com.apress.projsf.ch2.renderer.html.HtmlInputDateRenderer`—is automatically added to the standard default HTML Basic `RenderKit`.

Custom Action Tag Handlers

Since the default page description language is JSP, most JSF components will have a JSP custom action. When the JSP container encounters a custom action, it asks for the JSF tag handler associated with this action. The main purpose of the JSF tag handler is to create an instance of the component, using the renderer-specific subclass, and associate the component with a `Renderer` at the first page request.

Request-Processing Lifecycle

As a component writer, it is essential you have a clear understanding about the lifecycle of JSF. A page constructed with JSF components will go through a well-defined request-processing lifecycle. This lifecycle consists of six phases—Restore View, Apply Request Values, Process Validations, Update Model Values, Invoke Application, and Render Response, as shown in Figure 1-8.

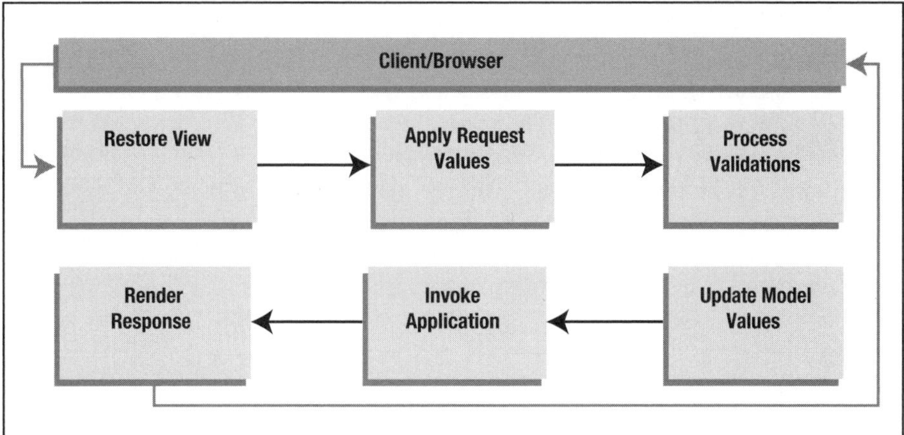

Figure 1-8. *Formal lifecycle of JSF*

Here's the process broken down:

1. *Restore View*: This phase is responsible for restoring the component hierarchy from the previous request and attaching it to the `FacesContext`. If no saved state is available, then the Restore View phase is responsible for creating a new `UIViewRoot`, which is the root node in the component hierarchy, and storing it on the `FacesContext`.
2. *Apply Request Values*: In this phase, each component has the opportunity to update its current state with information included in the current request.
3. *Process Validations*: This phase is in charge of processing any validators or converters attached to components in the component hierarchy.
4. *Update Model Values*: During this phase, all suitable model data objects will have their values updated to match the local value of the matching component, and the component local values will be cleared.
5. *Invoke Application*: At this phase, any remaining events broadcast to the application need to be performed (for example, actions performed by an `HtmlCommandButton`).
6. *Render Response*: This phase is responsible for rendering the response to the client and storing the new state for processing of any subsequent requests.

To put these phases into a real-life context, we'll use a simple example where the user will access an application built with JSF and JSP. This application contains a simple login page with some input fields for a username and password and a button to log in. On successful login, the user is redirected to a second page that will display the user's username.

Building an Application Using JSF

This application contains three essential pieces—the application description (JSP), a JSF configuration file, and a managed bean. This application has two JSP pages—`login.jspx` and `result.jspx`. Code Sample 1-16 shows the login page.

Code Sample 1-16. *The Login Page*

```
<?xml version="1.0" encoding="utf-8"?>
<jsp:root xmlns:jsp="http://java.sun.com/JSP/Page" version="2.0"
          xmlns:f="http://java.sun.com/jsf/core"
          xmlns:h="http://java.sun.com/jsf/html">
  <jsp:output omit-xml-declaration="true" doctype-root-element="HTML"
              doctype-system="http://www.w3.org/TR/html4/loose.dtd"
              doctype-public="-//W3C//DTD HTML 4.01 Transitional//EN"/>
  <jsp:directive.page contentType="text/html;charset=utf-8"/>
  <f:view>
    <html>
      <body>
        <h:form>
          <h:outputText value="Application Login" />
          <h:inputText value="#{credentials.username}" />
```

```
        <h:inputText value="#{credentials.password}" />
        <h:commandButton value="Login"
                         action="success"
                         actionListener="#{credentials.onLogin}" />
      </h:form>
    </body>
  </html>
 </f:view>
</jsp:root>
```

The structure of the page is simple and describes a page containing two input fields for a username and password and a login button. Figure 1-9 shows what the page looks like when rendered.

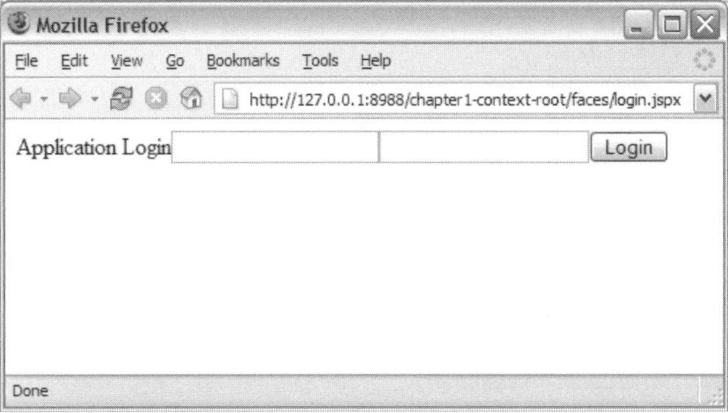

Figure 1-9. *The login page*

The second page in the application, shown in Code Sample 1-17, is simple and merely illustrates navigation and completion of the lifecycle. The page contains an `<h:outputText>` component that will render the entered value from the username `<h:inputText>` component on the initial page on successful login.

Code Sample 1-17. *Navigation Rules and Managed Beans for the Application*

```
<?xml version="1.0" encoding="utf-8"?>
<jsp:root xmlns:jsp="http://java.sun.com/JSP/Page" version="2.0"
          xmlns:f="http://java.sun.com/jsf/core"
          xmlns:h="http://java.sun.com/jsf/html">
  <jsp:output omit-xml-declaration="true" doctype-root-element="HTML"
              doctype-system="http://www.w3.org/TR/html4/loose.dtd"
              doctype-public="-//W3C//DTD HTML 4.01 Transitional//EN"/>
  <jsp:directive.page contentType="text/html;charset=utf-8"/>
  <f:view>
    <html>
```

```
        <body>
          <h:form>
              <h:outputText value="#{credentials.username}" />
          </h:form>
        </body>
      </html>
    </f:view>
</jsp:root>
```

To be able to navigate from one page to another, you have to define a navigation case in the JSF configuration file—`faces-config.xml`. You also need to create a mapping to the back-end code using a managed bean. Code Sample 1-18 shows how to do this.

Code Sample 1-18. *Navigation Rules and Managed Beans for the Application*

```
<navigation-rule>
  <from-view-id>/login.jspx</from-view-id>
  <navigation-case>
    <from-outcome>success</from-outcome>
    <to-view-id>/result.jspx</to-view-id>
  </navigation-case>
</navigation-rule>
<managed-bean>
  <managed-bean-name>credentials</managed-bean-name>
  <managed-bean-class>
    com.apress.projsf.ch1.application.CredentialsBean
  </managed-bean-class>
  <managed-bean-scope>session</managed-bean-scope>
</managed-bean>
```

As you can see, Code Sample 1-18 defines that from the `login.jspx` page, on an outcome of `success`, the user of the application will be sent to the `result.jspx` page. It also defines a managed bean that points to a class—`CredentialsBean`—containing some simple application logic. Code Sample 1-19 shows the application logic.

Code Sample 1-19. *The Application Logic*

```
package com.apress.projsf.ch1.application;

import javax.faces.event.AbortProcessingException;
import javax.faces.event.ActionEvent;

public class CredentialsBean
{
  public void onLogin(
    ActionEvent event)
```

```
    {
      If (!"duke".equalsIgnoreCase(_username))
         throw new AbortProcessingException("Unrecognized username!");
      // clear out the password, for good measure!
      _password = null;
    }

    public void setUsername(
      String username)
    {
      _username = username;
    }

    public String getUsername()
    {
      return _username;
    }

    public void setPassword(
      String password)
    {
      _password = password;
    }

    public String getPassword()
    {
      return _password;
    }

    private String _username;
    private String _password;
}
```

Web Application Start-Up

Upon receiving a JSF request, the JSF implementation must *launch*, or acquire, references to several processes/services that must be available to a JSF Web application running in a servlet or portlet environment. To get access to these references, the JSF implementation will call several factories that are responsible for creating instances needed to launch the JSF application.

When a JSF Web application starts, four factories are instantiated; each of these factories is responsible for different areas within a JSF Web application:

> *ApplicationFactory*: The `ApplicationFactory` class is responsible for the creation of the `Application` instance, which can be seen as a service that allows, for example, the `Lifecycle` instance to create and restore JSF views (component hierarchies) on incoming requests and to store the state of the JSF view.

LifecycleFactory: The LifecycleFactory is in charge of returning a Lifecycle instance for a lifecycle identifier. The default Lifecycle instance is in charge of invoking processing logic to implement the required functionality for each phase of the JSF request-processing lifecycle.

RenderKitFactory: The RenderKitFactory is responsible for returning a RenderKit for the JSF Web application. A RenderKit is a library of Renderers with a common rendering technology.

FacesContextFactory: The FacesContextFactory provides the JSF implementation with a way to create an instance of FacesContext that is used to represent contextual information associated with the incoming request and eventually with the response.

Figure 1-10 shows the players involved at application start-up.

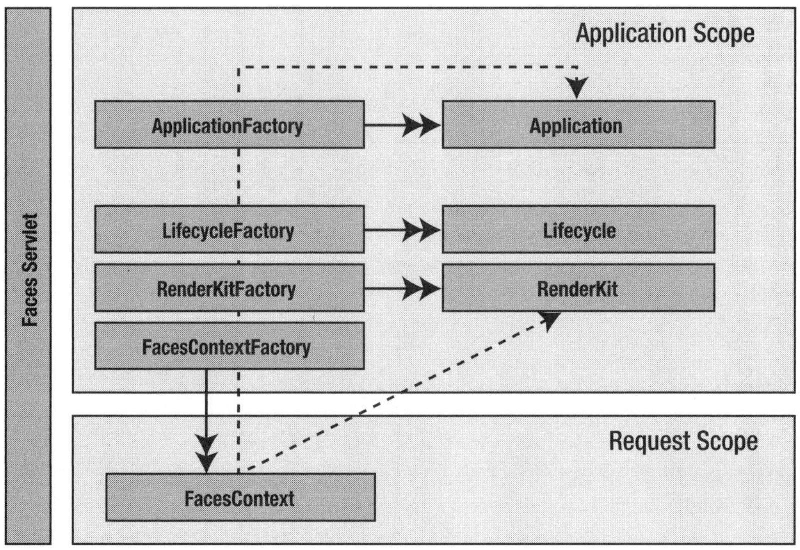

Figure 1-10. *Application creation*

Each JSF Web application has one ApplicationFactory. This factory class is responsible for creating and replacing the Application instance that is required by all applications utilizing JSF. The Application instance will then serve other processes with services supported by this instance. Likewise, the JSF configuration file—faces-config.xml—is read once during the creation of the Web application and stored in the Application instance.

The RenderKitFactory is responsible for returning a RenderKit instance based on the RenderKit identifier for this JSF Web application. For each JSF implementation, there has to be one default RenderKit—the HTML RenderKit that is identified by a string constant—RenderKitFactory.HTML_BASIC_RENDER_KIT. The LifecycleFactory is in charge of creating (if needed) and returning a Lifecycle. This Lifecycle instance is in charge of invoking processing logic to implement the required functionality for each phase (refer to Figure 1-8) of the request-processing lifecycle. The last factory class—`FacesContextFactory`—is providing the JSF implementation with a way to create an instance of `FacesContext` that is used to represent contextual information associated with the incoming request and eventually creating the response.

Initial Request

When the user accesses the application for the first time, an initial request is sent to the `FacesServlet`, which dispatches the request to the JSF `Lifecycle` instance (refer to Figure 1-10).

Restore View Phase

The first phase of the JSF lifecycle is the Restore View phase (see Figure 1-11) whose responsibility it is to check whether this page has been requested earlier or if this is a new request.

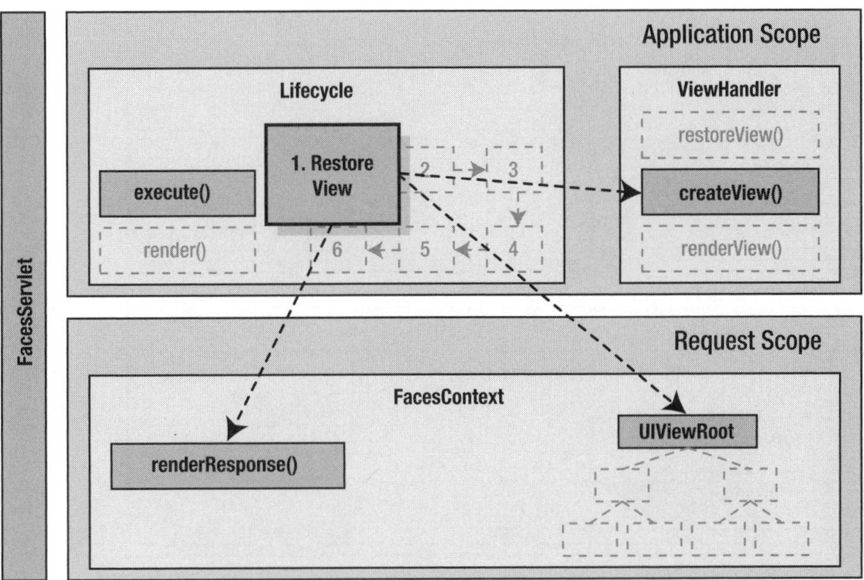

Figure 1-11. *Restore View phase during initial request*

In Figure 1-11, you are looking at the process for an incoming request and how the first phase—Restore View—in the JSF lifecycle is responsible for restoring a view from the server and client state. During the first request for this view, the `ViewHandler.restoreView()` method will return `null`, since there is no stored state.

■ **Note** The JSF lifecycle phase identifiers are part of the JSF public API in the `PhaseId` class.

If the return value is null, the Restore View phase will call renderResponse() on the FacesContext for this request. The renderResponse() method will indicate that when this phase is done, the render() method is called to execute phase 6—Render Response—without proceeding with phases 2 through 5. Subsequently, the Restore View phase will call the ViewHandler.createView() method to create the component hierarchy root—UIViewRoot—and attach it to the FacesContext. The UIViewRoot component performs no rendering but plays an important role in event delivery during a postback request.

Render Response Phase

When the renderResponse() method is called during the Restore View phase, the lifecycle skips directly to the render() method, which is responsible for performing the Render Response phase, as shown in Figure 1-12.

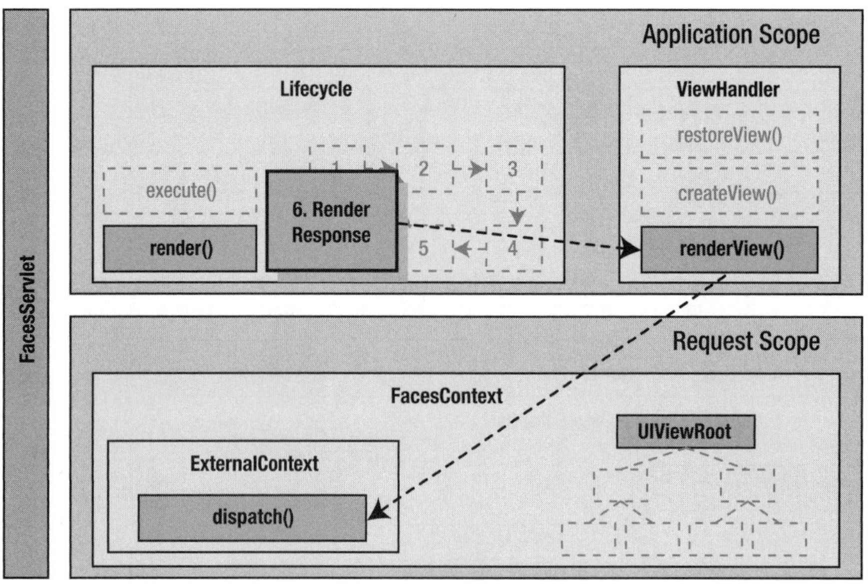

Figure 1-12. *Render Response phase during initial request*

During this phase, the ViewHandler.renderView() method is called to execute the JSP document. The renderView() method will pass the value of the viewId property acquired from the UIViewRoot node as a context-relative path to the dispatch() method of the ExternalContext associated with this request. The dispatch() method will forward the value of viewId property (for example, /login.jspx as a context-relative path) to the Web container.

Since the JSF-specific mapping is not part of the forwarded request, the request is ignored by the FacesServlet and passed to the JSP container, which in turn will locate the JSP based on the context-relative path and execute the JSP page matching the viewId (for example, /login.jspx). Figure 1-13 shows the processing of the JSF JSP document.

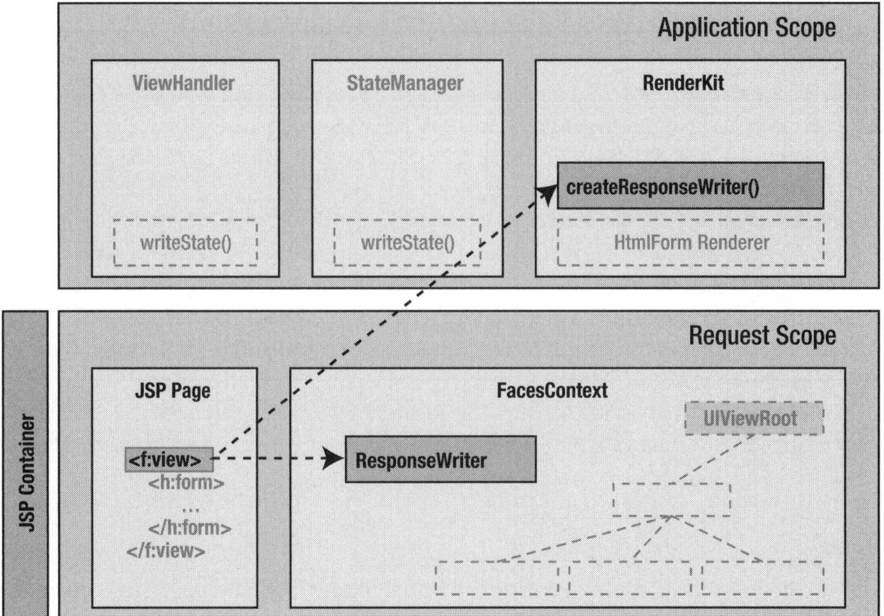

Figure 1-13. *Setting the* `ResponseWriter` *on the* `FacesContext`

THE JSF VIEW IDENTIFIER: VIEW ID

Depending on which mapping is used—prefix or suffix—the `UIViewRoot` view identifier is derived slightly differently from the request uniform resource identifier (URI). If prefix mapping is used, such as `/faces/*` (which is the most common) for the `FacesServlet`, the `viewId` property is set from the path information coming after the mapping; for example, `/context-rootfaces/login.jspx` will set a view identifier equal to `/login.jspx`. If suffix mapping is used, such as `*.jsf`, the `viewId` property is set from the servlet path information of the request URI, after replacing the suffix with the value of the context initialization parameter named by the symbolic constant `ViewHandler.DEFAULT_SUFFIX_NAME`. For example, `/context-root/login.jsf` will set a view identifier equal to `/login.jsp` by default but can leverage the context initialization parameter to use `.jspx` as the default suffix instead.

Before processing and executing the JSF JSP document, the JSP runtime first determines the content type and character encoding to use. For JSF to work in harmony with the JSP lifecycle, the `<f:view>` tag needs to be present. The `<f:view>` tag is a JSP body tag that buffers all the rendered output from the nested JSF components. Simply put, the `<f:view>` tag serves as a container for all other JSF components. The `<f:view>` tag is responsible for creating and storing an instance of the `ResponseWriter` on the `FacesContext`.

The `createResponseWriter()` method creates a new instance of the `ResponseWriter` for the specified content type and character encoding. The `ResponseWriter` is responsible for writing the generated markup to the requesting client, in this case the `<f:view>` body content buffer.

CONTENT TYPE AND CHARACTER ENCODING

When a server sends a document to an HTTP browser client, it also passes information in the Content-Type HTTP header about the Multipurpose Internet Mail Extensions (MIME) type, such as `text/html`, and the character set, such as `UTF-8` or `ISO-8859-1`. The client uses this information to correctly process the incoming bytes from the server.

A list of acceptable content types and character encodings is sent in the Accept HTTP header from the client to the server. This can be used to dynamically select an appropriate content type for the response, or the application developer can specify a static content type for the document.

In JSF, the `<f:view>` tag passes `null` to the `RenderKitFactory` as the list of acceptable content types, even though the JSP container is aware of the complete list accepted by the requesting browser. So, the default `RenderKit`—the standard HTML Basic `RenderKit`—must assume the content type has already been set to `text/html` since it is rendering only HTML. The `RenderKit` uses information about the content type and character encoding to create a `ResponseWriter` that can produce correctly formatted markup to the client.

For each JSF JSP tag within `<f:view>` during the initial render, a JSF component is created and attached to the component hierarchy. As you remember, the `UIViewRoot` was created in the first phase and attached to the `FacesContext`, so you can safely assume that the components will be attached to the component hierarchy. Figure 1-14 shows execution of the `<h:form>` start tag.

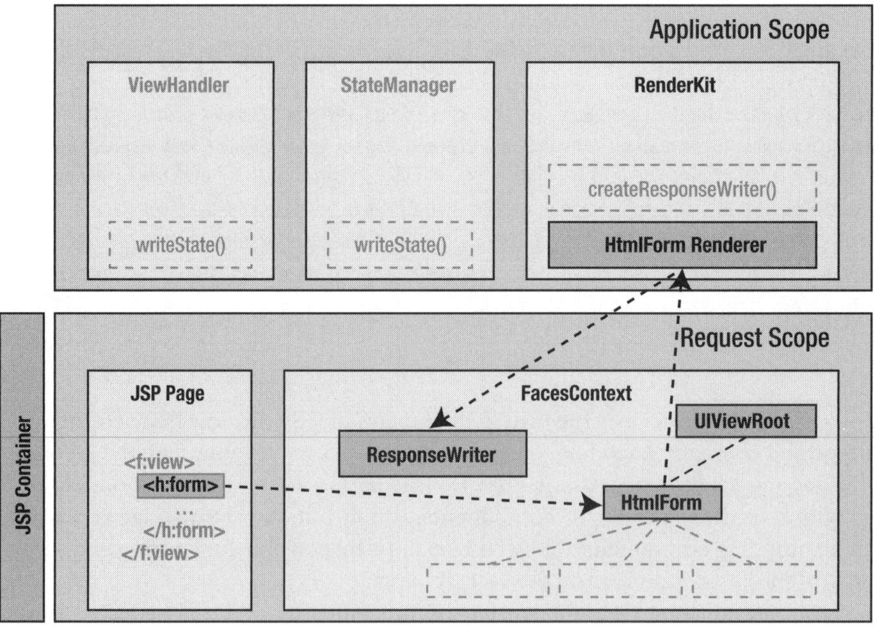

Figure 1-14. *Writing `<form>` start element to the `<f:view>` body content buffer*

In the login JSP document, the next JSF JSP tag to be executed is the `<h:form>` tag. The JSF JSP tag calls the `Application.createComponent()` method that takes a string representing the component type, for example `javax.faces.HtmlForm` (see the section "Component Family and Component Type"). The component type is mapped to a class defined in the `faces-config.xml` file, and an instance of the `HtmlForm` component is created and attached to the `UIViewRoot`. Next, a `Renderer` for the newly created component needs to be found. A `Renderer` is located by component family and renderer type, which together define a unique identifier for the `Renderer` (see the section "Renderer Types").

Note Let's use the `HtmlInputText` component to illustrate the relationship between the component family and renderer type. The `HtmlInputText` component has the component family `javax.faces.Input` and the renderer type `javax.faces.Text`. Together, they uniquely identify the appropriate `Renderer` class within the HTML Basic `RenderKit—javax.faces.renderer.html.HtmlInputText`.

The renderer type is already known by the `<h:form>` tag, and the component family can be located in the component's superclass, `UIForm`. The tag then calls a method called `encodeBegin()` on the component, which in turn calls the `encodeBegin()` method on the `HtmlForm` renderer. The `encodeBegin()` method on the `Renderer` calls methods on the `ResponseWriter` to write the markup for the HTML form element—`<form method="" action="">`. All markup output from the `ResponseWriter` ends up in the `<f:view>` body content buffer. Figure 1-15 shows the closing process of the `<h:form>` tag.

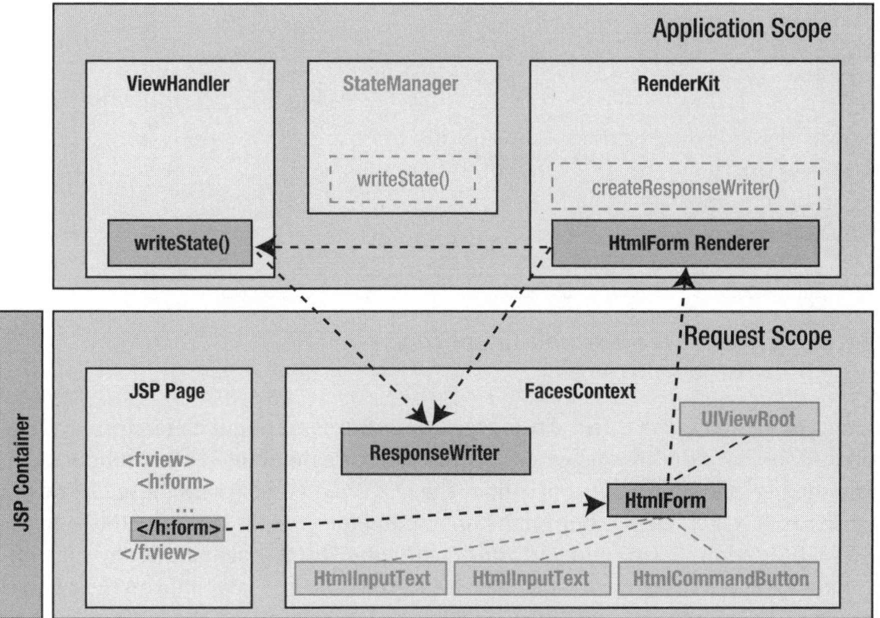

Figure 1-15. *Output token and closing the `</form>` element*

The process continues, and all nested components within the HtmlForm component are rendered and added to the <f:view> body content buffer. Then, the closing tag for the <h:form> tag is executed. The <h:form> tag calls the encodeEnd() method on the Renderer, HtmlFormRenderer, which in turn calls the writeState() method on the ViewHandler. The writeState() method passes a token to the ResponseWriter, which is added to the <f:view> body content buffer. The encodeEnd() method then calls methods on the ResponseWriter to write the closing tag for the HTML form element—</form>. Figure 1-16 shows the closing of the <f:view> tag.

■ **Note** The ViewHandler represents the view technology, and in this case the view technology is JSP. Nothing in the JSF specification prevents anyone from implementing an alternate ViewHandler for another view technology, such as XML.

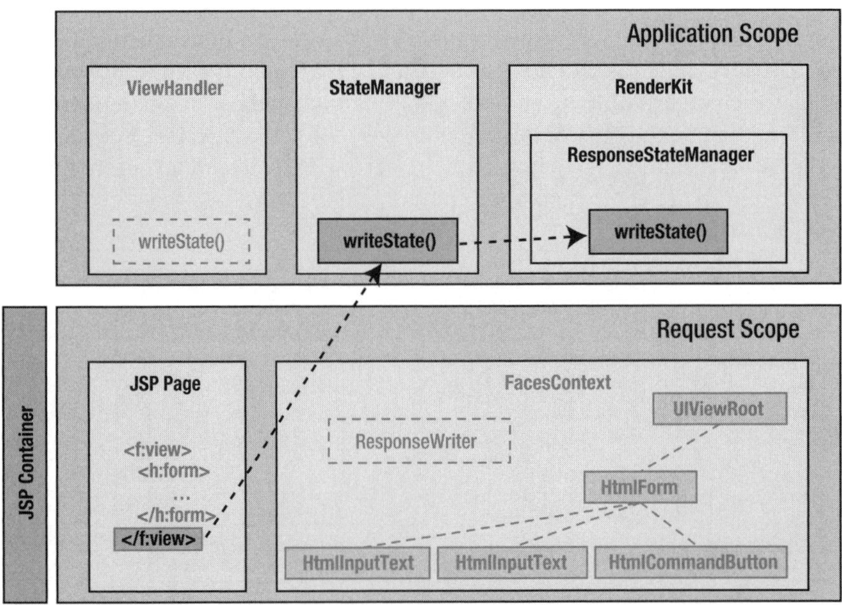

Figure 1-16. *Replacing token with serialized state and closing* </f:view>

By the time you get to the </f:view> closing tag, the entire component hierarchy is available. It is not until you have the complete tree that you can store the state of the component hierarchy representing this page of the application. The </f:view> end tag calls the writeState() method on the StateManager. Depending on the init parameter—STATE_SAVING_METHOD—for state saving (see the section "Saving and Restoring State"), the StateManager stores the state in the session on the server or delegates to the ResponseStateManager to save state on the client replacing the token with the serialized state. After the state has been saved, the buffer is flushed out to the client, and execution of any remaining non-JSF JSP tags will take place. The login page is now rendered in the browser.

Note In JSF 1.2, the `<f:view>` tag is no longer responsible for buffering the output. Instead, buffering is achieved by using a `ServletResponse` wrapper. In addition, the component hierarchy is no longer created inline during rendering. Instead, during the Render Response phase of JSF 1.2, the component hierarchy is created first and rendered next. Therefore, during rendering, the full component hierarchy is available, so the state is written directly into the buffered response, rather than needing to use a placeholder token to be replaced by the real state in `</f:view>`.

Postback Request

So far, the only thing the user has seen is the initial rendering of the first requested page. After receiving the page, the user enters a username and password and clicks the login button. A postback is performed, and you will now look at how JSF handles postback. Some parts are similar to what we have already been covering in the initial request, but there are obviously differences and additions, especially in the JSF request lifecycle. At postback, all six phases of the JSF request lifecycle get called (unless somewhere in the process the `FacesContext.renderResponse()` method is called causing the lifecycle to jump directly to the Render Response phase). This is different from the initial request where only the first and last phases are called.

Restore View Phase

The first part of a postback is the same as for the initial request; the Restore View phase executes and calls the `restoreView()` method on the `ViewHandler` to restore any state available from the previous request. Figure 1-17 shows restoring the saved state of the component hierarchy.

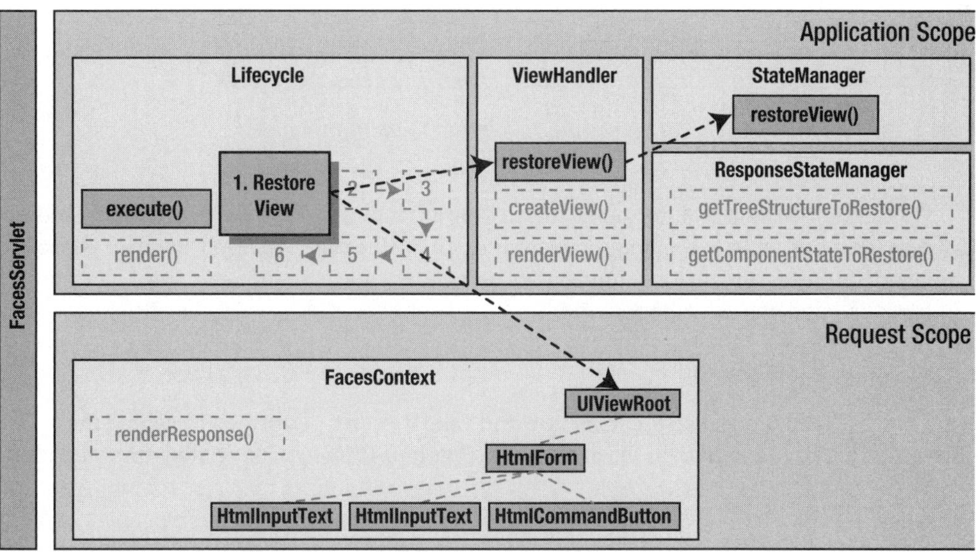

Figure 1-17. *Restoring the saved state of the component hierarchy*

Here is where the similarities end; instead of returning `null`, the `restoreView()` method will return the current state of the component hierarchy associated with a particular `viewId` and `FacesContext` from the `StateManager`, and if the init parameter—`STATE_SAVING_METHOD`—is set to client-side state-saving, call the `ResponseStateManager` to retrieve the state from the current request. The restored component hierarchy is then passed to the `FacesContext` by the Restore View phase.

Apply Request Values Phase

In the Apply Request Values phase, each input component establishes the submitted value from the request parameters, and each command component queues an event to be delivered in the Invoke Application phase. Figure 1-18 shows how the Apply Request Values phase passes new values to the components.

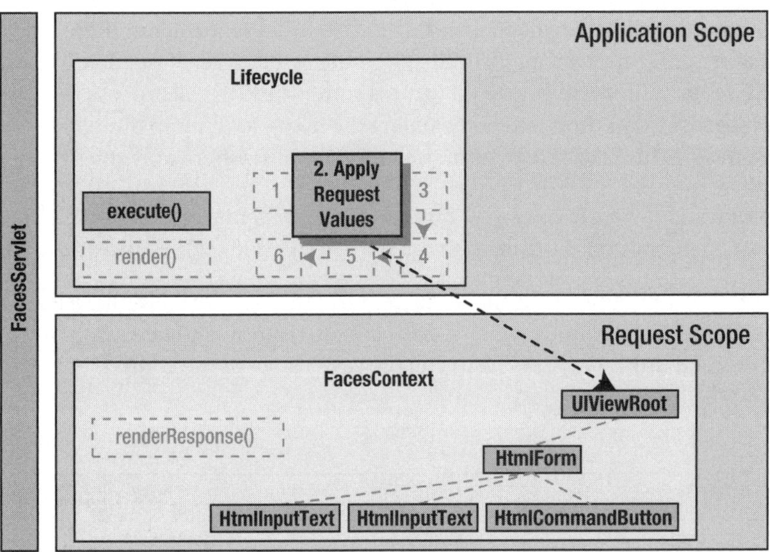

Figure 1-18. *Applying new values passed on the request to the components*

The submitted value is at this point stored only as "submitted" on the component, and no value has been pushed into the underlying model yet. By the time the Apply Request phase is completed, the `Renderers` no longer need to observe the request parameters, since all values have been updated on each component.

Process Validation Phase

In the Process Validations phase, conversion and validation are performed by calling the `processValidators()` method on the `UIViewRoot`. Figure 1-19 shows conversion and validation.

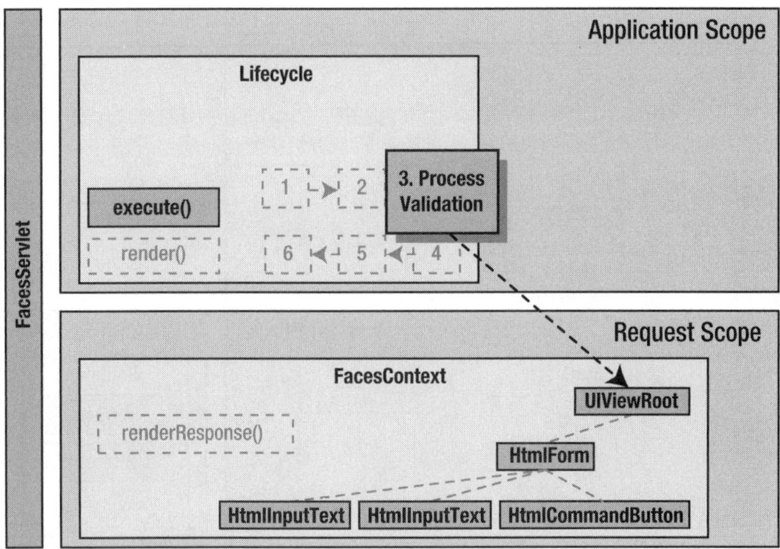

Figure 1-19. *Performing conversion and validation*

This process will continue calling the `processValidators()` method recursively on each component in the component hierarchy. During validation of each `HtmlInputText` component, type conversion will occur first on the component's submitted value (for example, a string to a strongly typed object). The new object is set as a local value on the component, and the submitted value is cleared. The new strongly typed object is then validated. If there are no errors, then the next step is to queue a `ValueChangeEvent` that will be delivered at the end of the Apply Request Values phase.

If a conversion or validation error occurs, a corresponding JSF message is attached to the `FacesContext` using the component `clientId`, and then the `renderResponse()` method is called to indicate that the lifecycle should skip directly to the Render Response phase after the Process Validations phase is complete.

Update Model Phase

At this point in the lifecycle, all submitted values have been successfully converted and validated, so it is safe to push them into the underlying data model. During the Update Model phase, the JSF lifecycle walks over the component hierarchy, calling the `processUpdates()` method on each component. Figure 1-20 shows the Update Model phase updating the underlying model.

To determine where to store the new value, the `processUpdates()` method will use the value binding, which is defined in the `value` attribute on the component (for example, `#{credentials.username}`). The value binding points to a property on a managed bean (for example, `username`). Using the value binding, the locally stored value on the component is pushed into the data model, and the locally stored value on the component is cleared.

Any JSF messages and errors on the model—for example, validations implemented by the model—are attached to the `FacesContext` with the component's client ID. The `renderResponse()` method is then called to indicate that the lifecycle should skip directly to the Render Response phase after the Update Model phase is complete.

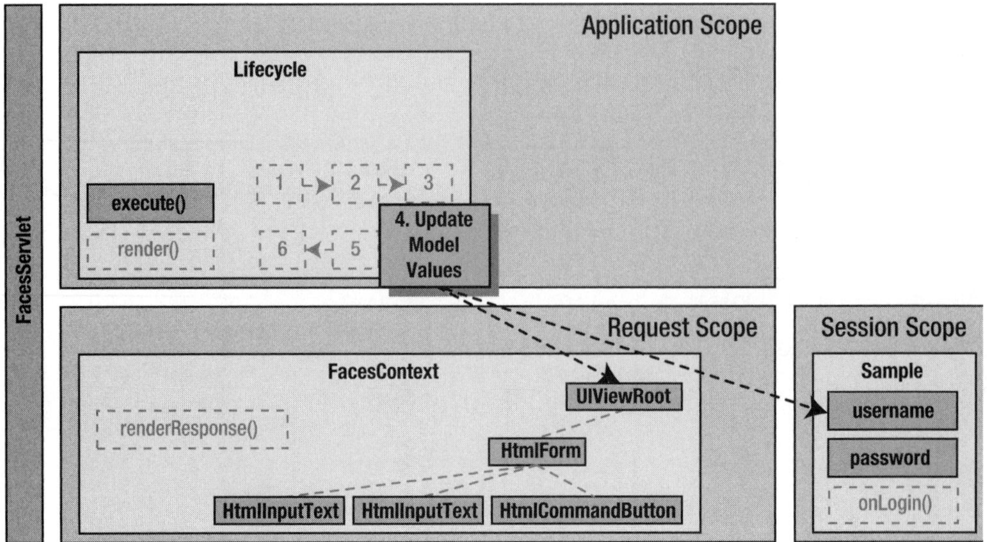

Figure 1-20. *Updating underlying model*

Invoke Application Phase

In the Invoke Application phase, you have no need to walk the component hierarchy, since this phase will handle only the queued events from previous phases and, depending on the outcome, will either continue to the last phase—Render Response—or redirect to another page. Figure 1-21 shows the broadcasting of events queued for this phase and the processing of action method bindings.

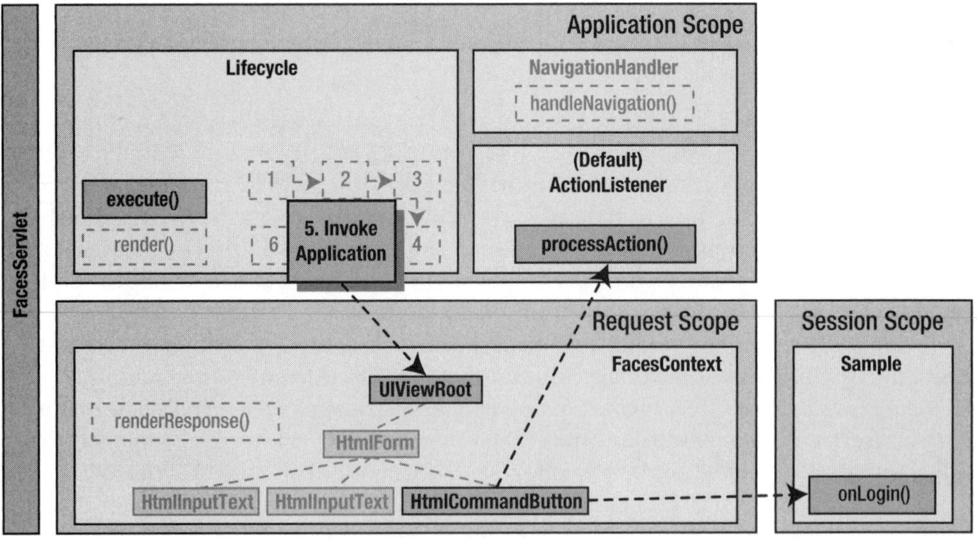

Figure 1-21. *Performing application logic*

As mentioned in the earlier section "Converters, Validators, Events, and Listeners," you have two methods that will be processed when an `ActionEvent` occurs. The first thing that happens is a call to the `processApplication()` method on the `UIViewRoot` that takes each queued event and broadcasts to the target component for the event (for example, `commandButton.broadcast(FacesEvent)`). The `UICommand` component knows about the `action` and `actionListener` attributes, as well as the default `ActionListener` attached to the `Application` object.

First all previously registered `ActionListeners` are called, then the `actionListener` method binding is executed (for example, `#{credentials.onLogin}`), and finally the component calls the `processAction()` method on the default `ActionListener` to process the action method binding and handle navigation. It is important that the action method binding is called at the end of this process, since it defines possible navigation, and you don't want to navigate before you have processed all events.

Postback with Navigation

When the default `ActionListener` is processing an `ActionEvent`, it invokes the action method binding and gets the `outcome`, which is a `String` object. If the `outcome` returns `null`, then the default `ActionListener` will continue with the next queued event. After all events have been broadcast, the Invoke Application phase is complete and lifecycle processing continues to the last phase—Render Response. If the `outcome` is not `null`, then the default `ActionListener` passes `FacesContext`, `fromAction` (which is the method-binding expression text—for example, `credentials.doLogin`), and `outcome` to the `NavigationHandler`. Figure 1-22 shows navigation on postback.

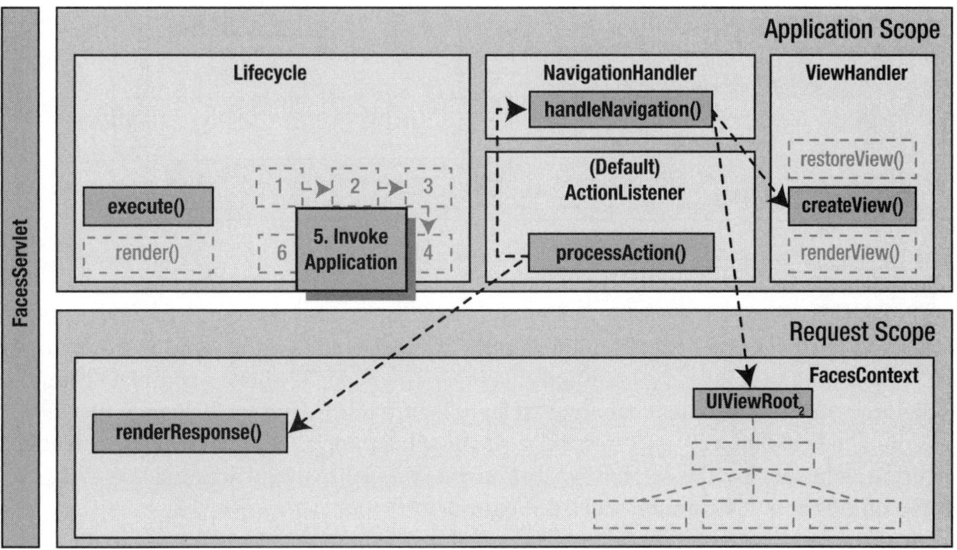

Figure 1-22. *Navigation on postback*

Navigation rules are defined in `faces-config.xml`, which is read at start-up, and all information is stored in the `Application` object (see the section "Navigation Model"). The first thing the `NavigationHandler` does is to check for a navigation rule that matches the combination of `fromViewId` (which it will get from the `FacesContext`), `fromAction`, and `outcome`.

You can handle navigation in two ways. Redirecting means a new request (and as a bonus you can bookmark the new page) and starts the JSF request lifecycle all over again; you can also have the `handleNavigation()` method create a new `UIViewRoot`, set the new `UIViewRoot` on the `FacesContext`, and let the default `ActionListener` call `renderResponse()` to initiate the Render Response phase. This solution is replicating the behavior of the initial request in the Render Response phase but with a new view identifier. Figure 1-23 shows the JSP execution during postback.

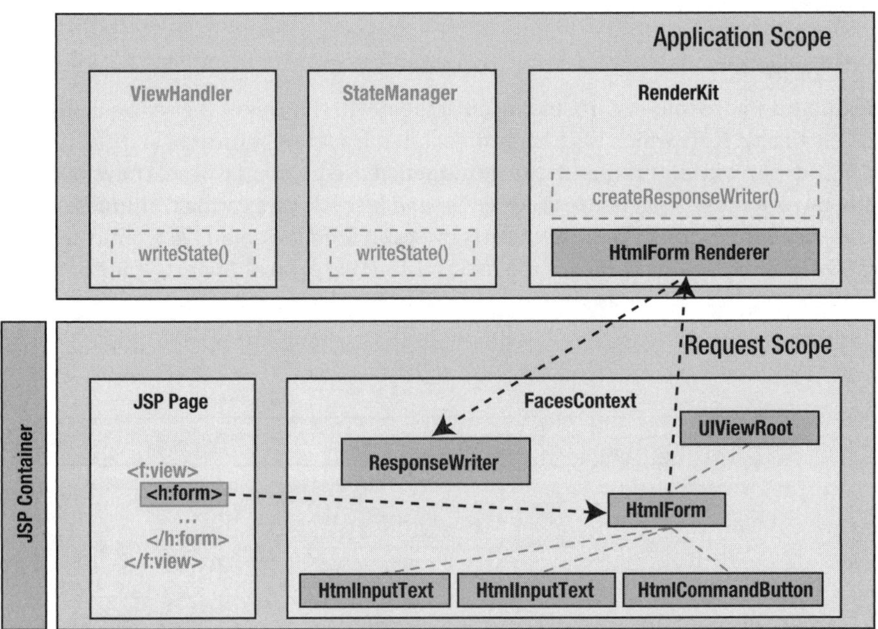

Figure 1-23. *Render Response on postback*

During a postback, the first part of the Render Response phase is the same as that of the initial request until the `dispatch()` method call, except that you now have a complete component hierarchy and not just the `UIViewRoot` (refer to Figure 1-13). After the dispatch, the JSP page is executed, and the `<f:view>` start tag does the same thing as at initial request—creating and storing an instance of the `ResponseWriter` on the `FacesContext` and acting as a buffer for rendered output from the components (see Figure 1-14).

Instead of creating new components and attaching them to the `UIViewRoot` as in the initial request, individual component tags nested within the `<f:view>` tag will have to locate their counterparts that already exist in the component hierarchy. This takes place during JSP page execution, by traversing up the tag tree to find the closest enclosing parent component tag. From the parent component tag, the child component tag can find its component counterpart, via either the component identifier or the facet name (see the section "Facets").

Apart from mapping components to component tags rather than creating new component instances, the processing proceeds in the same way as the initial request—rendering components to the `<f:view>` body content buffer, storing the state either at the client or in the session at the server, and finally flushing the buffered markup to the parent JSP container for rendering (refer to Figure 1-15).

JSF and JSP

In JSF, a component writer can set a `boolean` property called `rendersChildren` on a component. This property decides whether a component should render its children. For components in the JSF implementation, the value of `rendersChildren` is set to `false`. This means each component is responsible for rendering the right output to the `ResponseWriter` and buffering in the `<f:view>`, not caring how its children are rendered. If `rendersChildren` is set to `true` on a component, then the `encodeBegin()` method is called in the closing tag instead of the start tag (refer to Figure 1-14) to ensure that no children are rendered to the buffer until the parent has closed the loop on its children. Once the parent knows about its children, they will be rendered to the `<f:view>` body content buffer. One component that uses this is the `dataTable` component, because it needs to have access to all its child components before any rendered output is generated.

Considering that some components may require that `rendersChildren` is set to `true`, this will have an impact on how you can construct your page description. Remember the login page? Let's add some labels to the input fields and adjust the layout a bit so the components will be aligned vertically instead of horizontally, as shown in Code Sample 1-20.

Code Sample 1-20. *The Login Page Modified with Some JSP Tags*

```
<?xml version='1.0' encoding='windows-1252'?>
<jsp:root xmlns:jsp="http://java.sun.com/JSP/Page" version="2.0"
          xmlns:f="http://java.sun.com/jsf/core"
          xmlns:h="http://java.sun.com/jsf/html">
  <jsp:output omit-xml-declaration="true" doctype-root-element="HTML"
              doctype-system="http://www.w3.org/TR/html4/loose.dtd"
              doctype-public="-//W3C//DTD HTML 4.01 Transitional//EN"/>
  <jsp:directive.page contentType="text/html;charset=windows-1252"/>
  <f:view>
    <html>
      <body>
        <h:form>
          <h:outputText value="Application Login" />
          <h:panelGrid columns="2">

            <jsp:text>Username</jsp:text>
            <h:inputText value="#{sample.username}" />
```

```
            <jsp:text>Password</jsp:text>
            <h:inputText value="#{sample.password}" />

          </h:panelGrid>
          <h:commandButton value="Submit" action="#{credentials.onLogin}" />
        </h:form>
      </body>
    </html>
  </f:view>
</jsp:root>
```

This sample wraps the components with a <h:panelGrid> tag. The component created by this tag renders its children in a two-dimensional grid, with two columns. The HtmlPanelGrid component has rendersChildren set to true, so it can observe all the children before rendering the markup for each column. It also adds two non-JSF tags—<jsp:text>—that will add a label to each input field. At runtime the page looks like Figure 1-24.

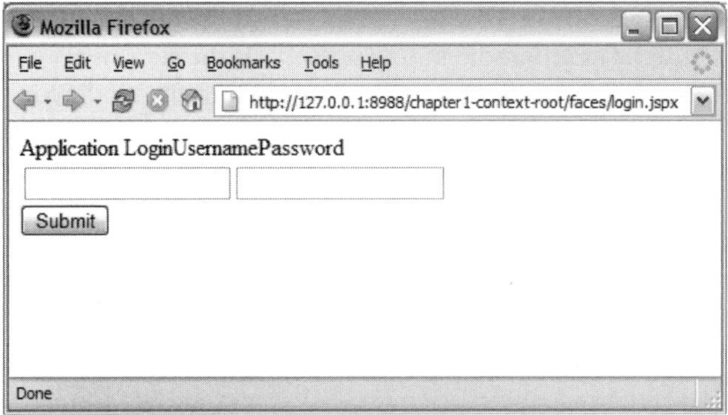

Figure 1-24. *Rendering of non-JSF content with* rendersChildren *set to* true

As you can see, the Username and Password labels have been incorrectly placed at the top of the page. During execution of this page, any JSF component within the HtmlPanelGrid component will be delayed from rendering to the buffer until the closing tag of the HtmlPanelGrid (for example, </h:panelGrid>). Note that no other arbitrary tags or text nested within the HtmlPanelGrid component will be delayed. Therefore, <jsp:text> is rendered to the buffer immediately. You can circumvent this behavior by wrapping an <f:verbatim> tag around non-JSF content, as shown in Code Sample 1-21.

Code Sample 1-21. *The Login Page with* <f:verbatim> *Tag Wrapped Around Non-JSF Content*

```
<h:form>
  <h:outputText value="Application Login"/>
  <h:panelGrid columns="2">
```

```
    <f:verbatim><jsp:text>Username</jsp:text></f:verbatim>
    <h:inputText value="#{credentials.username}" />
    <f:verbatim><jsp:text>Password</jsp:text></f:verbatim>
    <h:inputText value="#{credentials.password}" />

  </h:panelGrid>
  <h:commandButton value="Submit" action="#{credentials.onLogin}" />
</h:form>
```

The `<f:verbatim>` tag takes non-JSF content and adds it to the component hierarchy as a `UIOutput` component. At runtime the updated page looks like Figure 1-25.

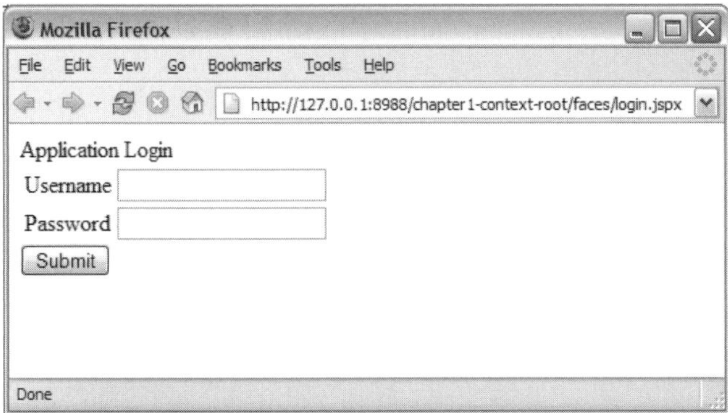

Figure 1-25. *Rendering of non-JSF content using the* `<f:verbatim>` *tag*

Note The issue with `rendersChildren` has been resolved by the JSF Expert Group (EG) in the JSF 1.2 release. The new content-interweaving feature accommodates the differences between JSF and JSP rendering strategies, making it no longer necessary to add the `<f:verbatim>` wrapper tags.

Summary

This chapter acts as a mini-guide for the rest of the book; it also gives you a foundation for your continued journey into the world of JSF beyond this book.

One of the key differentiators JSF has over other view technologies is its openness and ability to adopt newly emerging technologies such as XUL, HTC, and Ajax, as well as other future view technologies. JSF has clear benefits over other technologies because an application built with JSF can continue to live while the surrounding technologies pass away and new ones arise. JSF can reduce maintenance costs for application development since there is only one programming model needed—JSF and Java—even though the systems may require different user agents such as Telnet, instant messaging, mobile agents, browsers, and other types of agents such as barcode readers.

This chapter touched on details that make up a JSF application—JSF components, navigation model, and backend logic via managed beans. We also explored the ins and outs of the JSF component model and its clear separation between presentation and behavior, and we discussed the structure of JSF components—`UIComponent`, `Renderer`, the renderer-specific subclass `RenderKit`, and the JSP tag handler. The chapter also detailed the JSF request lifecycle on initial request and postback, including navigation.

It is crucial to understand the separation between presentation and behavior in order to grasp the full potential of JSF components.

CHAPTER 2

■ ■ ■

Defining the Date Field Component

By allowing the developer to separate the functionality of a solution into components, located where it is most logical for the solution, component-based design removes many of the constraints that used to hinder the deployment and maintenance of the solution.

—Microsoft Developer Network (MSDN)

Having introduced JSF in Chapter 1, this chapter will explore the concepts of component design and its applicability in JSF.

The main focus for this chapter is to get you up to speed with the building blocks needed to design and create a reusable JSF component. Creating JSF components is not hard; you just need to follow a well-defined blueprint, which we will provide in this chapter. Specifically, we will cover how to create a `Renderer`, how to create a renderer-specific subclass, how to create a JSP tag handler, and how to register your custom JSF component.

To illustrate this process, we will show how to create a simple date field component that you will use throughout the book. In subsequent chapters, we will show how to enhance this date field component until you arrive at a rich, full-fledged JSF component that supports Ajax, XUL, and HTC. Nevertheless, at the end of this chapter, you should have your first functional component to show to your friends and developer peers.

Requirements for the Date Field Component

You can build your own reusable component in many ways, but for JSF the most common approach is to locate a component that already has the behavior you need and expand upon it. So, what type of behavior is required of the component you will build in this chapter? For example, is it for inputting values, selecting one value, selecting many values, or navigating?

Well, you'll build a component that can take a value, process that value, and then push it back to the underlying model as a strongly typed `Date` object. The component should allow an application developer to attach a converter in order to set the desired date format (such as `mm/dd/yyyy`) for which the end user has to comply. Basically, you'll build a simple input component that can convert and validate the date entered by users.

Having confirmed that this is what you need, it is easy to search existing components for this particular behavior. Table 2-1 lists all the behavioral superclasses available in the JSF specification.

Table 2-1. *JSF Specification: Behavioral Superclasses**

Name**	Description
`UIColumn`	`UIColumn` (extends `UIComponentBase`) is a component that represents a single column of data with a parent `UIData` component. The child components of a `UIColumn` will be processed once for each row in the data managed by the parent `UIData`.
`UICommand`	`UICommand` (extends `UIComponentBase`; implements `ActionSource`) is a control that, when activated by the user, triggers an application-specific "command" or "action." Such a component is typically rendered as a button, a menu item, or a hyperlink.
`UIData`	`UIData` (extends `UIComponentBase`; implements `NamingContainer`) is a component that represents a data binding to a collection of data objects represented by a `DataModel` instance. Only children of type `UIColumn` should be processed by renderers associated with this component.
`UIForm`	`UIForm` (extends `UIComponentBase`; implements `NamingContainer`) is a component that represents an input form to be presented to the user and whose child components (among other things) represent the input fields to be included when the form is submitted. The `encodeEnd()` method of the renderer for `UIForm` must call `ViewHandler.writeState()` before writing out the markup for the closing tag of the form. This allows the state for multiple forms to be saved.
`UIGraphic`	`UIGraphic` (extends `UIComponentBase`) is a component that displays a graphical image to the user. The user cannot manipulate this component; it is for display purposes only.
`UIInput`	`UIInput` (extends `UIOutput`, implements `EditableValueHolder`) is a component that both displays the current value of the component to the user (as `UIOutput` components do) and processes request parameters on the subsequent request that needs to be decoded.
`UIMessage`	`UIMessage` (extends `UIComponentBase`) encapsulates the rendering of error message(s) related to a specified input component.
`UIMessages`	`UIMessage` (extends `UIComponentBase`) encapsulates the rendering of error message(s) not related to a specified input component or all queued messages.
`UIOutput`	`UIOutput` (extends `UIComponentBase`; implements `ValueHolder`) is a component that has a value, optionally retrieved from a model tier bean via a value-binding expression that is displayed to the user. The user cannot directly modify the rendered value; it is for display purposes only.
`UIPanel`	`UIPanel` (extends `UIComponentBase`) is a component that manages the layout of its child components.
`UIParameter`	`UIParameter` (extends `UIComponentBase`) is a component that represents an optionally named configuration parameter that affects the rendering of its parent component. `UIParameter` components do not generally have rendering behavior of their own.
`UISelectBoolean`	`UISelectBoolean` (extends `UIInput`) is a component that represents a single boolean (`true` or `false`) value. It is most commonly rendered as a checkbox.

Name**	Description
UISelectItem	UISelectItem (extends UIComponentBase) is a component that may be nested inside a UISelectMany or UISelectOne component and represents exactly one SelectItem instance in the list of available options for that parent component.
UISelectItems	UISelectItems (extends UIComponentBase) is a component that may be nested inside a UISelectMany or UISelectOne component and represents zero or more SelectItem instances for adding selection items to the list of available options for that parent component.
UISelectMany	UISelectMany (extends UIInput) is a component that represents one or more selections from a list of available options. It is most commonly rendered as a multiple selection list or a series of checkboxes.
UISelectOne	UISelectOne (extends UIInput) is a component that represents zero or one selections from a list of available options. It is most commonly rendered as a combo box or a series of radio buttons.

* *Source: The JSF 1.1 specification*
** *The full class name of this component is* javax.faces.component.

The key behavior of the date field component you'll create in this chapter is for the user to input a new date. Examining Table 2-1, you can see that one component describes the behavior you're looking for in the date field component—the behavioral superclass UIInput. Instead of having to create a new component that introduces existing behavior, you can use this UIInput component from the JSF specification. Therefore, the new component will be called an *input date component* and will follow the same naming conventions as standard JSF components, such as the input text component.

USING UIINPUT

The UIInput component defines the contract for how an application interacts with your component or any component extending this superclass. The UIInput component comes with a default renderer that will at runtime display the component as a text input field into which the user can enter data. Its component type is javax.faces.Input, and the default renderer type is javax.faces.Text.

The UIInput component can display values to the client in much the same way as the UIOutput component does. In fact, the UIInput component extends the UIOutput component. The UIInput component also processes, on a postback, request parameters that need to be decoded and managed. If a value passed on the request is different from the previous value, then a ValueChangeEvent event is raised by the component. You can attach a ValueChangeListener to receive notification when the ValueChangeEvent is broadcast by the UIInput component.

The Input Date Component

The intent with this input date component is to give you a solid foundation for more advanced work with JSF later in the book. Visually the component will be a simple input text field with an icon overlay to indicate it is a date field and will have some useful type conversion and date validation functionality.

To comply with these new requirements, this chapter will introduce one new Renderer, a renderer-specific subclass, and a new tag handler. The input date component also introduces a non-Java element to your design of components—the use of a style sheet. After completing this chapter, you should understand the JSF lifecycle and have enough knowledge to create a new Renderer, a renderer-specific subclass, and a corresponding JSP tag handler.

Figure 2-1 shows the five classes you'll create in this chapter; they are HtmlInputDateRenderer, ProInputDate, UIComponentTagSupport, and ProInputDateTag, as well as two you'll be extending: Renderer and UIInput.

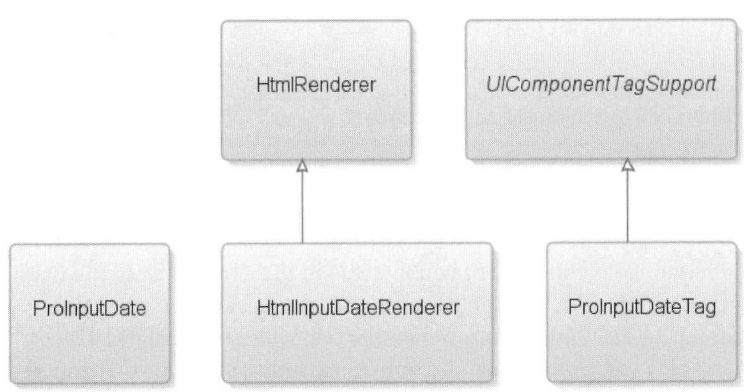

Figure 2-1. *Class diagram showing classes created in this chapter*

- The ProInputDate is the renderer-specific subclass.
- The HtmlRenderer superclass provides some convenience methods for encoding resources.
- The HtmlInputDateRenderer is your new custom Renderer, which is in charge of the markup rendered to the client.
- The ProInputDateTag is the tag handler.
- And finally, the abstract UIComponentTagSupport tag handler class is a support tag handler superclass providing functionality that is common among all components.

Designing the Input Date Component Using a Blueprint

Before creating your first custom JSF component, you need to understand the steps required to complete a JSF component. Table 2-2 outlines the blueprint needed to successfully implement a custom JSF component. During the course of this book, we'll expand this blueprint with additional steps, and these first steps will be the foundation for all custom components you'll create later. For now, you'll focus only on the steps needed to successfully implement the input date component.

Table 2-2. *Steps in the Blueprint for Creating a New JSF Component*

Step	Task	Description
1	Creating a UI prototype	Create a prototype of the UI and intended behavior for your component using the appropriate markup.
2	Creating a client-specific `Renderer`	Create the `Renderer` you need that will write out the client-side markup for your JSF component.
3	Creating a renderer-specific subclass	(Optional) Create a renderer-specific subclass. Although this is an optional step, it is good practice to implement it.
4	Registering `UIComponent` and `Renderer`	Register your new `UIComponent` and `Renderer` in the `faces-config.xml` file.
5	Creating a JSP tag handler and TLD	This step is needed in case you are using JSP as your default view handler. An alternative solution is to use Facelets (`http://facelets.dev.java.net/`).

The first step in Table 2-1 is probably the most important one since that is where you will prototype and test to see whether your ideas will work in the intended client. When you have a prototype working, your next goal is to implement your solution in JSF, which in this case means you need to provide a new `Renderer` to write the intended markup to the client and provide a renderer-specific subclass as a convenience for application developers. Finally, you have to register the custom component and provide a JSP tag handler.

You'll start with the first step in the blueprint to define the new component, implementing it in the intended markup that will eventually be sent to the client.

Step 1: Creating a UI Prototype

When developing a new component, it is a good practice to first create a prototype of the intended markup that will need to be rendered to the client. By doing so, you will not only find out which elements your component has to generate but also which renderer-specific attributes you will need in order to parameterize the generated markup.

As you can see in Code Sample 2-1, the prototype markup consists of an HTML form `<input>` element, an `<img>` element, a `<div>` element, and a `<style>` element. By examining the HTML prototype, as shown in Code Sample 2-2, you can see that three HTML attributes—`title`, `name`, and `value`—are needed to parameterize the generated markup.

Code Sample 2-1. *HTML Prototype for the Input Date Component*

```
<style type="text/css" >
  .overlay
  {
    position:relative;
    left:-10px;
    bottom:-10px;
  }
</style>
```

```
...
<div title="Date Field Component" >
<input name="dateField" value="26 January 2005" >
  <img class="overlay" src="inputDateOverlay.gif" >
</div>
```

Code Sample 2-2. *Parameterized HTML for the Input Date Component*

```
<style type="text/css" >
  .overlay
  {
    position:relative;
    left:-10px;
    bottom:-10px;
  }
</style>
...
<div title="[title]">
<input name="[clientId]" value="[converted value]" >
<img class="overlay" src="inputDateOverlay.gif" >
</div>
```

In Code Sample 2-2, you map the HTML attributes to their corresponding `UIComponent` attributes that are used during rendering.

■ **Note** For more information about HTML elements and all their supported attributes, please visit the W3C Web site at `http://www.w3.org/MarkUp/`.

Figure 2-2 shows the result of your prototype, which displays a simple page with an input field that has an icon indicating this is a date field.

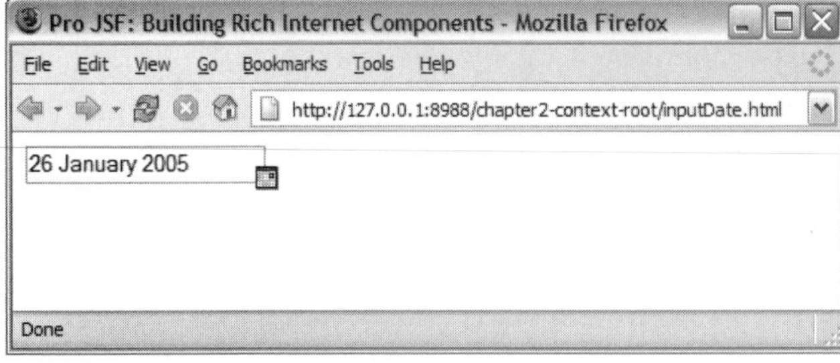

Figure 2-2. *The date field component prototype implemented in HTML with an icon overlay*

Before you create the input date component, you'll take a sneak peak at the final result and how you will use it in a JSP page. Code Sample 2-3 uses the input date component, <pro:inputDate>, and applies a JSF core converter, <f:convertDateTime>, that converts the string entered by the user to a strongly typed Date object. Another <f:convertDateTime> displays the formatted date just below the submit button.

Code Sample 2-3. *Sample Page with the Date Field Component*

```
<pro:inputDate id="dateField"
               title="Date Field Component"
               value="#{backingBean.date}" >
  <f:convertDateTime pattern="dd MMMMM yyyy" />
</pro:inputDate>
<br></br>
<h:message for="dateField" />
<br></br>
<h:commandButton value="Submit" />
<br></br>
<h:outputText value="#{backingBean.date}" >
  <f:convertDateTime pattern="dd MMMMM yyyy" />
</h:outputText>
```

The code in bold is the input date component you will create in this chapter.

Step 2: Creating a Client-Specific Renderer

As discussed in Chapter 1, a Renderer is responsible for the output (presentation) to the client, whether that is WML markup for a mobile device or traditional HTML markup for a browser client. A Renderer also provides client-side attributes that are not supported by the behavioral UIComponent class, such as style, width, height, and disabled.

In cases where no new behavior is needed, only a Renderer is required to create a "new" component. The renderer-specific component subclass described later in this chapter (see the "Step 3: Creating a Renderer-Specific Subclass" section) is merely a convenience class for application developers. Although not strictly necessary, it is common practice to implement the client-specific component subclass to make some aspects of application development easier.

For this input date component, you'll reuse the UIInput component superclass because it provides the component behavior you need. Now it is time to focus on providing the UIInput component with a custom input date Renderer. Based on the earlier blueprint, you have now reached the second step, and it is time to start looking at the code that comprises the Renderer.

Figure 2-3 shows the custom Renderer, HtmlInputDateRenderer, that you will create in this chapter. The custom Renderer extends the HtmlRenderer utility superclass, which extends the standard Renderer class (javax.faces.render.Renderer).

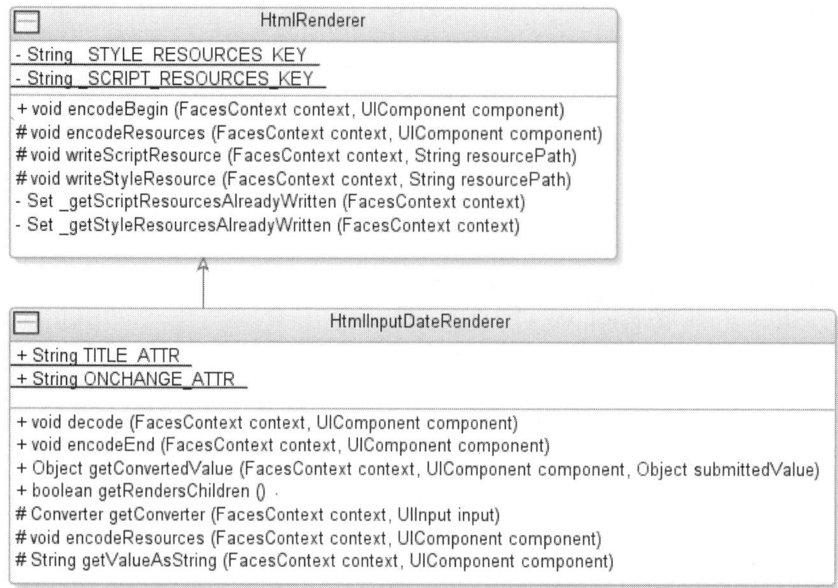

Figure 2-3. *Class diagram over the* `HtmlInputDateRenderer` *class created in this chapter*

The HtmlRenderer Superclass

The `HtmlRenderer` superclass provides some convenience methods for encoding resources needed by the HTML `Renderer`. An application developer might add two or more input date components to the page; therefore, if not taken care of, any resource (for example, a style sheet) used by the input date component will be written to the client multiple times.

The semantics behind the methods provided by the `HtmlRenderer` implementation will make sure these resources are written only once. In this chapter, you'll create the semantics, which guarantees that style and script resources are written only once during rendering.

Code Sample 2-4 shows the convenience methods to be used by subclasses to write out their resources.

Code Sample 2-4. `HtmlRenderer` *Superclass Providing Convenience Methods for Other HTML Renderers*

```
package com.apress.projsf.ch2.render.html;

import java.io.IOException;

import java.util.HashSet;
import java.util.Map;
import java.util.Set;
```

```
import javax.faces.application.ViewHandler;
import javax.faces.component.UIComponent;
import javax.faces.context.ExternalContext;
import javax.faces.context.FacesContext;
import javax.faces.context.ResponseWriter;
import javax.faces.render.Renderer;

/**
 * HtmlRenderer is a base class for all Renderers that output HTML markup.
 */
public class HtmlRenderer extends Renderer
{
  /**
   * Begins the encoded output for this component.
   *
   * @param context    the Faces context
   * @param component  the Faces component
   *
   * @throws IOException  if an I/O error occurs during rendering
   */
  public void encodeBegin(
    FacesContext context,
    UIComponent  component) throws IOException
  {
    // write out resources
    encodeResources(context, component);
  }

  /**
   * Override hook for subclasses to write out their resources.
   *
   * @param context    the Faces context
   * @param component  the Faces component
   */
  protected void encodeResources(
    FacesContext context,
    UIComponent  component) throws IOException
  {
    // empty hook for subclasses to override as needed
  }
```

The `encodeResources()` method is called automatically during `encodeBegin()` and can be overridden by your subclass to add any HTML resources needed during rendering of this component. Next you'll look at the `writeStyleResource()` method (see Code Sample 2-5), which essentially checks to see whether this style resource has already been written to the client; if it has, there is no need to write it again.

Code Sample 2-5. *Writing Style Resources to Client*

```
/**
 * Writes a style sheet resource at-most-once within a single
 * RenderResponse phase.
 *
 * @param context       the Faces context
 * @param resourcePath  the style sheet resource path
 *
 * @throws IOException  if an error occurs during rendering
 */
protected void writeStyleResource(
  FacesContext context,
  String       resourcePath) throws IOException
{
  Set styleResources = _getStyleResourcesAlreadyWritten(context);

  // Set.add() returns true only if item was added to the set
  // and returns false if item was already present in the set
  if (styleResources.add(resourcePath))
  {
    ViewHandler handler = context.getApplication().getViewHandler();
    String resourceURL = handler.getResourceURL(context, resourcePath);
    ResponseWriter out = context.getResponseWriter();
    out.startElement("style", null);
    out.writeAttribute("type", "text/css", null);
    out.writeText("@import url(" + resourceURL + ");", null);
    out.endElement("style");
  }
}
```

The `writeStyleResource()` method first calls the `_getStyleResourceAlreadyWritten()` method, which returns a resource set, identified by a key, containing resources written to the client, if any. If the style resource is already present in the resource set, the `styleResource.add()` returns `false`, and no resource is written to the client.

Although not used in this chapter, a similar method, the `writeScriptResource()` method (see Code Sample 2-6), makes the same write-once guarantee for script resources.

Code Sample 2-6. *Writing Script Resource to the Client*

```
/**
 * Writes a script library resource at-most-once within a single
 * RenderResponse phase.
 *
 * @param context       the Faces context
```

```
 * @param resourcePath  the script library resource path
 *
 * @throws IOException  if an error occurs during rendering
 */
protected void writeScriptResource(
  FacesContext context,
  String       resourcePath) throws IOException
{
  Set scriptResources = _getScriptResourcesAlreadyWritten(context);

  // Set.add() returns true only if item was added to the set
  // and returns false if item was already present in the set
  if (scriptResources.add(resourcePath))
  {
    ViewHandler handler = context.getApplication().getViewHandler();
    String resourceURL = handler.getResourceURL(context, resourcePath);
    ResponseWriter out = context.getResponseWriter();
    out.startElement("script", null);
    out.writeAttribute("type", "text/javascript", null);
    out.writeAttribute("src", resourceURL, null);
    out.endElement("script");
  }
}
```

The `_getStyleResourceAlreadyWritten()` method implements the at-most-once semantics by adding a key—`_STYLE_RESOURCE_KEY`—with an associated `Map` to the request scope. This `Map` is populated by the `writeStyleResource()` method described in Code Sample 2-7.

Code Sample 2-7. *Implements At-Most-Once Semantics for Each Style Resource*

```
// Implements at-most-once semantics for each style resource on
// the currently rendering page
private Set _getStyleResourcesAlreadyWritten(
  FacesContext context)
{
  ExternalContext external = context.getExternalContext();
  Map requestScope = external.getRequestMap();
  Set written = (Set)requestScope.get(_STYLE_RESOURCES_KEY);

  if (written == null)
  {
    written = new HashSet();
    requestScope.put(_STYLE_RESOURCES_KEY, written);
  }

  return written;
}
```

Code Sample 2-8 shows a similar method, the `_getScriptResourceAlreadyWritten()` method, that creates a similar key-`Map` pair as the previously mentioned `_getStyleResourceAlreadyWritten()` method and guarantees that script resources are written only once.

Code Sample 2-8. *Implements At-Most-Once Semantics for Each Script Resource*

```
// Implements at-most-once semantics for each script resource on
// the currently rendering page
private Set _getScriptResourcesAlreadyWritten(
  FacesContext context)
{
  ExternalContext external = context.getExternalContext();
  Map requestScope = external.getRequestMap();
  Set written = (Set)requestScope.get(_SCRIPT_RESOURCES_KEY);

  if (written == null)
  {
    written = new HashSet();
    requestScope.put(_SCRIPT_RESOURCES_KEY, written);
  }

  return written;
}
```

The last part of the `HtmlRenderer` is the resource key implementation shown in Code Sample 2-9. You create the keys using the fully qualified class name of the `HtmlRenderer` class, `com.apress.projsf.ch2.render.html.HtmlRenderer`, and appending either `STYLE_WRITTEN` or `SCRIPTS_WRITTEN` to distinguish between style and script resources.

Code Sample 2-9. *The Unique Keys Used to Identify Resources*

```
  static private final String _STYLE_RESOURCES_KEY =
                       HtmlRenderer.class.getName() + ".STYLES_WRITTEN";
  static private final String _SCRIPT_RESOURCES_KEY =
                       HtmlRenderer.class.getName() + ".SCRIPTS_WRITTEN";
}
```

The HtmlInputDateRenderer Class

With the utility class out of the way, you'll start with the basic foundation of writing an HTML `Renderer` for the `UIInput` component that can handle the basic requirements for the input date field. Code Sample 2-10 shows the `import` statements for the renderer package.

Code Sample 2-10. `import` *Statements*

```
package com.apress.projsf.ch2.renderer.html.basic;

import javax.faces.component.UIComponent;
```

```
import javax.faces.component.UIInput;
import javax.faces.context.ExternalContext;
import javax.faces.context.FacesContext;
import javax.faces.context.ResponseWriter;
import javax.faces.convert.Converter;
import javax.faces.convert.ConverterException;
import javax.faces.convert.DateTimeConverter;

import com.apress.projsf.ch2.render.html.HtmlRenderer;
```

The UIComponent class and the Renderer class are both part of the contract when writing client-specific Renderers. The FacesContext is part of the contract when creating the decode(), encodeBegin(), encodeChildren(), and encodeEnd() methods, and all markup is written to the client using a ResponseWriter. The FacesContext contains all information about the per-request state related to a JSF request process and the corresponding render response.

The UIInput class is the behavioral superclass you'll provide with a new Renderer. You also need access to the ExternalContext to access request parameters. The ExternalContext class allows JSF-based applications to run in either a servlet or a portlet environment and gives you access to (for example) session instance, response object, and path information.

For the input date component, you also want to convert to a strongly typed Date object the actual String passed on the request using a Converter and possibly throw a ConverterException for invalid input values. In case the application developer does not specify a converter, you must provide a default DateTimeConverter.

When you have access to all the classes needed for the input date component, it is time to code. In this chapter, you will create an HTML-specific renderer that has the component type set to Input and that is designated to take a value of type Date, so an appropriate name of this class is HtmlInputDateRenderer.

Encode Begin and Encode End

During the initial request, only two phases are at work—Restore View and Render Response—so the decode() method of the renderer will not be called since it is called in the Apply Request Value phase. The only methods called are encodeBegin(), getRendersChildren(), encodeChildren(), and encodeEnd():

- encodeBegin() is generally used to write the opening client markup element(s) for the UIComponent (for example, <table>).
- encodeEnd() is generally used to write the closing client markup element(s) for the UIComponent (for example, </table>).
- getRendersChildren() is used as a flag to indicate whether a UIComponent/Renderer is responsible for rendering its children.
- encodeChildren() is called only if the rendersChildren property returns true. In that case, the UIComponent (or its Renderer, if present) is responsible for rendering its child components.

THE RENDERSCHILDREN PROPERTY

The previously mentioned method—encodeChildren()—depends on a read-only UIComponent property called rendersChildren. If the component has a renderer, then the component delegates to the Renderer to determine whether rendersChildren is true. A Renderer returns true for rendersChildren if it needs access to its children components to correctly render the output to the client. One example from the JSF standard is h:dataTable, where the number of column children is needed in advance to correctly render the HTML markup.

If rendersChildren is true, the Renderer controls rendering for its entire subtree of components. This means when the JSP engine executes a tag that manages a component with rendersChildren set to true, instead of continuing to iterate through the component hierarchy, asking each component to render, it has to first create the component hierarchy so that the child component hierarchy is available to the parent component and its Renderer.

An application developer can attach a custom Converter or Validator to an input component in the JSP document. It is important not to reference either the Converter or the Validator during rendering until encodeEnd() because a custom Converter or Validator will not be attached to the component until after encodeBegin() has completed. Therefore, you will avoid using encodeBegin() for your HtmlInputDateRenderer and instead do the majority of the rendering in encodeEnd(). Code Sample 2-11 shows the endcodeEnd() method's two arguments.

Code Sample 2-11. *The* encodeEnd() *Method's Arguments*

```
public class HtmlInputDateRenderer extends HtmlRenderer
{
  public void encodeEnd(
    FacesContext  context,
    UIComponent  component) throws IOException
  {
```

The encodeEnd() method takes two arguments—FacesContext context and UIComponent component. The Render Response phase will call the encodeEnd() method on the UIComponent, which in turn will delegate to the encodeEnd() method on the Renderer, passing the FacesContext and the UIComponent instance. In this case, you are guaranteed to be passed an instance of UIInput, but you might also be passed a renderer-specific subclass of UIInput. If a cast is needed, you always cast to the behavioral superclass, rather than to a renderer-specific subclass.

Looking Up Attribute Values

A component such as the one you are creating usually contains a set of renderer-specific attributes, such as title, width, and height. For the inputDate component, you previously determined that you needed HTML attributes—value, title, and name.

These HTML attributes are rendered using the behavioral component's clientId and converted value attribute. You must also render the markup-specific attributes, so in Code Sample 2-12, you look up the renderer-specific title attribute in the UIComponent attribute's Map.

WHY NOT CAST TO A RENDERER-SPECIFIC SUBCLASS IN THE RENDERER?

Optionally, you can cast the component to a renderer-specific subclass and use the getters directly to look up the renderer-specific attributes. However, for similar reasons as those described in Chapter 1, you need to make sure your `Renderer` works even if an application developer creates a new `UIInput` programmatically, sets the renderer type, and adds it to the component hierarchy.

The following code is an extract from a sample backing bean and illustrates how an application developer would add a `UIInput` component to the component hierarchy programmatically:

```
public void setBinding(
  UIPanel panel)
{
  UIInput input = new UIInput();
  input.setRendererType("com.apress.projsf.Date");
  Map attrs = input.getAttributes();
  attrs.put("title", "Programmatic Date Field");
  panel.getChildren().add(input);
}
```

This sample would cause a `ClassCastException` to occur if you always cast to the renderer-specific component subclass in your `Renderer`, instead of casting to the `UIInput` behavioral superclass.

Code Sample 2-12. *Getting Attribute Values from the* `UIComponent`

```
Map attrs = component.getAttributes();
String title = (String)attrs.get(TITLE_ATTR);
String valueString = getValueAsString(context, component);
```

The `getAttributes()` method returns a mutable `Map` of attributes (and properties) associated with this `UIComponent`, keyed by attribute name. On the `Map` you can then look up the values of the attribute specified (for example, `title`). In Code Sample 2-12, you are using the `TITLE_ATTR` constant with the value `title`. The `getValueAsString()` method is defined by the `HtmlInputDateRenderer` and returns either the component's `submittedValue` attribute after a previously unsuccessful postback or the component's value attribute, formatted as a string.

Identifying Component

Since there is only one `Renderer` instance per `Renderer` class (singleton), you need to make sure that during postback you decode the request and apply values entered by the user to the right component. To achieve this, you must include a unique identifier in the generated component markup. So, on encoding, before you start writing markup to the client, you need to determine which `UIComponent` in the component hierarchy you are encoding. The `clientId` is a globally unique identifier for the component markup that remains consistent across postback. In Code Sample 2-13, you calculate the `clientId` of a component.

Code Sample 2-13. `UIComponent clientId` *Lookup*

```
String clientId = input.getClientId(context);
```

The `getClientId()` method calculates the `clientId` of a component by walking up the component hierarchy to the first `NamingContainer` parent component (for example, `UIForm`). The `getClientId()` method obtains the `clientId` from the `UIComponent` that implements `NamingContainer`. The `clientId` of this parent component is then appended as a prefix to the child component's ID (for example, `[NamingContainer clientId]:[id]`).

■ Note If the application developer has not defined an ID on a component, the `getClientId()` method will call the `createUniqueId()` method on the `UIViewRoot` to create a unique `clientId`. By default, JSF will generate `clientIds` that start with _ to help to avoid conflicts with IDs specified by the application developer (for example, `_id1`, `_id2`, and so on).

Figure 2-4 illustrates a simplified version of the page description shown in Figure 2-1.

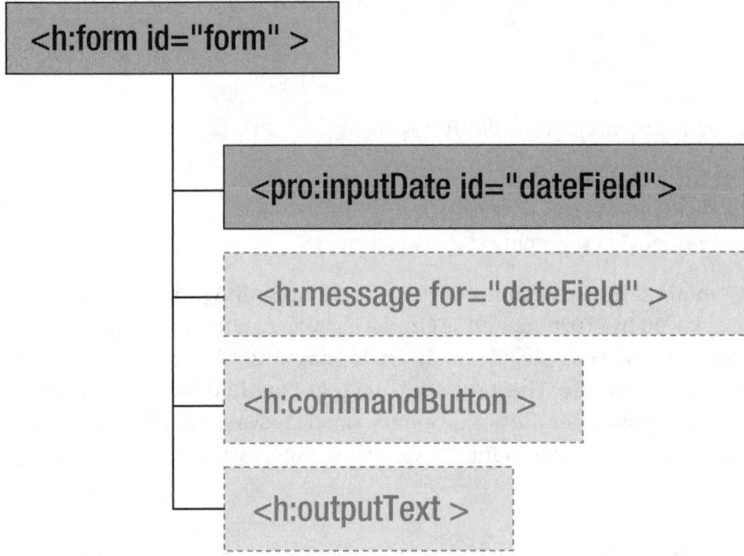

Figure 2-4. *Unique IDs within* `NamingContainer`

The identifier written to the client for the `inputDate` component, based on Figure 2-4, will be `form:dateField`. Since the other components do not contain any user-defined IDs, a component ID will be generated by the `createUniqueId()` method on `UIViewRoot` (for example, `_id1`).

JSF NAMINGCONTAINER

To ensure each component's uniqueness, JSF provides a `NamingContainer` marker interface. Within a component implementing `NamingContainer`, each child component is required to have a locally unique identifier. This is enforced by the `renderView()` method on `ViewHandler`, and in JSP-based applications it is also enforced by the `UIComponentTag`. The only time it would be useful to implement `NamingContainer` for your own component would be if your component stamped out its children in a similar fashion to the `HtmlDataTable` component.

In case the JSF default-generated client ID (for example, `_id1`, `_id2`, and so on) is not understood by the client markup, the component writer can decide to override a method called `convertClientId()`. If the `UIComponent` has a `Renderer`, the last call made by the `getClientId()` method is to the `convertClientId()` method. This ensures the `Renderer` can make the final call about which client ID gets sent to the client. For example, the XHTML rules for fragment identifiers are much stricter than HTML because XHTML does not allow identifiers to start with underscores or colons. (See the XHTML 1.0 specification at `http://www.w3.org/TR/xhtml1/#C_8`).

Note As good practice, always set IDs on `<h:form>` components in the JSP page description.

Writing Output to the Client

You have now verified the value, the client ID, and the additional renderer-specific attributes, so it is time to write the necessary markup and resources back to the browser via the JSP buffered body tag. Using the `ResponseWriter` class, you can leverage some convenience methods to generate proper markup. In this sample, you will use the `startElement()`, `writeAttribute()`, and `endElement()` methods. However, these are not the only methods implemented by the `ResponseWriter` class. Table 2-3 lists useful methods provided by the JSF `ResponseWriter` class.

Table 2-3. *Useful* `ResponseWriter` *Methods**

Method Name	Description
`getContentType()`	Returns the content type used to create this `ResponseWriter`.
`getCharacterEncoding()`	Returns the character encoding used to create this `ResponseWriter`.
`startDocument()`	Writes appropriate characters at the beginning of the current response.
`endDocument()`	Writes appropriate characters at the end of the current response.
`startElement()`	Writes the beginning of a markup element, such as the < character, followed by the element name such as `table`, which causes the `ResponseWriter` implementation to note internally that the element is open. This can be followed by zero or more calls to `writeAttribute()` or `writeURIAttribute()` to append an attribute name and value to the currently open element. The element will be closed with the trailing > character added on any subsequent call to `startElement()`, `writeComment()`, or `writeText()`.

Continued

Table 2-3. *Continued*

Method Name	Description
`endElement()`	Closes the specified element. The element name must match the previous call to `startElement`.
`writeComment()`	Writes a comment string wrapped in appropriate comment delimiters, after converting the comment object to a `String` first. Any currently opened element is closed first.
`writeAttribute()`	Adds an attribute name-value pair to an element that was opened with a previous call to `startElement()`. The `writeAttribute()` method causes character encoding to be performed in the same manner as that performed by the `writeText()` methods.
`writeURIAttribute()`	Assumes that the attribute value is a URI and performs URI encoding (such as percent encoding for HTML).
`writeText()`	Writes text (converting from `Object` to `String` first, if necessary), performing appropriate character encoding and escaping. Any currently open element created by a call to `startElement()` is closed first.

** Source: The JSF 1.1 specification. For more detailed information about these methods, please refer to the JSF specification.*

From the context you can get the `ResponseWriter`—`getResponseWriter()`—for this request. The `ResponseWriter` class extends the `java.io.Writer` class and adds methods that generate markup elements, such as start and end elements for HTML and XML.

You could ignore these convenience methods provided by the `ResponseWriter` and instead control the output of the markup directly. However, this is not a recommended approach for several reasons. First, you will get better performance if you don't have to keep your own objects in memory to handle what gets written, and when, to the client. Second, you will also get better portability of your code between markup languages that have only subtle differences, such as between HTML and XHTML. Finally, by using the `startElement()` and `endElement()` API, it is easier to detect and debug the generated markup by verifying that all `startElement()` and `endElement()` calls are balanced. You can do this by using a decorating `ResponseWriter` class.

■ Note Depending on the supported content type of the client browser, JSF 1.2 will create a content-specific `ResponseWriter` that will format markup such as XHTML. By using the `startElement()` method and the `endElement()` method, a component writer will not need to provide multiple solutions for HTML and XHTML content types; the `ResponseWriter` will handle this.

It is usually good practice to create helper classes for client-specific elements and attributes. For example, the MyFaces project has a utility class—`org.apache.myfaces.renderkit.html.HTML`—that contains public constants, such as `HTML.INPUT_ELEM` for the `input` element. For clarity you will be entering the element name directly as shown in Code Sample 2-14.

Code Sample 2-14. *Writing Output to the JSP Buffered Body Tag*

```
  ResponseWriter out = context.getResponseWriter();
  out.startElement("div", component);
  if (title != null)
    out.writeAttribute("title", title, TITLE_ATTR);
  out.startElement("input", component);
  out.writeAttribute("name", clientId, null);
  if (valueString != null)
    out.writeAttribute("value", valueString, null);
  out.endElement("input");

  ViewHandler handler = context.getApplication().getViewHandler();
  String overlayURL = handler.getResourceURL(context,
                                   "/projsf-ch2/inputDateOverlay.gif");
  out.startElement("img", null);
  out.writeAttribute("class", "ProInputDateOverlay", null);
  out.writeAttribute("src", overlayURL, null);
  out.endElement("img");
  out.endElement("div");
}
```

The `startElement()` method takes the following arguments—`name`, `UIComponent`, and `componentForElement`. The `name` parameter is the name of the element generated (for example, `"div"`), and the `componentForElement` is the `UIComponent` this element represents. In Code Sample 2-14, this is represented by the `UIInput` component that was passed to the `encodeEnd()` method by the Render Response phase. In this section of the `encodeEnd()` method, you also write the image that will be used as an overlay for the input date component.

■ Note The `componentForElement` parameter is optional and can be set to `null`, but the presence of the `componentForElement` parameter allows visual design-time environments to track generated markup for a specific component. This is also useful for advanced Ajax manipulation of markup at runtime. Chapter 4 covers Ajax technologies.

After adding applicable attributes, you close your elements using the `endElement()` method on the `ResponseWriter`. You are now done with the `encodeEnd()` method.

Writing Out Resources

You need to override the `encodeResources()` method, as shown in Code Sample 2-15, to write a reference to the CSS style sheet used by this component. This style sheet defines the `ProInputDateOverlay` style used by the overlay image.

Code Sample 2-15. *The* encodeResources() *Method*

```
/**
 * Write out the HtmlInputDate resources.
 *
 * @param context    the Faces context
 * @param component  the Faces component
 */
protected void encodeResources(
  FacesContext context,
  UIComponent  component) throws IOException
{
  writeStyleResource(context, "/projsf-ch2/inputDate.css");
}
```

The writeStyleResource() method provided by the HtmlRenderer superclass guarantees that a style resource is written only once during rendering, even if multiple ProInputDate components appear on the same page. In Code Sample 2-15, the encodeResources() method writes a CSS style sheet resource needed by your HtmlInputDate component—inputDate.css.

Looking Up the Value String

The getValueAsString() method, shown in Code Sample 2-16, will return the string representation of the value to be encoded. By calling the getSubmittedValue() method on the UIInput component, you can get the submitted value, if any.

Code Sample 2-16. *The* getValueAsString() *Method*

```
/**
 * Returns the submitted value, if present, otherwise returns
 * the value attribute converted to string.
 *
 * @param context    the Faces context
 * @param component  the Faces component
 *
 * @return  the value string for the specified component
 *
 * @throws IOException  if an I/O exception occurs during rendering
 */
protected String getValueAsString(
  FacesContext context,
  UIComponent  component) throws IOException
{
  // look up the submitted value
  UIInput input = (UIInput)component;
  String valueString = (String)input.getSubmittedValue();
```

```
  // the submitted value will be null
  // on initial render (or after a successful postback)
  if (valueString == null)
  {
    // look up the strongly typed value for this input
    Object value = input.getValue();
    if (value != null)
    {
      // if present, convert the strongly typed value
      // to a string for rendering
      Converter converter = getConverter(context, input);
      valueString = converter.getAsString(context, component, value);
    }
  }

  return valueString;
}
```

For your `HtmlInputDateRenderer`, the submitted `value` attribute represents the string value entered by the user that needs to be converted to a strongly typed `Date` object. If the submitted value is `null`, which it will be on initial request or after a successful postback, you call the `getValue()` method on the `UIInput` component.

If a value is returned by the `getValue()` method, you need to convert the value from a strongly typed `Date` object to a string representation suitable for rendering. You do this by using the JSF `Converter` object returned by the `getConverter()` method.

In case of an unsuccessful postback, the submitted value is non-null and should be redisplayed to give the user an opportunity to address the conversion or validation error.

Converting Values

For the `inputDate` component, you have decided to make sure values entered by the user always get converted properly to `Date` objects, whether that is with one you have implemented or with a `Converter` that the application developer has attached. By adding the `getConverter()` method to the `HtmlInputDateRenderer` class, you will be able to control the conversion of entered values, as shown in Code Sample 2-17.

Code Sample 2-17. *The* `getConverter()` *Method*

```
private Converter getConverter(
  FacesContext context,
  UIInput      input)
{
  Converter converter = input.getConverter();
  if (converter == null)
  {
    // default the converter
    DateTimeConverter datetime = new DateTimeConverter();
```

```
      datetime.setLocale(context.getViewRoot().getLocale());
      datetime.setTimeZone(TimeZone.getDefault());
      converter = datetime;
    }
    return converter;
  }
```

The first task to perform is to check whether the application developer has attached a Converter to the input date component (for example, <f:convertDateTime>). If not, then you will create a new DateTimeConverter and from the context get the locale for the client, getLocale(), and set it on the new Converter, setLocale(). You then set the time zone on the new converter and return the Converter.

Controlling Rendering of Child Components

You can use the rendersChildren property of the UIComponent or Renderer as a flag to indicate whether the UIComponent/Renderer is responsible for rendering its children. If this flag is true, then the parent or ancestor component must render the content of its child components. In the case of the input date component, it does not make sense to nest other components within it, since it is a leaf component. You can solve this in two ways; one way is to not do anything and let the rendersChildren property be set to default, which in the JSF 1.1 specification is false. In this case, if the application developer adds a child to this component, it will be rendered underneath it. The second way to solve this is to set rendersChildren to true and implement an empty encodeChildren() method, as shown in Code Sample 2-18.

Code Sample 2-18. *Controlling Rendering of Child Components*

```
public boolean getRendersChildren()
 {
   return true;
 }

 public void encodeChildren(
   FacesContext  context,
   UIComponent  component) throws IOException
 {
  // do not render children
 }
```

This way, any attached children will not be rendered since you are ignoring them with an empty encodeChildren() method.

Decode on Postback

The UIInput component renderer must also manage new values entered by the user. During postback, the JSF request lifecycle steps through all six phases, starting with the Restore View phase followed by the Apply Request Values phase.

■ **Note** If the `renderResponse()` method is called during any `Lifecycle` phase, then the `Lifecycle` will jump directly to the Render Response phase after the current phase is completed. If the `responseComplete()` is called during any `Lifecycle` phase, then the `Lifecycle` will not execute any more phases after the current phase is completed.

During the Apply Request Values phase, a method—`processDecodes()`—will be called on the `UIViewRoot` at the top of the component hierarchy (see Figure 2-5).

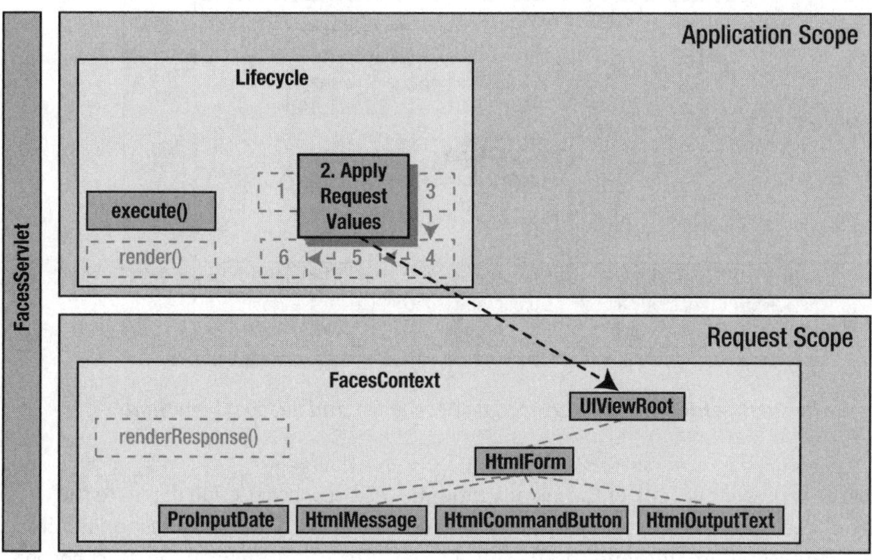

Figure 2-5. *Apply Request Values phase*

The `processDecodes()` method on the `UIViewRoot` is responsible for recursively calling `processDecodes()` on each `UIComponent` in the component hierarchy.

■ **Note** `UIViewRoot` is the `UIComponent` that represents the root of the `UIComponent` tree. This component has no renderer.

For each `UIComponent` in the component hierarchy, the `processDecodes()` method will first check to see whether any children are attached to the component. If there are, it calls `processDecodes()` on its children. After that, it will call the `decode()` method on the `UIComponent` (see Figure 2-6).

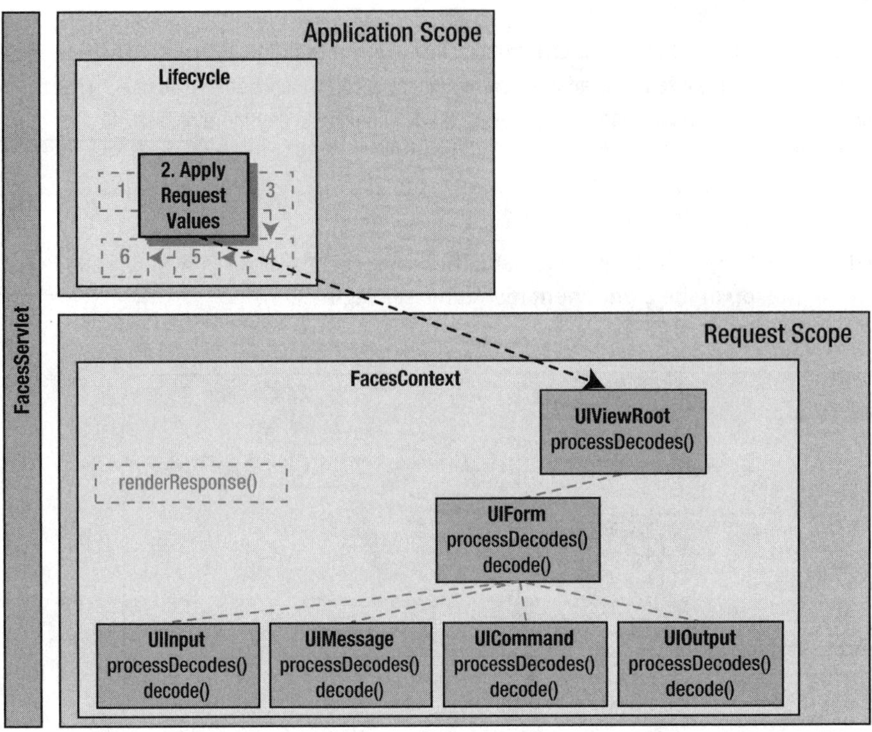

Figure 2-6. *Apply Request Values phase—the* `processDecodes()` *and* `decode()` *methods*

If a `Renderer` is present for any of these components, the `UIComponent` will delegate the responsibility of decoding to the `Renderer`. It is the `Renderer` `decode()` method's responsibility to observe the request parameters and set the submitted value accordingly on the `UIComponent`. After the `processDecodes()` method is finished, the JSF lifecycle continues to the Process Validations phase. Code Sample 2-19 shows the `decode()` method in the `HtmlInputDateRenderer` class.

Code Sample 2-19. *The* `decode()` *Method in the* `HtmlInputDateRenderer` *Class*

```
public void decode(
  FacesContext context,
  UIComponent  component)
{
  ExternalContext external = context.getExternalContext();
  Map requestParams = external.getRequestParameterMap();

  UIInput input = (UIInput)component;
  String clientId = input.getClientId(context);

  String submittedValue = (String)requestParams.get(clientId);
  input.setSubmittedValue(submittedValue);
}
```

By adding the decode() method to the HtmlInputDateRenderer class, you can control the decode processing of the inputDate component. To get the request parameters, you first need to look up the external context. From the external context, you can look up the Map containing the parameters passed on the request. You then get the client ID from the UIComponent—getClientId(context)—and use that client ID to get the submitted request parameter value for this component. This parameter value is then stored on the UIComponent using setSubmittedValue() so that it can be processed further in subsequent phases of the JSF lifecycle.

■ **Note** The setSubmittedValue() method should be called only from the decode() method of your component's Renderer. Once the decode() method is completed, no other phase should be using the ExternalContext to observe any request parameter values associated with your component. The getSubmittedValue() method should be called only from the encode methods of your component's Renderer.

Process Validation and Conversion During Postback

After the Apply Request Values phase, the application enters the Process Validation phase (see Figure 2-7), in which conversion and validation are performed by calling the processValidators() method on the UIViewRoot. The processValidators() method on the UIViewRoot is responsible for recursively calling processValidators() on each UIComponent in the component hierarchy.

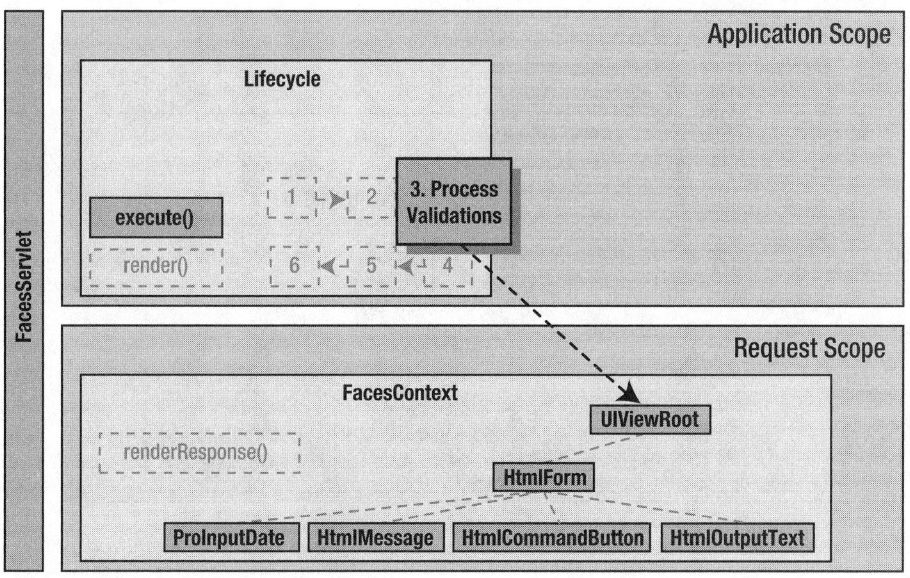

Figure 2-7. *Process Validations phase*

■ **Note** Generally, if a `UIComponent` has the property `rendered` set to `false`, then no processing, such as calls to `processDecodes()` or `processValidators()`, will occur on the component or on any of its child components.

During the validation of a `UIInput`, type conversion will first occur on the component's submitted value. For example, a string is converted to a strongly typed object and then validated.

On each `UIInput` in the `UIComponent` tree, the `processValidators()` method will also call the `validate()` method to type convert and validate the component's submitted value (see Figure 2-8). The `validate()` method will first call the `getSubmittedValue()` method on the `UIComponent`, and if it returns `null` (when no value was submitted for the `UIComponent`), it will exit without further processing. If the submitted value is not `null`, then the `validate()` method calls the `getConvertedValue()` method and passes the newly submitted value from the decode process.

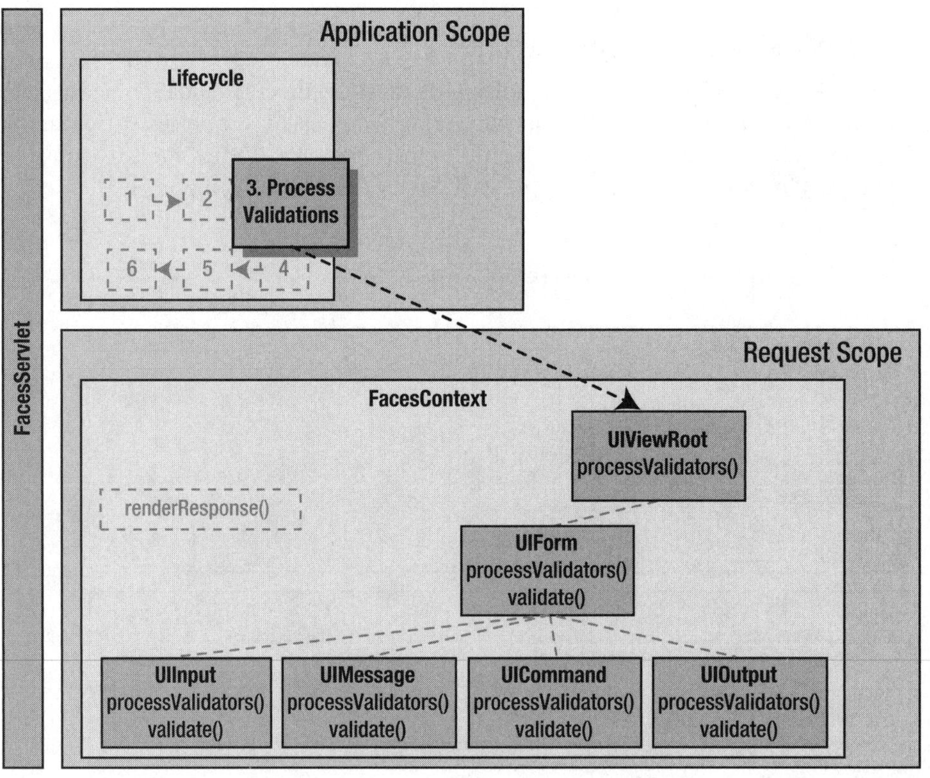

Figure 2-8. *Process Validations phase—the* `processValidators()` *and* `validate()` *methods*

The getConvertedValue() method converts the submitted value to a strongly typed object (for example, Date). If the UIComponent has a Renderer attached, then the UIComponent delegates to the Renderer's getConvertedValue() method to return the converted value. By default, the base Renderer implementation returns the submittedValue directly without any conversion. Code Sample 2-20 shows the getConvertedValue() method as implemented in the HtmlInputDateRenderer.

Code Sample 2-20. *The Renderer* getConvertedValue() *Method*

```
public Object getConvertedValue(
  FacesContext context,
  UIComponent component,
  Object       submittedValue) throws ConverterException
{
  UIInput input = (UIInput)component;
  Converter converter = getConverter(context, input);
  String valueString = (String)submittedValue;
  return converter.getAsObject(context, component, valueString);
}
```

In the HtmlInputDateRenderer class, you will add the previous getConvertedValue() method so you can make sure the value passed to the underlying model is a strongly typed object of type Date. This is similar to what you did in the encode method (see the section "Encode Begin and Encode End") except that you are now reversing the process. First you get the Converter for the UIComponent in question, and then you convert the submitted value to an Object using the getAsObject() method on the Converter.

The new object returned by the getConvertedValue() method is set as a local value on the component, clearing the submitted value. The new strongly typed object is then validated. If there are no errors, a ValueChangeEvent is queued to be delivered at the end of the Process Validations phase. If there are conversion errors, the getConvertedValue() method throws a ConverterException.

■ **Note** You can use a ValueChangeListener to capture the event raised by the ValueChangeEvent before the new local value is pushed into the model in the Update Model Values phase.

Update Model

After the Process Validations phase, the application enters the Update Model Values phase, in which conversion and validation are performed by calling the processUpdates() method on the UIViewRoot (see Figure 2-9). The processUpdates() method on the UIViewRoot is responsible for recursively calling processUpdates() on each UIComponent in the component hierarchy.

The processUpdates() method calls the updateModel() method, which is in charge of updating the model data associated with the UIComponent.

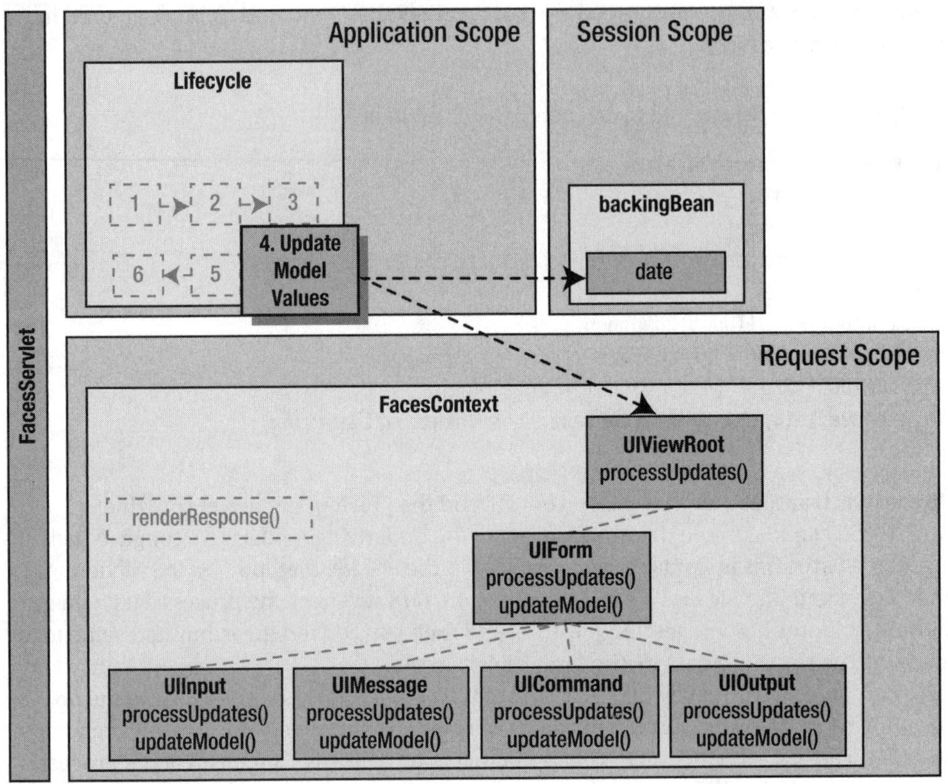

Figure 2-9. *Update Model Values phase—the* processUpdates() *and* updateModel() *methods*

If the value property on the UIComponent has an associated ValueBinding, the setValue() method of that ValueBinding will be called during the Update Model Values lifecycle phase to push the local value from the component to the underlying model. The local value is then cleared so that any subsequent getValue() calls delegate to the ValueBinding, allowing the most current data to be retrieved from the data model.

Render Response Phase During Postback

During the Render Response phase in the initial request, the only possible value for the inputDate component was from the getValue() method. However, during the Render Response phase on postback, it is possible that the submitted value was not a valid date if conversion to the strongly typed Date object failed. In this case, the submittedValue is non-null and is rendered directly as the value in the markup. When there is no `submittedValue`, then the type conversion to `Date` was successful, and the code behaves in the same way as an initial request. Code Sample 2-21 shows the `encodeEnd()` method of the `HtmlInputDateRenderer` class.

> **VALUEBINDING**
>
> To bind a component's attribute value to a property on a bean, or to an element of another data source, JSF leverages value-binding expressions. A value-binding expression can point to both read and write properties on a bean. The `ValueBinding` class encapsulates the actual evaluation of a value binding. Instances of `ValueBinding` for specific references are acquired from the `Application` instance by calling the `createValueBinding()` method.

Code Sample 2-21. *Collecting Data for Rendering*

```
public void encodeEnd(
  FacesContext context,
  UIComponent component)
{
  String valueString = (String)input.getSubmittedValue();
  if (valueString == null)
  {
    Object value = input.getValue();
    if (value != null)
    {
      Converter converter = getConverter(context, input);
      valueString = converter.getAsString(context, component, value);
    }
  }
  ...
}
```

By adding the code in bold to the `encodeEnd()` method, you will now be able to render the `submittedValue` for the input date component, even though it is an invalid date string.

Step 3: Creating a Renderer-Specific Subclass

Based on the earlier blueprint, it is time to provide a renderer-specific subclass. Although this is an optional step, it is good practice since there might be cases when an application developer would like to use it for convenience. The class provides getters and setters for all renderer-specific attributes on the JSF component, such as `style`, `disabled`, `readonly`, and so on.

Figure 2-10 shows the `ProInputDate` renderer-specific subclass that you will create and its inheritance. Code Sample 2-22 shows the source of this renderer-specific subclass.

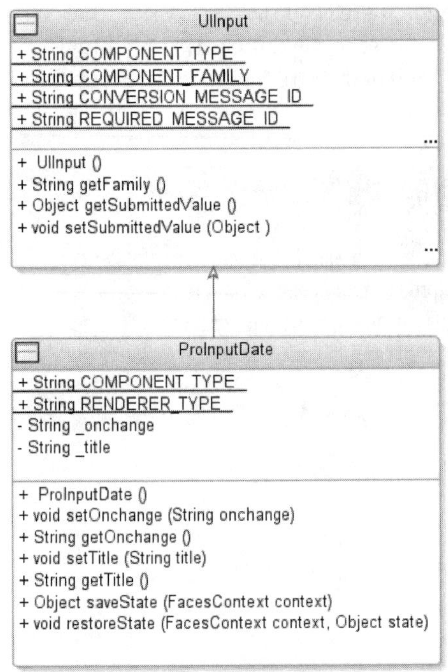

Figure 2-10. *Class diagram over the* `ProInputDate` *renderer-specific subclass*

Code Sample 2-22. *Creating a New Renderer-Specific Subclass*

```
package com.apress.projsf.ch2.component.pro;

import javax.faces.component.UIInput;
import javax.faces.context.FacesContext;
import javax.faces.el.ValueBinding;

/**
 * The ProInputDate component.
 */
public class ProInputDate extends UIInput
{
  /**
   * The component type for this component.
   */
  public static final String COMPONENT_TYPE = "com.apress.projsf.ProInputDate";

  /**
   * The renderer type for this component.
   */
  public static final String RENDERER_TYPE = "com.apress.projsf.Date";
```

```
  /**
   * Creates a new ProInputDate.
   */
  public ProInputDate()
  {
    setRendererType(RENDERER_TYPE);
  }
```

The first tasks you have to do is to make sure you have access to the required classes for the input date component and extend the right component superclass, which in this case is `UIInput`. After that, you define a `public static final String` constant named `COMPONENT_TYPE` to match the standard `UIComponent` implementation strategy defined by the JSF specification.

Caution Renderer-specific components must not define a `COMPONENT_FAMILY` constant or override the `getFamily()` method they inherit from their superclass.

The next constant is the `RENDERER_TYPE`, which will be used to associate the correct renderer for the `UIComponent` when it is created. As you can see in Code Sample 2-22, you pass the `RENDERER_TYPE` to the `setRendererType()` method in the constructor of the renderer-specific subclass.

Renderer-Specific Attributes and ValueBinding

In the earlier section "Looking Up Attribute Values," we covered the `Renderer` part of handling markup-specific attributes, such as `title`. The purpose of the renderer-specific component subclass is to provide convenience getters and setters for each renderer-specific attribute, as shown in Code Sample 2-23.

Code Sample 2-23. *Creating Properties and Accessors for Client-Side Attributes*

```
/**
 * The title attribute value.
 */
private String _title;

/**
 * Sets the title attribute value.
 *
 * @param title  the new title attribute value
 */
public void setTitle(
  String title)
{
  _title = title;
}
```

```
/**
 * Returns the title attribute value.
 *
 * @return  the title attribute value
 */
public String getTitle()
{
  if (_title != null)
    return _title;

  ValueBinding binding = getValueBinding("title");
  if (binding != null)
  {
    FacesContext context = FacesContext.getCurrentInstance();
    return (String)binding.getValue(context);
  }

  return null;
}
```

Creating getters and setters for your markup-specific attributes is similar to creating a regular JavaBean with some properties. First you declare the storage fields on the `ProInputDate` subclass (for example, `private String _title`). Then you create the public accessor and mutator for this attribute, `setTitle()` and `getTitle()`.

The main differences from a regular JavaBean are the attribute accessors. The method signature and purpose of the method (to read a property) are the same. However, the component attribute accessors add support for `ValueBinding`s. The application developer can assign a `ValueBinding` to attributes in order to retrieve information from an underlying model.

To handle this correctly, you first need to see whether there is a local value stored directly in the component. This will take precedence over any `ValueBinding` defined for the attribute (for example, `#{sample.myAttribute}`). If no local value is available, then you must call the `getValueBinding()` method on the `UIComponent` and pass the name of the attribute. If a `ValueBinding` exists, then you need to call the `getValue()` method on the `ValueBinding` to resolve the actual value. If no local attribute value is stored directly in the component, and no `ValueBinding` exists for the attribute, then `null` is returned.

Save and Restore State

State management is one of the primary benefits of using JSF to build applications. JSF provides automatic state handling through a class called `StateManager`, which saves and restores state for a particular view (hierarchy of `UIComponents`) between requests on the server. Each `UIComponent` controls what internal state is saved, so you need to perform some work on your `ProInputDate` component to save its internal state.

Note By default state saving for a `UIComponent` is turned on, but an application developer can opt out of this by setting a flag—`transient`—to `true`. When a component is marked transient, it will not be present in the component hierarchy during the next postback request.

Since you are extending the `UIInput` component with a client-specific subclass, you need to manage the state saving in the `saveState()` method on your `ProInputDate` class, as shown in Code Sample 2-24.

Code Sample 2-24. *Saving State in the* `ProInputDate` *Component*

```
/**
 * Returns the saved state for this component.
 *
 * @param context the Faces context
 */
public Object saveState(
  FacesContext context)
{
  Object values[] = new Object[2];
  values[0] = super.saveState(context);
  values[1] = _title;
  return values;
}
```

It is important to include the saved state from the `UIInput` superclass, as well as your renderer-specific attribute value, `_title`.

Likewise, you also need to restore the state on a subsequent postback request by adding the `restoreState()` method to your `ProInputDate` class, as shown in Code Sample 2-25.

Code Sample 2-25. *Restoring State in the* `ProInputDate` *Component*

```
  /**
   * Restores the state of this component.
   *
   * @param context the Faces context
   * @param state   the saved state
   */
  public void restoreState(
    FacesContext context,
    Object       state)
  {
    Object values[] = (Object[])state;
    super.restoreState(context, values[0]);
    _title = (String)values[1];
  }
}
```

The StateManager will pass the stored state to the restoreState() method on your ProInputDate instance. This will allow you to extract and restore the previously stored state for the UIInput superclass, before you restore the value of your renderer-specific attribute, title.

Step 4: Registering UIComponent and Renderer

As discussed in Chapter 1, the Application instance will store resources defined in the JSF configuration file—faces-config.xml—at application start-up. The JSF implementation processes any configuration files available accordingly to the following rules—first by searching for all resources named META-INF/faces-config.xml in the ClassLoader resource paths for this web application.

Then, it checks for the existence of a context initialization parameter named javax.faces.CONFIG_FILES. If this parameter exists, it will be treated as a comma-delimited list of ServletContext relative resource paths (starting with /) and load each of the specified resources into the Application instance. Finally, the JSF implementation will check for the existence of a Web application configuration resource named /WEB-INF/faces-config.xml and load it if the resource exists. JSF then merges the metadata definitions found in these faces-config.xml files.

The benefit of this aggregated approach is that it allows developers to package a faces-config.xml file with their custom component library, which in turn has the benefit of simpler installation of custom component libraries as a single JAR file. It also allows application developers to override component-specific configurations in the application-specific WEB-INF/faces-config.xml file since it takes precedence over all other faces-config.xml files.

Register the Renderer

To register your new HtmlInputDateRenderer class as a renderer for JSF, you need to add the faces-config.xml file, as shown in Code Sample 2-26, in a META-INF directory somewhere on your resource path.

Code Sample 2-26. *Registration of the* ProInputDateRenderer *in a* faces-config.xml *File*

```
<?xml version="1.0" encoding="UTF-8" ?>
<!DOCTYPE faces-config
   PUBLIC "-//Sun Microsystems, Inc.//DTD JavaServer Faces Config 1.1//EN"
          "http://java.sun.com/dtd/web-facesconfig_1_1.dtd">

<faces-config>

  <render-kit>
    <!-- no renderkit-id, so these renderers are added to
         the default renderkit -->
    <renderer>
      <component-family>
        javax.faces.Input
```

```
    </component-family>
    <renderer-type>
      com.apress.projsf.Date
    </renderer-type>
    <renderer-class>
      com.apress.projsf.ch2.render.html.basic.HtmlInputDateRenderer
    </renderer-class>

    <!-- Renderer-specific attributes -->
    <attribute>
      <attribute-name>title</attribute-name>
      <attribute-class>java.lang.String</attribute-class>
    </attribute>
  </renderer>

</faces-config>
```

As already covered in Chapter 1, Renderers are grouped into RenderKits. A RenderKit is in charge of creating the markup-specific ResponseWriter, which is used to write markup to the client. The RenderKit is also responsible for storing and returning the Renderers. By default, it will store only one Renderer instance for each renderer type and component family combination. In your previous configuration, you have omitted the <render-kit-id> element, which will default your client-specific renderer to use the default RenderKit (with identifier RenderKitFactory.HTML_BASIC_RENDER_KIT) provided by the JSF implementation.

You also set the <component-family>, which is a string—javax.faces.Input—that represents the behavior of the component (for example, an input component), and the <renderer-type>, which is also a string—com.apress.projsf.Date—that represents the presentation of the component. In combination with the component family, the render type uniquely identifies which Renderer class to use with the component—the HtmlInputDateRenderer class. For more information about this, please refer to Chapter 1.

Register the Renderer-Specific Subclass

The ProInputDate component is registered as shown in Code Sample 2-27 in the faces-config.xml file.

Code Sample 2-27. *Defining the Component Type and Component Class*

```
<faces-config>
  ...
  <component>
    <component-type>
      com.apress.projsf.ProInputDate
    </component-type>
    <component-class>
      com.apress.projsf.ch2.component.pro.ProInputDate
    </component-class>
```

The code in bold registers your new component by defining the component type, com.apress.projsf.ProInputDate, and the corresponding component class, com.apress.projsf.ch2.component.pro.ProInputDate. You should add this metadata to the faces-config.xml file you created earlier for your renderer, since they will both be included in the same JAR for easier installation.

Note that you have not closed the <faces-config> element because you are still going to add more metadata for your new component, as shown in Code Sample 2-28.

Code Sample 2-28. UIComponent-*Inherited Attributes*

```
<!-- UIComponent attributes -->
<attribute>
  <description>
    The component identifier for this component.  This value must be
    unique within the closest parent component that is a naming
    container.
  </description>
  <attribute-name>id</attribute-name>
  <attribute-class>java.lang.String</attribute-class>
</attribute>
<attribute>
  <description>
    Flag indicating whether or not this component should be rendered
    (during Render Response Phase), or processed on any subsequent
    form submit.
  </description>
  <attribute-name>rendered</attribute-name>
  <attribute-class>boolean</attribute-class>
  <default-value>true</default-value>
</attribute>
<attribute>
  <description>
     The value-binding expression linking this component to a
     property in a backing bean.
  </description>
  <attribute-name>binding</attribute-name>
  <attribute-class>javax.faces.el.ValueBinding</attribute-class>
</attribute>
```

Although good practice, it is not required to add these attributes to the faces-config.xml file. If they are not added, tools will not be able to provide any additional help or information about the component during design time. This metadata defines attributes that are inherited from the UIComponent base class and that will be used by the application developer.

Code Sample 2-29 shows metadata that defines the UIInput-inherited attributes available to the application developer.

Code Sample 2-29. UIInput-*Inherited Attributes*

```
<!-- UIInput attributes -->
<attribute>
  <description>
    Converter instance registered with this component.
  </description>
  <attribute-name>converter</attribute-name>
  <attribute-class>javax.faces.convert.Converter</attribute-class>
</attribute>
<attribute>
  <description>
    Flag indicating that this component's value must be
    converted and validated immediately (that is, during
    Apply Request Values phase), rather than waiting
    until Process Validations phase.
  </description>
  <attribute-name>immediate</attribute-name>
  <attribute-class>boolean</attribute-class>
</attribute>
<attribute>
  <description>
    Flag indicating that the user is required to provide a submitted
    value for this input component.
  </description>
  <attribute-name>required</attribute-name>
  <attribute-class>boolean</attribute-class>
</attribute>
<attribute>
  <description>
    MethodBinding representing a validator method that will be called
    during Process Validations to perform correctness checks on the
    value of this component.  The expression must evaluate to a public
    method that takes FacesContext, UIComponent, and Object parameters,
    with a return type of void.
  </description>
  <attribute-name>validator</attribute-name>
  <attribute-class>javax.faces.validator.Validator</attribute-class>
</attribute>
<attribute>
  <description>
    The current value of this component.
  </description>
  <attribute-name>value</attribute-name>
  <attribute-class>java.lang.Object</attribute-class>
</attribute>
```

```
<attribute>
  <description>
    MethodBinding representing a value change listener method that will be
    notified when a new value has been set for this input component.  The
    expression must evaluate to a public method that takes a
    ValueChangeEvent parameter, with a return type of void.
  </description>
  <attribute-name>valueChangeListener</attribute-name>
  <attribute-class>javax.faces.event.ValueChangeListener</attribute-class>
</attribute>
```

Finally, in Code Sample 2-30, you add the renderer-specific attribute you need for your `ProInputDate` component, `title`. You also set the object type for the attribute, `java.lang.String`.

Code Sample 2-30. `ProInputDate` *Attributes*

```
    <!-- ProInputDate attributes -->
    <attribute>
      <description>
        The title, or tooltip, to use for the rendered markup of
        this component.
      </description>
      <attribute-name>title</attribute-name>
      <attribute-class>java.lang.String</attribute-class>
    </attribute>
  </component>
  ...
</faces-config>
```

Step 5: Creating a JSP Tag Handler and TLD

The last step in your initial blueprint is to create a JSP tag handler. To build a JSF application, you need some way of describing the structure of your application, and the default view technology for page descriptions, which must be provided by any JSF implementation, is JSP. One of the benefits of making JSP the default language is its broad adoption among Web application developers, and by leveraging this broad developer knowledge about JSP, building JSF applications using JSP as page description is increasing rapidly.

■ **Note** JSF implementations must support (although JSF-based applications need not utilize) JSP as the page description language for JSF pages. You can enable this JSP support by providing custom actions so that a JSF user interface can be easily defined in a JSP page by adding tags that correspond to JSF UI components. For JSP version 2.0 and onward, the file extension `.jsf` is reserved and may optionally be used (typically by tools) to represent JSP pages containing JSF content. When running in a JSP 1.2 environment, JSP authors must give their JSP pages that contain JSF content a filename ending in `.jsp`, according to the JSF 1.2 specification.

An application developer will use a custom action (a.k.a. *tag*) in a JSP page description to indicate which JSF `UIComponent` is needed for the application. The custom action has a corresponding tag handler class, which is responsible for creating the `UIComponent` and transferring each declarative JSP tag attribute to the `UIComponent` instance. The syntax of the custom action has both behavioral attributes and renderer-specific attributes. Therefore, each such custom action is tied to a particular component family and renderer type combination. For example, the standard HTML `RenderKit` provided by the JSF implementation supports three `Renderer` types for the `UIInput` component (`Text`, `TextArea`, and `Secret`), which require three separate custom actions (`inputText`, `inputTextArea`, and `inputSecret`). You are extending the `UIInput` component and adding a new `Renderer` type—`com.apress.projsf.Date`—and you must therefore also provide a new JSP custom action, `inputDate`.

Figure 2-11 shows a class diagram over the tag handler and its support class that you will create.

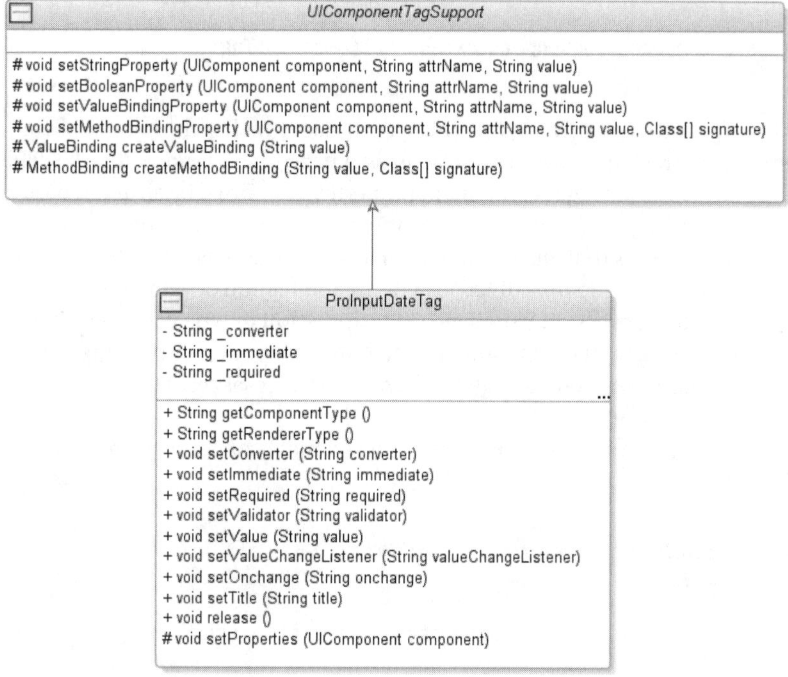

Figure 2-11. *Class diagram over the* `ProInputDate` *tag handler and its support class*

The UIComponentTagSupport Class

Before you start with the actual tag handler for your custom action, you'll learn about your abstract `UIComponentTagSupport` tag handler class. If you planned to just create one component, you would not need the support tag handler class shown in Code Sample 2-31, but since you are planning on adding more components to your JSF component library, it makes sense to separate what functionality is common among all components into a support tag handler superclass.

Code Sample 2-31. *The* `UIComponentTagSupport` *Class*

```
package com.apress.projsf.ch2.taglib;

import java.util.Map;

import javax.faces.application.Application;
import javax.faces.component.UIComponent;
import javax.faces.context.FacesContext;
import javax.faces.el.MethodBinding;
import javax.faces.el.ValueBinding;
import javax.faces.webapp.UIComponentTag;

/**
 * UIComponentTagSupport provides common helper methods for
 * JavaServer Faces UIComponent tag handlers.
 */
abstract public class UIComponentTagSupport extends UIComponentTag
{
```

The `UIComponentTagSupport` class extends the `UIComponentTag`, which is the base class for all JSP custom actions that correspond to UI components in a page that is rendered by JSF. The `UIComponentTag` handler base class manages component properties supported by all `UIComponents` (for example, `id`, `rendered`, and `binding`). The `UIComponentTagSupport` class provides helper methods to your tag handler classes that will be registered in the TLD as custom actions.

For each of the attributes available on a `UIComponent`, an application developer can set either a static value or a JSF Expression Language (EL) expression of type value binding or method binding. To ensure that you can handle the attributes for your components, you can implement four utility methods—`setStringProperty()`, `setBooleanProperty()`, `setValueBindingProperty()`, and `setMethodBindingProperty()`.

Code Sample 2-32 shows the `setStringProperty()` method that is handling `String` attributes and properties.

Code Sample 2-32. *Method Handling String Attributes and Properties*

```
/**
 * Sets a component string property as a value binding, or string literal.
 *
 * @param component  the Faces component
 * @param attrName   the attribute name
 * @param value      the attribute value
 */
protected void setStringProperty(
  UIComponent component,
  String      attrName,
  String      value)
{
  if (value == null)
    return;
```

```
  if (isValueReference(value))
  {
    component.setValueBinding(attrName, createValueBinding(value));
  }
  else
  {
    component.getAttributes().put(attrName, value);
  }
}
```

You can use this `setStringProperty()` method to assign any component attribute that can take either a static value or a value binding (for example, `#{sample.Date}`). If the value is `null`, then you avoid explicitly storing the value in the component. To check whether the value is a JSF EL expression, you can use a method called `isValueReference()`. This method is provided by the `UIComponentTag` class and will return `true` if the specified value conforms to the syntax requirements of a value-binding expression. When the string is a valid value-binding expression, you create and store a corresponding `ValueBinding` instance as the attribute value.

JSF 1.2 SETPROPERTIES

JSF 1.2 supports the direct use of JSP 2.1 `ValueExpression` and `MethodExpression`, rather than passing a `String` to the tag handler and requiring it to parse the expression internally. As a result, the `UIComponentTagSupport` `setStringProperty()` method described in this chapter would change as follows for JSF 1.2:

```
protected void setStringProperty(
  UIComponent     component,
  String          attrName,
  ValueExpression value)
{
  if (value == null)
    return;

  if (!value.isLiteralText())
  {
    component.setValueExpression(attrName, value);
  }
  else
  {
    component.getAttributes().put(attrName, value.getExpressionString());
  }
}
```

If the `ValueExpression` is actually just literal text, then this text is pushed directly into the component attribute's map. Otherwise, the `ValueExpression` is set on the component for this attribute for deferred evaluation during the execution of the JSF lifecycle.

The setBooleanProperty() method, as shown in Code Sample 2-33, is essentially performing the same task as the aforementioned setStringProperty() method with one difference; instead of handling String object types, it handles boolean types.

Code Sample 2-33. *Method Handling Boolean Attributes and Properties*

```
/**
 * Sets a component boolean property as a value binding, or boolean literal.
 *
 * @param component  the Faces component
 * @param attrName   the attribute name
 * @param value      the attribute value
 */
protected void setBooleanProperty(
  UIComponent component,
  String      attrName,
  String      value)
{
  if (value == null)
    return;

  if (isValueReference(value))
  {
    component.setValueBinding(attrName, createValueBinding(value));
  }
  else
  {
    component.getAttributes().put(attrName, Boolean.valueOf(value));
  }
}
```

The setValueBindingProperty() method, as shown in Code Sample 2-34, is simpler in its construction since it will be used by only those attributes that do not support a literal value and accept only a value-binding expression. If the value passed does not conform to EL expression syntax, it throws an IllegalArgumentException.

Code Sample 2-34. *Method Handling* ValueBinding *Attributes and Properties*

```
/**
 * Sets a component property as a value binding.
 *
 * @param component  the Faces component
 * @param attrName   the attribute name
 * @param value      the attribute value
 */
```

```
protected void setValueBindingProperty(
  UIComponent component,
  String      attrName,
  String      value)
{
  if (value == null)
    return;

  if (!isValueReference(value))
    throw new IllegalArgumentException();
  component.setValueBinding(attrName, createValueBinding(value));
}
```

For the `ProInputDate` component, you want to provide support for the `valueChangeListener` attribute, and therefore you need to handle method-binding expressions, as illustrated in Code Sample 2-35.

Code Sample 2-35. *Method Handling* `MethodBinding` *Attributes and Properties*

```
/**
 * Sets a component property as a method binding.
 *
 * @param component  the Faces component
 * @param attrName   the attribute name
 * @param value      the attribute value
 * @param signature  the method signature
 */
protected void setMethodBindingProperty(
  UIComponent component,
  String      attrName,
  String      value,
  Class[]     signature)
{
  if (value == null)
    return;

  Map attrs = component.getAttributes();
  attrs.put(attrName, createMethodBinding(value, signature));
}
```

A major difference between a `MethodBinding` and a `ValueBinding` is that not only do you have to provide the method expression, but you also have to provide the `signature` for the method specified by the method expression. For a `valueChangeListener` method, this means you need to pass the signature as a class array with one class—`ValueChangeEvent.class`.

METHODBINDING

`UICommand` components use method-binding expressions to reference, for example, an `Action` method or an `ActionListener` method. The `MethodBinding` class encapsulates the actual evaluation of a method binding. You can acquire instances of `MethodBinding` for specific references from the `Application` instance by calling the `createMethodBinding()` method. Note that instances of `MethodBinding` are immutable and contain no references to a `FacesContext` (which is passed in as a parameter when the reference binding is evaluated).

To complete the `UIComponentTagSupport` class, you need to add two methods that can create and return a `ValueBinding` and a `MethodBinding`. Code Sample 2-36 shows the `createValueBinding()` and `createMethodBinding()` methods.

Code Sample 2-36. *The* `createValueBinding()` *and* `createMethodBinding()` *Methods*

```
/**
  * Returns a ValueBinding for the string value.
  *
  * @param value  the attribute string value
  *
  * @return  a parsed ValueBinding
  */
 protected ValueBinding createValueBinding(
   String value)
 {
   FacesContext context = FacesContext.getCurrentInstance();
   Application application = context.getApplication();
   return application.createValueBinding(value);
 }

 /**
  * Returns a MethodBinding for the string value.
  *
  * @param value      the attribute string value
  * @param signature  the method binding signature
  *
  * @return  a parsed MethodBinding
  */
 protected MethodBinding createMethodBinding(
   String  value,
   Class[] signature)
 {
   FacesContext context = FacesContext.getCurrentInstance();
   Application application = context.getApplication();
   return application.createMethodBinding(value, signature);
 }
}
```

The createMethodBinding() method evaluates the specified method-binding expression and creates a MethodBinding instance. The method referenced by the expression is called when the MethodBinding is executed. When the method is called, certain parameters are passed to the backing bean method, such as a ValueChangedEvent for the MethodBinding attached to the valueChangeListener attribute. The MethodBinding must dynamically look up the right method signature to make sure it calls the right method.

JSF 1.2 VALUEEXPRESSION AND METHODEXPRESSION

JSF 1.2 now directly leverages JSP EL in JSP 2.1. JSP EL has native support for both immediate ${}-syntax expressions and deferred #{}-syntax expressions. Therefore, JSF 1.2 tag handlers use the new JSP EL ValueExpression and MethodExpression types as parameters, letting the JSP container take responsibility for parsing the expressions. Two new tag handler base classes, UIComponentELTag and UIComponentELBodyTag, have been introduced in JSF 1.2 to replace UIComponentTag and UIComponentBodyTag in JSF 1.1.

The ProInputDateTag Class

Your new component needs a new custom action, inputDate, with a corresponding tag handler class, ProInputDateTag. On initial rendering, the ProInputDateTag is responsible for creating your new renderer-specific component subclass—ProInputDate—and transferring all JSP custom action attributes from the tag handler to the component instance.

The ProInputDateTag uses the Application to create the component by defining the component type—com.apress.projsf.ProInputDate. This will create a ProInputDate instance, which has a default renderer type of com.apress.projsf.Date. However, it is possible for the local Web application faces-config.xml to override the component class that should be created for this component type. Therefore, the tag handler must explicitly set the renderer type on the newly created component instance and not rely on the default renderer type specified in the ProInputDate constructor. This will guarantee your HtmlProInputDateRenderer is used for the component instance created by the ProInputDateTag when using the default HTML basic RenderKit.

The ProInputDateTag class extends your UIComponentTagSupport, which is the helper class for all your JSP custom actions that correspond to UI components in a page that is rendered by JSF. As shown in Code Sample 2-37, the ProInputDateTag manages all other behavioral properties and the renderer-specific attributes for your component, and you must ensure this tag handler uses the right component type and renderer type.

Code Sample 2-37. *The* ProInputDateTag *Class*

```
package com.apress.projsf.ch2.taglib.pro;

import javax.faces.component.UIComponent;
import javax.faces.event.ValueChangeEvent;

import com.apress.projsf.ch2.component.pro.ProInputDate;
import com.apress.projsf.ch2.taglib.UIComponentTagSupport;
```

```
/**
 * ProInputDateTag component tag handler.
 */
public class ProInputDateTag extends UIComponentTagSupport
{
  /**
   * Returns the component type.
   *
   * @return  the component type
   */
  public String getComponentType()
  {
    return ProInputDate.COMPONENT_TYPE;
  }

  /**
   * Returns the renderer type.
   *
   * @return  the renderer type
   */
  public String getRendererType()
  {
    return ProInputDate.RENDERER_TYPE;
  }
```

As shown in Code Sample 2-38, your `ProInputDateTag` provides tag attribute setters and internal field storage for the behavioral `UIInput` component's attributes (for example, `converter`, `validator`, `valueChangeListener`, `value`, `immediate`, and `required`), as well as the renderer-specific `ProInputDate` attribute (for example, `title`).

Code Sample 2-38. *Behavioral and Renderer-Specific Attributes*

```
/**
 * The converter attribute.
 */
private String _converter;

/**
 * Sets the converter attribute value.
 *
 * @param converter  the converter attribute value
 */
public void setConverter(
  String converter)
{
  _converter = converter;
}
```

```
/**
 * The immediate attribute.
 */
private String _immediate;

/**
 * Sets the immediate attribute value.
 *
 * @param immediate  the immediate attribute value
 */
public void setImmediate(
  String immediate)
{
  _immediate = immediate;
}

/**
 * The required attribute.
 */
private String _required;

/**
 * Sets the required attribute value.
 *
 * @param required  the required attribute value
 */
public void setRequired(
  String required)
{
  _required = required;
}

/**
 * The validator attribute.
 */
private String _validator;

/**
 * Sets the validator attribute value.
 *
 * @param validator  the validator attribute value
 */
public void setValidator(
  String validator)
{
  _validator = validator;
}
```

```
/**
 * The value attribute.
 */
private String _value;

/**
 * Sets the value attribute value.
 *
 * @param value  the value attribute value
 */
public void setValue(
  String value)
{
  _value = value;
}

/**
 * The valueChangeListener attribute.
 */
private String _valueChangeListener;

/**
 * Sets the valueChangeListener attribute value.
 *
 * @param valueChangeListener  the valueChangeListener attribute value
 */
public void setValueChangeListener(
  String valueChangeListener)
{
  _valueChangeListener = valueChangeListener;
}

/**
 * The title attribute.
 */
private String _title;

/**
 * Sets the title attribute value.
 *
 * @param title  the title attribute value
 */
public void setTitle(
  String title)
{
  _title = title;
}
```

THE IMMEDIATE ATTRIBUTE

In some cases, you don't want to go through the entire request-processing lifecycle, for example when the user decides to cancel the current transaction. The `immediate` attribute gives the application developer a way to override the `PhaseId` defined by the `FacesEvent` instance. This attribute can be set on `UICommand` components and takes `true` or `false` as valid values, and by setting the `immediate` attribute to `true`, an application developer can short-circuit the processing lifecycle, cancel a process, and navigate to another view.

The `immediate` attribute is also available on the `UIInput` components. If set to `true`, validation will occur during decode and cause the conversion and validation processing (including the potential to fire `ValueChangeEvent` events) to occur during the Apply Request Values phase instead of in the Process Validations phase.

The `setProperties()` method, as shown in Code Sample 2-39, transfers properties and attributes from this tag to the specified component, if the corresponding properties of this tag handler instance were explicitly set.

Code Sample 2-39. *The* `setProperties()` *Method*

```
  /**
   * Transfers the property values from this tag to the component.
   *
   * @param component  the target component
   */
  protected void setProperties(
    UIComponent component)
  {
    super.setProperties(component);

    // Behavioral properties
    setValueBindingProperty(component, "converter", _converter);
    setBooleanProperty(component, "immediate", _immediate);
    setBooleanProperty(component, "required", _required);
    setValueBindingProperty(component, "validator", _validator);
    setStringProperty(component, "value", _value);
    setMethodBindingProperty(component, "valueChangeListener",
                             _valueChangeListener,
                             new Class[] { ValueChangeEvent.class });

    // Renderer-specific attributes
    setStringProperty(component, "title", _title);
  }
}
```

Any JSF tag handler subclasses that support additional properties on top of what is provided by the UIComponentTag handler must ensure that the base class setProperties() method is still called—super.setProperties().

Code Sample 2-40 shows the release() method, which resets all the internal storage, allowing this tag handler instance to be reused during JSP page execution.

Code Sample 2-40. *The* release() *Method*

```
/**
 * Releases the internal state used by the tag.
 */
public void release()
{
  _converter = null;
  _immediate = null;
  _required = null;
  _validator = null;
  _value = null;
  _valueChangeListener = null;
  _title = null;
}
```

The Tag Library Description

You have now defined the behavior of your ProInputDateTag handler class, so it is time to register the name of the custom action and define some rules for how it can be used. A TLD allows component providers to group custom actions to make up a JSF tag library. When creating a tag library for JSF custom components, the TLD file defines one custom action per Renderer. For the purposes of this chapter, the TLD, as shown in Code Sample 2-41, will define just one custom action—<pro:inputDate>.

Code Sample 2-41. *TLD*

```
<?xml version="1.0" encoding="UTF-8" ?>
<!DOCTYPE taglib
   PUBLIC "-//Sun Microsystems, Inc.//DTD JSP Tag Library 1.2//EN"
          "http://java.sun.com/dtd/web-jsptaglibrary_1_2.dtd" >

<taglib>

  <tlib-version>1.0</tlib-version>
  <jsp-version>1.2</jsp-version>
  <short-name>pro</short-name>
  <uri>http://projsf.apress.com/tags</uri>
  <description>
    This tag library contains the JavaServer Faces component tag for the
    ProJSF Input Date component.
  </description>
```

The TLD must declare a tag library version, the JSP version that the library depends on, a short name that will be used as the default namespace prefix for any custom actions defined in this tag library (for example, pro), and finally a unique URI (http://projsf.apress.com/tags) that will be used by application developers as the taglib directive.

For each custom action in the TLD, you need a <tag> element. Code Sample 2-42 shows how the name of the custom action element is defined in the nested name element (for example, <name>inputDate</name>), and the tag handler class is defined in the <tag-class> element. The <body-content> element describes how this tag should be processed.

Code Sample 2-42. *Custom Action*

```
<tag>
  <name>inputDate</name>
  <tag-class>com.apress.projsf.ch2.taglib.pro.ProInputDateTag</tag-class>
  <body-content>JSP</body-content>
  <description>
    ProJSF Input Date component tag.
  </description>
```

JSP 2.0 ${} EXPRESSIONS AND JSF 1.1 #{} EXPRESSIONS

JSP already has an expression language to provide dynamic values for tag attributes using the ${}-syntax expressions. These expressions are fully evaluated to literal values before the tag handler can observe them. As a result, all information about the underlying data model is lost, preventing the JSF component from being able to post back values to the data model.

Therefore, a different style of expression is required, the JSF #{}-syntax. This syntax is ignored by the JSP engine and passed as a String literal to the tag attribute. The JSF tag handler has an opportunity to parse the expression and retain knowledge of the underlying data model for use during postback. If the value is a literal, such as true, then the JSF tag handler converts this to a strongly typed literal value, such as Boolean.TRUE, before storing it as the component attribute value. The <rtexprvalue>, or runtime expression value, metadata is always set to false because JSP expression syntax is not supported by JSF tag handlers, and this will cause the JSP runtime to enforce that requirement.

If the custom action has attributes, the attributes have to be defined with the <attribute> element. For each attribute in the TLD, as shown in Code Sample 2-43, the <rtexprvalue> element must be set to false, and the attribute class must be left unspecified, allowing it to default to String.

Code Sample 2-43. UIComponent *Attributes*

```
<!-- UIComponent attributes -->
<attribute>
  <name>id</name>
  <required>false</required>
  <rtexprvalue>false</rtexprvalue>
  <description>
```

```
      The component identifier for this component.  This value must be
      unique within the closest parent component that is a naming
      container.
    </description>
  </attribute>
  <attribute>
    <name>rendered</name>
    <required>false</required>
    <rtexprvalue>false</rtexprvalue>
    <description>
      Flag indicating whether or not this component should be rendered
      (during Render Response Phase), or processed on any subsequent
      form submit.
    </description>
  </attribute>
  <attribute>
    <name>binding</name>
    <required>false</required>
    <rtexprvalue>false</rtexprvalue>
    <description>
      The value-binding expression linking this component to a
      property in a backing bean.
    </description>
  </attribute>
```

The previously listed tag attributes are inherited from the parent `UIComponentTag` handler class, and they have to be declared in the TLD to be used with your renderer-specific tag handler class. The tag attributes shown in Code Sample 2-44 are required to support the behavioral `UIInput` attributes.

Code Sample 2-44. `UIInput` *Attributes*

```
<!-- UIInput attributes -->
<attribute>
  <name>converter</name>
  <required>false</required>
  <rtexprvalue>false</rtexprvalue>
  <description>
    Converter instance registered with this component.
  </description>
</attribute>
<attribute>
  <name>immediate</name>
  <required>false</required>
  <rtexprvalue>false</rtexprvalue>
  <description>
```

```
      Flag indicating that this component's value must be
      converted and validated immediately (that is, during
      Apply Request Values phase), rather than waiting
      until Process Validations phase.
    </description>
  </attribute>
  <attribute>
    <name>required</name>
    <required>false</required>
    <rtexprvalue>false</rtexprvalue>
    <description>
      Flag indicating that the user is required to provide a submitted
      value for this input component.
    </description>
  </attribute>
  <attribute>
    <name>validator</name>
    <required>false</required>
    <rtexprvalue>false</rtexprvalue>
    <description>
      MethodBinding representing a validator method that will be called
      during Process Validations to perform correctness checks on the
      value of this component.  The expression must evaluate to a public
      method that takes FacesContext, UIComponent, and Object parameters,
      with a return type of void.
    </description>
  </attribute>
  <attribute>
    <name>value</name>
    <required>false</required>
    <rtexprvalue>false</rtexprvalue>
    <description>
      The current value of this component.
    </description>
  </attribute>
  <attribute>
    <name>valueChangeListener</name>
    <required>false</required>
    <rtexprvalue>false</rtexprvalue>
    <description>
      MethodBinding representing a value change listener method that will be
      notified when a new value has been set for this input component.  The
      expression must evaluate to a public method that takes a
      ValueChangeEvent parameter, with a return type of void.
    </description>
  </attribute>
```

Finally, in Code Sample 2-45, you define your ProInputDate renderer-specific attributes.

Code Sample 2-45. ProInputDate *Attributes*

```
    <!-- ProInputDate attributes -->
    <attribute>
      <name>title</name>
      <required>false</required>
      <rtexprvalue>false</rtexprvalue>
      <description>
        Advisory title information about markup elements generated
        for this component.
      </description>
    </attribute>
  </tag>
</taglib>
```

JSP 2.1 DEFERRED-VALUE AND DEFERRED-METHOD

JSF 1.2 now directly leverages JSP EL in JSP 2.1. JSP EL has native support for both immediate ${}-syntax expressions and deferred #{}-syntax expressions. A JSF 1.2 tag library can now leverage the <deferred-value> syntax available in JSP 2.1 tag library descriptors, such as the following to indicate that #{}-syntax is supported by this JSP 2.1 tag attribute and that it defines the evaluation type to be Boolean:

```
<deferred-value>
  <type>java.lang.Boolean</type>
</deferred-value>
```

This will result in a ValueExpression being passed as a parameter to the JSP 2.1 tag handler setter method for this attribute. You can also use the <deferred-method> syntax for method invocations, as follows, to indicate that #{}-syntax is supported by this JSP 2.1 tag attribute and to define the signature of the deferred method:

```
<deferred-method>
  <method-signature>
    void doAction(javax.faces.event.ActionEvent)
  </method-signature>
</deferred-method>
```

This will result in a MethodExpression being passed as a parameter to the JSP 2.1 tag handler setter method for this attribute.

This approach replaces the classic JSF 1.1 <rtexprvalue>false</rtexprvalue> and default java.lang.String tag attribute type in JSP 2.0.

Building an Application with the Input Date Component

To use the custom component in a JSP document, the application developer must use the standard JSP taglib directive to declare the URI for your tag library. To identify the custom action to be used within the tag library, the application developer needs to append the namespace prefix. Note that the JSP page shown in Code Sample 2-46 is the same page described at the beginning of this chapter.

Code Sample 2-46. *JSF Document Using the* `<pro:inputDate>` *Tag*

```
<?xml version = '1.0' encoding = 'windows-1252'?>
<jsp:root xmlns:jsp="http://java.sun.com/JSP/Page" version="1.2"
          xmlns:pro="http://projsf.apress.com/tags"
          xmlns:f="http://java.sun.com/jsf/core"
          xmlns:h="http://java.sun.com/jsf/html" >
  <jsp:directive.page contentType="text/html"/>
  <f:view>
    <html>
      ...
      <body>
        <h:form>
          <pro:inputDate id="dateField"
                         title="Date Field Component"
                          value="#{backingBean.date}" >
            <f:convertDateTime pattern="dd MMMMM yyyy" />
          </pro:inputDate>
          <br></br>
          <h:message for="dateField" />
          ...
        </h:form>
      </body>
    </html>
  </f:view>
</jsp:root>
```

Running this page will render the page shown in Figure 2-12 to the browser.

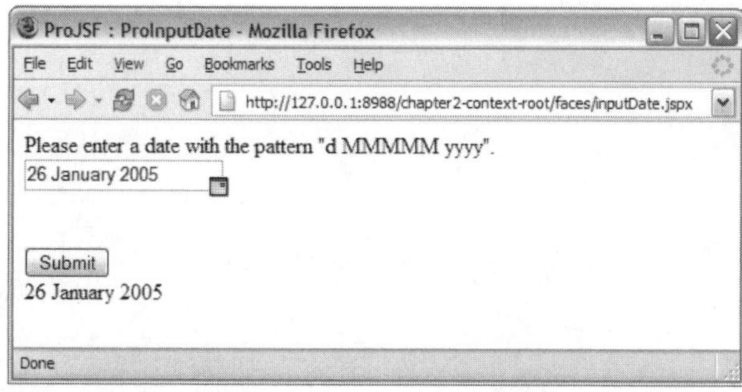

Figure 2-12. *The date field component with an additional* `commandButton` *and an* `outputText` *field*

Summary

This chapter gave you a blueprint and an understanding of what is required to write a JSF custom component. It covered topics including creating `Renderers`, creating renderer-specific subclasses, using external resources, registering component objects, and creating JSP tag handlers and TLDs. In later chapters, you will leverage this knowledge as the foundation for building more advanced JSF components.

The structure of how to build components will remain the same throughout the book. First you analyze the markup needed to create the intended behavior and user interface. Then you create the client-specific `Renderer` with all attributes needed for your component. Optionally, but recommended, you create the renderer-specific subclass that the application developer can use to customize the component at runtime. Finally, you implement support for the page description of choice—JSP. You should also now understand how to use `ValueBinding` and `MethodBinding` and how to support these concepts in your own JSF tag handlers.

CHAPTER 3

Defining the Deck Component

One of the most important aspects of most nontrivial applications (especially UI type apps) is the ability to respond to events that are generated by the various components of the application, both in response to user interactions and other system components . . . .

—Terry Warren, SCOUG, 1999

This chapter expands on the blueprint for building components outlined in the previous chapter. For this chapter, we will show how to create a component that can act as an accordion, or *deck*, which is commonly used within applications and integrated development environments (IDEs) to show and hide information, such as information about selected files in a file explorer or JSF components in a component palette. Figure 3-1 shows an expandable deck used in Microsoft's Windows Explorer.

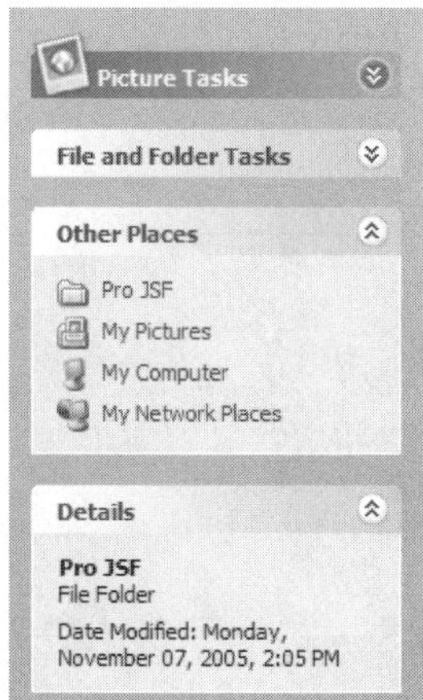

Figure 3-1. *Expandable deck used in Microsoft Windows Explorer*

A deck component has the benefit of being stackable and of being able to store more information than the equivalent space in a traditional HTML page. From a component writer's point of view, this type of component introduces several key areas of component design, such as handling events, rendering children, and loading external resources.

Requirements for the Deck Component

The design of the deck component will allow a user to expose specific information that is currently hidden by clicking one of the displayed decks and exposing a set of items associated with the clicked deck. These child items can be anything, including links, text, and even graphics. The component should be intelligent enough to detect an already open deck and close it before opening the one requested by the user. From an application developer's point of view, the component needs to be extensible, meaning the application developer can add as many decks as needed and include any number of children within these decks. The application developer should also be able to add any number of deck groups to a page.

The Deck Component

As you remember from the first chapter, the only reason for creating new behavioral superclasses is if the behavior and the definition have not been introduced before. According to the requirements in the previous section, the deck component should be able to selectively show nested components or groups of components, based on the user selection, and only one group will be shown at any time. To achieve this, you have to create a new `Renderer` to handle the selective display and a new event type to handle the user selection with an accompanying listener interface for that particular event type. Since the behavior of showing and hiding children has not been introduced yet, we will cover two new behavioral superclasses to handle the show-one-item behavior (see Table 2-1 in Chapter 2).

After completing this chapter, you should understand the JSF event model and know how to create new behavioral superclasses and your own event type with a corresponding listener interface. Figure 3-2 shows the 11 classes you will create in this chapter.

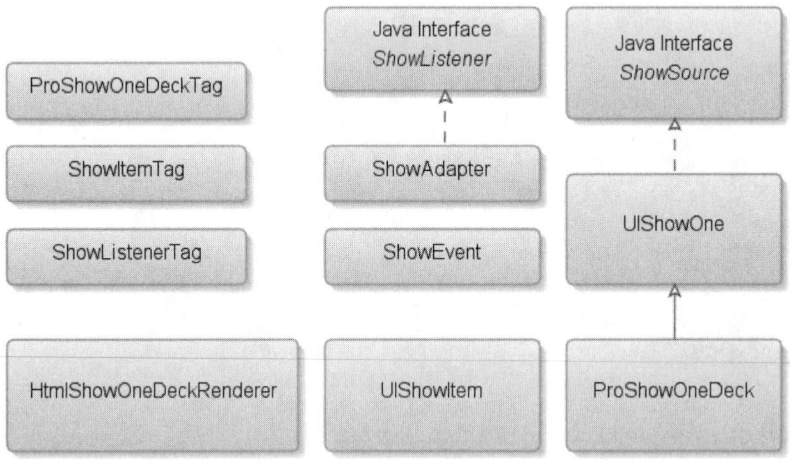

Figure 3-2. *Class diagram showing classes created in this chapter*

The classes are as follows:

- The ProShowOneDeckTag class represents the ProShowOneDeck component.
- The ShowItemTag class represents leaf nodes of the deck component.
- The ShowListenerTag class represents a custom action that the application developer will use to register a ShowListener instance to a UIShowOne component.
- The HtmlShowOneDeckRenderer is the new custom Renderer, which is in charge of the markup rendered to the client.
- The ShowListener is a Listener interface.
- The ShowAdapter supports adding a MethodBinding as a ShowListener.
- The ShowEvent is the custom event class.
- The UIShowItem is a behavioral superclass and represents each of the child components to the UIShowOne component.
- The ShowSource class isolates the event listener management methods.
- The UIShowOne class is a behavioral superclass that acts as a top-level container, controlling which one of its child components to display when activated.
- And finally, the ProShowOneDeck class is your renderer-specific subclass.

Designing the Deck Component Using a Blueprint

When you design a component that requires a new behavior or new functionality, it is wise to start implementing this before creating the actual Renderer for this behavior, and as such, these two steps precede the client-specific Renderer step in the blueprint, as shown in Table 3-1.

Table 3-1. *Steps in the Blueprint for Creating a New JSF Component*

#	Step	Description
1	Creating a UI prototype	Create a prototype of the UI and intended behavior for your component using the appropriate markup.
2	**Creating events and listeners**	(Optional) Create custom events and listeners in case your specific needs are not covered by the JSF specification.
3	**Creating a behavioral superclass**	(Optional) If the component behavior is not to be found, create a new behavioral superclass (for example, UIShowOne).
4	Creating a client-specific Renderer	Create the Renderer you need that will write out the client-side markup for your JSF component.
5	Creating a renderer-specific subclass	(Optional) Create a renderer-specific subclass. Although this is an optional step, it is good practice to implement it.

Continued

Table 3-1. *Continued*

#	Step	Description
6	Registering a `UIComponent` and `Renderer`	Register your new `UIComponent` and `Renderer` in the `faces-config.xml` file.
7	Creating a JSP tag handler and TLD	This step is needed in case you are using JSP as your default view handler. An alternative solution is to use Facelets (`http://facelets.dev.java.net/`).

As you can see, the blueprint has two additional steps: creating events and listeners and creating a behavioral superclass. According to the blueprint, you still need to first implement the component in the intended markup.

Step 1: Creating a UI Prototype

Let's take a moment to reflect on what you want to achieve and create a prototype of the intended markup needed for the client (in this case, a web browser). Remember, by doing so, you will find out what elements the `Renderer` has to generate, what renderer-specific attributes the application developer will need, and what behavior is expected to build an application with the deck component.

Figure 3-3 shows the end result of the deck component implemented in HTML.

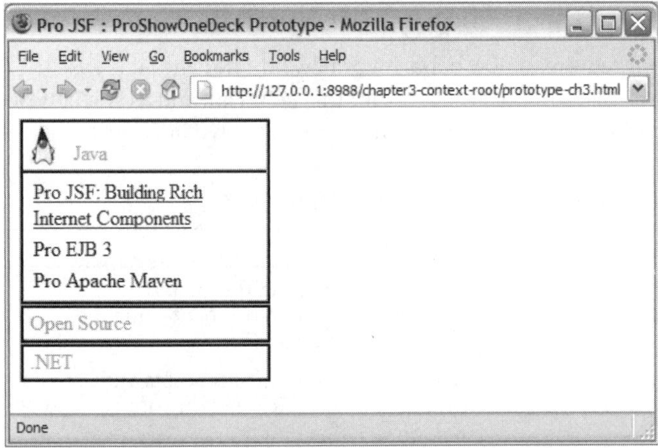

Figure 3-3. *The deck component, implemented in HTML, showing the Java item expanded*

Let's first focus on the presentation of the prototype. As you can see in Figure 3-3, the deck has three labels—Java, Open Source, and .NET. Each label represents an expandable region, and in Figure 3-3 the Java region is currently expanded and shows its content. These labels are containers, since they can hold more than just text (for example, a combination of images and text). Within the expanded Java region is a mix of plain text and links. Styles control the actual look and feel. Code Sample 3-1 shows the HTML needed to create the deck component.

Code Sample 3-1. *The Deck HTML Prototype Implementation*

```
<html>
  <head>
    <title>Pro JSF : ProShowOneDeck Prototype</title>
    <style type="text/css" >
      .ProShowOne { ... }
      .ProShowItem { ... }
      .ProShowItemHeader { ... }
      .ProShowItemContent { ... }
    </style>
  </head>
  <body>
    <div style="width:200px;" >
      <div class="ProShowOne">
        <div class="ProShowItem">
          <div class="ProShowItemHeader"
               onclick="alert('first')" >
            <img src="resources/java_small.jpg"
                 alt="The Duke"
                 style="margin-right: 8px; vertical-align:bottom;" />
            Java
          </div>
          <div class="ProShowItemContent">
            <table>
              <tbody>
                <tr>
                  <td>
                    <a href="http://www.apress.com/...">
                      Pro JSF: Building Rich Internet Components
                    </a>
                  </td>
                </tr>
                <tr>
                  <td>Pro EJB 3</td>
                </tr>
                <tr>
                  <td>Pro Apache Maven</td>
                </tr>
              </tbody>
            </table>
          </div>
```

```
        </div>
        <div class="ProShowItem">
          <div class="ProShowItemHeader"
               onclick="alert('second')" >
            Open Source
          </div>
        </div>
        <div class="ProShowItem">
          <div class="ProShowItemHeader"
               onclick="alert('third')">
            .NET
          </div>
        </div>
      </div>
    </div>
  </body>
</html>
```

As you can see, `<div ...>` elements represent the label containers and their contents. The reason for choosing `<div>` elements instead of anchor elements (`<a href>`) is so you can more easily control the look and feel of the deck nodes. If you implemented this using anchor elements, you would have to deal with browser-specific behaviors to handle links, such as the look of visited links, not visited links, and so on.

Apart from the obvious visual aspect, you do not need to identify which label the user has activated, since only one node can be expanded at any time. In the prototype in Code Sample 3-1, we have simulated this behavior by adding an alert (for example, `onclick="alert('first')"`) to the `<div>` element representing the label of the expandable region.

By examining the HTML source in Code Sample 3-1, you can also see that you need to expose attributes for four style classes—`ProShowOne`, `ProShowItem`, `ProShowItemHeader`, and `ProShowItemContent`. Code Sample 3-2 show how to map some of the visible HTML attributes to their corresponding `UIComponent` attributes.

Code Sample 3-2. *Parameterized HTML for the* `showOneDeck` *Renderer*

```
<div class=[showOne.styleClass]>
 <div class=[showOne.itemStyleClass]>
   <div class=[showOne.itemHeaderStyleClass]
        onclick="alert([showItem.id])" >
     <img src="resources/java_small.jpg"
          alt="The Duke"
          style="margin-right: 8px; vertical-align:bottom;" />
     Java
   </div>
   <div class=[showOne.itemContentStyleClass]>
     <table>
       <tbody>
```

```
          <tr>
            <td>
              <a href="http://www.apress.com/...">
                Pro JSF: Building Rich Internet Components
              </a>
            </td>
          </tr>
          <tr>
            <td>Pro EJB 3</td>
          </tr>
          <tr>
            <td>Pro Apache Maven</td>
          </tr>
        </tbody>
      </table>
    </div>
  </div>
  <div class="[showOne.itemStyleClass]" >
    class="[showOne.itemHeaderStyleClass]"
         onclick="alert([showItem.id])" >
      Open Source
    </div>
  </div>
  <div class="[showOne.itemStyleClass]" >
    <div class="[showOne.itemHeaderStyleClass]"
         onclick="alert([showItem.id])" >
      .NET
    </div>
  </div>
</div>
```

Part of the design of the component is that it should allow the user to expand only one item at a time. For this you need to first identify the item activated by the user; this takes place with the `alert()` function attached to each item, and `[showItem.id]` illustrates the identifier. In addition, you need a way to keep track of each item and to ensure that only one is expanded at any time.

To achieve this, you need a parent container that can listen for the event identifying the activated item and then expand it and close the previously opened item. The prototype uses the `<div class=[showOne.styleClass]>` element as the logical parent container. This design of having a logical container for multiple items is modeled after `HtmlDataTable` and `UIColumn` in the JSF specification. The attributes in the prototype are associated with one of these components (in other words, the parent container, `showOne`) or one of its children (`showItem`).

It is important to note that although the prototype describes the user interface requirements, some attributes and functionality still might not be visible or make sense in the actual prototype. For the HTML source in Code Sample 3-2, one attribute is not visible but still needed by the implementation—`showOne.showItemId`. It will be used to set the default expanded item on the initial request. Additionally, you need to let application developers listen for events on the component `showOne.showListener` and invoke application logic when an item has been activated.

Before you start creating the deck component, take a sneak peak at the final result and how it will be used in a JSP page, as shown in Code Sample 3-3.

Code Sample 3-3. *Deck Component As It Would Be Used in a JSF JSP Document*

```
<?xml version="1.0" encoding="UTF-8" ?>
<jsp:root ...>
  <jsp:directive.page contentType="text/html" />
  <f:view>
    ...
    <pro:showOneDeck showItemId="first"
                     showListener="#{backingBean.doShow}" >
      <pro:showItem id="first" >
        <f:facet name="header" >
          <h:panelGroup>
            <h:graphicImage url="/resources/java_small.jpg"
                            alt="The Duke"
                            style="margin-right: 8px; vertical-align:bottom;" />
            <h:outputText value="Java" />
          </h:panelGroup>
        </f:facet>
        <h:panelGrid columns="1" >
          <h:outputLink value="http://www.apress.com" >
            <h:outputText value="Pro JSF: Building Rich Internet Components" />
          </h:outputLink>
          <h:outputText value="Pro EJB 3" />
          <h:outputText value="Pro Apache Maven" />
        </h:panelGrid>
      </pro:showItem>
      <pro:showItem id="second" >
        <f:facet name="header">
          <h:outputText value="Open Source" />
        </f:facet>
        <h:panelGrid columns="1" >
          <h:outputText value="Foundations of AJAX" />
          <h:outputText value="Pro Apache Ant" />
          <h:outputText value="Pro PHP Security" />
        </h:panelGrid>
      </pro:showItem>
      <pro:showItem id="third" >
        <f:facet name="header">
```

```
          <h:outputText value=".NET" />
        </f:facet>

        <h:panelGrid columns="1" >
          <h:outputText value="Pro .NET Extreme Programming" />
          <h:outputText value=".NET for Delphi Programmers" />
        </h:panelGrid>
      </pro:showItem>

      <pro:showListener
           type="com.apress.projsf.ch3.application.MyShowListener" />
    </pro:showOneDeck>
  ...
  </f:view>
</jsp:root>
```

The tags highlighted in bold represent the JSF components you will learn how to create in this chapter. As you can see, the sample is a fairly simple application with one parent component—`<pro:showOneDeck ... >`—that keeps track of which item is currently open and which node is set to be expanded by default. In the page the parent component has three children—`<pro:showItem ... >`. Each `<pro:showItem ... >` child component has its own unique identifier (for example, `first`, `second`, and `third`). Each `<pro:showItem ... >` has a facet—`<f:facet name="header">`—associated with it representing the "header" of the clickable area of the item (see Chapter 1 for more about facets).

Part of the deck component's requirements is to allow application developers to use any component to represent the actual clickable header, and as examples we have used regular `<h:outputText>` and `<h:panelGroup>` components. Nested within each `<pro:showItem ... >` is a set of children, which will be displayed when the user selects an item. When the user selects any of the `<pro:showItem ... >` components, an event will be delivered to the event queue for processing in the Invoke Application phase.

To be able to react to this event, a new listener—`<pro:showListener ... />`—listens for the aforementioned event.

Step 2: Creating Events and Listeners

To be able to create the component, you need to understand two new behavioral superclasses—`UIShowOne` and `UIShowItem`. The `UIShowOne` behavioral superclass keeps track of which node the user has selected, and the `UIShowItem` acts as a clickable parent container that will either show or hide its children. For these new `UIComponents`, you also need a new event type, `ShowEvent`, with a corresponding event listener interface, `ShowListener`, to notify application developers and to attach application code to the component. The new event instance needs to keep track of which item the user has selected. On top of this, you need to create a new `Renderer` to handle the selective rendering with accompanying renderer-specific subclasses and JSP tag handlers.

Figure 3-4 shows the classes needed for the event and listener implementation that you will learn how to create in this chapter.

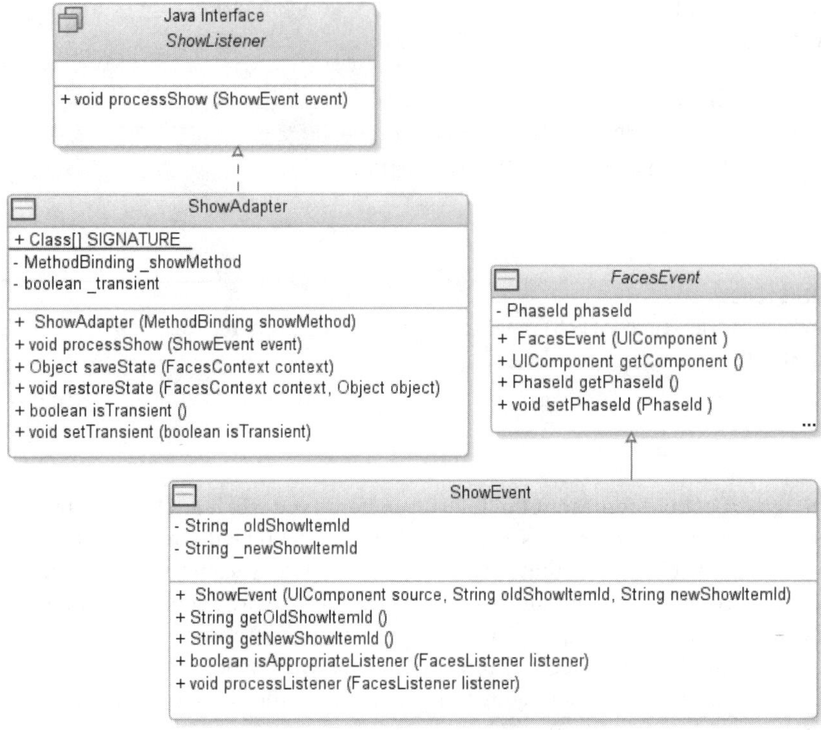

Figure 3-4. *Class diagram showing all classes needed for the event and listener implementation*

Event Handling Overview

This section will cover a few topics regarding the JSF event model before you see the code for the event and listener implementation for the deck component.

If you have experience developing applications with the Swing toolkit or Oracle's ADF Swing framework, you will notice that the event model implemented by JSF is similar. In fact, JSF implements a model for event notification and listener registration based on the naming convention in the JavaBeans specification, version 1.0.1. Essentially, this means an application developer can write application code and register it to listen for a specific event. A `UIComponent` delivers the event itself (for example, when a user clicks a button, which is similar to the approach taken in other UI toolkits). Application developers will immediately recognize the benefits of such a model, since it has proven to be easy to maintain and develop. It allows application developers to write application code for specific events in well-defined blocks of code like the ones used in Microsoft Visual Basic.

The main difference between the Swing framework and JSF is that Swing operates in a stateful mode and is always listening for events fired by the client; by contrast, JSF works in a stateless environment. With no permanent connection between the client and the backend server, JSF cannot always listen to events and has to rely on postbacks to be notified about any changes on the client that might cause an event to be delivered. This limitation of HTTP has forced JSF to implement a strict event model to handle client-generated events, based on the JSF request-processing lifecycle described in Chapter 1.

During postback, all six phases of the JSF request lifecycle are called (unless somewhere in the process `renderResponse()` is called, in which case the lifecycle will directly jump to the Render Response phase). When the Restore View phase is executed, it restores any state available from the previous request. During the Apply Request Values phase (see Figure 3-5), the submitted value from the request parameters is established and added to each input component, and any events are queued.

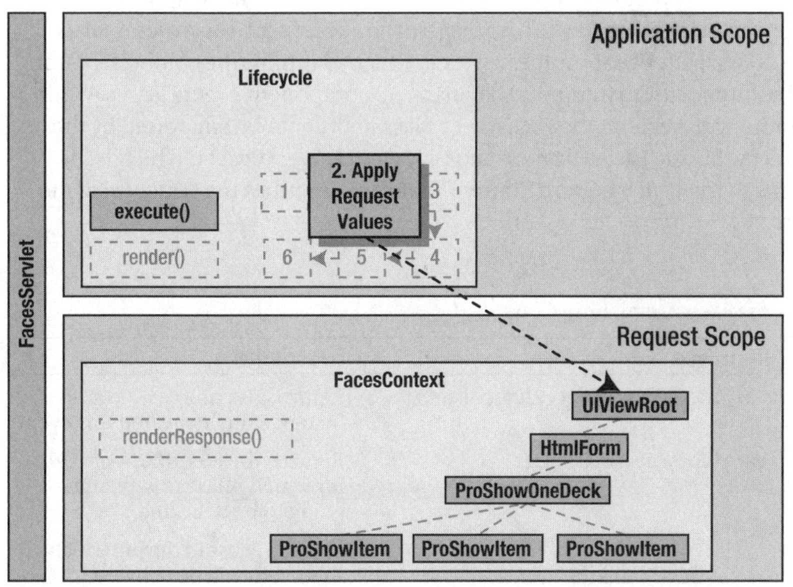

Figure 3-5. *Applying new values passed on the request to the components*

By default, at the end of each one of these phases, the appropriate `UIViewRoot` lifecycle management method (`processDecodes()`, `processValidators()`, `processUpdates()`, and `processApplication()`) will loop over events queued in the phase and notify any registered listeners on the component that queued the event (for example, a `ProShowOneDeck`). Application logic in these listeners can also queue events, and the `UIViewRoot` lifecycle management method will continue looping through the queued list of events until it is empty before continuing to the next phase.

■ **Note** It is important to understand that events can be queued and delivered during any of the following request lifecycle phases: Apply Request Values, Process Validations, Update Model Values, and Invoke Application.

Events

Application developers can use event instances to be notified about changes to the UI or underlying model. The JSF specification defines two default event types—`javax.faces.event.ActionEvent` and `javax.faces.event.ValueChangeEvent`. The `ActionEvent` is usually delivered when a user activates a `UICommand` component, and the `ValueChangeEvent` indicates that a value has changed in any of the `UIInput` components.

The FacesEvent Base Class

The `javax.faces.event.FacesEvent` class is the abstract base class for UI and application events within JSF that can be delivered by `UIComponents`. The `FacesEvent` constructor takes one argument—the `UIComponent` event source instance, which identifies the component from which the event will be broadcast to interested listeners. All component event classes within JSF—default or custom—must extend the `FacesEvent` class in order to be supported by the request-processing lifecycle. The `FacesEvent` extends `java.util.EventObject`, which is the base class for all events in the Java Standard Edition. Table 3-2 describes the structure of the `FacesEvent` base class.

Table 3-2. *Method Summary of the* `FacesEvent` *Base Class**

Method	Return Type	Description
`getComponent()`	`javax.faces.component.UIComponent`	Returns the source `UIComponent` instance that delivered this event
`getPhaseId()`	`javax.faces.event.PhaseId`	Returns the identifier—`phaseId`—for which phase this event is going to be delivered
`setPhaseId`	`void`	Sets the `PhaseId` during which this event will be delivered
`isApproriateListener()`	`boolean`	Checks whether this listener is of a listener instance that this event supports
`processListener()`	`void`	Broadcasts this event to the specified listener
`queue()`	`void`	Convenience method that queues this event for broadcast at the end of the current request-processing lifecycle phase

* *Source: The API Java documentation for the JSF specification*

The phaseId Property

By default events are delivered in the phase in which they were queued, but component authors can decide to have events delivered at any of the JSF request-processing lifecycle phases by setting the `phaseId` property of the `FacesEvent` class, which has a data type of `PhaseId`. This data type is a type-safe enumeration and stores a value representing which request lifecycle phase should deliver the event. Table 3-3 shows the valid values.

Table 3-3. *Valid* PhaseId *Values*

PhaseId value	Description
PhaseId.ANY_PHASE	This is the default value if the component author has not set anything. The event will be delivered in the phase in which it was queued.
PhaseId.APPLY_REQUEST_VALUES	Delivers the event at the end of the Apply Request Values phase.
PhaseId.PROCESS_VALIDATIONS	Delivers the event at the end of the Process Validations phase.
PhaseId.UPDATE_MODEL_VALUES	Delivers the event at the end of the Update Model Values phase.
PhaseId.INVOKE_APPLICATION	Delivers the event at the end of the Invoke Application phase.
PhaseId.RENDER_RESPONSE	Delivers the event at the end of the Render Response phase.

At the end of each phase, the `UIViewRoot` component will loop over all events in the queue, starting with events that have `phaseId` set to `ANY_PHASE` and thereafter with events that have `phaseId` set to that particular phase.

Broadcast Events

As described previously, at the end of each phase, the `UIViewRoot` component will loop over the list of queued events, and it will "broadcast" events to any listeners registered for that particular event. In practice, it means the `UIViewRoot` will call a method—`broadcast()`—on the `UIComponent` instance delivering the event, as shown in Code Sample 3-4.

Code Sample 3-4. *The* `broadcast()` *Method Signature*

```
public abstract void broadcast(
  FacesEvent event) throws AbortProcessingException;
```

This method notifies any listeners registered for a specific event type, and it takes one argument of type `FacesEvent`.

Event Subclass

In Chapter 2, the second step in the blueprint was to create a client-specific `Renderer`. In this chapter, you need to extend the custom component blueprint by adding the creation of new event types and behavioral superclasses.

Based on the analysis of the HTML source, you need to be able to handle client-side user events and keep track of what has been expanded and what the user wants to expand next. Before you create the new behavioral superclass, you need to define a new event class and a new listener interface that can be used to execute application code specific to this new type of user events. You also have to decide on a name for the new event class; the convention used in the JavaBeans specification is to prefix the name with the actual event behavior, which in this case is to show something (`Show`) followed by the name `Event` (for example, `ShowEvent`). Code Sample 3-5 shows the new event class.

Code Sample 3-5. *The* ShowEvent *Subclass*

```
package com.apress.projsf.ch3.event;

import javax.faces.component.UIComponent;
import javax.faces.event.FacesEvent;
import javax.faces.event.FacesListener;
import javax.faces.event.PhaseId;

/**
 * The ShowEvent event.
 */
public class ShowEvent extends FacesEvent
{
  /**
   * Creates a new ShowEvent.
   *
   * @param source         the source of the event
   * @param oldShowItemId  the previously showing item identifier
   * @param newShowItemId  the currently showing item identifier
   */
  public ShowEvent(
    UIComponent source,
    String      oldShowItemId,
    String      newShowItemId)
  {
    super(source);
    setPhaseId(PhaseId.INVOKE_APPLICATION);
    _oldShowItemId = oldShowItemId;
    _newShowItemId = newShowItemId;
  }

  public String getOldShowItemId()
  {
    return _oldShowItemId;
  }

  public String getNewShowItemId()
  {
    return _newShowItemId;
  }

  public boolean isAppropriateListener(
    FacesListener listener)
  {
    return (listener instanceof ShowListener);
  }
```

```
  public void processListener(
    FacesListener listener)
  {
    ((ShowListener) listener).processShow(this);
  }

  private String _oldShowItemId;
  private String _newShowItemId;
}
```

When you introduce a new event class, you need to make sure it extends javax.faces.event.FacesEvent so that the event can participate in the JSF request-processing lifecycle. The FacesEvent base class constructor takes one argument—the source of the UIComponent instance delivering the event. This means the new event class—ShowEvent—has to take the UIComponent instance source as an argument and pass it on to its superclass—super(source);. If not set, the default value for phaseId is PhaseId.ANY_PHASE, which means the event will be delivered in the phase in which it was queued. To ensure that the deck component's ShowEvent event is not delivered before the entire component hierarchy has been processed, you have to set phaseId to PhaseId.INVOKE_APPLICATION. This is important since the deck node needs to know about its children and allow them to be updated and validated in order to render properly.

To make life easier on application developers using the ShowEvent class, you can also add two properties—oldShowItemId and newShowItemId—with corresponding getter methods, which are not required by the FacesEvent base class. These accessors are there for convenience so that application developers can find out which item is collapsed and which item is currently expanded.

You also override two methods in the FacesEvent base class—isApproriateListener() and processListener(). The isApproriateListener() method returns true if the listener is an instance of ShowListener (more about this listener in a second). The isAppropriateListener() method allows component writers to verify that the signature of the listener associated with the component is compatible with the event being broadcast. If the listener is compatible, the processListener() method is called during UIComponent.broadcast() to deliver this event to the ShowListener instance's processShow() method, implemented by the application developer.

Listeners

For an application to react to events raised by the user, JSF supports a Listener. For each event type (for example, ValueChangeEvent) defined by either the JSF implementation or a custom UIComponent, there has to be a corresponding Listener interface (for example, ValueChangeListener). The Listener implemented by the application developer implements one or more of these Listener interfaces, along with the event handling method(s) specified by those interfaces, which will be called during event broadcast.

The FacesListener Interface

The javax.faces.event.FacesListener interface (extends java.util.EventListener) is the base interface for all default and custom listener interfaces in JSF. The FacesListener interface (extends java.util.EventListener) is a marker interface and is used only for type safety. Commonly, most implementations of this listener interface take a single argument of the event type for which the listener is being created (for example, `public void processShow(ShowEvent event);`).

Event Listener Interface

Any custom event type that extends the `FacesEvent` base class has to provide a `Listener` interface for that event type, which makes sense since there is no meaning in delivering an event unless there is a way to act on it.

Code Sample 3-6 extends the `FacesListener` interface and creates a listener interface—`ShowListener`—that adds the `processShow()` method that takes a `ShowEvent` instance as an argument. As you can see, this follows the same naming convention used for the `ShowEvent` class with a prefix of the intended event name and a suffix of `Listener` to indicate the purpose of this class.

Code Sample 3-6. *The* `ShowListener` *Interface*

```
package com.apress.projsf.ch3.event;

import javax.faces.event.FacesListener;

/**
 * The ShowListener listener.
 */
public interface ShowListener extends FacesListener
{
  /**
   * Processes a ShowEvent.
   *
   * @param event  the show event
   */
  public void processShow(
    ShowEvent event);
}
```

Event Listener Adapter

As described in Chapter 2, the `UIInput` component delivers a `ValueChangeEvent` to all registered event listeners. In addition, the `ValueChangeEvent` is also delivered to the backing bean via a `MethodBinding` stored in the `UIInput`'s `valueChangeListener` attribute. The `valueChangeListener` attribute is exposed as a tag attribute on the standard input tags, such as `<h:inputText valueChangeListener="#{backingBean.doValueChange}" >`. In JSF 1.2, the `valueChangeListener` attribute is deprecated on the `UIInput` component but is still present on the JSP tag as a JSP 2.1 `MethodExpression`, so an adapter class is needed to adapt the `MethodExpression` into a `ValueChangeListener` instance. This allows the backing bean to still be called when a `ValueChangeEvent` occurs but without needing a separate `valueChangeListener` attribute on the `UIInput` component. This simplifies and clarifies component development by more closely following the JavaBeans specification while preserving `MethodBinding` support for application development.

We will show how to follow this design pattern to adapt a JSF 1.1 MethodBinding into a ShowListener instance. Code Sample 3-7 shows the implementation of this design pattern, ShowAdapter.

Code Sample 3-7. *The* ShowAdapter *Class*

```
package com.apress.projsf.ch3.event;

import javax.faces.component.StateHolder;
import javax.faces.component.UIComponentBase;
import javax.faces.context.FacesContext;
import javax.faces.el.MethodBinding;

/**
 * The ShowAdapter calls a MethodBinding with the same signature
 * as the <code>processShow</code> method.
 */
public class ShowAdapter implements ShowListener,
                                    StateHolder
{
  /**
   * The MethodBinding signature for ShowListener methods.
   */
  public static Class[] SIGNATURE = new Class[] { ShowEvent.class };

  /**
   * Creates a new ShowAdapter.
   *
   * @param showMethod  the MethodBinding to adapt
   */
  public ShowAdapter(
    MethodBinding showMethod)
  {
    _showMethod = showMethod;
  }

  /**
   * Processes a ShowEvent.
   *
   * @param event  the show event
   */
  public void processShow(
    ShowEvent event)
  {
    FacesContext context = FacesContext.getCurrentInstance();
    _showMethod.invoke(context, new Object[]{event});
  }
```

```
/**
 * Saves the internal state of this ShowAdapter.
 *
 * @param context  the Faces context
 *
 * @return  the saved state
 */
public Object saveState(
  FacesContext context)
{
  return UIComponentBase.saveAttachedState(context, _showMethod);
}

/**
 * Restores the internal state of this ShowAdapter.
 *
 * @param context  the Faces context
 * @param object   the state to restore
 */
public void restoreState(
  FacesContext context,
  Object       object)
{
  _showMethod = (MethodBinding)
     UIComponentBase.restoreAttachedState(context, object);
}

/**
 * Returns true if this ShowAdapter is transient and should
 * not be state saved, otherwise false.
 *
 * @return  the value of transient
 */
public boolean isTransient()
{
  return _transient;
}

/**
 * Indicates whether this ShowAdapter is transient and should
 * not be state saved.
 *
 * @param isTransient  the new value for transient
 */
public void setTransient(
  boolean isTransient)
{
```

```
    _transient = isTransient;
  }

  private MethodBinding _showMethod;
  private boolean       _transient;
}
```

The ShowAdapter implements the processShow method, calling the specified MethodBinding with the ShowEvent parameter. It is important that the MethodBinding passed to the ShowAdapter constructor matches the signature of the processShow method. Therefore, the ProShowOneDeckTag uses the SIGNATURE constant to create the MethodBinding with the correct signature.

It is important to implement the StateHolder interface on this adapter class so that the state can be properly saved and restored when an instance is registered as a listener on a component in the component hierarchy.

You must provide an implementation of the saveState() method to store to the MethodBinding state as the UIShowAdapter state, so you need to use a static method from UIComponentBase called saveAttachedState(). This convenience method does the work of state saving attached objects that may or may not implement the StateHolder interface.

You must also provide an implementation of the restoreState() method that takes the FacesContext and the state object as arguments. Note that using the saveAttachedState() method to save the MethodBinding state implies that you use the restoreAttachedState() method to restore the MethodBinding state.

Event Delivery in Practice

Let's use the same page as in Code Sample 3-3 to step through the event delivery mechanism provided by JSF. We will now show how to use the same code to dive into the JSF event and listener model. The page contains the source in Code Sample 3-8.

Code Sample 3-8. *Page Source with the* showListener *Tag*

```
<h:form>
  ...
    <pro:showOneDeck showItemId="first"
                     showListener="#{backingBean.doShow}" >
      <pro:showItem id="first" >
        ...
      </pro:showItem>

      <pro:showListener
            type="com.apress.projsf.ch3.application.MyShowListener" />
    </pro:showOneDeck>
  ...
</h:form>
```

The <pro:showOneDeck ...> contains one attribute that is associated with the ShowEvent event type—ShowListener. This sample sets the <pro:showOneDeck> attribute showListener to #{backingBean.doShow}. This is a common approach of assigning a listener to a component via an attribute. The MethodBinding is pointing to a method—doShow()—that follows the signature of the ShowListener interface but without directly implementing it. Code Sample 3-9 shows the source for the ShowListener method—doShow().

Code Sample 3-9. *A* ShowListener *Method*—doShow()

```
package com.apress.projsf.ch3.application;

import com.apress.projsf.ch3.event.ShowEvent;

/**
 * ShowOneDeckBean is a backing bean for the showOneDeck.jspx document.
 */
public class ShowOneDeckBean
{
  /**
   * The ShowListener method binding.
   *
   * @param event  the show event
   */
  public void doShow(
    ShowEvent event)
  {
    String oldShowItemId = event.getOldShowItemId();
    String newShowItemId = event.getNewShowItemId();
    System.out.println("BackingBean [oldShowItemId=" + oldShowItemId + "," +
                                   "newShowItemId=" + newShowItemId + "]");
  }
}
```

This way of implementing a listener is provided as a convenience for application developers. However, it is also limiting in that the showListener attribute on the <pro:showOneDeck /> takes only one method binding; by contrast, associating a listener using a specific listener tag—such as <pro:showListener ...>—allows application developers to associate as many listeners as needed (for example, to log information about the event) and to associate one to actually process the event. From an application developer's point of view, an implementation of the ShowListener could look something like Code Sample 3-10.

Code Sample 3-10. *Implementation of the* ShowListener *Interface*

```
package com.apress.projsf.ch3.application;

import com.apress.projsf.ch3.event.ShowEvent;
import com.apress.projsf.ch3.event.ShowListener;

public class MyShowListener implements ShowListener
{
  public void processShow(
    ShowEvent event)
```

```
  {
    String oldShowItemId = event.getOldShowItemId();
    String newShowItemId = event.getNewShowItemId();
    System.out.println("MyShowListener " +
                       "[oldShowItemId=" + oldShowItemId + "," +
                        "newShowItemId=" + newShowItemId + "]");
  }

}
```

This listener—MyShowListener—implements the ShowListener interface and takes an instance of ShowEvent as an argument, and it gets the IDs of the new and old items used in the deck component from the event instance and prints them to the system log window.

Event Handling in the JSF Lifecycle

When a user interacts with the deck component (for example, expanding an item), a request is sent to the server with information about the action performed. By now you know that the first phase, Restore View, will restore the component hierarchy on postback. The second phase is the interesting phase—the Apply Request Values phase (see Figure 3-6).

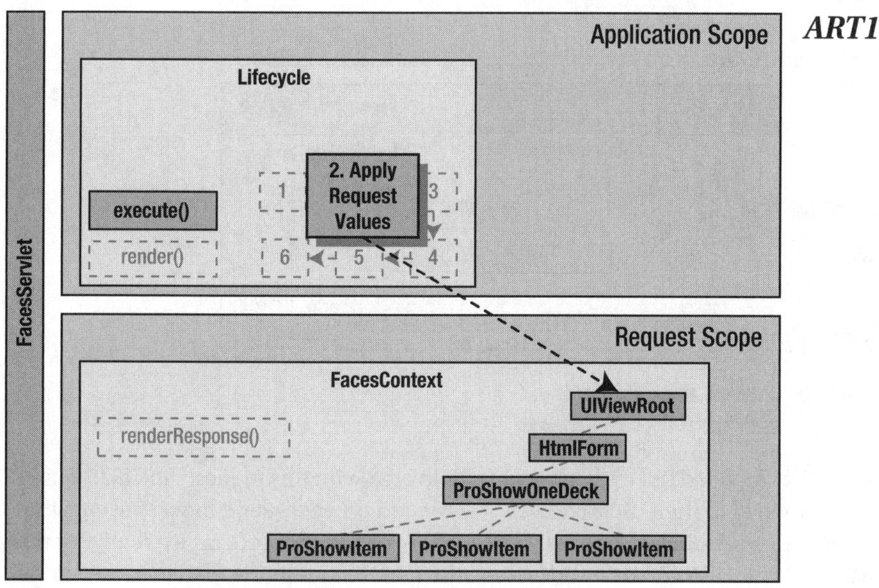

Figure 3-6. *Event handling in the Apply Request Values phase*

In this phase, the incoming request parameters are decoded and mapped to their counterpart UIComponent in the component hierarchy. When the Renderer for a component discovers that the user has triggered an event, the component's Renderer creates an instance of the corresponding FacesEvent subclass and queues the event to the source component.

For example, when the `Renderer` for the `UIShowOne` component discovers that the user has activated, or clicked, the header of an item in the rendered markup, the `UIShowOne`'s `Renderer` creates an instance of `ShowEvent`, passing the source `UIShowOne` component instance to the constructor, and calls the `queue()` method on the newly created event instance. This causes the `ShowEvent` instance to be stored in the event queue by the `UIViewRoot` until it is delivered during the Invoke Application phase (see Figure 3-7).

Note If no `Renderer` is associated with the `UIComponent`, it is the responsibility of the component's `decode()` method to queue the event, usually targeting the Invoke Application phase for delivery.

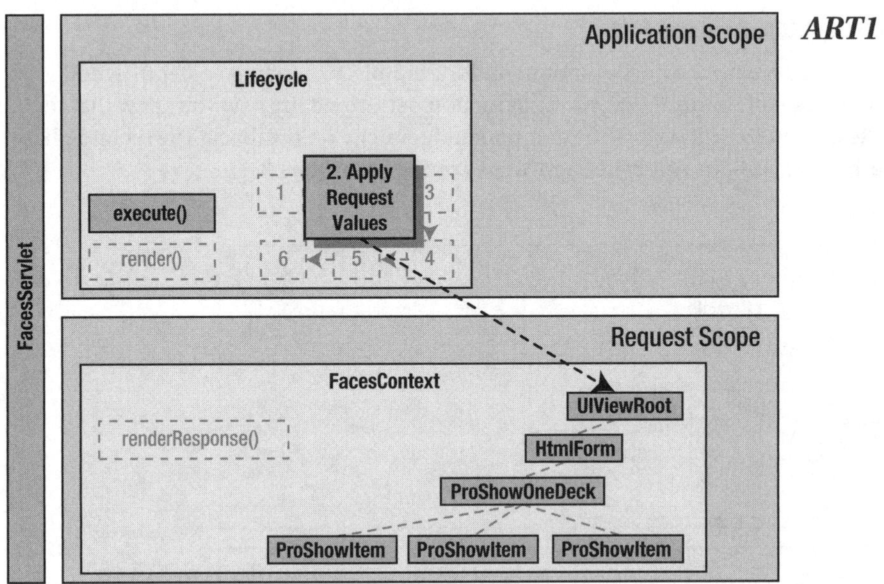

Figure 3-7. *Event handling in the application*

After you have completed queuing any events delivered with this request, and all request values have been applied to their `UIComponents`, it is time to broadcast and process events that have `phaseId` set to the default value (`PhaseId.ANY_PHASE`) or have `phaseId` set explicitly for this phase (`PhaseId.APPLY_REQUEST_VALUES`)—the Apply Request Values phase. If there are events to deliver in this phase, the `processDecodes()` method on the `UIViewRoot` is called first. This method takes all queued events and broadcasts to each component in the component hierarchy. In the application, the only event fired during this request is the `ShowEvent` delivered by the `UIShowOne` component `Renderer`.

The `UIShowOne` component has the phase identifier set to `PhaseId.INVOKE_APPLICATION`, which indicates to the request-processing lifecycle that this event must be delivered in the Invoke Application phase. In this phase, the `processApplication()` method on the `UIViewRoot` is called first. This method broadcasts any events that have been queued for the Invoke Application phase of the request-processing lifecycle by calling the `UIShowOne.broadcast(ShowEvent)` method.

If the `UIShowOne` has listeners attached when a `ShowEvent` is broadcast, each registered `ShowListener` is called in turn to deliver the event. A `ShowAdapter` may be registered as a listener to execute a method binding (for example, `#{backingBean.doShow}`) that references a public method with a `void` return type and a single parameter of type `ShowEvent`.

Step 3: Creating a Behavioral Superclass

You are now done with the `Event` and `Listener` implementation, so it is time to introduce the two new behavioral superclasses—`UIShowOne` and `UIShowItem`. At the moment you decide you need additional behavioral superclasses, you also need to decide what naming convention to use for these new classes. The convention used by the JSF specification is to prefix any top-level behavioral component with `UI`, followed by the actual behavior (for example, `UIInput`). Internal components, such as `UISelectItem`, that are useful only inside a particular parent component often use part of their parent component's name and the suffix `Item` to indicate they are not a top-level behavioral component.

During prototyping, it was decided that the deck component needs two new `UIComponents`. The first new component acts as a top-level container, controlling which one of its child components to display when activated. Following the naming conventions, this is called `UIShowOne`. The second component represents each of the child components that are displayed in collapsed form when inactive and in expanded form when activated. Following the naming conventions, this is called `UIShowItem`.

You will now look at the `UIShowOne` component implementation; Figure 3-8 shows the classes you will create for the `UIShowOne` component implementation.

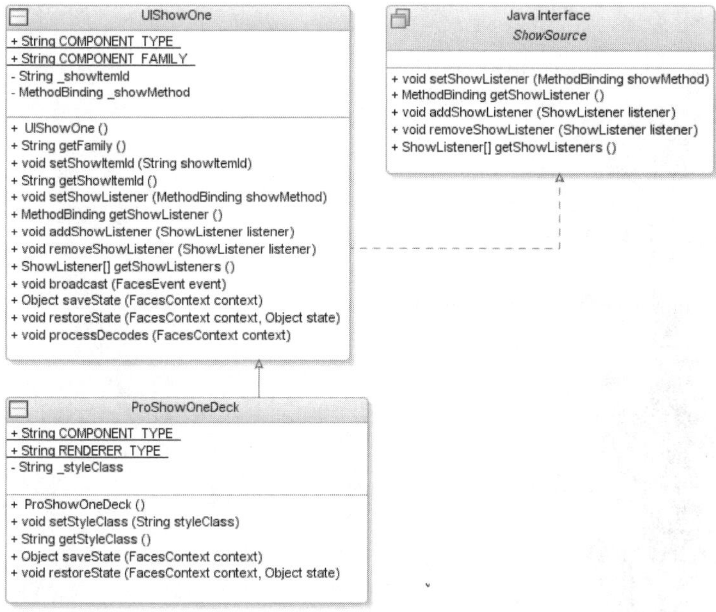

Figure 3-8. *Class diagram showing the* `UIShowOne` *implementation*

The classes are as follows:

- The UIShowOne class is the behavioral superclass.
- The ProShowOneDeck class is the client-specific subclass.
- And the ShowSource class isolates the event listener management methods.

Tip Several good resources are available in the JSF community; in particular, organizations such as Apache MyFaces (http://myfaces.apache.org/) and community sites such as JSF Central (http://jsfcentral.com/) are invaluable sources of information.

The ShowSource Interface

In case a component writer would like to create a component that uses ShowEvent and ShowListener (for example, maybe for a UIShowMany component), you should follow best practices by isolating the event listener management methods into an interface. The naming convention for this interface is based on the event and listener names, with a Source suffix. In this case, the listener management interface is called ShowSource, as shown in Code Sample 3-11.

Code Sample 3-11. *The* ShowSource *Interface*

```
import com.apress.projsf.ch3.event.ShowListener;

import javax.faces.el.MethodBinding;

/**
 * A ShowSource is the source of ShowEvents.
 */
public interface ShowSource
{
  /**
   * Adds a ShowListener to this ShowSource component.
   *
   * @param listener  the show listener to be added
   */
  public void addShowListener(
    ShowListener listener);

  /**
   * Removes a ShowListener to this ShowSource component.
   *
   * @param listener  the show listener to be removed
   */
```

```
  public void removeShowListener(
    ShowListener listener);

  /**
   * Returns all ShowListeners for this ShowSource component.
   *
   * @return the show listener array
   */
  public ShowListener[] getShowListeners();
}
```

The ShowSource interface will make sure you follow the standard JavaBeans design pattern for EventListener registration—add<ListenerType>(<ListenerType> listener) and remove<ListenerType>(<ListenerType> listener)—to allow application developers to programmatically add and remove listeners from any behavioral component that needs to deliver ShowEvents. The last method—public ShowListener[] getShowListeners();—is added so that anyone who might have interest in knowing which listeners are attached to this component can find out (for example, via an IDE).

The UIShowOne Behavioral Superclass

The UIShowOne component is a behavioral superclass, and it defines the contract for how an application interacts with the component or any component extending this superclass. It is important to understand that behavioral UIComponent subclasses, such as UISelectOne, do not define anything that is renderer-specific, so they can be reused for many different client technologies.

As you remember from Chapter 1, the component family returned by the getFamily() method is a string that represents the component's behavior and is used to select a Renderer for the particular UIComponent. The component type returned by the getComponentType() method is a string that is used by the Application object as an identifier for the UIComponent subclass (for example, UIShowOne). Following the naming convention from the previous chapters, the component family and component type are both called com.apress.projsf.ShowOne. Code Sample 3-12 introduces the first behavioral superclass—UIShowOne.

Code Sample 3-12. *Extending the* UIComponentBase *Class*

```
import java.util.Iterator;
import java.util.List;

import javax.faces.component.NamingContainer;
import javax.faces.component.UIComponentBase;
import javax.faces.context.FacesContext;
import javax.faces.el.MethodBinding;
import javax.faces.el.ValueBinding;
import javax.faces.event.AbortProcessingException;
import javax.faces.event.FacesEvent;

import com.apress.projsf.ch3.event.ShowEvent;
import com.apress.projsf.ch3.event.ShowListener;
```

```
/**
 * The UIShowOne behavioral component.
 */
public class UIShowOne extends UIComponentBase
                       implements ShowSource
{
  /**
   * The component type for this component.
   */
  public static final String COMPONENT_TYPE = "com.apress.projsf.ShowOne";

  /**
   * The component family for this component.
   */
  public static final String COMPONENT_FAMILY = "com.apress.projsf.ShowOne";

  /**
   * Creates a new UIShowOne.
   */
  public UIShowOne()
  {
  }

  /**
   * Returns the component family for this component.
   *
   * @return the component family
   */
  public String getFamily()
  {
    return COMPONENT_FAMILY;
  }
```

The `UIComponent` and `UIComponentBase` classes are the foundation of all JSF components, and they define the behavioral contract and state information for all components. The `UIComponentBase` class (`javax.faces.component.UIComponentBase`) is a convenience subclass that implements almost all methods of the `UIComponent` class. The `UIShowOne` class extends the `UIComponentBase` class, which is recommended since it will protect the `UIComponent` subclass—`UIShowOne`—from any changes to the signature of the `UIComponent` implementation that might occur in the future. The `ShowSource` interface is implemented to make sure you comply with the rules for which custom listeners can be attached to the component.

Lastly, you set two constants for the `UIShowOne` component, one for the component family and one for the component type.

■ **Note** You can find more information about component family and component type in Chapter 1.

Next, add bean properties to handle access to the behavioral attribute, showItemId, as shown in Code Sample 3-13. Remember that the requirement for this component is to show one item at a time.

Code Sample 3-13. *Accessor and Mutator for the* showItemId *Behavioral Attributes*

```
/**
 * Sets the show item child id to show.
 *
 * @param showItemId  the new show item child id to show.
 */
public void setShowItemId(
  String showItemId)
{
  _showItemId = showItemId;
}

/**
 * Returns the show item child id to show.
 *
 * @return  the show item child id to show
 */
public String getShowItemId()
{
  if (_showItemId != null)
    return _showItemId;

  ValueBinding binding = getValueBinding("showItemId");
  if (binding != null)
  {
    FacesContext context = FacesContext.getCurrentInstance();
    return (String)binding.getValue(context);
  }

  return null;
}
```

The UIShowOne component is the parent container that will control which items to display. The showItemId bean property will set the new item selected by the user (or set the default identifier at the initial request) and get the showItemId for the currently showing item.

Handling of Associated Listeners

Part of the implementation of the UIShowOne component is to provide a ShowEvent that will be delivered as a result of a user selecting an item in the deck component. Part of the contract you have with the ShowSource interface is to implement methods to allow programmatic access to add and remove listeners to the UIShowOne component, as shown in Code Sample 3-14.

Code Sample 3-14. *Implementing the* ShowSource *Interface*

```
/**
 * Adds a ShowListener to this UIShowOne component.
 *
 * @param listener  the show listener to be added
 */
public void addShowListener(
  ShowListener listener)
{
  addFacesListener(listener);
}

/**
 * Removes a ShowListener to this UIShowOne component.
 *
 * @param listener  the show listener to be removed
 */
public void removeShowListener(
  ShowListener listener)
{
  removeFacesListener(listener);
}

/**
 * Returns all ShowListeners for this UIShowOne component.
 *
 * @return the show listener array
 */
public ShowListener[] getShowListeners()
{
  return (ShowListener[])getFacesListeners(ShowListener.class);
}
```

Later in this chapter (see the section "The ShowListenerTag Class"), we will show how to build a ShowListener tag handler using the addShowListener() method, which you can use to associate a listener to the deck component or to any custom component that implements the ShowSource interface.

State Saving

By now you should know that JSF provides facilities to store the state of components used by application developers. You have two alternatives for storing the state of a view—doing it on the client side and doing it on the server side. The server-side implementation leverages the JSP and Servlet specifications and is managed by a class called StateManager. The ResponseStateManager class, which is part of a RenderKit, manages the client-side state saving.

The StateManager saves and restores state for a particular view (hierarchy of UIComponents) between requests on the server, as shown in Code Sample 3-15. The UIComponent (for example, UIShowOne) controls which internal state to save, so the component writer has some work to do.

Code Sample 3-15. *Managing State Saving*

```
public Object saveState(
  FacesContext context)
{
  Object values[] = new Object[2];
  values[0] = super.saveState(context);
  values[1] = _showItemId;

  return values;
}

public void restoreState(
  FacesContext context,
  Object       state)
{
  Object values[] = (Object[])state;
  super.restoreState(context, values[0]);
  _showItemId = (String)values[1];
}
```

Since you are extending the UIComponentBase class, you need to manage the state of the behavioral attributes, and you need to make sure any state for the base component is stored.

Processing Decodes

From implementing the ProInputDate component (see Chapter 2), you should have learned that during the Apply Request Values phase the processDecodes() method will be called on the UIViewRoot component. The processDecodes() method, on the UIViewRoot, is responsible for recursively calling processDecodes() on each UIComponent in the component hierarchy. As such, you need to make sure you have implemented this method in the component to make sure you can handle any request parameters passed to the UIShowOne component, as shown in Code Sample 3-16.

Code Sample 3-16. *Processing Decodes*

```
  public void processDecodes(
    FacesContext context)
  {
    if (context == null)
      throw new NullPointerException();
```

```
    if (!isRendered())
      return;

    String showItemId = getShowItemId();
    if (showItemId != null && getChildCount() > 0)
    {
      List children = getChildren();
      for (Iterator iter = children.iterator(); iter.hasNext();)
      {
        UIShowItem showItem = (UIShowItem)iter.next();
        if (showItemId.equals(showItem.getId()))
          showItem.processDecodes(context);
      }
    }

    // decode the showOne component last
    decode(context);
  }

  private String         _showItemId;
  private MethodBinding _showMethod;
}
```

Components that were not previously rendered to the client should not be processed as part of the postback. Therefore, you use the `isRendered()` method in the `processDecodes()` implementation to ensure that the component will not participate in the postback when the `rendered` property is `false`. This prevents a malicious user from attacking the system by attempting to trigger an event on a component that was not previously rendered. If `UIShowOne`'s `rendered` property is `true`, you first call `processDecodes()` on the currently active `UIShowItem` child component (if any) and then call the `decode()` method on the `UIShowOne` component itself. If a `Renderer` is present for the `UIShowOne` component, the `decode()` method delegates to the `Renderer`.

The UIShowItem Behavioral Superclass

The `UIShowItem` component is needed to allow the application developer to add labeled items to the deck component. The `UIShowItem` component is similar to the `UISelectItem` component provided by the JSF specification, except in this case `UIShowItem` acts as a container for other JSF components added by the application developer. Figure 3-9 shows the behavioral `UIShowItem` superclass.

The `UIShowItem` component does not render anything, so you do not need to implement a `Renderer` or a renderer-specific subclass. Instead, the parent `UIShowOne` component is responsible for rendering the `header` facet of each `UIShowItem` child component, as well as the children of the currently active `UIShowItem` child component, as shown in Code Sample 3-17.

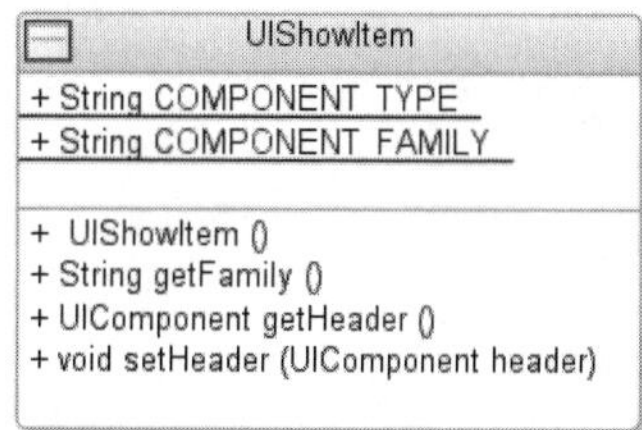

Figure 3-9. *Class diagram of the* `UIShowItem` *implementation*

Using a `header` facet rather than a `headerText` attribute gives application developers more flexibility to decide how best to visualize the header. For example, using a facet allows an icon and text to both be used in the header, rather than just text.

Code Sample 3-17. `UIShowItem` *Component*

```
package com.apress.projsf.ch3.component;

import javax.faces.component.UIComponent;
import javax.faces.component.UIComponentBase;

public class UIShowItem extends UIComponentBase
{
  /**
   * The component type for this component.
   */
  public static final String COMPONENT_TYPE = "com.apress.projsf.ShowItem";
  public static final String COMPONENT_FAMILY = "com.apress.projsf.ShowItem";

  /**
   * Creates a new UIShowItem.
   */
  public UIShowItem()
  {
  }

  /**
   * Returns the component family for this component.
   *
   * @return  the component family
   */
  public String getFamily()
  {
    return COMPONENT_FAMILY;
  }
```

```
  /**
   * Returns the header facet.
   *
   * @return the header facet
   */
  public UIComponent getHeader()
  {
    return getFacet("header");
  }

  /**
   * Sets a new header facet.
   *
   * @param header  the new header facet
   */
  public void setHeader(UIComponent header)
  {
    getFacets().put("header", header);
  }
}
```

As mentioned, you add the component family and component type to be able to select a Renderer and as an identifier for the UIComponent subclass. In this case, it might seem redundant to have these defined in the UIShowItem component, but part of the contract when building new behavioral components is that the new component introduces its own component family. Basically, the component family is needed for every new behavioral component and indicates its behavioral grouping. In addition, every component (behavioral or renderer-specific) should have a registered component type in faces-config.xml.

As you can see, you also add convenience getter and setter methods for the header facet using the getFacet() method inherited from UIComponentBase. The getFacet() method returns the named facet (for example, header) if it exists; otherwise, it returns null. In general, facets associate a child component with its parent component by a named purpose (for example, header) without implying anything about the rendered position of this facet relative to the other child components.

Step 4: Creating a Client-Specific Renderer

You now have a foundation for the JSF deck component with the behavioral components, including event and listener support. It is time to start looking at rendering the deck component. Following the naming pattern, discussed earlier in this chapter, the fully qualified class name for the UIShowOne component's Renderer is com.apress.projsf.ch3.render.html.basic.HtmlUIShowOneDeckRenderer.

The HtmlShowOneDeckRenderer Class

Figure 3-10 shows the HtmlShowOneDeckRenderer extending the HtmlRenderer introduced in Chapter 2.

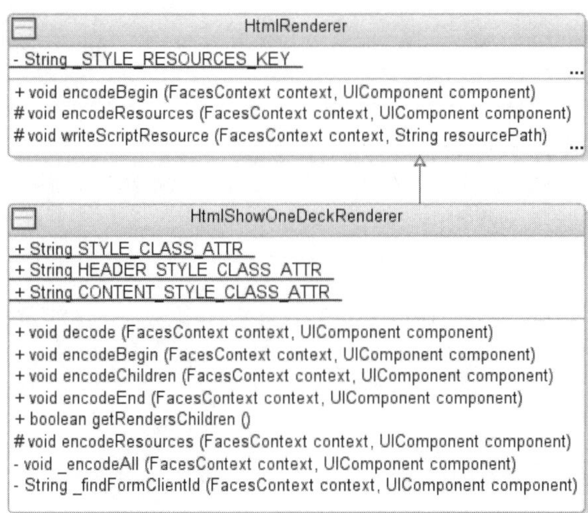

Figure 3-10. *Class diagram showing the* `HtmlShowOneDeckRenderer` *extending the* `HtmlRenderer`

Since the `UIShowOne` component is a container component, it needs to render its children, so you will implement `encodeBegin()`, `encodeChildren()`, and `encodeEnd()` in the new `Renderer`. Code Sample 3-18 shows the `encodeBegin()` method for the `HtmlShowOneDeckRenderer`.

Code Sample 3-18. *The* `encodeBegin()` *Method*

```
package com.apress.projsf.ch3.render.html.basic;

import java.io.IOException;
import java.util.Iterator;
import java.util.List;
import java.util.Map;

import javax.faces.component.UIComponent;
import javax.faces.component.UIForm;
import javax.faces.context.ExternalContext;
import javax.faces.context.FacesContext;
import javax.faces.context.ResponseWriter;

import com.apress.projsf.ch2.render.html.HtmlRenderer;
import com.apress.projsf.ch3.component.UIShowItem;
import com.apress.projsf.ch3.component.UIShowOne;
import com.apress.projsf.ch3.event.ShowEvent;

/**
 * Renders the UIShowOne component as a Deck.
 */
public class HtmlShowOneDeckRenderer extends HtmlRenderer
```

```
{
  /**
   * The styleClass attribute.
   */
  public static String STYLE_CLASS_ATTR = "styleClass";

  /**
   * The itemStyleClass attribute.
   */
  public static String ITEM_STYLE_CLASS_ATTR = "itemStyleClass";

  /**
   * The itemHeaderStyleClass attribute.
   */
  public static String ITEM_HEADER_STYLE_CLASS_ATTR = "itemHeaderStyleClass";

  /**
   * The itemContentStyleClass attribute.
   */
  public static String ITEM_CONTENT_STYLE_CLASS_ATTR = "itemContentStyleClass";

  public void encodeBegin(
    FacesContext context,
    UIComponent  component) throws IOException
  {
    // first write out resources
    super.encodeBegin(context, component);

    ResponseWriter out = context.getResponseWriter();
    out.startElement("div", component);
    Map attrs = component.getAttributes();
    String styleClass = (String)attrs.get(STYLE_CLASS_ATTR);
    if (styleClass != null)
      out.writeAttribute("class", styleClass, STYLE_CLASS_ATTR);
  }
```

The encodeBegin() method takes two arguments—FacesContext context and UIComponent component. The Render Response phase will call the encodeBegin() method on the UIShowOne component, which in turn will delegate to the encodeBegin() method on the HtmlShowOneDeckRenderer, passing the FacesContext and the UIShowOne component instance.

You get the ResponseWriter, write out the first HTML <div> element representing the component, and attach the styleClass defined by the application developer, if any. Before you continue to write anything to the client, you also need to get the component's unique identifier—clientId. You do this by calling the getClientId() method on the UIShowOne instance passed as an argument to the Renderer. You then include this unique identifier in the generated markup to ensure that on a postback you will be able to decode the request and apply any values or events to the right component. For more information about the clientId, see Chapter 2.

According to the requirements, the UIShowOne component is controlling which item—UIShowItem—to expand. This is managed by a JavaScript resource written to the response by the encodeResources() method, as shown in Code Sample 3-19.

Code Sample 3-19. *The* encodeResources() *Method*

```
/**
 * Write out the HtmlShowOneDeck resources.
 *
 * @param context    the Faces context
 * @param component  the Faces component
 */
protected void encodeResources(
  FacesContext context,
  UIComponent  component) throws IOException
{
  writeScriptResource(context, "/projsf-ch3/showOneDeck.js");
  writeStyleResource(context, "/projsf-ch3/showOneDeck.css");
}
```

The writeScriptResource() method provided by the HtmlRenderer superclass guarantees that a script resource is written only once during rendering, even if multiple ProShowOneDeck components appear on the same page. In Code Sample 3-19, the encodeResources() method writes out a JavaScript resource needed to render the ProShowOneDeck component—showOneDeck.js. You also encode a CSS style sheet resource—showOneDeck.css—to define the ProShowItem, ProShowItemHeader, and ProShowItemContent CSS style classes that are shared by all ProShowOneDeck components on the same page.

■ **Note** Use the ResponseWriter's startElement() and endElement() methods. This will improve your performance, make your code more portable between markup languages that have only subtle differences (for example, between HTML and XHTML), and make it easier to detect and debug the generated markup by verifying that all startElement() and endElement() calls are balanced.

The JavaScript Implementation

Before you continue with encoding the children of the UIShowOne component, take a closer look at the new JavaScript file, showOneDeck.js, as shown in Code Sample 3-20. You can see only one function in this file, showOneDeck(); it takes three arguments:

- The formClientId argument represents the clientId of the parent UIForm component.
- The showOneClientId argument represents the clientId of the containing UIShowOne component.
- The itemId argument is the node selected by the user.

Later in the encodeChildren() method, you will see how you attach this JavaScript function to the generated HTML and pass these values to it. Using a JavaScript function, you can respond to user actions and trigger a postback to the FacesServlet by submitting the form.

Code Sample 3-20. *The Source of the* showOneDeck.js *File*

```
/**
 * The onclick handler for HtmlShowOneDeckRenderer.
 *
 * @param formClientId  the clientId of the enclosing UIForm component
 * @param clientId      the clientId of the ProShowOneDeck component
 * @param itemId        the id of the UIShowItem that was clicked
 */
function _showOneDeck_click(
  formClientId,
  clientId,
  itemId)
{
  var form = document.forms[formClientId];
  var input = form[clientId];
  if (!input)
  {
    input = document.createElement("input");
    input.type = 'hidden';
    input.name = clientId;
    form.appendChild(input);
  }
  input.value = itemId;
  form.submit();
}
```

During rendering, after the HTML document has been fully parsed, the browser provides array access to various collections of related HTML elements in the page (for example, images and forms). You can use the document.forms array to access the form being submitted. Each form also provides array access to the input fields managed by that form. In the JavaScript implementation, you will be using a hidden form field to store the clientId of the selected UIShowItem. When the form is submitted, this value will be passed to the server and used during decode to detect which UIShowItem should be expanded, causing its child components to be displayed.

Potentially, an application developer might be adding more than one HtmlShowOneDeck component to the page, and by giving the hidden form field the same name as the clientId of the HtmlShowOneDeck component, you ensure you expand the correct HtmlShowOneDeck component. You first get the form—document.forms[formClientId]. Then, knowing the form, you can access the hidden input field, if it exists, and set the clientId of the selected UIShowItem component—input.value = itemId. You finish the function by submitting the form and passing the new values to the server-side component hierarchy for processing.

■ **Tip** For more information about JavaScript and the DOM, please visit `http://www.w3.org/DOM/`. Another good source if you are new to JavaScript is `http://developer.mozilla.org/en/docs/Main_Page`.

This function is defined only once, in a separate JavaScript file, for all `UIShowOneDeck` components on the page. We will show you how to package and leverage resources such as JavaScript files, CSS files, and images in Chapter 5.

Encode Children

Encoding the children of the `UIShowOne` component is where the real grunt work takes place in the creation of the expandable `UIComponent`. It is in the `encodeChildren()` method that you will set styles, set images, and decide which `UIShowItem` component will appear "expanded," showing its children. In Code Sample 3-21, we have highlighted in bold some areas that are of greater importance, since these are new areas not covered before or that need some extra explanation.

Code Sample 3-21. *Getting the IDs of the* `UIForm` *and* `UIShowOne` *Components*

```
public void encodeChildren(
  FacesContext context,
  UIComponent  component) throws IOException
{
  if (component.getChildCount() > 0)
  {
    UIShowOne showOne = (UIShowOne)component;
    String showItemId = showOne.getShowItemId();

    // the renderer-specific attributes
    Map attrs = showOne.getAttributes();
    String itemStyleClass = (String)attrs.get(ITEM_STYLE_CLASS_ATTR);
    if (itemStyleClass == null)
      itemStyleClass = "ProShowItem";
    String itemHeaderStyleClass = (String)
                                attrs.get(ITEM_HEADER_STYLE_CLASS_ATTR);
    if (itemHeaderStyleClass == null)
      itemHeaderStyleClass = "ProShowItemHeader";
    String itemContentStyleClass = (String)
                                attrs.get(ITEM_CONTENT_STYLE_CLASS_ATTR);
    if (itemContentStyleClass == null)
      itemContentStyleClass = "ProShowItemContent";

    String formClientId = _findFormClientId(context, component);
    String showOneClientId = component.getClientId(context);
```

In the encodeChildren() method, you first check to see whether this UIShowOne component has any children at all. If the application developer has not added any UIShowItem children, then you do not need to do any further work in this method. You then collect information about the CSS style classes used to display the items, as well as the default UIShowItem identifier to display, the clientId of the actual parent UIForm component, and the clientId of the UIShowOne component instance, as shown in Code Sample 3-21. You then collect all children of the UIShowOne component, iterate over the list of children, and check whether each child is an instance of UIShowItem (see Code Sample 3-22). If not, the child will not be rendered.

Code Sample 3-22. *Rendering the Start of Each* UIShowItem *Child Component*

```
List children = component.getChildren();
for (Iterator iter = children.iterator(); iter.hasNext();)
{
  UIComponent child = (UIComponent) iter.next();
  if (child instanceof UIShowItem)
  {
    UIShowItem showItem = (UIShowItem)child;
    String id = showItem.getId();
    Map attrs = showItem.getAttributes();

    boolean isActive = id.equals(showItemId);
    ResponseWriter out = context.getResponseWriter();
    out.startElement("div", showItem);
    out.writeAttribute("class", itemStyleClass,
                      ITEM_STYLE_CLASS_ATTR);

    out.startElement("div", null);
    out.writeAttribute("class", itemHeaderStyleClass,
                      ITEM_HEADER_STYLE_CLASS_ATTR);
```

If the child is a UIShowItem component instance, you gather the clientId and all attributes available on the UIShowItem component. The clientId is then used to set a flag—isActive—to true or false to determine whether the clientId of the soon-to-be-rendered UIShowItem component matches the showItemId. This flag will later indicate whether this UIShowItem component should render its children. The rest of the code, shown in Code Sample 3-22, is rendering the two start <div> elements, setting the style classes, and representing the UIShowItem container and header.

Before you append any JavaScript function to the UIShowItem component, check whether a UIForm is available; if not, you can just omit the JavaScript function so that no unnecessary markup is rendered to the client (see Code Sample 3-23).

Code Sample 3-23. *Processing Facet and Children of the* UIShowItem *Component*

```
    if (formClientId != null)
    {
```

```
          out.writeAttribute("onclick",
                             "_showOneDeck_click('" + formClientId + "'," +
                                                "'" + showOneClientId + "'," +
                                                "'" + id + "')",
                             null);
        }

        UIComponent header = showItem.getHeader();
        if (header != null)
        {
          _encodeAll(context, header);
        }
        else
        {
          out.writeText("Header", null);
        }

        out.endElement("div");

        if (isActive)
        {
          out.startElement("div", null);
          out.writeAttribute("class", itemContentStyleClass,
                             ITEM_CONTENT_STYLE_CLASS_ATTR);
          List kids = showItem.getChildren();
          Iterator it = kids.iterator();
          while (it.hasNext())
          {
            UIComponent kid = (UIComponent)it.next();
            _encodeAll(context, kid);
          }
          out.endElement("div");
        }

        out.endElement("div");
      }
    }
  }
}
```

The requirement for the component is to activate the item when clicked. By appending the `_showOneDeck_click()` function to the `onclick` event handler of the `<div>` element representing the `UIShowItem` header, you create a clickable `<div>` element. The `_showOneDeck_click()` function takes three arguments, which represent the identifier of the surrounding form component, the identifier of the parent `UIShowOne` component, and the `clientId` of the `UIShowItem` instance.

You then get the `header` facet from the `UIShowItem` component by calling the `getHeader()` method. If the `getHeader()` method returns a non-`null` facet, you call the `_encodeAll()` method to render the facet and its child components.

■Note You can add code to restrict which components can be rendered within a facet, but it is good practice to allow application developers to nest any components—standard or custom—within a facet. If you need to recommend a certain type of component to application developers, you can use `faces-config.xml` to list any recommended components using metadata defined by JSR-276.

After rendering the `header` facet, you use the `isActive` flag to determine whether this is the currently expanded `UIShowItem` component. If it is, you use the `_encodeAll()` method to render each of the `UIShowItem`'s child components.

Encode End

With the input date component implementation, it did not make sense to handle children, so you could combine all the rendered output into a single `encodeEnd()` method, as shown in Code Sample 3-24. With the `UIShowOne` component, the `Renderer` is in charge of rendering its children using the `encodeChildren()` method. This has the consequence that you also need to implement the `encodeEnd()` method to write out the closing element of the component.

Code Sample 3-24. *The* `HtmlShowOneDeckRenderer encodeEnd()` *Method*

```
public void encodeEnd(
  FacesContext context,
  UIComponent  component) throws IOException
{
  ResponseWriter out = context.getResponseWriter();
  out.endElement("div");
}
```

If you take a close look at the actual output required by the deck component, you will see that all the children that were added are at the end of the generated markup. Therefore, not much is required for the `UIShowOne` component's `Renderer` but to close the generated markup.

Renders Children

In the JSF 1.1 specification, the default value of the `rendersChildren` property is `false`.

For the `UIShowOne` component, the `Renderer` is responsible for rendering its children, and thus this flag needs to be set to `true`, as shown in Code Sample 3-25.

Code Sample 3-25. *Setting* `rendersChildren` *to* `true`

```
public boolean getRendersChildren()
{
  return true;
}
```

Locate Form ClientId

The `_findFormClientId` method is used in the `encodeChildren()` method to return the `clientId` of the closest enclosing `UIForm` component, as shown in Code Sample 3-26.

Code Sample 3-26. *The* `_findFormClientId` *Method*

```
private String _findFormClientId(
  FacesContext context,
  UIComponent  component)
{
  while (component != null &&
         !(component instanceof UIForm))
  {
    component = component.getParent();
  }

  return (component != null) ? component.getClientId(context) : null;
}
```

In the `_findFormClientId()` method, you first check whether the component is an instance of `UIForm`; if it is not, you walk the component hierarchy to find the parent `UIForm` component by calling `component.getParent()`. When you have the parent `UIForm` component, you return the `clientId`. If not, you return `null`.

Encode Children

In the `encodeChildren()` method, you call the method `_encodeAll()` to render the `header` facet and each of the active `UIShowItem`'s child components, as shown in Code Sample 3-27. This method takes two arguments—the `FacesContext` for the current request and the `UIComponent` to render.

Code Sample 3-27. *The* `_encodeAll()` *Method*

```
  /**
   * Encodes a component and all of its children.
   *
   * @param context the Faces context
   * @param component the Faces component
   *
   * @throws IOException if an I/O error occurs during rendering
   */
  private void _encodeAll(
    FacesContext context,
    UIComponent  component) throws IOException
  {
    component.encodeBegin(context);
    if (component.getRendersChildren())
```

```
      {
        component.encodeChildren(context);
      }
      else
      {
        List kids = component.getChildren();
        Iterator it = kids.iterator();
        while (it.hasNext())
        {
          UIComponent kid = (UIComponent)it.next();
          _encodeAll(context, kid);
        }
      }
      component.encodeEnd(context);
    }
  }
```

The requirement for the deck component is to make it flexible enough to handle any type of child component added to the `UIShowItem` component by the application developer. The `UIShowItem` component itself is not responsible for rendering its children, but sometimes an application developer has added a child container component for rendering its children (for example, an `HtmlPanelGrid` component).

To be able to achieve this, you first call `encodeBegin()` to start rendering the generated markup for the current component. You then check whether the component is responsible for rendering its children. If it is, you call `encodeChildren()` on the component to render all of its children. However, if the component is not responsible for rendering its children, then you iterate over the child components and recursively call `_encodeAll()` for each one. Finally, you complete the generated markup by calling the `encodeEnd()` method on the component.

■ **Note** A new method, `UIComponent.encodeAll(FacesContext)`, has been added to the JSF 1.2 release and implements equivalent functionality to the `_encodeAll(FacesContext, UIComponent)` method shown in Code Sample 3-27.

Decode

During the Apply Request Values phase, a method—`processDecodes()`—will be called on the `UIViewRoot` at the top of the component hierarchy. The `processDecodes()` method on the `UIViewRoot` will recursively call `processDecodes()` on each `UIComponent` in the component hierarchy. If a `Renderer` is present for any of these components, then the `UIComponent` will delegate the responsibility of decoding to the `Renderer`. For more information about `processDecodes()`, please refer to Chapter 2. Code Sample 3-28 shows how you can manage information passed on the request during decode.

Code Sample 3-28. *Decoding the Request*

```
public void decode(
  FacesContext context,
  UIComponent  component)
{
  ExternalContext external = context.getExternalContext();
  Map requestParams = external.getRequestParameterMap();
  String clientId = component.getClientId(context);
  String newShowItemId = (String)requestParams.get(clientId);
  if (newShowItemId != null && newShowItemId.length() > 0)
  {
    UIShowOne showOne = (UIShowOne)component;
    String oldShowItemId = showOne.getShowItemId();
    if (!newShowItemId.equals(oldShowItemId))
    {
      showOne.setShowItemId(newShowItemId);
      ShowEvent event = new ShowEvent(showOne, oldShowItemId, newShowItemId);
      event.queue();
    }
  }
}
```

From the external context, you can get hold of the `Map` containing all the parameters passed on this request. In the JavaScript function, you set the value of the hidden input form field, representing the `UIShowOne` component, to the ID of the selected `UIShowItem` component. So, by using the `clientId` of the `UIShowOne` component, you can retrieve the value stored in the hidden input form field passed on the request—`String newShowItemId = (String)requestParams.get(clientId)`. This value represents the new identifier of the `UIShowItem` component to be expanded during the Render Response phase.

The requirements stated that an application developer should be able to add any number of `UIShowOneDeck` components to a page. Potentially, an application developer can have any number of forms with a `UIShowOneDeck` component or have multiple `UIShowOneDeck` components within the same form. When you put a second deck into a form and click one of the item headers, there will be no hidden field for the first `UIShowOneDeck`; therefore, the `newShowItemId` will contain `null`, and the `newShowItemId != null` code path is skipped as desired. When any other component causes a form submission for the same form, you get back `""` (an empty string), and with the additional check for nonempty string, (`newShowItemId.length() > 0`), this works even in a single form. If the value is either `null` or the empty string `""`, it will do nothing.

Passing this control, you compare the new ID—`newShowItemId`—with the value stored in the `showItemId` property; if it matches, the user clicked the same item that was already expanded, and there is nothing for you to do except to return. If the value passed on the request is a new ID, you set the `showItemId` property on the `UIShowOne` component to this new value to store the currently open `UIShowItem` component. After setting the new identifier, you create a new instance of the `ShowEvent` event, passing the `UIShowOne` component instance, the old `UIShowItem` ID, and the new `UIShowItem` ID. Finally, you queue the `ShowEvent` event instance for later processing in the Invoke Application phase. If application developers have used the `ShowListener`, they will be able to invoke some application logic based on this user action.

Step 5: Creating a Renderer-Specific Subclass

To follow best practices, you will now learn how to create the renderer-specific subclass for the deck component—`com.apress.projsf.ch3.component.pro.ProShowOneDeck` (see Figure 3-11). This class provides a getter and a setter for one renderer-specific attribute on the JSF component—`styleClass`.

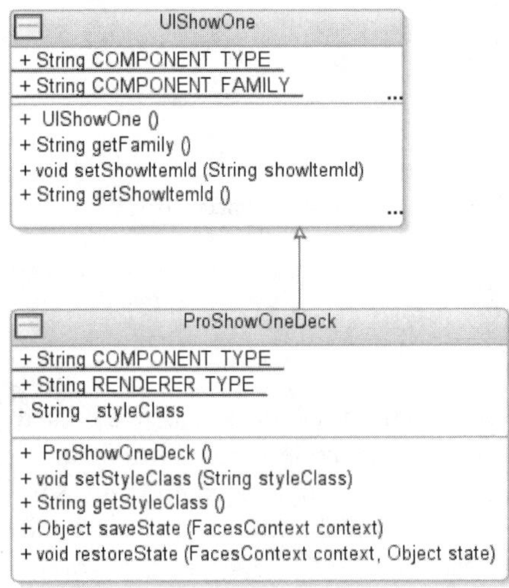

Figure 3-11. *Class diagram showing the* `ProShowOneDeck` *class*

You can now start to see the pattern you are using to build these components; for example, Code Sample 3-29 follows the same design as the `ProInputDate` subclass created in Chapter 2.

Code Sample 3-29. *The* `ProShowOneDeck` *Client-Specific Subclass*

```
package com.apress.projsf.ch3.component.pro;

import javax.faces.context.FacesContext;
import javax.faces.el.ValueBinding;

import com.apress.projsf.ch3.component.UIShowOne;

/**
 * The ProShowOneDeck renderer-specific component.
 */
```

```
public class ProShowOneDeck extends UIShowOne{

  public static final String COMPONENT_TYPE = "com.apress.projsf.ProShowOneDeck";
  public static final String RENDERER_TYPE = "com.apress.projsf.Deck";

  /**
   * Creates a new ProShowOneDeck.
   */
  public ProShowOneDeck()
  {
    setRendererType(RENDERER_TYPE);
  }


  /**
   * The styleClass attribute value.
   */
  private String _styleClass;

  /**
   * Sets the CSS style class.
   *
   * @param styleClass  the new style class
   */
  public void setStyleClass(
    String styleClass)
  {
    _styleClass = styleClass;
  }

  /**
   * Returns the CSS style class.
   *
   * @return  the style class
   */
  public String getStyleClass()
  {

    if (_styleClass != null)
      return _styleClass;

    ValueBinding binding = getValueBinding("styleClass");
    if (binding != null)
    {
      FacesContext context = FacesContext.getCurrentInstance();
      return (String)binding.getValue(context);
    }
```

```
    return null;
  }

  public Object saveState(
    FacesContext context)
  {
    Object values[] = new Object[2];
    values[0] = super.saveState(context);
    values[1] = _styleClass;
    return values;
  }

  public void restoreState(
    FacesContext context,
    Object       state)
  {
    Object values[] = (Object[])state;
    super.restoreState(context, values[0]);
    _styleClass = (String)values[1];
  }

}
```

The first thing you do is to make sure you extend the right component superclass, which is UIShowOne. You then define constants for the component type and renderer type so that the correct Renderer is associated with the UIComponent when it is created. The UIShowOne component is a container only for the UIShowItem component and has only one renderer-specific attribute—styleClass.

The UIShowItem component has no Renderer, so it has no renderer-specific facets or attributes and requires no renderer-specific component subclass.

Step 6: Registering a UIComponent and Renderer

Registering a behavioral superclass follows the same rules as registering a renderer-specific subclass (see Chapter 2). The UIShowOne and the UIShowItem components are registered in faces-config.xml, as shown in Code Sample 3-30.

Code Sample 3-30. *Registering* UIShowOne *and* UIShowItem

```
<?xml version="1.0" encoding="UTF-8" ?>
<!DOCTYPE faces-config
   PUBLIC "-//Sun Microsystems, Inc.//DTD JavaServer Faces Config 1.1//EN"
          "http://java.sun.com/dtd/web-facesconfig_1_1.dtd">

<faces-config>

...
```

```
<component>
  <component-type>com.apress.projsf.ShowOne</component-type>
  <component-class>com.apress.projsf.ch3.component.UIShowOne</component-class>

  <!-- UIComponent attributes -->
  <attribute>
    <description>
      The component identifier for this component. This value must be unique
      within the closest parent component that is a naming container.
    </description>
    <attribute-name>id</attribute-name>
    <attribute-class>java.lang.String</attribute-class>
  </attribute>
  <attribute>
    <description>
      Flag indicating whether or not this component should be rendered (during
      Render Response Phase), or processed on any subsequent form submit.
    </description>
    <attribute-name>rendered</attribute-name>
    <attribute-class>boolean</attribute-class>
    <default-value>true</default-value>
  </attribute>
  <attribute>
    <description>
      The value binding expression linking this component to a property in a
      backing bean.
    </description>
    <attribute-name>binding</attribute-name>
    <attribute-class>javax.faces.el.ValueBinding</attribute-class>
  </attribute>

  <!-- UIShowOne attributes -->
  <attribute>
    <description>
      The currently active showItem identifier.
    </description>
    <attribute-name>showItemId</attribute-name>
    <attribute-class>java.lang.String</attribute-class>
  </attribute>

</component>

<component>
  <component-type>com.apress.projsf.ShowItem</component-type>
  <component-class>com.apress.projsf.ch3.component.UIShowItem</component-class>
```

```
    <!-- UIShowItem facets -->
    <facet>
      <description>The header of the showItem component.</description>
      <display-name>header</display-name>
      <facet-name>header</facet-name>
      <facet-extension>
        <facet-metadata>
          <preferred-children>h:outputText h:graphicImage</preferred-children>
        </facet-metadata>
      </facet-extension>
    </facet>

    <!-- UIComponent attributes -->
    <attribute>
      <description>
        The component identifier for this component. This value must be unique
        within the closest parent component that is a naming container.
      </description>
      <attribute-name>id</attribute-name>
    </attribute>
    <attribute>
      <description>
        Flag indicating whether or not this component should be rendered (during
        Render Response Phase), or processed on any subsequent form submit.
      </description>
      <attribute-name>rendered</attribute-name>
      <attribute-class>boolean</attribute-class>
      <default-value>true</default-value>
    </attribute>
    <attribute>
      <description>
        The value binding expression linking this component to a property in a
        backing bean.
      </description>
      <attribute-name>binding</attribute-name>
    </attribute>
  </component>
</faces-config>
```

The code in bold registers the new components (`com.apress.projsf.ShowOne` and `com.apress.projsf.ShowItem`) by defining the component type and the corresponding component classes (`com.apress.projsf.ch3.component.UIShowOne` and `com.apress.projsf.ch3.component.UIShowItem`). The code sample also adds metadata for the `UIShowItem` facet—header—that can be picked up by any IDE supporting JSF to assist application developers in adding components to the header facet. The code sample also defines metadata for attributes inherited from the `UIComponentBase` class, which will be used by application developers.

■ **Note** A JSR is currently under development (JSR-276: Design-Time Metadata for JavaServer Faces Components) that focuses on defining a standard mechanism for associating design-time information with JSF components.

Registering the HtmlShowOneDeckRenderer

The HtmlShowOneDeckRenderer class is registered in faces-config.xml, as shown in Code Sample 3-31.

Code Sample 3-31. *Registering* HtmlShowOneDeckRenderer

```
<?xml version="1.0" encoding="UTF-8" ?>
<!DOCTYPE faces-config
   PUBLIC "-//Sun Microsystems, Inc.//DTD JavaServer Faces Config 1.1//EN"
          "http://java.sun.com/dtd/web-facesconfig_1_1.dtd">

<faces-config>

  <render-kit>
    <!-- no renderkit-id, so these renderers are added to
         the default renderkit -->
    <renderer>
      <component-family>
        com.apress.projsf.ShowOne
      </component-family>
      <renderer-type>
        com.apress.projsf.Deck
      </renderer-type>
      <renderer-class>
        com.apress.projsf.ch3.render.html.basic.HtmlShowOneDeckRenderer
      </renderer-class>
    </renderer>
  </render-kit>

</faces-config>
```

To register the new HtmlShowOneDeckRenderer class as a Renderer for JSF, you need to add the metadata shown in bold to the same faces-config.xml file you used to register the UIShowOne and UIShowItem components. Code Sample 3-31 also omits the <render-kit-id> element, which will make the client-specific Renderer use the default RenderKit (with the identifier RenderKitFactory.HTML_BASIC_RENDER_KIT) provided by the JSF implementation.

You also set <component-family> to com.apress.projsf.ShowOne, which represents the behavior of the UIShowOne component, and set <renderer-type> to com.apress.projsf.Deck, which represents the presentation of the UIShowOne component. The combination of component family and render type uniquely identifies which Renderer class to use with the component—com.apress.projsf.ch3.render.html.basic.HtmlShowOneDeckRenderer. For more information about this, please refer to Chapter 1.

Registering the ProShowOneDeck Renderer-Specific Subclass

The renderer-specific ProShowOneDeck subclass is registered in faces-config.xml, as shown in Code Sample 3-32.

Code Sample 3-32. *Registering the* ProShowOneDeck *Renderer-Specific Subclass*

```
<?xml version="1.0" encoding="UTF-8" ?>
<!DOCTYPE faces-config
   PUBLIC "-//Sun Microsystems, Inc.//DTD JavaServer Faces Config 1.1//EN"
          "http://java.sun.com/dtd/web-facesconfig_1_1.dtd">

<faces-config>

  <component>
    <component-type>
      com.apress.projsf.ProShowOneDeck
    </component-type>
    <component-class>
      com.apress.projsf.ch3.component.pro.ProShowOneDeck
    </component-class>

    <!-- UIComponent attributes -->
    <attribute>
      <attribute-name>id</attribute-name>
      <description>
        The component identifier for this component.  This value must be
        unique within the closest parent component that is a naming
        container.
      </description>
    </attribute>
    <attribute>
      <attribute-name>rendered</attribute-name>
      <attribute-class>boolean</attribute-class>
      <default-value>true</default-value>
      <description>
        Flag indicating whether or not this component should be rendered
        (during Render Response Phase), or processed on any subsequent
        form submit.
      </description>
    </attribute>
    <attribute>
      <attribute-name>binding</attribute-name>
```

```
      <description>
        The value binding expression linking this component to a
        property in a backing bean.
      </description>
    </attribute>

    <!-- UIShowOne attributes -->
    <attribute>
      <description>
        The currently active showItem identifier.
      </description>
      <attribute-name>showItemId</attribute-name>
      <attribute-class>java.lang.String</attribute-class>
    </attribute>
    <attribute>
      <description>
        MethodBinding representing a show listener method that will be
        notified when the active UIShowItem changes for this UIShowOne
        component.  The expression must evaluate to a public method that
        takes a ShowEvent parameter, with a return type of void.
      </description>
      <attribute-name>showListener</attribute-name>
      <attribute-class>com.apress.projsf.ch3.event.ShowListener</attribute-class>
    </attribute>

    <!-- ProShowOneDeck attributes -->
    <attribute>
      <description>
        The styleClass for this ProShowOneDeck component.
      </description>
      <attribute-name>styleClass</attribute-name>
      <attribute-class>java.lang.String</attribute-class>
    </attribute>
  </component>
</faces-config>
```

The bold code registers the new component by defining the component type (`com.apress.projsf.ProShowOneDeck`) and the corresponding component class (`com.apress.projsf.ch3.component.pro.ProShowOneDeck`). The metadata defines attributes that are inherited from the `UIComponent` base class, which will be used by application developers.

Step 7: Creating a JSP Tag Handler and TLD

To recap from the previous chapter, a custom action has a corresponding tag handler class, which is responsible for creating the `UIComponent` and transferring each declarative JSP tag attribute to the `UIComponent` instance. The design of the deck component is a renderer-specific parent component (`ProShowOneDeck`) that manages which child to display to the user and a behavioral child component (UIShowItem) that has a header facet and contains any child components that application developers might have added. You also have the custom event (ShowEvent) with the associated listener interface (ShowListener). Figure 3-12 shows the three tag handlers.

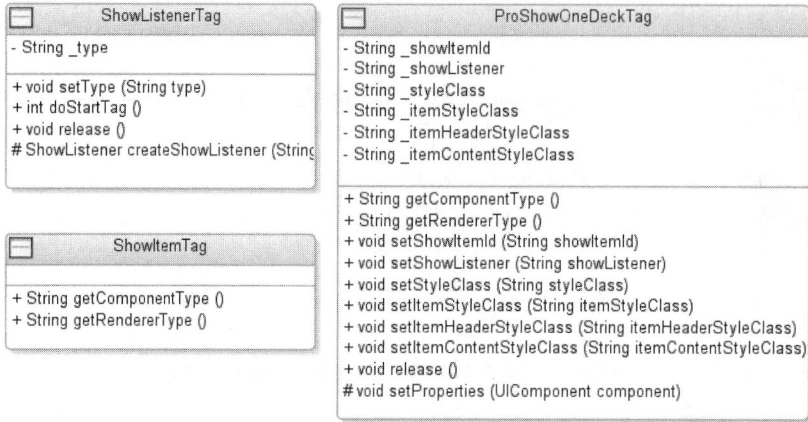

Figure 3-12. *Class diagram showing the three tag handlers*

You need to create custom actions for the renderer-specific ProShowOneDeck component and the behavioral UIShowItem component; in addition, you need to create a custom action for adding a ShowListener to the ProShowOneDeck component.

The ProShowOneDeckTag Class

The ProShowOneDeck component needs a custom action, showOneDeck, with a corresponding tag handler class, ProShowOneDeckTag. On initial render, the ProShowOneDeckTag is responsible for creating a new instance of the new renderer-specific component subclass (ProShowOneDeck) and transferring all JSP custom action attributes to and from the tag handler to the component instance (see Code Sample 3-33).

Code Sample 3-33. *The* ProShowOneDeckTag *Class*

```
package com.apress.projsf.ch3.taglib.pro;

import javax.faces.component.UIComponent;
import javax.faces.el.MethodBinding;

import com.apress.projsf.ch2.taglib.UIComponentTagSupport;
import com.apress.projsf.ch3.component.UIShowOne;
import com.apress.projsf.ch3.component.pro.ProShowOneDeck;
import com.apress.projsf.ch3.event.ShowAdapter;
```

```
/**
 * ProShowOneDeckTag component tag handler.
 */
public class ProShowOneDeckTag extends UIComponentTagSupport
{

  /**
   * Returns the component type.
   *
   * @return  the component type
   */
  public String getComponentType()
  {
    return ProShowOneDeck.COMPONENT_TYPE;
  }

  /**
   * Returns the renderer type.
   *
   * @return  the renderer type
   */
  public String getRendererType()
  {
    return ProShowOneDeck.RENDERER_TYPE;
  }

  /**
   * Sets the showItemId attribute value.
   *
   * @param showItemId  the currently showing item identifer
   */
  public void setShowItemId(
    String showItemId)
  {
    _showItemId = showItemId;
  }

  /**
   * Sets the showListener attribute value.
   *
   * @param showListener  the showListener attribute value
   */
  public void setShowListener(
    String showListener)
  {
    _showListener = showListener;
  }
```

```
/**
 * Sets the CSS style class.
 *
 * @param styleClass  the new style class
 */
public void setStyleClass(String styleClass)
{
  _styleClass = styleClass;
}

/**
 * Sets the item CSS style class.
 *
 * @param itemStyleClass  the new item style class
 */
public void setItemStyleClass(
  String itemStyleClass)
{
  _itemStyleClass = itemStyleClass;
}

/**
 * Sets the CSS style class for the item header facet.
 *
 * @param itemHeaderStyleClass  the new style class for the item header facet
 */
public void setItemHeaderStyleClass(
  String itemHeaderStyleClass)
{
  _itemHeaderStyleClass = itemHeaderStyleClass;
}

/**
 * Sets the CSS style class for the item content.
 *
 * @param itemContentStyleClass  the new style class for the item content
 */
public void setItemContentStyleClass(
  String itemContentStyleClass)
{
  _itemContentStyleClass = itemContentStyleClass;
}

/**
 * Releases the internal state used by the tag.
 */
public void release()
{
```

```
    _showItemId = null;
    _showListener = null;
    _styleClass = null;
    _itemStyleClass = null;
    _itemHeaderStyleClass = null;
    _itemContentStyleClass = null;
  }

  protected void setProperties(
    UIComponent component)
  {
    super.setProperties(component);

    // Behavioral properties
    setStringProperty(component, "showItemId", _showItemId);

    // Behavioral listeners
    if (_showListener != null)
    {
      UIShowOne showOne = (UIShowOne) component;
      MethodBinding showMethod = createMethodBinding(_showListener,
                                                ShowAdapter.SIGNATURE);
      showOne.addShowListener(new ShowAdapter(showMethod));
    }
    // Renderer-specific attributes
    setStringProperty(component, "styleClass", _styleClass);
    setStringProperty(component, "itemStyleClass", _itemStyleClass);
    setStringProperty(component, "itemHeaderStyleClass", _itemHeaderStyleClass);
    setStringProperty(component, "itemContentStyleClass", _itemContentStyleClass);
  }

  private String _showItemId;
  private String _showListener;
  private String _styleClass;
  private String _itemStyleClass;
  private String _itemHeaderStyleClass;
  private String _itemContentStyleClass;
}
```

First you extend the `UIComponentTagSupport` tag handler class introduced in Chapter 2. This gives you access to the `setStringProperty()` method, which can be used to assign any component attribute that takes either a static value or a value binding. It also gives you access to the `createMethodBinding()` method, which is used to create a `MethodBinding` instance from a string expression and a `Class` array describing the signature of the referenced backing bean method.

The `ProShowOneDeckTag` also provides tag attribute setters and internal field storage for the `ProShowOneDeck` component's attributes (for example, `showItemId`). The `setProperties()` method transfers properties and attributes from this tag to the specified component, if the corresponding properties of this tag handler instance were explicitly set. Notice that you use the ShowAdapter to add the showListener MethodBinding to the UIShowOne component as a ShowListener.

Any JSF tag handler subclasses that support additional properties on top of what is provided by the UIComponentTag handler must ensure that the base class setProperties() method is still called—super.setProperties().

The ShowItemTag Class

If the syntax of the custom action has both behavioral attributes and renderer-specific attributes, then it is tied to a particular component family and renderer type combination, which implies you need one custom action per Renderer. This is true in most cases; however, in the case of the UIShowItem component, no Renderer is available. The UIShowOne component's Renderer manages the rendering, but you still need a custom action for the UIShowItem component so that application developers can add it as a child to the UIShowOne component (see Code Sample 3-34).

Code Sample 3-34. *The* ShowItemTag *Class*

```
package com.apress.projsf.ch3.taglib;

import com.apress.projsf.ch2.taglib.UIComponentTagSupport;
import com.apress.projsf.ch3.component.UIShowItem;

/**
 * ShowItemTag is the UIShowItem component tag handler.
 */
public class ShowItemTag extends UIComponentTagSupport
{
  /**
   * Returns the component type.
   *
   * @return  the component type
   */
  public String getComponentType()
  {
    return ProShowItem.COMPONENT_TYPE;
  }

  /**
   * Returns the renderer type.
   *
   * @return  the renderer type
   */
  public String getRendererType()
  {
    return null;
  }
}
```

It is important to note that in Code Sample 3-34 you still have to follow the contract of a JSF custom action and provide accessors for the component type and render type. In the case of `ShowItemTag`, you have set the return value for the render type to `null`, since this component does not come with a `Renderer`. On initial render, the `ShowItemTag` is responsible for creating an instance of the behavioral `UIShowItem` component.

The ShowListenerTag Class

The `ShowListenerTag` tag handler class represents the custom action `showListener` that will be used by the application developer to register a `ShowListener` instance to a `UIShowOne` component, as shown in Code Sample 3-35. It is also important to ignore any attempt by application developers to nest children within this new `ShowListenerTag`, since it cannot handle children. You also need to establish the fully qualified class name of the listener tag—`com.apress.projsf.ch3.taglib.ShowListenerTag`.

Code Sample 3-35. *The* `ShowListenerTag` *Class*

```
package com.apress.projsf.ch3.taglib;

import javax.faces.application.Application;
import javax.faces.component.UIComponent;
import javax.faces.context.FacesContext;
import javax.faces.el.ValueBinding;
import javax.faces.webapp.UIComponentTag;

import javax.servlet.jsp.JspException;
import javax.servlet.jsp.tagext.TagSupport;

import com.apress.projsf.ch3.component.ShowSource;
import com.apress.projsf.ch3.event.ShowListener;

/**
 * ShowListenerTag listener tag handler.
 */
public class ShowListenerTag extends TagSupport
{
  /**
   * The fully qualified class name of the {@link ShowListener}
   * instance to be created.
   */
  private String _type;

  /**
   * Sets the fully qualified class name of the
   * {@link ShowListener} instance to be created.
   *
   * @param type  the class name
   */
```

```
  public void setType(
    String type)
  {
    _type = type;
  }
```

The ShowListenerTag class extends the TagSupport class, which is a utility class intended to be used as the base class for new tag handlers. The TagSupport class implements the Tag interface and adds convenience methods including getter methods for the properties in Tag. The type property represents the fully qualified class name of the ShowListener instance to be created.

Tip For more information about the TagSupport and Tag classes, please refer to the J2EE 1.4 API specification.

The doStartTag() method, as shown in Code Sample 3-36, is part of the contract with the TagSupport class and is invoked by the JSP page implementation when all properties have been set.

Code Sample 3-36. *The* doStartTag() *Method*

```
public int doStartTag() throws JspException
{
  UIComponentTag tag = UIComponentTag.getParentUIComponentTag(pageContext);
  if (tag == null)
    throw new JspException("Not inside UIComponentTag");

  if (tag.getCreated())
  {
    UIComponent component = tag.getComponentInstance();
    if (component == null)
      throw new JspException("Component instance is null");

    String className = _type;

    if (UIComponentTag.isValueReference(_type))
    {
      FacesContext context = FacesContext.getCurrentInstance();
      Application application = context.getApplication();
      ValueBinding vb = application.createValueBinding(_type);
      className = (String)vb.getValue(context);
    }

    ShowListener listener = createShowListener(className);
```

```
    if (!(component instanceof ShowSource))
      throw new JspException("Component is not a ShowSource");

        showSource.addShowListener(listener);
  }

  return (SKIP_BODY);
}
```

In this case, the type property is required, so it is expected to be non-null. You start by retrieving the parent UIComponentTag to the ShowListener custom action using the getParentUIComponentTag() method. This method will return the nearest enclosing UIComponentTag, if any; if no UIComponentTag is available, it will return null.

■ **Note** The UIComponentTag is an implementation of javax.servlet.jsp.tagext.Tag and must be the base class for any JSP custom action that corresponds to a JSF UIComponent. For more information about the UIComponentTag, please refer to the JSF 1.1 specification.

You evaluate whether the parent UIComponentTag has a matching UIComponent by invoking the getCreated() method. This method returns true if the parent UIComponentTag created an instance of a UIComponent during its execution, which in this case is a UIShowOne component. This statement is implemented to avoid the case where a UIComponentTag is not creating a new instance of a UIComponent, which happens on postback, since the component hierarchy already exists.

The next important part of the doStartTag() method is to see whether the property _type is a fully qualified class name (for example, com.apress.projsf.ch3.application.MyShowListener) or whether it is a ValueBinding reference (for example, #{myBean.returnListener}). This class name is passed as an argument to the createShowListener() method, which returns a new instance of this ShowListener class.

■ **Note** JSF 1.2 adds a binding attribute to all standard converter, validator, and listener tags. You can use the binding attribute on a listener tag to reference a managed bean that is also an instance of the corresponding listener interface.

After this you check to see whether the component created by the UIComponentTag is an instance of the ShowSource. You can check to see whether the component was of instance UIShowOne, but remember that UIShowOne implements ShowSource, and you want to make sure you can reuse tags such as the ShowListener for other components you might want to create in the future (for example, UIShowMany). Finally, and this is important, you always return SKIP_BODY.

At this point the only thing you know about the listener, defined by the application developer, is a `String` representing the fully qualified class name—`com.apress.projsf.ch3.application.MyShowListener`. To be able to use this class, you first need to load the class defined in the string from the class path and then create and return a new instance of this class. In the `createShowListener()` method, you first need to get hold of the `ClassLoader` for this thread to be able to load the class from the class path, as shown in Code Sample 3-37. You then invoke the `loadClass()` method on the `ClassLoader` instance, passing the fully qualified class name defined in the `String` object. When you have the class, you can create a new instance of it by invoking the `newInstance()` method. You then cast this new instance to `ShowListener` before you return the listener instance.

Code Sample 3-37. *The* `createShowListener` *Method*

```
  protected ShowListener createShowListener(
    String className) throws JspException
  {
    try
    {
      ClassLoader loader = Thread.currentThread().getContextClassLoader();
      Class clazz = loader.loadClass(className);
      return ((ShowListener) clazz.newInstance());
    }
    catch (Exception e)
    {
      throw new JspException(e);
    }
  }
}
```

■ **Note** For more information about the classes `java.lang.Thread` and `java.lang.ClassLoader`, please refer to the J2SE 1.4 API specification (`http://java.sun.com/j2se/1.4.2/docs/api/index.html`).

The `release()` method (see Code Sample 3-37) is part of the `Tag` handler contract and as such is not a JSF-specific feature, but since the `ShowListener` tag handler class is directly extending the `Tag` handler subclass, `TagSupport`, it makes sense to discuss the `release()` method now.

Code Sample 3-38. *Release Stored State*

```
/**
 * Releases the internal state used by the tag.
 */
public void release()
{
  _type = null;
}
```

This method is called on a Tag handler to release state. The page compiler guarantees that JSP page implementation objects will invoke this method on all tag handlers to release any state currently stored, which in this case means setting the _type property to null.

Tag Library Descriptor

You have now implemented three tag handler classes—ProShowOneDeckTag, ShowItemTag, and ShowListenerTag—and as with all JSP tag handler classes, you need to declare them in a TLD, as shown in Code Sample 3-39. The custom actions for the three new tag handlers will be added to the same TLD and follow the same pattern as the ProInputDateTag tag handler declared in Chapter 2.

Code Sample 3-39. *The TLD*

```
<?xml version="1.0" encoding="UTF-8" ?>
<!DOCTYPE taglib
   PUBLIC "-//Sun Microsystems, Inc.//DTD JSP Tag Library 1.2//EN"
          "http://java.sun.com/dtd/web-jsptaglibrary_1_2.dtd" >

<taglib>

  <tlib-version>1.0</tlib-version>
  <jsp-version>1.2</jsp-version>

  <short-name>pro</short-name>
  <uri>http://projsf.apress.com/tags</uri>
  <description>
    This tag library contains JavaServer Faces component tags for the
    ProJSF ShowOne Deck Renderer, and ShowOne Listener.
  </description>

  <tag>
    <name>showOneDeck</name>
    <tag-class>com.apress.projsf.ch3.taglib.pro.ProShowOneDeckTag</tag-class>
    <body-content>JSP</body-content>
    <description>
      The ProShowOneDeck component tag handler.
    </description>

    <!-- UIComponent attributes -->
    <attribute>
      <name>id</name>
      <required>false</required>
      <rtexprvalue>false</rtexprvalue>
```

```
    <description>
      The component identifier for this component.  This value must be
      unique within the closest parent component that is a naming
      container.
    </description>
  </attribute>
  <attribute>
    <name>rendered</name>
    <required>false</required>
    <rtexprvalue>false</rtexprvalue>
    <description>
      Flag indicating whether or not this component should be rendered
      (during Render Response Phase), or processed on any subsequent
      form submit.
    </description>
  </attribute>
  <attribute>
    <name>binding</name>
    <required>false</required>
    <rtexprvalue>false</rtexprvalue>
    <description>
       The value binding expression linking this component to a
       property in a backing bean.
    </description>
  </attribute>

  <!-- UIShowOne attributes -->
  <attribute>
    <name>showItemId</name>
    <required>false</required>
    <rtexprvalue>false</rtexprvalue>
    <description>
       The initial item to show.
    </description>
  </attribute>

  <!-- ProShowOneDeck attributes -->
  <attribute>
    <name>styleClass</name>
    <required>false</required>
    <rtexprvalue>false</rtexprvalue>
    <description>
       The CSS style class for the ProShowOneDeck component.
    </description>
  </attribute>
```

```
    <attribute>
      <name>itemStyleClass</name>
      <required>false</required>
      <rtexprvalue>false</rtexprvalue>
      <description>
         The CSS style class for the UIShowItems.
      </description>
    </attribute>

    <attribute>
      <name>itemHeaderStyleClass</name>
      <required>false</required>
      <rtexprvalue>false</rtexprvalue>
      <description>
         The CSS style class for the header facet of the UIShowItems.
      </description>
    </attribute>

    <attribute>
      <name>itemContentStyleClass</name>
      <required>false</required>
      <rtexprvalue>false</rtexprvalue>
      <description>
         The CSS style class for the content of the UIShowItems.
      </description>
    </attribute>
  </tag>

  <tag>
    <name>showItem</name>
    <tag-class>com.apress.projsf.ch3.taglib.ShowItemTag</tag-class>
    <body-content>JSP</body-content>
    <description>
      The UIShowItem component tag handler.
    </description>

    <!-- UIComponent attributes -->
    <attribute>
      <name>id</name>
      <required>false</required>
      <rtexprvalue>false</rtexprvalue>
      <description>
        The component identifier for this component.  This value must be
        unique within the closest parent component that is a naming
        container.
      </description>
    </attribute>
```

```
    <attribute>
      <name>rendered</name>
      <required>false</required>
      <rtexprvalue>false</rtexprvalue>
      <description>
        Flag indicating whether or not this component should be rendered
        (during Render Response Phase), or processed on any subsequent
        form submit.
      </description>
    </attribute>
    <attribute>
      <name>binding</name>
      <required>false</required>
      <rtexprvalue>false</rtexprvalue>
      <description>
        The value binding expression linking this component to a
        property in a backing bean.
      </description>
    </attribute>

    <!-- UIShowItem attributes (none) -->
  </tag>

  <tag>
    <name>showListener</name>
    <tag-class>com.apress.projsf.ch3.taglib.ShowListenerTag</tag-class>
    <body-content>JSP</body-content>
    <description>
      The ShowListener tag handler.
    </description>

    <attribute>
      <name>type</name>
      <required>false</required>
      <rtexprvalue>false</rtexprvalue>
      <description>
        The fully qualified class name for the show listener.
      </description>
    </attribute>
  </tag>
</taglib>
```

To recap from Chapter 2, each custom action in the TLD needs a <tag> element. The name of the custom action element is defined in the nested name element (for example, <name>showListener</name>), and the Tag handler class is defined in the <tag-class> element. If the custom action has attributes, they have to be defined with the <attribute> element. Remember also that the runtime expression value—<rtexprvalue>—must be set to false, and the attribute class must be left unspecified to avoid any conflicts with either Java or JSP EL expressions and to allow the tag handler to convert the expression to either a `ValueBinding` or a `MethodBinding`.

This was the final touch on the HTML version of the deck component. We are aware of the complexity of this deck component, but we thought it was necessary to show all aspects of designing new reusable components from the bottom up, starting with the new event `ShowEvent` and its corresponding `Listener` interface, `ShowListener`, followed by two new behavioral superclasses, `UIShowOne` and `UIShowItem`. We also introduced the concept of facets and leveraged JavaScript to give you an understanding of JSF's power and flexibility.

You can reuse most of the work you have put into this component (for example, `UIShowOne`, `UIShowItem`, `ShowListener`, and `ShowEvent`). Moving forward, we will show how to extend these behavioral superclasses with new `Renderers` so that you can support richer functionality.

Summary

This chapter extended the blueprint given to you in Chapter 2. The blueprint now contains seven steps covering everything from analyzing the UI prototype to writing the JSP TLD. Remember that in most cases you will need to use only five out of these seven steps, since the most common scenario is to extend an existing behavioral `UIComponent` rather than to create a new one.

As part of the blueprint, you also created a client-specific `Renderer` (`HtmlShowOneDeckRenderer`) with all the attributes needed for the component and a renderer-specific subclass (`ProShowOneDeck`). Finally, you implemented support for the page description of choice—JSP. All of this followed the same pattern introduced in Chapter 2; as you probably noticed, it is not hard to create a component if you have a blueprint to follow, although there is a certain amount of repetition.

From this chapter, you also gained an understanding of the JSF event model and how to implement support for custom events and listeners in your own JSF tag handlers.

PART 2

Designing Rich Internet Components

Although the Web has gained widespread adoption as the default deployment solution for enterprise-class applications, users increasingly demand a more interactive browser experience and broader support for the vast array of Internet-enabled devices. This part of the book will teach you how to deliver reusable, rich Internet components using JSF. These are components that provide application developers with a set of building blocks for creating rich Internet applications with JSF without sacrificing productivity, and they can be deployed to any platform.

CHAPTER 4

Using Rich Internet Technologies

Ajax—in Greek mythology Ajax was a powerful warrior who fought in the Trojan War and supposedly was second only to Achilles, the Greeks' best warrior. Although characterized as slow-witted, Ajax was one of the best fighters among the Greeks and was famed for his steadfast courage in the face of adversity.

—Laboratori Nazionali di Frascati (`http://www.lnf.infn.it`)

It will always be the user who will feel the effect of the technology you choose, and the first priority of any Web or desktop application developer should be the user experience. Users are not interested in what technology is being used or whether the application is a traditional desktop application or a Web application. Users demand a feature-rich and interactive interface.

Traditionally, desktop applications have been able to provide users with the richness required to fulfill their demands, but an increasing number of desktop applications are migrating to the Web. Therefore, Web application developers have to provide richer Web interfaces.

To make you fully appreciate JSF and what it brings to the Internet community, you need to understand the current status of rich Internet applications. Web application developers today are faced with a demand for richer functionality using technologies such as HTML, CSS, JavaScript, and the DOM. However, these technologies were not developed with enterprise applications in mind. The increasing demand from consumers for applications with features not fully supported by these technologies is pushing Web application developers to explore alternative solutions.

New breeds of Web technologies that enhance the traditionally static content provided by Web applications have evolved from these consumer requirements. These technologies are often referred to as *Rich Internet Technologies* (RITs).

In the absence of a standard definition and with the lack of extensibility of the traditional Web technologies, new technologies have emerged, such as Mozilla's XUL, Microsoft's HTC, Java applets, Flex, and OpenLaszlo. These technologies support application-specific extensions to traditional HTML markup while still leveraging the benefits of deploying an application to a central server. Another solution that has returned under a newly branded name is Ajax (recently an acronym for Asynchronous JavaScript and XML and formerly known as XMLHTTP). Applications built with these technologies are often referred to as *Rich Internet Applications* (RIAs).

In this chapter, we will introduce three RITs: Ajax, Mozilla XUL, and Microsoft HTC. This chapter will give a high-level overview of these technologies, and it will show some simple examples to highlight the core feature of each technology. In later chapters, you will get into the details of each technology to improve the user experience of two JSF components—`ProInputDate` and `ProShowOneDeck`.

The following are the four main players in this chapter:

Ajax[1]: Ajax is the new name of an already established technology suite—the DOM, JavaScript, and `XMLHttpRequest`. Ajax is used to create dynamic Web sites and to asynchronously communicate between the client and server.

XUL: XML User Interface Language (XUL) which, pronounced *zuul*, was created by the Mozilla organization (Mozilla.org) as an open source project in 1998. With XUL, developers can build rich user interfaces that may be deployed either as "thin client" Web applications, locally on a desktop or as Internet-enabled "thick client" desktop applications.

XBL: Extensible Binding Language (XBL) is a language used by XUL to define new components. XBL is also used to bridge the gap between XUL and HTML, making it easy to attach behavior to traditional HTML markup.

HTC: Introduced in Microsoft Internet Explorer 5, HTCs provide a mechanism to implement components in script as DHTML behaviors. Saved with an `.htc` extension, an HTC file is an HTML file that contains script and a set of HTC-specific elements that define the component.

After reading this chapter, you should understand what these RITs are, what they provide, and how you can create rich user interface components with them.

Introducing Ajax

Ajax has been minted as a term describing a Web development technique for creating richer and user-friendlier Web applications. In this chapter, we will give you an overview of Ajax.

Ajax was first coined in February 2005 and has since taken the software industry by storm. One of the reasons Ajax has gained momentum and popularity is the `XMLHttpRequest` object and the way this object makes it possible for developers to asynchronously communicate with underlying servers and any business services used by Web applications. Popular sites such as Google GMail and Google Suggest are using Ajax techniques to provide users with rich interfaces that have increased the awareness of Ajax.

Although the name *Ajax* is new, the technologies listed as the foundation of this technique—JavaScript, `XMLHttpRequest`, and the DOM—have been around for some time. In fact, the latest addition to this suite of technologies—the `XMLHttpRequest` object—was introduced by Microsoft in 1999 with the release of Internet Explorer 5.0 and was implemented as an ActiveX component.

The `XMLHttpRequest` object, although widely used, is not a standard; it could at best be called a "de facto" standard, since most modern browsers, including Firefox, Internet Explorer,

[1] This term was first coined in an article by James Garrett of Adaptive Path.

Opera, and Safari, support it. However, a standard has been proposed that covers some of the functionality provided by the `XMLHttpRequest` object—the DOM Level 3 Load and Save specification.

■ **Note** The `XMLHttpRequest` object is not a W3C standard. The W3C DOM Level 3 Load and Save specification contains some similar functionality, but this is not implemented in any browsers yet. So, at the moment, if you need to send an HTTP request from a browser, you will have to use the `XMLHttpRequest` object.

With the `XMLHttpRequest` object, developers can now send requests to the Web server to retrieve specific data and use JavaScript to process the response. This ability to send data between the client and the Web server reduces the bandwidth to a minimum and saves time on the server since most of the processing to update the user interfaces takes place on the client using JavaScript.

The XMLHttpRequest Object

Since the `XMLHttpRequest` object is not a standard, each browser may implement support for it slightly differently; thus, the behavior might vary among browsers. You will notice when creating the sample application in this chapter that Microsoft's Internet Explorer implements the `XMLHttpRequest` object as an ActiveX object, whereas Mozilla Firefox treats it like a native JavaScript object. However, most implementations support the same set of methods and properties. This eases the burden on application developers, since the only difference is in creating an instance of the `XMLHttpRequest` object. Creating an instance of the `XMLHttpRequest` object can look like Code Sample 4-1 or Code Sample 4-2.

Code Sample 4-1. *Creating an Instance of the* `XMLHttpRequest` *Object*

```
var xmlhttp = new XMLHttpRequest();
```

Code Sample 4-2. *Creating an Instance of the* `XMLHttpRequest` *Object Using* `ActiveXObject`

```
var xmlhttp = new ActiveXObject("Microsoft.XMLHTTP");
```

It is also worth noting that the `XMLHttpRequest` object is not exclusive to standard HTML. The `XMLHttpRequest` object can potentially be used by any HTML/XML-based Web technology such as XUL or HTC.

Methods

An `XMLHttpRequest` object instance provides methods that can be used to asynchronously communicate with the Web server (see Table 4-1).

Table 4-1. `XMLHttpRequest` *Object Methods*

Method	Description
`open("method", "URL")`	Assigns destination URL, method, and other optional attributes of a pending request
`send(content)`	Transmits the request, optionally with a string that can be posted or DOM object data
`abort()`	Stops the current request
`getResponseHeader("headerLabel")`	Returns the string value of a single header label
`getAllResponseHeaders()`	Returns a complete set of headers (labels and values) as a string
`setRequestHeader("label", "value")`	Assigns a label/value pair to the header to be sent with a request

In Table 4-1, the `open()` and `send()` methods are the most common ones. The `open("method", "URL"[, "asynch"[, "username"[, "password"]]])` method sets the stage for the request and upcoming operation. Two parameters are required; one is the HTTP method for the request (`GET` or `POST`), and the other is the URL for the connection. The optional `asynch` parameter defines the nature of this request—`true` being the default and indicating that this is an asynchronous request. The other two optional parameters—`username` and `password`—allow application developers to provide a username and password, if needed.

The `send()` method makes the request to the server and is called after you have set the stage with a call to the `open()` method. Any content passed to this method is sent as part of the request body.

Properties

Once an `XMLHttpRequest` has been sent, scripts can look to several properties that all implementations have in common (see Table 4-2).

Table 4-2. `XMLHttpRequest` *Object Properties*

Property	Description
`onreadystatechange`	Event handler for an event that fires at every state change
`readyState`	Object status integer: `0` = uninitialized, `1` = loading, `2` = loaded, `3` = interactive, `4` = complete
`responseText`	String version of data returned from server process
`responseXML`	DOM-compatible document object of data returned from server process
`status`	Numeric code returned by server, such as 404 for "Not Found" or 200 for "OK"
`statusText`	String message accompanying the status code

As with the `XMLHttpRequest` object methods, two properties will be used more frequently than the others—`responseText` and `responseXML`. You can use these two properties to access data returned with the response. The `responseText` property provides a string representation of the data, which is useful in case the requested data comes in as plain text or HTML. Depending on the context, the `responseXML` property offers a more extensive representation of the data. The `responseXML` property will return an XML document object, which can be examined using W3C DOM node tree methods and properties.

Traditional Web Application Development

Before getting into the details of Ajax, you need to first understand how a traditional Web application works and what issues users, and application developers, face when a Web application contains form elements. HTML forms are used to pass data to an underlying Web server. You have probably encountered Web applications with forms, such as when you have filled in a survey, ordered products online from Web sites such as eBay (`http://www.ebay.com`), or filled in an expense report with a company's HR application.

A form in a traditional Web application is defined by a special HTML tag (`<form>`) that has a set of parameters—`action`, `method`, `enctype`, and `target`. The `action` parameter defines the destination URL to pass the form data, the `method` parameter defines the HTTP method used for the form postback, the `enctype` parameter defines the content type to be used for encoding the data, and the `target` parameter defines the frame that should receive the response.

Regular Postback

You can use two methods when submitting a form—`POST` and `GET`. With the HTTP `GET` method, the form data set is appended to the URL specified by the `action` attribute (for example, `http://forums.oracle.com/forums/forum.jspa?forumID=83`), and this new URL is sent to the server. In JSF the value of the `action` attribute is provided by `ViewHandler.getActionURL(viewId)` during rendering.

■ Note The `<h:form>` tag defined by the JSF specification does not have the `method` and `action` attributes.

With the HTTP `POST` method, the form data set is included in the body of the request sent to the server. The `GET` method is convenient for bookmarking, but should be used only when you do not expect form submission side effects as defined in the W3C HTTP specification (`http://www.w3.org/Protocols/`). If the service associated with the processing of a form causes side effects (for example, if the form modifies a database row or subscribes to a service), you should use the `POST` method.

Another reason for choosing the `POST` method over the `GET` method is that it allows browsers to send an unlimited amount of data to a Web server by adding data as the message body after the request headers on an HTTP request. The `GET` method is restricted to the URL length, which cannot be more than 2,048 characters. `POST` removes any limitations from the transmitted data length.

Note The `GET` method restricts form data set values to ASCII characters. Only the `POST` method (with `enctype="multipart/form-data"`) is specified to cover the entire [ISO10646] character set.

When the user submits a form (for example, by clicking a submit button), as shown in Figure 4-1, the browser processes the controls within the submitted form and builds a form data set. A form data set is a sequence of control-name/current-value pairs constructed from controls within the form. The form data set is then encoded according to the content type specified by the `enctype` attribute of the `<form>` element (for example, `application/x-www-form-urlencoded`).

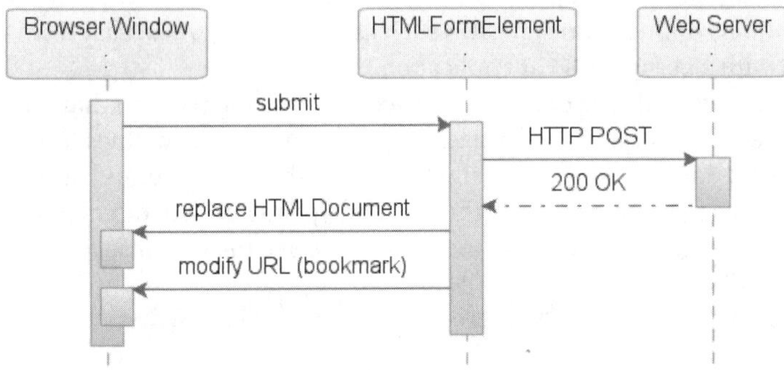

Figure 4-1. *Sequence diagram over a regular postback*

The encoded data is then sent as a `url-formencoded` stream back to the server (HTTP `POST`). The server response contains information about the response status indicating that the request has succeeded (HTTP status code 200 "OK") and sends a full-page response. The browser will then parse the HTML sent on the response to the HTML DOM and render the page in the browser window. Any resources required by the page will be reverified and possibly downloaded again from the server. After the HTML document has been replaced in the browser window, the URL in the browser location bar is also modified to reflect the page from the previous page form action.

Alternatively, the server response can contain information indicating that the request has failed (for example, HTTP status code 404 "Not Found").

Side Effects of Regular Postback

The obvious undesired side effect of regular postback is that it will cause the page to flicker when the page is reloaded in the browser window, and at worst the user will have to wait while the page downloads all the required resources to the client browser again. Other less prominent, but still annoying, side effects are the loss of scroll position and cursor focus.

■ **Note** Most browsers today have excellent client-side caching functionalities that work well to prevent pages from reloading resources from the Web server, unless caching is turned off or the application is using HTTPS, in which case content may be prevented from being cached on the client.

As part of a page design, it might be required to have multiple forms on a page. When multiple forms are available on a page, only one form will be processed during postback, and the data entered in other forms will be discarded.

One benefit is that bookmarking is possible with regular postbacks. However, the user is often fooled by the URL set in the location bar, since it reflects what was last requested and not what is returned on the response. When the user selects the bookmark, it will return to the previously submitted page. A regular postback also allows the user to click the browser back button to return to the previous page with the only side effect that a form post warning will occur.

Ajax Web Application Development

Developing sophisticated Ajax-enabled applications is not something for the everyday application developer, and just as the Trojans feared Ajax on the battlefield, even the most experienced Web designer dreads to attack Ajax. A major part of the Ajax framework is the client-side scripting language JavaScript. As many Web designers have experienced, JavaScript is not an industrial-strength language and is claimed by many to lack support in professional development tools.

However, in our opinion, at least two really good JavaScript tools are available—Microsoft's Visual Studio and Mozilla's Venkman. What is true, though, is that maintaining Ajax applications is difficult; the lack of browser consistency in JavaScript implementations makes maintaining browser-specific code a challenge.

MOZILLA'S VENKMAN DEBUGGER

Venkman is the code name for Mozilla's JavaScript debugger (`http://www.mozilla.org/projects/venkman/`). Venkman aims to provide a powerful JavaScript debugging environment for Mozilla-based browsers, including the Netscape 7.*x* series of browsers and Mozilla milestone builds. It does not include Gecko-only browsers such as K-Meleon and Galeon. The debugger is available as an add-on package in XPI format and has been provided as part of the Mozilla install distribution since October 3, 2001.

Ajax Postback

Now that you have familiarized yourself with regular postbacks, it is time to look at Ajax. This section will give you an overview of how to use Ajax postbacks to handle events. You can use Ajax to take control of the form submit action, and instead of using the regular form submit action, you use an `XMLHttpRequest` object to asynchronously submit your request to the Web server. As a side effect, when the user submits a form (for example, by clicking a submit button), no browser helps you process the controls within the submitted form. You now need to handle any form fields that need to be part of the postback and use them to build a form data set—control-name/current-value pairs. You then take the form data set and simulate the encoding (`url-formencoded`) to provide the same syntax as a regular postback (see Figure 4-2).

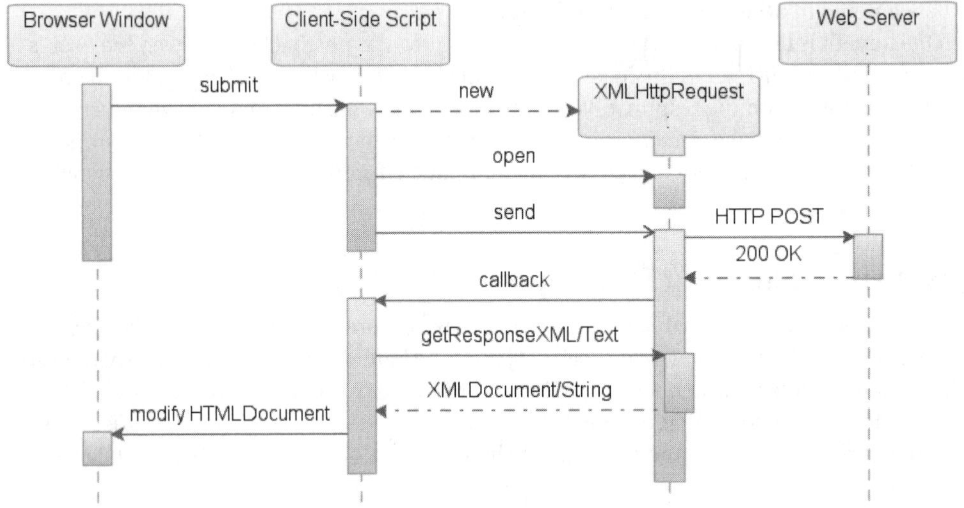

Figure 4-2. *Sequence diagram over an* `XMLHttpRequest` *postback*

After you have created the `XMLHttpRequest` object, you use the `open()` method to set the HTTP method—`GET` or `POST`—intended for the request and the URL for the connection. After you have set the stage for your `XMLHttpRequest` operation, you send the encoded data, using the `XMLHttpRequest` object, as a `url-formencoded` stream back to the server (HTTP `POST`). For the Web server, the request will appear as a traditional HTTP `POST`, meaning that the Web server cannot tell the difference between a regular postback and your Ajax postback. For a JSF solution, this means an Ajax request can be picked up the same way as a regular postback request, allowing server code (for example, JSF request lifecycle) to be unaffected.

If the request is successful, the ready state on your `XMLHttpRequest` object is set to `4`, which indicates that the loading of the response is complete. You can then use two properties to access data returned with the response—`responseText` and `responseXML`.

The `responseText` property provides a string representation of the data, which is useful in case the requested data comes in the shape of plain text or HTML. Depending on the context, the `responseXML` property offers a more extensive representation of the data.

The `responseXML` property will return an XML document object, which is a full-fledged document node object (a DOM `nodeType` of `9`) that can be examined using the W3C DOM node tree methods and properties. In this traditional Ajax approach, the Ajax handler is in charge of sending the data, managing the response, and modifying the HTMLDocument object node tree.

■ **Note** DOM elements can be different types. An element's type is stored in an integer field of nodeType (for example, COMMENT_NODE = 8 and DOCUMENT_NODE = 9). For more information about the different nodeTypes, please visit http://www.w3.org/.

Side Effects of Ajax Postback

As with the regular postback, desired and undesired side effects exist when using Ajax for postback. The most prominent and desired side effect is the XMLHttpRequest object's strength and ability to set or retrieve parts of a page. This will remove flickering when data is reloaded and increase performance of the application, since there is no need to reload the entire page and all its resources. The undesired side effect of this is that users will typically no longer be able to bookmark a page or use the back button to navigate to the previous page/state.

Another important, but less immediately obvious, implication of using XMLHttpRequest in your application is that clients such as mobile phones, PDAs, screen readers, and IM clients lack support for this technology. Also, Ajax requires additional work to make applications accessible; for example, screen readers expect a full-page refresh to work properly.

■ **Note** With XMLHttpRequest, you do not need the form element in an application, but one function requires a form regardless of regular postbacks or Ajax postbacks—file upload. If you need file-upload functionality in your application, you have to use form.submit(). In the context of Ajax, you can do this by using a hidden <iframe> tag and the form.submit() function and setting target.

Ajax Is Not a Magic Wand

As you know, the XMLHttpRequest object is an important player in Ajax, since it transports data asynchronously between the client and the server. It is important to understand that the XMLHttpRequest is not a magic wand that automatically solves all your problems. You still need to watch performance and scalability carefully using the XMLHttpRequest object. If you are aware of this, it is easy to understand that it is what you send on the request, receive upon the response, and manage on the client that will affect your performance.

Building Ajax Applications

Traditional Web applications are in most cases slower than their desktop application counterparts. With Ajax, you can now send requests to the Web server to retrieve only the data needed using JavaScript to process the response, which creates a more responsive Web application. Figure 4-3 illustrates a page using Ajax to asynchronously communicate with the back-end and provide a Book Titles drop-down list that includes certain books based on what category the user enters.

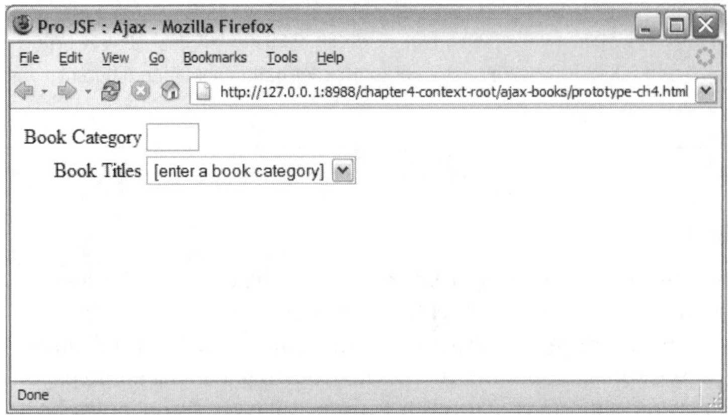

Figure 4-3. *An HTML page using Ajax to filter a list of books based on category*

When the user tabs out of the Book Category field, the drop-down list is populated with books based on the entered category without a page refresh.

Figure 4-4 shows the result of entering *Ajax* as the category and tabbing out of the Book Category field.

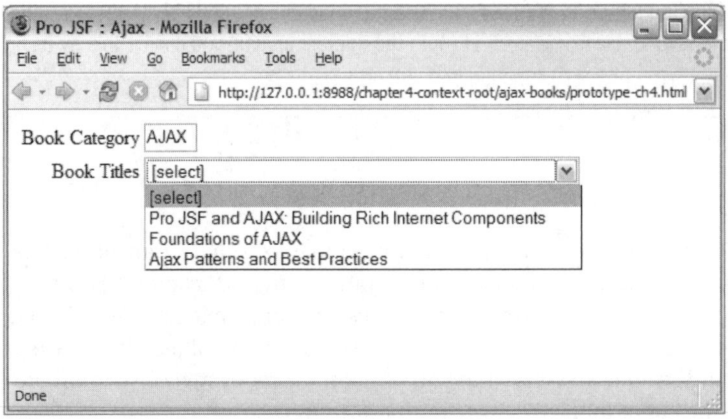

Figure 4-4. *An HTML page using Ajax to filter a list of books based on category*

As you can see, the Book Titles drop-down list has been populated with books about the related topic.

A traditional Ajax application leverages standard HTML/XHTML as the presentation layer and JavaScript to dynamically change the DOM, which creates an effect of “richness” in the user interface with no dependency on a particular runtime environment. Code Sample 4-3 shows the actual HTML source behind this simple application.

Code Sample 4-3. *An HTML Page Leveraging Ajax to Update a* `<select>` *Element*

```
<!DOCTYPE HTML PUBLIC "-//W3C//DTD HTML 4.01 Transitional//EN">
<html>
  <head>
    <script type="text/javascript"
            src="projsf-ch4/dynamicBookList.js" >
    </script>
    <title>Select a book</title>
  </head>
  <body>
    <form name="form" method="get">
      <table>
        <tr>
          <td align="right">Book Category</td>
          <td>
            <input type="text" size="3" maxlength="8"
                   onchange="populateBookList('/chapter4-context-root/projsf-ch4',
                                              'bookListId', this.value);" />
          </td>
        </tr>
        <tr>
          <td align="right">Book Title</td>
          <td >
            <select id="bookListId" >
              <option value="[none]">
                [enter a book category]
              </option>
            </select>
          </td>
        </tr>
      </table>
    </form>
  </body>
</html>
```

At the top of this page, you have a reference to your Ajax implementation—`dynamicBookList.js`. This code adds an `onchange` event handler to the `<input>` element that will call a JavaScript function, `populateBookList()`, which is invoked when the cursor leaves the input field. The `populateBookList()` function takes three arguments—the service URL for retrieving the book list data, the book category entered in the input field `this.value`, and the ID of the `select` element to populate with books (`'bookListId'`).

The Ajax Book Filter Implementation

The Ajax book filter implementation consists of three JavaScript functions—`populateBookList()`, `createHttpRequest()`, and `transferListItems()`—and a data source containing information about the books. As soon as the cursor leaves the Book Category field, the `getBookList()` function is invoked (see Figure 4-5).

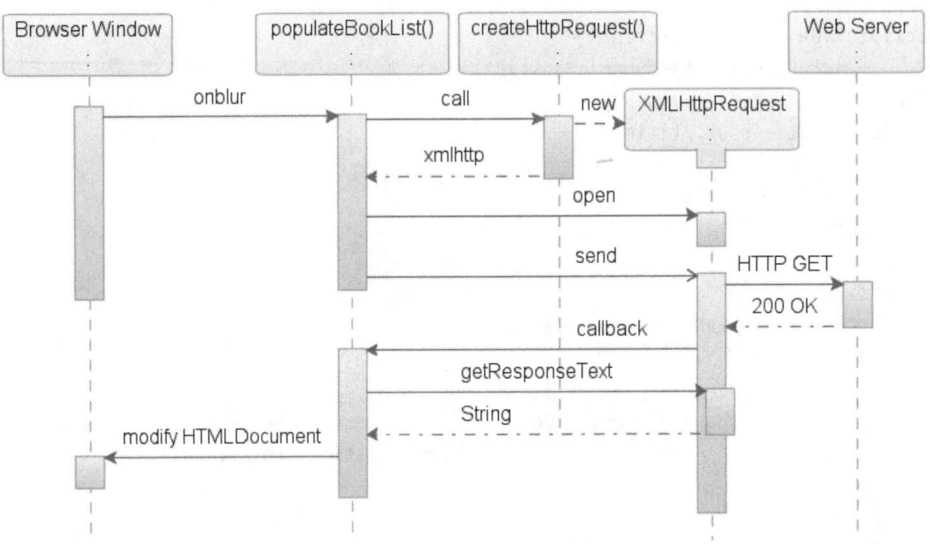

Figure 4-5. *Sequence diagram over the book filter* `XMLHttpRequest`

The `populateBookList()` function will call the `createHttpRequest()` function, which will create a new instance of the `XMLHttpRequest` object. You then use this `XMLHttpRequest` object to set the stage for your request and send the encoded data as a `url-formencoded` stream back to the server (HTTP GET). If the request is successful, the `XMLHttpRequest` object calls your callback function. This function will get the response text from the `XMLHttpRequest` object and use the content passed (for example, a list of books) to modify the HTML document and populate the `<select>` element with data. Code Sample 4-4 shows the actual code behind this book filter.

Code Sample 4-4. *The* `populateBookList()` *Function*

```
/**
 * Populates the select element with a list of books in a specific book category.
 *
 * @param serviceURL  the service URL for retrieving JSON data files
 * @param selectId    the id of the target select element to populate
 * @param category    the book category for the populated books
 */
function populateBookList(
  serviceURL,
  selectId ,
```

```
  category)
{
  var xmlhttp = createHttpRequest();

  // You can use any type of data source, but for the sample
  // you are going to use a simple JSON file that contains your data.
  var requestURL = serviceURL + '/booklist-' + category.toLowerCase() + '.json';
  xmlhttp.open("GET", requestURL);
  xmlhttp.onreadystatechange=function()
  {
    if (xmlhttp.readyState == 4)
    {
      if (xmlhttp.state == 200)
      {
        transferListItems(selectId, eval(xmlhttp.responseText));
      };
    };
  };
  xmlhttp.send(null);
};
```

With this code, you first create a new instance of the XMLHttpRequest object by calling a function called createHttpRequest(). You initiate your request by calling the open("GET", requestURL) method on the XMLHttpRequest object instance and passing two arguments. The GET string indicates the HTTP method for this request, and the requestURL variable represents the URL to your data source, which in this case is a simple text file. If a request is successful, the readyState on your XMLHttpRequest object is set to 4, and the state is set to 200. You use the onreadystatechange event handler to invoke the transferListItems() function when readyState is set to 4, passing the responseText property from the XMLHttpRequest object. The transferListItems() function will take the returned string and populate the <select> element with data.

Creating an instance of the XMLHttpRequest object is simple, although as shown in Code Sample 4-5, you have a few things to consider.

Code Sample 4-5. *The* createHttpRequest() *Function That Creates the* XMLHttpRequest *Object*

```
/**
 * Creates a new XMLHttpRequest object.
 */
function createHttpRequest()
{
  var xmlhttp = null;
  if (window.ActiveXObject)
  {
    xmlhttp = new ActiveXObject("Microsoft.XMLHTTP");
  }
  else if (window.XMLHttpRequest)
```

```
  {
    xmlhttp = new XMLHttpRequest();
  }
  return xmlhttp;
};
```

Code Sample 4-5 creates the `XMLHttpRequest` object, and as in many browsers with JavaScript support, different browsers support the `XMLHttpRequest` object slightly differently. This means you need to implement support for different browsers in your `createHttpRequest()` function. For Microsoft Internet Explorer, you have to create the `XMLHttpRequest` object using `new ActiveXObject("Microsoft.XMLHTTP")`. With any browser supporting the Mozilla GRE, you can use a native call—`new XMLHttpRequest()`—to create an instance of the `XMLHttpRequest` object.

The `transferListItems()` function, shown in Code Sample 4-6, returns the data requested by the user and populates the `<select>` element with data.

Code Sample 4-6. *The* `transferListItems()` *Function That Populates the* `<select>` *Element*

```
/**
 * Transfers the list items from the JSON array
 * to options in the select element.
 *
 * @param selectId    the id of the target select element to populate
 * @param listArray   the retrieved list of books
 */
function transferListItems (
  selectId,
  listArray)
{
  var select = document.getElementById(selectId);

  // reset the select options
  select.length = 0;
  select.options[0] = new Option('[select]');

  // transfer the book list items
  for(var i=0; i < listArray.length; i++)
  {
    // create the new Option
    var option = new Option(listArray[i]);
    // add the Option onto the end of the select options list
    select.options[select.length] = option;
  };
};
```

The `transferListItems()` function takes two arguments—`selectId` and `listArray`. The `listArray` represents the data returned by your request, and `selectId` represents the `<select>`

element that is being populated with this data. Code Sample 4-7 is just showing your simple data source, in JavaScript Object Notation (JSON) syntax, so that you can replicate the sample application.

Code Sample 4-7. *Source for Your Ajax Titles*—`ajax.json`

```
['Pro JSF and Ajax: Building Rich Internet Components',
 'Foundations of Ajax',
 'Ajax Patterns and Best Practices']
```

This file contains a JavaScript expression that defines a new array of Ajax related books.

■ **Note** JSON is a lightweight data interchange format. It is based on a subset of the JavaScript programming language (standard ECMA-262, third edition). JSON is a text format that is completely language independent but uses conventions familiar to programmers of the C family of languages, including C, C++, C#, Java, JavaScript, Perl, Python, and many others.

Ajax Summary

You should now understand what Ajax is and be familiar with the `XMLHttpRequest` object, which is a vital part of the Ajax technique, and the lifecycle of a regular `XMLHttpRequest`. You should also have enough knowledge to be able to create simple Ajax solutions. In the coming chapters, you will dive deeper into Ajax.

Introducing Mozilla XUL

What is Mozilla XUL? Is it a crossbreed between a dinosaur and an evil Ghostbuster spirit? No, Mozilla XUL is an open source project that is known as the development platform for the Mozilla Firefox browser and Mozilla Thunderbird email client. In the following sections of this chapter, you will get a high-level overview of Mozilla XUL and its subcomponents. In 1998 the Mozilla organization (`Mozilla.org`) created an open source project called XUL, which is an extensible UI language based on XML and, as such, can leverage existing standards including XSLT, XPath, the DOM, and even Web Services (SOAP).

Using XUL, developers can build rich user interfaces that can be deployed as Web applications, as desktop applications locally, or as desktop applications on other Internet-enabled devices. XUL leverages the support of the Mozilla Gecko Runtime Environment (GRE) in order to fully provide the consumer with a rich user interface. The Firefox browser and the Thunderbird email client, as well as numerous plug-ins, are available for these clients and are two good examples of applications based on XUL and the Mozilla GRE.

One of the great features of XUL is its extensibility. Using XBL, XUL provides a declarative way to create new and extend existing XUL components. XBL can also bridge the gap between XUL and HTML, since it is not possible to embed XUL components directly into an HTML page. The following section introduces how to build XUL applications and some of the components used when building XUL applications.

Tip An excellent sample to look at to get a feel for what is possible with XUL is the Mozilla Amazon Browser (MAB) at `http://www.faser.net/mab/`.

Building XUL Applications

The idea behind XUL is to provide a markup for building user interfaces, much like HTML, while leveraging technologies such as CSS for the look and feel and JavaScript for the event and behavior. Also, APIs are available to give developers access to read from and write to file systems over the network and give them access to Web Services. As an XML-based language, developers can also use XUL in combination with other XML languages such as XHTML and SVG. You can load an application built with XUL in three ways:

- You can load the XUL page the traditional way from the local file system.
- You can load it remotely using an HTTP URL to access content on a Web server.
- You can load it using the chrome URL provided by the Mozilla GRE.

XUL Components

XUL comes with a base set of components (see Table 4-3) that are available through the Mozilla GRE, and as such, XUL does not need to download components to draw an application in the browser. You can also design your own components with XUL; these *will* need to be downloaded upon request and cached in the browser.

MOZILLA XUL'S CHROME SYSTEM

In addition to loading files from the local file system or from a Web server, the Mozilla engine has a special way of installing and registering applications as a part of its *chrome system*. The chrome system allows developers to package applications and install them as plug-ins to clients supporting the Mozilla GRE. XUL applications deployed in this way gain read and write access to the local file system, and so on. This type of access can be hard to achieve in a traditional Web application unless the application has been signed with a digital certificate, and the end-user grants access permission.

An important distinction exists between accessing an application via an HTTP URL (`http://`) and accessing it via a chrome URL (`chrome://`). The chrome URL always refers to packages or extensions that are installed in the chrome system of the Mozilla engine. An example of an application that can be reached by a chrome URL is `chrome://browser/content/bookmarks/bookmarksManager.xul`. This chrome URL will open the Bookmarks Manager available in the Firefox browser.

Table 4-3. *Subset of Available XUL Components**

Component Name	Description
<button>	A button that can be clicked by the user. Event handlers can be used to trap mouse, keyboard, and other events. A button is typically rendered as a gray outset rectangle. You can specify the label of the button by using the `label` attribute or by placing content inside the button.
<window>	Describes the structure of a top-level window. It is the root node of a XUL document, and it is by default a horizontally oriented box. Because it is a box, it takes all the box attributes. By default, the window will have a platform-specific frame around it.
<menubar>	A container that usually contains menu elements. On a Mac, the menu bar is displayed along the top of the screen, and all non-menu-related elements inside the menu bar will be ignored.
<menu>	An element, much like a button, that is placed on a menu bar. When the user clicks the <menu> element, the child <menupopup> of the menu will be displayed. This element is also used to create submenus.
<menupopup>	A container used to display menus. It should be placed inside a menu, menu list, or menu-type button element. It can contain any element but usually will contain <menuitem> elements. It is a type of box that defaults to vertical orientation.
<menuitem>	A single choice in a <menupopup> element. It acts much like a button, but it is rendered on a menu.
<radio>	An element that can be turned on and off. Radio buttons are almost always grouped together in clusters. Only one radio button within the same <radiogroup> can be selected at a time. The user can switch which radio button is turned on by selecting it with the mouse or keyboard. Other radio buttons in the same group are turned off. A label, specified with the `label` attribute, can be added beside the radio button to indicate its function to the user.
<radiogroup>	A group of radio buttons. Only one radio button inside the group can be selected at a time. The radio buttons can direct either children of the <radiogroup> or descendants. Place the <radiogroup> inside a <groupbox> if you would like a border or caption around the group. The <radiogroup> defaults to vertical orientation.
<checkbox>	An element that can be turned on and off. The user can switch the state of the check box by selecting it with the mouse. A label, specified with the `label` attribute, may be added beside the check box to indicate to the user its function.
<box>	A container element that can contain any number of child elements. If the box has an `orient` attribute that is set to `horizontal`, the child elements are laid out from left to right in the order they appear in the box. If `orient` is set to `vertical`, the child elements are laid out from top to bottom. Child elements do not overlap. The default orientation is `horizontal`.
<splitter>	An element that should appear before or after an element inside a container. When the splitter is dragged, the sibling elements of the splitter are resized.
<image>	An element that displays an image, much like the HTML <img> element. The `src` attribute can be used to specify the URL of the image.

* *Source:* `http://xulplanet.com/references/elemref/`

We will cover the details of XBL shortly, but the sample XUL file in Code Sample 4-8 demonstrates how to embed standard, namespaced HTML elements into base XUL controls.

Code Sample 4-8. *A Simple XUL File with Embedded HTML Elements*

```
<?xml version="1.0"?>
<?xml-stylesheet href="chrome://global/skin/" type="text/css" ?>
<xul:window title="Pro JSF and AJAX: Mozilla XUL" align="start"
     xmlns:xul="http://www.mozilla.org/keymaster/gatekeeper/there.is.only.xul"
     xmlns:html="http://www.w3.org/1999/xhtml" >
  <xul:groupbox>
    <xul:caption label="Search" />
    <xul:hbox>
      <html:input id="find-text" />
      <xul:button label="Search" />
    </xul:hbox>
  </xul:groupbox>
</xul:window>
```

Code Sample 4-8 shows how to use a namespaced HTML input element—`<html:input id="find-text"/>`—embedded in a XUL page and mixed with regular XUL components.

To be able to deploy and run a XUL application on a remote server, the Web server needs to be configured to send files with the content type of `application/vnd.mozilla.xul+xml`. A browser that uses the Mozilla GRE (Netscape and Firefox, in other words) will use this content type to determine the markup used by the requesting application. A browser with the GRE does not use the file extension unless the file is read from the file system.

Events, State, and Data

Depending on what type of client is being developed—thick or thin—the event handling will be slightly different. This section, however, is showing XUL for Web deployment, and you use JavaScript to handle events and application logic.

Using XUL event handling is not that different from using HTML event handling. The GRE implementation supports DOM Level 2 (and partially DOM Level 3), which is virtually the same for HTML and XUL. Changes to the state and events are propagated through a range of DOM calls. XUL elements come with predefined event handlers, much like the event handlers provided with the standard HTML elements.

Code Sample 4-9 shows a simple use case where a button will launch an alert that will display the value entered by the user in an input field.

Code Sample 4-9. *A Simple Use Case of an Event and Predefined Event Handler*

```
<?xml version="1.0"?>
<?xml-stylesheet href="chrome://global/skin/" type="text/css"?>
```

```
<xul:window title="Pro JSF and AJAX : Mozilla XUL" align="start"
      xmlns:xul="http://www.mozilla.org/keymaster/gatekeeper/there.is.only.xul"
      xmlns:html="http://www.w3.org/1999/xhtml" >
  <xul:groupbox>
    <xul:caption label="Search" />
    <xul:hbox>
      <html:input id="find-text" />
      <xul:button label="Search"
                  oncommand="alert('Book choice: ' +
                             document.getElementById('find-text').value)" />
    </xul:hbox>
  </xul:groupbox>
</xul:window>
```

Figure 4-6 shows the aforementioned code running in Mozilla Firefox.

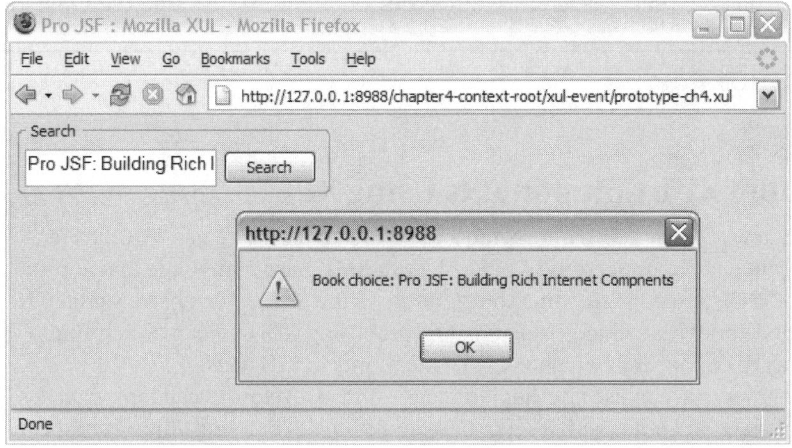

Figure 4-6. *A simple XUL file rendered in the Firefox browser*

As in HTML, developers can use JavaScript functions located in external files of the form `myScript.js`. You can access these methods and functions by using the `src` attribute on the `<script>` element or by embedding them in the page. Developers can refer to a remote server using the `http://` URL, as shown in Code Sample 4-10.

Code Sample 4-10. *Script Reference Using* `http://`

```
<script type="text/javascript" src="http://www.apress.com/projsf/js/myScript.js">
```

A large set of event handler attributes is available, and some of them work only on specific XUL/HTML elements. An example is the XUL <window> element that listens for DOM events (for example, load). Table 4-4 lists a subset of the available predefined event handlers.

Table 4-4. *Listing of Predefined Event Handlers Provided by the GRE DOM Implementation**

Event Handler	Description
onload	An event handler property for window loading. This event is being sent when the window element is finished loading and when all objects in the document are available in the DOM tree. This event handler can also be used on image elements.
oncommand	This event replaces the onclick event handler and is called when an element is activated. The activation can vary from element to element, but essentially it can be called from different user interactions such as clicking and hitting the Enter key or shortcut keys, which is not the case for the onclick event handler.
onblur	The blur event is raised when an element loses focus.
onfocus	The opposite of the onblur event. This event is raised when an element gets focus.

* *Source:* http://www.xulplanet.com

Creating Custom XUL Components Using XBL

To fully understand how Mozilla XUL can provide a mechanism for JSF to use XUL as a rendering technology, you have to understand XBL. XBL is an XML-based language that allows developers to extend XUL and add "custom" components to the already extensive set of XUL elements. In XUL, developers can change the look and feel using CSS and can attach skins, but they have no way to change the behavior of XUL elements in XUL itself.

To do this, developers have to use another language—XBL. Developers can look at XUL as the "implementation" that comes with a set of base components or as tag libraries that can be used to build a user interface, much like the JSF Reference Implementation. XBL is the language developers use to extend XUL components and enable integration with HTML, similar to how Java is used to extend JSF components.

Creating XBL Bindings

XBL is an XML language, and a file created with XBL contains a set of bindings. These bindings each describe the behavior of a XUL component. Besides describing the behavior, these bindings also describe the XUL elements that make up the component along with properties and methods of the component. In Code Sample 4-11, the root shows that the <bindings> element contains one <binding> element.

Code Sample 4-11. *An XBL File Containing One Binding*—projsf-bindings.xml

```
<?xml version="1.0"?>
<xbl:bindings xmlns:xbl="http://www.mozilla.org/xbl"
      xmlns:xul="http://www.mozilla.org/keymaster/gatekeeper/there.is.only.xul"
      xmlns:html="http://www.w3.org/1999/xhtml" >

  <xbl:binding id="welcome" >
    <xbl:content>
      <xul:text value="Welcome, " />
      <xul:text value="Guest" xbl:inherits="value=name" />
      <xul:text value="!" />
    </xbl:content>
  </xbl:binding>
</xbl:bindings>
```

A <bindings> element can contain an infinite number of <binding> elements. The namespace in the <bindings> element defines what syntax will be used, and in Code Sample 4-11 it is XBL—xmlns=http://www.mozilla.org/xbl. The file also contains some XUL elements: <xul:text/>. This is extremely useful to simplify development by encapsulating several components that later can be referred to as one component.

The xbl:inherits attribute on one of the <xul:text> elements allows the <xul:text> element to inherit values from the bound element by defining a variable name and, in this case, assigning it to the value attribute. If no value is defined in the bound element in the page using this component, the text field will default to Guest.

The id attribute on the <xbl:binding> element (in Code Sample 4-11, welcome) will identify the binding.

Using the XBL Bindings

To attach an XBL component or behavior to a XUL application, XUL uses CSS. Using CSS, a developer can assign a binding to an element by setting the -moz-binding property to a URI pointing to the XBL document.

Note Netscape has submitted a proposal to the W3C to define how to attach custom behavior to an HTML element in "A Modular Way of Defining Behavior for XML and HTML" (http://www.w3.org/TR/NOTE-AS).

Code Sample 4-12 illustrates a CSS file that attaches a binding to the <pro:welcome> element.

Code Sample 4-12. *A Sample CSS File That Has the* `-moz-binding` *Property Set*—`projsf.css`

```
@namespace pro url('http://projsf.apress.com/tags');

pro|welcome
{
  -moz-binding: url('projsf-bindings.xml#welcome');
}
```

In Code Sample 4-12, the selector has the `-moz-binding` set to point to an XBL file named `projsf-bindings.xml` and uses `#welcome` to refer to a specific binding in the XBL file. This is similar to how anchors are referenced in HTML files.

■ Note To provide a consistent sample tag throughout the chapter's samples, Code Sample 4-12 uses CSS3 standard syntax to simulate the sample element—`<pro:welcome>`.

If the binding `id` is omitted when assigned to an element, XUL will default to the first binding listed. In Code Sample 4-12, the `welcome` binding has been declared as the `id`, and the element that has been assigned this binding is `<pro:welcome>`.

In Code Sample 4-13, the `projsf-bindings.css` style sheet has been attached to the XUL document, and two elements (`<pro:welcome id="guest" />` and `<pro:welcome id="duke" name="Duke" />`) are inserted in the page. The first element displays a welcoming greeting for the specified user, "Duke". The second element displays the "Welcome, " string defined in the XBL file plus a default value user, "Guest". One of the cool features of using encapsulation of behavior, as provided by XBL, is that it creates a document tree within the scope of the custom component that is separate from the XUL page. What this means is that the content of the XBL component is not "exploded" into the main document, losing encapsulation. Figure 4-7 shows the DOM using a DOM inspector.

Code Sample 4-13. *A Sample HTML File with XUL Components*—`prototype-ch4.xul`

```
<?xml version="1.0"?>
<?xml-stylesheet href="chrome://global/skin/" type="text/css" ?>
<?xml-stylesheet href="projsf-bindings.css" type="text/css" ?>
<xul:window title="Pro JSF : Mozilla XBL" align="start"
      xmlns:xul="http://www.mozilla.org/keymaster/gatekeeper/there.is.only.xul"
      xmlns:pro="http://projsf.apress.com/tags" >
  <xul:groupbox>
    <xul:caption label="Greeting" />
    <pro:welcome id="duke" name="Duke" />
    <pro:welcome id="guest" />
  </xul:groupbox>
</xul:window>
```

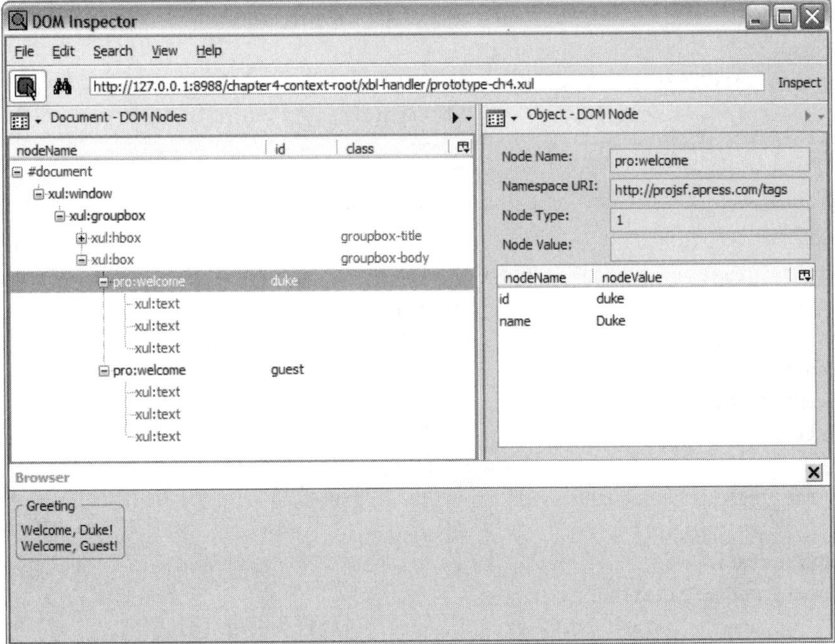

Figure 4-7. *A page's DOM tree with an XBL component*

The direct benefits of encapsulation are that the component author has full control over the behavior and look and feel and that the component is not exposing internal implementation details. In Figure 4-7, the nested `<xul:text>` elements are shown in the DOM inspector but never exposed in the actual main document.

Extending the XBL Bindings

Apart from creating a widget that is a collection of one or more XUL elements (as shown in the previous sections), you can also use XBL to add new properties and methods. XBL has three types of items that can be added to the binding—`fields`, `properties`, and `methods`:

- The `field` item is a simple container that can store a value, which can be retrieved and set.
- The `property` item is slightly more complex and is used to validate values stored in fields or values retrieved from XBL-defined element attributes. Since the `property` item cannot hold a value, you have no way to set a value directly on a `property` item without using the `onset` handler or the `onget` handler. Using these handlers, you can perform precalculation or validation of the value retrieved or modified.
- `Methods` are object functions, such as `window.open()`, that allow developers to add custom functions to custom elements.

In Code Sample 4-14, these three items are defined in an `<implementation>` element that is a child element of the `<binding>` element.

Code Sample 4-14. *Adding Properties and Methods—*pro-bindings.xml

```
<?xml version="1.0"?>
<xbl:bindings xmlns:xbl="http://www.mozilla.org/xbl"
      xmlns:xul="http://www.mozilla.org/keymaster/gatekeeper/there.is.only.xul"
      xmlns:html="http://www.w3.org/1999/xhtml" >

  <xbl:binding id="welcome" >
    <xbl:content>
      <xul:text id="greeting" value="Welcome, " />
      <xul:text value="Guest" xbl:inherits="value=name" />
      <xul:text value="!" />
    </xbl:content>
    <xbl:implementation>
      <xbl:constructor>
      <![CDATA[
        this._greetingNode = document.getElementById('greeting');
      ]]>
      </xbl:constructor>
      <xbl:property name="greeting"
                    onget="return this._greetingNode.getAttribute('value');"
                    onset="this._greetingNode.setAttribute('value', val);" />
    </xbl:implementation>
  </xbl:binding>
</xbl:bindings>
```

In Code Sample 4-14, you have added one method and one property. The method used in Code Sample 4-14 is a special method supported by XBL called constructor. A constructor is called whenever the binding is attached to an element. It is used to initialize the content such as loading preferences or setting the default values of fields. The property has been defined with an onget handler and an onset handler, which get and set the value attribute on your <pro:welcome> tag. To access these properties and call methods on the custom element, developers can use the getElementById() function. In Figure 4-8, a XUL button is added that triggers the oncommand event handler.

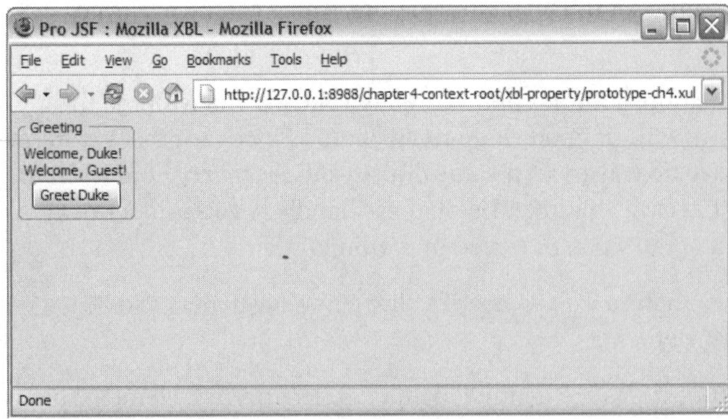

Figure 4-8. *A page using the welcome XBL component*

When the button Greet Duke is clicked, the text of the first `<pro:welcome>` tag changes and displays a new welcome message instead of the default message defined earlier in the `projsf-bindings.xml` file. Code Sample 4-15 shows the code behind this page.

Code Sample 4-15. *A Sample XUL File with XBL Components*—`prototype-ch4.xul`

```
<?xml version="1.0"?>
<?xml-stylesheet href="chrome://global/skin/" type="text/css" ?>
<?xml-stylesheet href="projsf-bindings.css" type="text/css" ?>
<xul:window title="Pro JSF : Mozilla XBL" align="start"
      xmlns:xul="http://www.mozilla.org/keymaster/gatekeeper/there.is.only.xul"
      xmlns:pro="http://projsf.apress.com/tags" >
  <xul:groupbox>
    <xul:caption label="Greeting" />
    <pro:welcome id="duke" name="Duke" />
    <pro:welcome id="guest" />
    <xul:button label="Greet Duke"
                oncommand="var duke = document.getElementById('duke');
                           duke.greeting = 'Howdy, ';" />
  </xul:groupbox>
</xul:window>
```

In Code Sample 4-15, a XUL button has been added that triggers the `oncommand` event handler. The `oncommand` event handler will execute the script encapsulated—`var duke = document.getElementById('duke'); duke.greeting = 'Howdy, ';`. This will set the value of the XUL element with the identifier greeting defined in your binding to "Howdy, " instead of the default greeting "Welcome, " causing Duke's greeting to change to "Howdy, Duke!" whereas the Guest greeting remains unchanged.

Event Handling and XBL Bindings

In XBL, developers can add event handlers directly to the XUL elements listed as children to the content element (for example, `<xul:button label="Press me!" oncommand= "alert('welcome')" />`). Sometimes developers need to add an event handler for all the child elements in the content element.

In XBL, you can do this by adding a `<handler>` element. The `<handler>` element is a child of the `<handlers>` element, and it can contain one or more event handlers. Each handler defines the action that will be taken for a particular event in the scope of the binding in which it is defined. If an event is not captured, it will just pass to the inner elements.

In Code Sample 4-15, you had a button and an event handler in the actual page source. Code Sample 4-16 shows how you can move this functionality into an XBL component.

Code Sample 4-16. *Adding Event Handlers*—`projsf-bindings.xml`

```
<?xml version="1.0"?>
<xbl:bindings xmlns:xbl="http://www.mozilla.org/xbl"
      xmlns:xul="http://www.mozilla.org/keymaster/gatekeeper/there.is.only.xul"
      xmlns:html="http://www.w3.org/1999/xhtml" >

  <xbl:binding id="welcome" >
    <xbl:content>
```

```
      <xul:text value="Welcome, " />
      <xul:text value="Guest" xbl:inherits="value=name" />
      <xul:text value="!" />
    </xbl:content>
    <xbl:handlers>
      <xbl:handler event="click" >
        if (this.hasAttribute('name'))
          alert('Nice to see you again, ' + this.getAttribute('name') + '.');
      </xbl:handler>
    </xbl:handlers>
  </xbl:binding>
</xbl:bindings>
```

In Code Sample 4-16, one handler has been added to capture all click events in the context of the welcome binding. The handler will display an alert only if the attribute name has been set on the <pro:welcome> tag. You now have a simple but well-defined and encapsulated XUL component. Code Sample 4-17 shows a simple XUL page that is using this new <pro:welcome> tag.

Code Sample 4-17. *A Simple XUL Page Using an XBL Binding with Attached Event Handler*

```
<?xml version="1.0"?>
<?xml-stylesheet href="chrome://global/skin/" type="text/css" ?>
<?xml-stylesheet href="projsf-bindings.css" type="text/css" ?>
<xul:window align="start"
      xmlns:xul="http://www.mozilla.org/keymaster/gatekeeper/there.is.only.xul"
      xmlns:pro="http://projsf.apress.com/tags" >
  <xul:groupbox>
    <xul:caption label="Greeting" />
    <pro:welcome id="duke" name="Duke" />
    <pro:welcome id="guest" />
  </xul:groupbox>
</xul:window>
```

In this page only one <pro:welcome> tag has the name attribute defined. So, when the page is launched in a browser (a Mozilla GRE-compliant browser), the click event will launch an alert only when the "Welcome, Duke!" text is clicked, as shown in Figure 4-9.

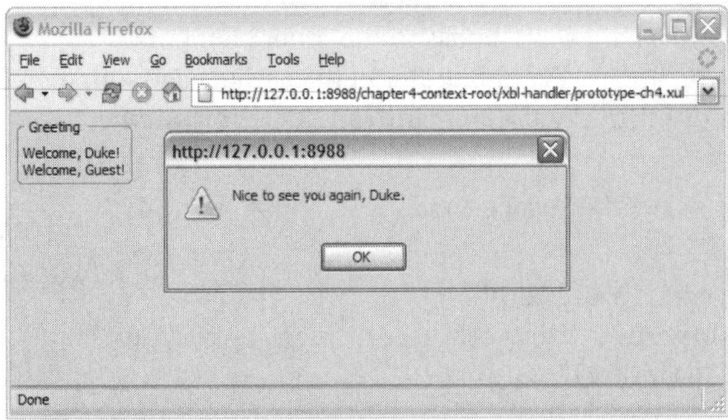

Figure 4-9. *Simple XUL page using a custom XBL binding with attached event handler*

XUL Summary

After reading the previous sections, you should understand the relationship between XUL and XBL. You should also know how to create custom XUL components using XBL and how to use them in the context of building XUL applications. In the next chapters, you will see how to build a new `RenderKit` for your JSF components by leveraging the component model provided by XUL and XBL.

Introducing Microsoft Dynamic HTML and HTC

In your continuing quest for a rich Internet component framework, the focus of this chapter now switches to Microsoft's offering. Microsoft has a similar offering to the Mozilla XUL technology through DHTML and HTC. These technologies rely on an underlying platform (in other words, Internet Explorer) to provide a foundation for extending HTML elements.

Applications built with these Microsoft technologies are deployed and downloaded from the Web. Microsoft's DHTML is designed to deliver an easy markup for building rich Internet applications.

When building applications with DHTML, developers will use regular HTML pages to describe their Web application but with the ability to dynamically change the rendering and content of the HTML page. HTC files can create reusable components that encapsulate dynamic behaviors, much the same way as XBL works for XUL. The following sections will give you an overview of Microsoft's DHTML solution and show how you can build reusable components with HTC.

WHY HTC AND NOT XAML?

Several reasons exist for not selecting XAML. One reason is that XAML requires .NET 2.0/Avalon, which ships with Microsoft's Vista release and is scheduled to be released at the end of 2006. Another project, XAMLON, provides a preview implementation of Avalon, which is the runtime engine needed to build XAML applications. This implementation provides an early look at XAML-like technologies on a .NET 1.1 runtime. The XAMLON preview implementation of XAML has two main drawbacks. First, it requires a .NET 1.1 runtime plug-in for Internet Explorer. Second, it does not integrate (well) with HTML pages. If you wanted to have a plug-in, you would use something that is established and can work cross-platform, such as Macromedia Flash, and be done.

HTC Structure

DHTML was introduced in Internet Explorer 5.0 and was Microsoft's first attempt to supply a medium in which to build RIAs. DHTML made it possible to transform the behavior of standard HTML elements by using the `behavior` attribute of a CSS entry or by using the `addBehavior` method in script.

■ **Note** Microsoft has submitted a proposal to add and extend HTML elements, using CSS as the bridge. This proposal is based on Microsoft's solution to add behavior to HTML, which is similar to the XUL solution. The proposal has been sent to the W3C and is named "Componentizing Web Applications" (`http://www.w3.org/ TR/1998/NOTE-HTMLComponents-19981023`), in collaboration with Netscape to define how to best add behavior and extend HTML elements—see "Behavioral Extensions to CSS" at `http://www.w3.org/TR/1999/WD-becss-19990804`.

HTC, as noted previously, provides a means of packaging dynamic behavior into a separate document. With DHTML and HTC, Microsoft has taken the approach of extending the HTML markup rather than coming up with yet another markup for RIAs. The fact that HTC leverages the HTML markup means you can focus purely on HTC, since HTML markup should be familiar to developers reading this book.

HTC File Structure and Elements

Plainly put, HTC is just an HTML page with the file extension `.htc`. The file shown in Code Sample 4-18 contains a set of HTC-specific elements, such as `<public:property>`, `<public:event>`, and `<public:method>`, that list properties, events, and methods that define the HTC component.

Code Sample 4-18. *HTC File Structure*

```
<html>
  <head>
    <public:component>
      <public:property ... />
      <public:event ... />
      <public:method ... />
      ...
    </public:component>
    <script language=" ">
      ...
    </script>
  </head>
  <body>
    ...
  </body>
</html>
```

The `<public:component>` is used to define two behavior types—element behavior and attached behavior. Code Sample 4-19 illustrates an attached behavior, which will modify an existing element by setting the color to green. The `<public:attach>` element couples an event raised on the client with an underlying function. In Code Sample 4-19 the function `onColor()` is attached to the `mouseover` event.

Code Sample 4-19. *A Simple HTC File*

```
<html>
  <head>
    <public:component>
      <public:attach event="onmouseover" onevent="onColors()" />
    </public:component>
    <script>
      function onColors()
      {
        runtimeStyle.color = "green";
      }
    </script>
  </head>
  <body>
  </body>
</html>
```

HTC comes with a set of public elements that can be used to define the component. Table 4-5 describes a subset of the available predefined elements.

Table 4-5. *HTC Public Elements**

Name	Description
COMPONENT	Identifies the content of the file as an HTC
PROPERTY	Defines a property of the HTC to be exposed to the containing document
DEFAULT	Sets default properties for an HTC
ATTACH	Binds a function to an event so that the function is called whenever the event fires on the specified object
METHOD	Defines a method of the HTC to be exposed to the containing document
EVENT	Defines an event of the HTC to be exposed to the containing document

* *Source: Microsoft MSDN* (`http://msdn.microsoft.com/workshop/author/behaviors/behaviors_node_entry.asp`)

Event Handling and HTC

Microsoft's implementation of the DOM is not standard, but it provides an implementation that is similar to DOM Level 2 event handling that includes, for example, event bubbling and cancellations. The following scripting languages are supported by HTC: Visual Basic Scripting Edition (VBScript), Microsoft JScript, JavaScript, and third-party scripting languages that support the Microsoft ActiveX Scripting interfaces.

Scripts are encapsulated in `<script>` elements the same way as in a regular HTML page. From these scripts, developers can access each HTC element as a script object, using the value of the HTC element's id attribute as the name of the script variable. This allows all attributes and methods of HTC elements to be dynamically modified as properties and methods of these objects.

In the DHTML object model, developers can declare an event handler function and assign a call to that function or do the reverse and declare event handling code to associate the function with the event.

A developer can assign a call to a function with HTC in three ways. Code Sample 4-20 and Code Sample 4-21 illustrate traditional HTML and JavaScript assignments, and Code Sample 4-22 illustrates an alternative solution in HTC.

Code Sample 4-20. *Assigning a Call to Function*

```
<script>
function onColor()
{
  ...
}
</script>
  ...
<input type="button" value="Press me!" onclick="onColor();" />
```

In Code Sample 4-20 the assignment has been done by the actual button using the `onclick` event handler. Code Sample 4-21 assigns the function in the `<script>` element to the `proButton` button.

Code Sample 4-21. *Associating Function with an Event*

```
<script for="proButton" event="onclick" >
function onColor()
{
  ...
}
</script>
  ...
<input id="proButton" type="button" value="Press me!" />
```

Developers can also use the `<public:attach>` element to associate an event globally in the component and assign it to a function, as shown in Code Sample 4-22.

Code Sample 4-22. *A Globally Assigned Event Handler*

```
<public:attach event="onclick" onevent="onColors()" />
```

This event handler will fire on all click events within this component.

Building DHTML Applications

In 1999, Netscape and Microsoft made a submission to the W3C to add behavioral extensions to the CSS specification. These proposals have not yet been rolled into the CSS standard (and are still a working draft for CSS 3), so Microsoft and Mozilla have implemented their own proposed solutions to add behavior to an HTML element—Microsoft via HTC and Mozilla via XBL. When Microsoft introduced the concept of DHTML with Internet Explorer 5.0, it used CSS to attach a behavior directly to an existing HTML element. This way of attaching behavior to an HTML element is referred to as an *attached behavior* and can be changed programmatically.

With the release of Internet Explorer 5.5, Microsoft introduced something called *element behavior*. With element behavior, developers can build custom components that can be used the same way as regular HTML elements but with the ability to add richer functionality via script. The default way of defining element behaviors is by using HTC files. It is important to not confuse the DHTML behavior—attached behavior—introduced in Internet Explorer 5.0 with element behaviors. Element behavior uses a different approach to bind to elements and has other distinctive characteristics.

Looking at the HTC solution, the element behavior is applied to a bound element using the `import` processing instruction. The `import` processing instruction imports a tag definition from an element behavior. Code Sample 4-23 illustrates how a behavior is bound to an element using this instruction.

Code Sample 4-23. *A Simple HTML File with Attached Behavior*

```
<!DOCTYPE HTML PUBLIC "-//W3C//DTD HTML 4.01 Transitional//EN" >
<html xmlns:pro >
  <?import namespace="pro" implementation="pro.htc" ?>
  <head>
    <title>Pro JSF : Microsoft HTC</title>
  </head>
  <body>
    <div><pro:welcome name="Duke" /></div>
    <div><pro:welcome/></div>
  </body>
</html>
```

An element behavior defines a custom tag, which can be used in a Web page like a standard HTML tag. By setting the `tagName` attribute on the `<public:component>` element, developers can turn an HTC file into a custom tag. The `<?import namespace="pro" implementation="pro.htc" ?>` element imports the `pro.htc` implementation and sets the identifier or prefix for the custom tags provided in the `.htc` file to the declared namespace—`pro`.

As shown in Code Sample 4-24, the `tagName` attribute specifies the name of the custom tag, which is defined in the HTC file.

Code Sample 4-24. *Defining Element Behavior*

```
<html>
  <head>
    <public:component tagName="welcome" >
      <public:property name="name" value="Guest" />
      <public:attach event="oncontentready" handler="_constructor" />
    </public:component>

    <script type="text/javascript" >
      function _constuctor()
      {
```

```
        nameSpan.innerText = element.name;
      }
    </script>
  </head>
  <body>
    Welcome, <span id="nameSpan"
               onclick="if (element.name != 'Guest')
                        {
                          alert('Nice to see you again, ' + element.name);
                        }" ></span>!
  </body>
</html>
```

Figure 4-10 shows the page running in the Internet Explorer, and you can see that it is only when the user clicks on Duke's greeting that the additional message is displayed.

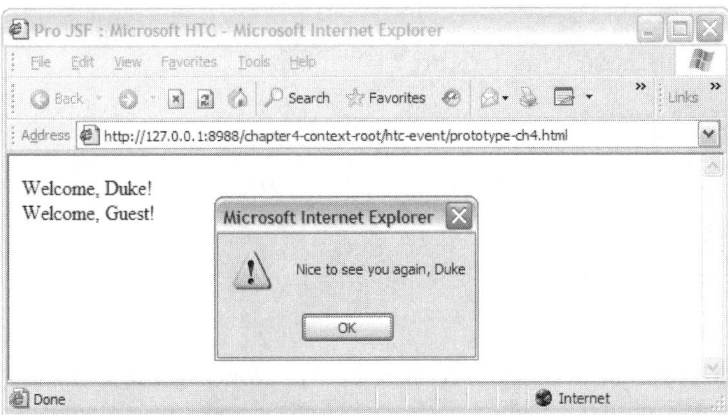

Figure 4-10. *A page using the welcome HTC component*

Importing HTC element behavior into an HTML page makes the custom element a first-class member in the DOM hierarchy and the element behavior permanently bound to the custom element. One of the key differentiators between element behavior and attached behavior is that an attached behavior is asynchronously bound to an element, allowing it to be attached and detached programmatically, whereas the element behavior is bound synchronously to a custom element, is seen as a regular HTML element, and cannot be detached from its custom element.

Component Encapsulation

When using HTC, developers can encapsulate a document tree within the HTC component, or they can decide to explode the content into the HTML page and as such expose internal implementations. In HTC, you can encapsulate a DOM tree inside the HTC component by setting the HTC declaration `<public:defaults>` to `<public:defaults viewLinkContent>`. By default, document fragments that are part of an HTC file are exploded into the HTML page, so developers will have to manually set the `viewlink` property on the `defaults` declaration.

Browser performance of the initial page parse should be faster with the property `viewlink` set on the `<public:defaults>` declaration (no exploding), but general interaction with the component might be a little slower because of the indirection. We recommend using the `viewlink` property if the interactivity performance is acceptable, since it allows for encapsulation and attendant benefits.

In Code Sample 4-25, `viewLinkContent` has been added to the `defaults` declaration, and as such the content of the `welcome` component will not be exploded into the main HTML page.

Code Sample 4-25. *HTC File with* `viewlink` *Set*

```
<html>
  <head>
    <public:component tagName="welcome" >
      <public:defaults viewlinkcontent="true" />
      <public:property name="name" value="Guest" />
      <public:attach event="oncontentready" handler="_constuctor" />
    </public:component>

    <script type="text/javascript" >
      function _constuctor()
      {
        nameSpan.innerText = element.name;
      }
    </script>
  </head>
  <body>
     Welcome, <span id="nameSpan"
                onclick="if (element.name != 'Guest')
                         {
                           alert('Nice to see you again, ' + element.name);
                         }" ></span>!
  </body>
</html>
```

Note Deploying Microsoft DHTML applications has no specific requirements except the dependency on Microsoft's browser Internet Explorer 5.0 and above.

HTC Summary

As with XUL, HTC comes with a well-defined component model allowing application developers to encapsulate behavior into a reusable entity. From the previous sections about Microsoft's DHTML and HTC, you now know about the HTC structure and about elements and event handling. You know the difference between element behavior and attached behavior. Later in this book (see Chapter 9), you will leverage this knowledge to build a set of `Renderers` for your JSF components that support HTC.

Comparing XBL and HTC

The lesson learned so far is that several technologies provide almost identical functionality although they are implemented completely differently. If you look at the semantics of XBL and HTC, you will see many similarities:

- Both use CSS to attach components or behavior to an HTML element.
- Both provide encapsulation of a document tree within the component, not exposing internal implementation details.
- Both depend on the underlying browser platform.

The critical differences are as follow:

- XBL is based on XML, whereas HTC is based on HTML.
- They support different platforms—XBL needs Mozilla GRE, and HTC needs Microsoft's Internet Explorer.

If you compare the pieces essential to creating a component and using it, they will fall into these categories—defining a component, implementing event handling, adding content, and attaching the component to the page.

Defining a Component

Although the two are similar, the way they define a component is different. In HTC the rule is one component per HTC file, whereas in XBL the recommendation is to have all related custom components in one file. This impacts how to define the component. In the HTC case, a developer sets the `tagName` attribute on `<public:component tagName="welcome" >` to specify the name of the tag for that particular HTC component.

In the XBL file, the binding ID will identify the component to be used with a specific element—`<binding id="welcome" >`. The element is then defined in a CSS file by using an anchor to couple the element to the right XBL binding/component.

Adding Content

In HTC the component content is encapsulated in the `<body>` element, and in XBL the content is encapsulated in the `<content>` element.

Event Handling

The two technologies both support DOM, although, once again, with some slight differences. XBL supports DOM Level 2 (and some Level 3), and HTC supports only DOM Level 1 and as such supports only bubbling of events and cancellation, not capturing or at target. (This is because no new version of Internet Explorer has been released over the past four years.)

■ **Note** The current version of Internet Explorer is 6.0. Microsoft is currently working on version 7.0 of its browser Internet Explorer, which is code-named Rincon. When it finally hits the shelves, it will be more than four years since the last release.

If you look at how event handling takes place in HTC and XBL, you will see some more distinct differences:

- HTC has three different approaches to event handling—a developer can use `<public:attach>` to declare a global event handler for the component, define a function using the HTML element `<script for="proButton" event="onclick">`, assign it to a specific element and event, and finally declare an event handler function and assign a call to that function (for example, `onclick="proButton()"`).
- XBL has two ways of defining event handlers—one is using a predefined event handler such as `onclick` or `onmouseover` on an element, and the other is defining an event handler globally for the component using the `<handler>` element. To add custom methods, a developer can use the `<method>` element to define a custom event handler for the component.

Attaching Components

Both technologies leverage CSS to attach behavior to an element. Attaching a component to the HTML page using XBL, developers have to use the `-moz-binding: url()` attribute; using HTC they have to use the `behavior: url()` attribute. Both of these approaches seem comparable, but the end result is poles apart. In XBL the style class name (for example, `pro\:welcome`) will become the tag `<pro:welcome>` and be interpreted as a first class element in the DOM tree, obscuring any internal implementations.

With HTC it is different, since the CSS approach is used to attach a behavior to an already existing HTML element (for example, `H1 {behavior:url(projsf.htc)}`) that is not declaring a first-class element in the DOM, and therefore it will expose internal implementations of that component. To create a first-class element, developers have to use the `<?import namespace="pro" implementation="pro.htc" ?>` element and the namespace `<html xmlns:pro >` to uniquely identify the imported component, and as mentioned earlier, the name of the tag is declared in the HTC file using the `tagName` attribute.

JSF—The Greatest Thing Since Sliced Bread!

Of the technologies described in this chapter, it is only XUL and HTC that allow developers to reuse components in Web applications. They allow the encapsulation of HTML, CSS, and script into components that application developers can reuse. Ajax, on the other hand, delivers asynchronous communication to the server that can be used to provide users with a responsive UI.

These technologies solve most of the requirements coming from consumers, but they are still lacking in support for the application developer.

What the market needs is a standard way of defining an RIA that can be deployed over the Web without vendor lock-in. A working group, called Web Hypertext Applications Technology (WHAT), is trying to create a standard tag library for extensions to HTML that work across all browsers by leveraging technologies such as Mozilla's XBL to achieve this. Technologies such as Mozilla's XBL allow for encapsulation of HTML, CSS, and script into components that application developers can reuse but that are not standards.

Note The WHAT working group (`http://www.whatwg.org/`) is addressing the need for a sound and rational development environment extending the standard HTML elements. This will take place through a set of technical specifications that can be used and implemented in Web browsers such as Firefox, Mozilla, and Internet Explorer.

Meanwhile, developers are falling back to the lowest common denominator—HTML—and using technologies such as Ajax to build dynamic Web applications. This approach of developing Web applications has one severe drawback—it has no good reuse model. Currently, this approach has no standard way for a developer to define reusable and easy-to-integrate HTML components that have rich functionality with existing server-side logic. Currently developers use JSP tag libraries to create reusable HTML components that access server-side logic, but this is still low-level and cumbersome.

What is needed is a standard that can encapsulate these RITs using components instead of markup in an effective model that allows application developers to build Web applications with prefabricated blocks of functionality without concern for implementation details. Prefabricated blocks, or components, allow application developers to build complex applications with reusable components. This also allows application developers to focus on the actual application structure rather than building the actual dynamic functionality themselves.

JSF is all about these kinds of reusable components!

Cross-Platform Support

An important aspect that developers and their managers need to take into account when building applications is cross-platform support. Consumer requirements are increasingly supporting handheld devices, Telnet clients, desktops, and so on. For developers with complete control over the consumer base and infrastructure, this may not be important, but in most cases it is.

Initially the term *cross-platform* meant the operating system the application runs on (for example, Windows, Linux, Mac OS, Unix, and so on), but the advancement of Internet-enabled devices means the cross-platform support matrix has become far more complex. Several cross-platform solutions such as Java are available.

In most cases, applications need to be designed to use features of a specific platform, which in turn is time-consuming and costly. For a developer to fully support an application on only one platform requires lengthy lifecycles for compiling and debugging. Adding more platforms to the mix, the time spent on developing a cross-platform application can grow exponentially.

For the technologies used in this chapter—Ajax, XUL, and HTC—Mozilla's XUL claims that it has cross-platform support. That is partially true; you can deploy a XUL application to any operating system that the Mozilla platform (GRE) supports.

Note XBL is already available for Firefox on the Mac, and it is coming to Safari 1.3/2.0.

You could also argue that Ajax provides cross-platform support, but it is the provider of the Ajax solution that needs to ensure that every browser-specific quirk is supported. So, although you have plenty of environments to deploy to, no true solution has full cross-platform support.

Imagination As the Only Limit

JSF standardizes the server side for the application developer, but you still have to wait for the presentation layer in the browser to standardize for component developers. JSF brings platform independence to the application developer by separating the user interface from the application, which makes it possible for the component author to change the presentation layer without tampering with the application.

This is not solving the browser inconsistency issue, the maintenance difficulties, or the cross-platform issue of the previously mentioned technologies, but it will help application developers build RIAs in a standard way.

The three technologies described in this chapter—Ajax, XUL, and HTC—have their advantages and drawbacks, so wouldn't it be great if you could combine the advantages into one reusable standard component?

A JSF component developer can use XUL or HTC for presentation and Ajax for communication and then dynamically fall back to a traditional HTML solution if the client does not support any of the three technologies. The application developer will be able to build one application supporting multiple rendering technologies with one common programming model—JSP and Java.

A JSF Application Supporting Ajax, XUL, and HTC

To finish this chapter and map back to the previously covered technologies, the JSF sample shown in Figure 4-11 illustrates a page containing your JSF input date component. In later chapters, you will implement the support shown in this section. This version of your component has been extended to include a pop-up calendar from which the user can pick a date. This improved component leverages Ajax for communication and XUL and HTC as rendering technologies.

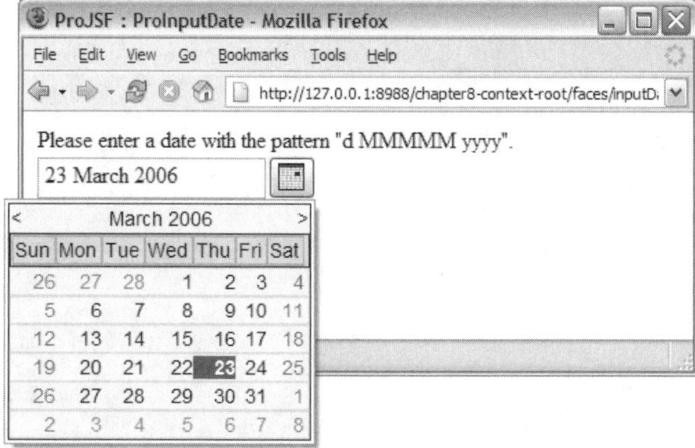

Figure 4-11. *A page built with JSF components using XUL as the rendering technology*

Figure 4-11 shows a JSF page—`inputDate.jspx`—that contains your `ProInputDate` component, which is rendering XUL content to the Mozilla Firefox browser.

Figure 4-12 shows the same page—`inputDate.jspx`—running in Internet Explorer. The interesting part with this simple application is that you are using the best rendering technology for each browser, and although not visible, the `ProInputDate` component is using Ajax to asynchronously communicate with the server to receive dates that are selectable.

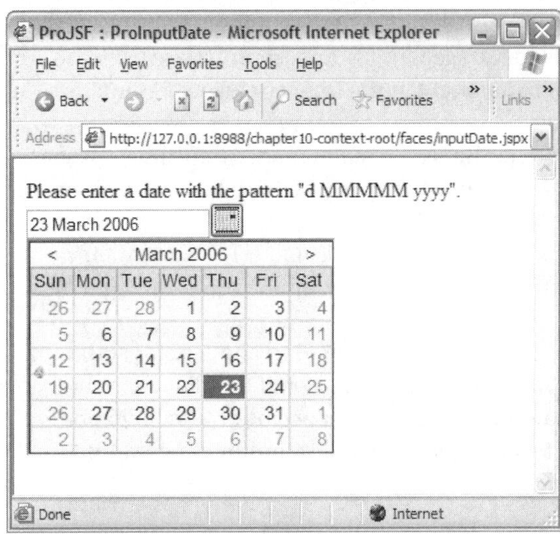

Figure 4-12. *The same page in Internet Explorer using HTC as the rendering technology*

The source of the page (see Code Sample 4-26) is not that different from what you have seen with XUL and HTC, but the main difference is that the application developer will not need to learn two, or even three, ways of supporting RIAs in today's browsers.

Code Sample 4-26. *JSF Page Matching the XUL and HTC Samples*

```
<?xml version="1.0" encoding="UTF-8" ?>
<jsp:root xmlns:jsp="http://java.sun.com/JSP/Page" version="1.2"
          xmlns:pro="http://projsf.apress.com/tags"
          xmlns:f="http://java.sun.com/jsf/core"
          xmlns:h="http://java.sun.com/jsf/html" >
  <jsp:directive.page contentType="application/x-javaserver-faces" />
  <f:view>
    <pro:document title="ProJSF : ProInputDate" >
      <h:form>
        Please enter a date with the pattern "d MMMMM yyyy".
        <br/>
        <pro:inputDate id="dateField"
                       title="Date Field Component"
                       value="#{inputDateBean.date}" >
```

```
        <f:convertDateTime pattern="d MMMMM yyyy" />
        <pro:validateDate availability="#{inputDateBean.getAvailability}" />
      </pro:inputDate>
      <br/>
      <h:message for="theDate" />
      <br/>
      <h:commandButton value="Submit" />
      <br/>
      <h:outputText value="#{inputDateBean.date}" >
        <f:convertDateTime pattern="d MMMMM yyyy" />
      </h:outputText>
    </h:form>
  </pro:document>
</f:view>
</jsp:root>
```

Apart from the obvious namespaces, the sample contains one namespace that maps to a custom component library (`xmlns:pro="http://projsf.apress.com/tags"`) and a custom component (`<pro:inputDate ..."/>`). Be patient—you will see the actual JSF implementation in the coming chapters.

Summary

This chapter gave you some insight into three of the market's leading view technologies for RIAs: XUL, HTC, and Ajax. These technologies have proven they are more than capable of providing users with rich and responsive interfaces. The chapter also touched on the issues with these technologies such as lack of standards, platform support, and maintenance.

Looking ahead, the potential for JSF as a technology is unlimited. Component developers can provide the community with a wide range of components supporting technologies from HTML to XUL, including wireless and even character-based solutions; your imagination is the only limit.

The chapter showed how to build reusable components with XBL and HTC, as well as how to implement event handling, how to implement encapsulation, and how to embed custom components in a page using the supported implementations (CSS and `import`) provided by the different technologies. You also gained knowledge about Ajax and its key player, the `XMLHttpRequest` object. For more information about these technologies, please visit the Mozilla Web site (`http://www.mozilla.org`), the Microsoft MSDN Web site (`http://msdn.microsoft.com/`), and Wikipedia.org (`http://en.wikipedia.org/wiki/AJAX`).

CHAPTER 5

Loading Resources with Weblets

If we have learned one thing from the history of invention and discovery, it is that in the long run—and often in the short one—the most daring prophecies seem laughably conservative.

—Arthur C. Clarke (1917–), *The Exploration of Space*, 1951

Web applications often use many different resource files, such as images, style sheets, or scripts, to improve the presentation and interactivity of the user interface. JSF component libraries that want to render attractive user interfaces will also leverage resource files.

The standard approach to providing resource files for a JSF component library is to serve them directly from the Web application root file system. These resources are usually packaged in an archive (such as a ZIP file) and are shipped separately from the JSF component library.

This chapter will introduce a new open source project—Weblets. The goal of this project (located at `http://weblets.dev.java.net`) is to provide component writers with the ability to serve resource files from a Java archive (JAR), rather than serving them from the Web application root file system. Unlike traditional Web applications, which have statically configured URL mappings defined in `web.xml`, JSF applications need dynamically configured URL mappings, based on the presence of a component library JAR file.

After reading this chapter, you should understand what weblets are, how resource loading with weblets works, and how to leverage weblets in your own JSF component library. We will show how to package the resources for a custom JSF component library to ensure you provide application developers with an easy way of successfully installing your custom JSF component library, including any resources needed by your component library.

Introducing Resource Loading

As you may remember from Chapters 2 and 3, we created two components—`ProShowOneDeck` and `ProInputDate`—that need resources served to the client. We will use both components in this chapter to illustrate how to use weblets.

For this example, the `HtmlShowOneDeckRenderer` component uses a JavaScript file, `showOneDeck.js`, to expand a `UIShowItem` when a user clicks the rendered component. As described in Chapter 3, this JavaScript file is traditionally served by the Web application via a relative path that is hard-coded into the actual `HtmlShowOneDeckRenderer` code. This requires the application developer to deploy additional resources that are delivered and packaged in a separate archive file (for example, a ZIP file), often referred to as an *installables* archive.

Note The JSF HTML Basic `RenderKit` does not have any images, styles, or scripts, so no standard solution exists for the JSF resource-packaging problem.

Code Sample 5-1 shows the `encodeResources()` method from the `HtmlShowOneDeckRenderer` class, which illustrates that the installable JavaScript resource files—`/projsf-ch3/showOneDeck.js` and `/projsf-ch3/showOneDeck.css`—are served from the Web application root file system.

Code Sample 5-1. *The* `encodeResources()` *Method in the* `HtmlShowOneDeckRenderer` *Code*

```
/**
* Write out the ProShowOneDeck resources.
*
* @param context    the Faces context
* @param component  the Faces component
*/
protected void encodeResources(
  FacesContext context,
  UIComponent  component) throws IOException
{
  writeScriptResource(context, "/projsf-ch3/showOneDeck.js");
  writeStyleResource(context, "/projsf-ch3/showOneDeck.css");
}
```

Although the installable approach is convenient for the JSF component writer, it increases the installation burden on the application developer, who must remember to extract the installables archive each time the component library is upgraded to a new version. Therefore, you need a way to package the additional resources into the same JAR file that contains the `Renderer` classes, thus simplifying deployment for application developers using your component library.

Using Existing Solutions

Some of the more advanced JSF component libraries available today, such as Apache MyFaces and Oracle ADF Faces, provide a custom servlet or filter solution for serving the resources needed by their specific renderers. However, each component library tends to solve the same problem in a slightly different way. The lack of any official standard solution therefore leads to an additional configuration and installation burden for each component library.

Using Weblets

The open source Weblets project aims to solve the resource-packaging problem in a generic and extensible way so that all JSF component writers can leverage it, and it places no additional installation burden on the application developer.

A *weblet* acts as a mediator that intercepts requests from the client and uses short URLs to serve resources from a JAR file. Unlike the servlet or filter approach, a weblet can be registered and configured inside a JAR file, so the component library Renderers, their resource files, and the weblet configuration file (weblets-config.xml) can all be packaged together in the same JAR file. You do not need to separately deploy additional installables when the component libraries are upgraded to new versions. For the application developer, no configuration steps are needed.

It is important to note that all resources served up by weblets are *internal* resources, used only by the Renderer. Any resources, such as images, that are provided by the application are supplied as component attribute values and loaded from the context root as *external* resources.

Exploring the Weblet Architecture

Although weblets were designed to be used by any Web client, the weblet implementation has been integrated with JSF using a custom ViewHandler, called WebletsViewHandler, as shown in Figure 5-1. During the rendering of the main JSF page, the WebletsViewHandler is responsible for converting weblet-specific resource URLs into the actual URLs used by a browser to request weblet-managed resources.

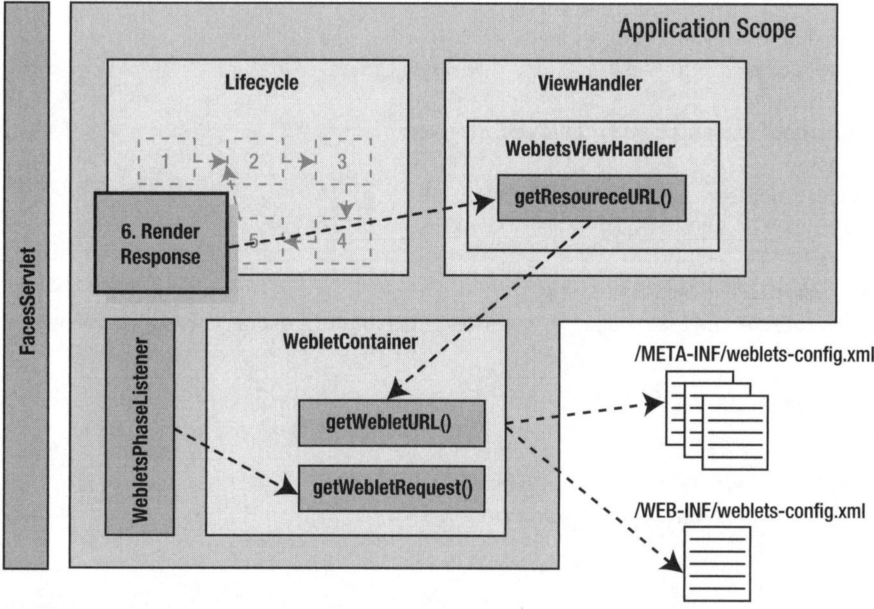

Figure 5-1. *High-level overview of weblet architecture*

After receiving the rendered markup for the main page, the browser downloads each additional resource using a separate request. Each request for a weblet-managed resource is intercepted by the `WebletsPhaseListener`, which then asks the `WebletContainer` to stream the weblet-managed resource file from the component library JAR file.

The weblet container is designed to leverage the browser cache where possible. This improves the overall rendering performance by minimizing the total number of requests made for weblet-managed resource files.

To ensure flexibility, ensure optimization, and avoid collisions with existing web application resources, application developers can configure weblets to override any default settings provided by the component writer.

Using Weblets in Your Component Library

You can configure weblets using a `weblets-config.xml` file, which must be stored in the `/META-INF` directory of the component library JAR file. Configuring a weblet is similar to configuring a servlet or a filter. Each weblet entry in the `weblets-config.xml` file has a weblet name, an implementation class, and initialization parameters. The weblet mapping associates a particular URL pattern with a specific weblet name, such as `com.apress.projsf.ch5`. The weblet name and default URL pattern define the public API for the weblet-managed resources and should not be modified between releases of the component library in order to maintain backward compatibility.

As shown in Code Sample 5-2, the example component library packages resources in the `com.apress.projsf.ch5.renderer.html.basic.resources` Java package and makes them available to the browser using the default URL mapping of `/projsf-ch5/*`.

Code Sample 5-2. *Weblets Configuration File—*`weblets-config.xml`

```
<?xml version="1.0" encoding="UTF-8" ?>
<weblets-config xmlns="http://weblets.dev.java.net/config" >
  <weblet>
   <weblet-name>com.apress.projsf.ch5</weblet-name>
   <weblet-class>
     net.java.dev.weblets.packaged.PackagedWeblet
   </weblet-class>
    <init-param>
      <param-name>package</param-name>
      <param-value>com.apress.projsf.ch5.render.html.basic.resources</param-value>
    </init-param>
  </weblet>

  <weblet-mapping>
    <weblet-name>com.apress.projsf.ch5</weblet-name>
    <url-pattern>/projsf-ch5/*</url-pattern>
  </weblet-mapping>
</weblets-config>
```

The `PackagedWeblet` is a built-in weblet implementation that can read from a particular Java package using the `ClassLoader` and then stream the result to the browser. The package initialization parameter tells the PackagedWeblet which Java package to use as a root when resolving weblet-managed resource requests.

Specifying Weblet MIME Types

When weblets are used to serve a JSF component resource file, it is important that the browser is correctly informed of the corresponding MIME type so the resource file can be processed correctly. By default, weblets have built-in knowledge of many common MIME types, such as text/plain, for common filename extensions, such as .txt. However, in some cases, a JSF component might need to package resources that either are not previously known by weblets or must be served using a different extension, preventing weblets from automatically recognizing the correct MIME type to use.

Code Sample 5-3 shows how to define a custom MIME type mapping for resources served by a weblet.

Code Sample 5-3. *Weblets Configuration File Defining a Custom MIME Type*

```
<?xml version="1.0" encoding="UTF-8" ?>
<weblets-config xmlns="http://weblets.dev.java.net/config" >
  <weblet>
   <weblet-name>com.apress.projsf.ch5</weblet-name>
   <weblet-class>
     net.java.dev.weblets.packaged.PackagedWeblet
   </weblet-class>
    <init-param>
      <param-name>package</param-name>
      <param-value>com.apress.projsf.ch5.render.html.basic.resources</param-value>
    </init-param>
    <mime-mapping>
      <extension>htc</extension>
      <mime-type>text/x-component</mime-type>
    </mime-mapping>
  </weblet>

  <weblet-mapping>
    <weblet-name>com.apress.projsf.ch5</weblet-name>
    <url-pattern>/projsf-ch5/*</url-pattern>
  </weblet-mapping>
</weblets-config>
```

Code Sample 5-3 defines a custom MIME type mapping of text/x-component for all resources with the .htc extension served by this weblet.

Specifying Weblet Versioning

Weblets also has built-in support for versioning of the component library. This allows the browser to cache packaged resources such as showOneDeck.js when possible, preventing unnecessary round-trips to the web server.

Each time the browser renders a page, the browser ensures that all resources used by that page are available. During the initial rendering of the page, the browser populates its cache with the contents of each resource URL by downloading a fresh copy from the Web server. As it does so, the browser records the `Last-Modified` and `Expires` time stamps from the response headers. The cached content is said to have expired if the current time is later than the expiration time stamp or if no expiration time stamp information exists.

On the next render of the same page, the browser checks to see whether the locally cached resource has expired. The locally cached copy is reused if it has not expired. Otherwise, a new request is made to the web server, including the last-modified information in the `If-Modified-Since` request header. The web server responds either by indicating that the browser cache is still up-to-date or by streaming the new resource contents to the browser with updated `Last-Modified` and `Expires` time stamps in the response headers.

Weblets use versioning to leverage the browser cache behavior so that packaged resources can be downloaded and cached as efficiently as possible. The browser needs to check for new updates only when the cache has been emptied or when the component library has been upgraded at the web server.

Code Sample 5-4 illustrates this versioning feature by adding a `1.0` version to the `com.apress.projsf.ch5` weblet.

Code Sample 5-4. *Weblets Configuration File Using* `1.0` *Versioning for Production*

```
<?xml version="1.0" encoding="UTF-8" ?>
<weblets-config xmlns="http://weblets.dev.java.net/config" >
  <weblet>
    <weblet-name>com.apress.projsf.ch5</weblet-name>
    <weblet-class>net.java.dev.weblets.packaged.PackagedWeblet</weblet-class>
    <weblet-version>1.0</weblet-version>
    <init-param>
      <param-name>package</param-name>
      <param-value>com.apress.projsf.ch5.render.html.basic.resources</param-value>
    </init-param>
  </weblet>

  <weblet-mapping>
    <weblet-name>com.apress.projsf.ch5</weblet-name>
    <url-pattern>/projsf-ch5/*</url-pattern>
  </weblet-mapping>
</weblets-config>
```

By specifying a weblet version, you indicate that the packaged resource will not change until the version number changes. Therefore, the version number is included as part of the resource URL determined at runtime by the `WebletsViewHandler` (for example, `/projsf-ch5$1.0/showOneDeck.js`). When the `WebletContainer` services this request, it extracts the version number from the URL and determines that the resource should be cached and should never expire. As soon as a new version of the component library is deployed to the web application, the resource URL created at runtime by the `WebletsViewHandler` changes (for example, `/projsf-ch5$2.0/showOneDeck.js`); thus, the browser's cached copy of `showOneDeck.js` for version 1.0 is no longer valid because the URL is different.

During development, the contents of packaged resources can change frequently, so it is important for the browser to keep checking with the web server to detect the latest resource URL contents. This check happens by default every time the main Web page is rendered if the weblet version is omitted from `weblets-config.xml`.

Alternatively, the weblet configuration allows component writers to append `-SNAPSHOT` to the version number. For example, `1.0-SNAPSHOT`, as shown in Code Sample 5-5, indicates that this file is under development and should behave as though the version number has been omitted.

Code Sample 5-5. *Weblets Configuration File Using* `SNAPSHOT` *Versioning for Development*

```
<?xml version="1.0" encoding="UTF-8" ?>
<weblets-config xmlns="http://weblets.dev.java.net/config" >
  <weblet>
    <weblet-name>com.apress.projsf.ch5</weblet-name>
    <weblet-class>net.java.dev.weblets.packaged.PackagedWeblet</weblet-class>
    <weblet-version>1.0-SNAPSHOT</weblet-version>
    ...
  </weblet>
  ...
</weblets-config>
```

Setting Up Security

When serving packaged resources from a JAR file, you must take extra care not to make Java class files or other sensitive information accessible by URL. In desktop Java applications, resource files are often stored in a subpackage called `resources` underneath the Java implementation classes that use the resource files. The same strategy is also appropriate for packaged resources in JSF component libraries, and this has the security benefit of ensuring that only the resource files are accessible by URL. All the other contents of the JAR file, including Java implementation classes, are not URL accessible because no Java classes exist either in the `resources` package or in any subpackage of `resources`.

Using the Weblet Protocol

Having learned how to configure weblets, it is time to look at how you can reference resources defined by the weblet in the two custom `Renderers`—`HtmlInputDateRenderer` and `HtmlShowOneDeckRenderer`. Code Sample 5-6 shows the syntax, defined by the weblet contract, for returning a proper URL to the JSF page.

Code Sample 5-6. *The Weblet Protocol Syntax*

```
weblet://<weblet name><resource>
```

The `weblet://` prefix indicates that this is a weblet-managed resource, and this is followed by the weblet name and the resource requested.

Using Weblets in the HtmlInputDateRenderer

Previously, in the `HtmlInputDateRenderer` class, you saw how to pass the URL `/projsf-ch2/inputDate.css` as an argument to the `writeStyleResource()` method. In Code Sample 5-7, you will see how to amend this to use the weblet protocol instead.

Code Sample 5-7. *Using the Weblet Protocol to Serve Up Resources*

```
/**
 * Write out the HtmlInputDate resources.
 *
 * @param context    the Faces context
 * @param component  the Faces component
 */
protected void encodeResources(
  FacesContext context,
  UIComponent  component) throws IOException
{
  writeStyleResource(context, "weblet://com.apress.projsf.ch5/inputDate.css");
}
```

The weblet protocol syntax is convenient and easy to understand. The syntax starts with `weblet://` followed by the weblet name (for example, `com.apress.projsf.ch5`) and finally the path information or resource file (for example, `/inputDate.css`).

■ **Note** Although the Weblets project uses a protocol-like syntax to describe resources in a public way, this is not a real protocol handler, so the `new URL("weblet::/...").openStream()` would not work from Java code. However, you don't need it to, since the client is not Java code.

Using Weblets in the HtmlShowOneDeckRenderer

As with the `HtmlInputDateRenderer`, in the `HtmlShowOneDeckRenderer` class you saw that we passed the URLs `/projsf-ch3/showOneDeck.js` and `/projsf-ch3/showOneDeck.css` as arguments to the `writeStyleResource()` method (see Code Sample 5-1). In Code Sample 5-8, you will see how to amend this to use the weblet protocol instead.

Code Sample 5-8. *Using the Weblet Protocol to Serve Up Resources*

```
/**
 * Write out the HtmlShowOneDeck resources.
 *
 * @param context    the Faces context
 * @param component  the Faces component
 */
```

```
protected void encodeResources(
  FacesContext context,
  UIComponent  component) throws IOException
{
  writeScriptResource(context, "weblet://com.apress.projsf.ch5/showOneDeck.js");
  writeStyleResource(context, "weblet://com.apress.projsf.ch5/showOneDeck.css");
}
```

Notice that neither the URL mapping nor the version number is included in the weblet resource syntax. The `WebletsViewHandler` uses the weblet URL mapping and version number to create a resource URL that the weblet will service.

When you are not using weblets, then you would not be using the `weblet://` resource path syntax, and you would distribute a separate installable ZIP file. When you move to weblets, you would start using the `weblet://` resource path syntax in the `Renderer` and include the resources in the JAR file. You get no benefit from using a mixture of these approaches for resources in the same version of the same component library.

Using Weblets in a JSF Application

To simplify setup for the application developer, component writers should select a default URL mapping for their component libraries. The application developer does not need to add *any* weblet-specific configuration to the `web.xml` file, since the `WebletsPhaseListener` will be invoked automatically to service incoming requests for weblet-managed resources.

Optimizing Weblets Using a Weblet Filter

Optionally, application developers can register the `WebletsFilter` in the `/WEB-INF/web.xml` file. By performing this simple step, they ensure that the weblet-based URLs are much shorter, such as `/projsf-ch5/showOneDeck.js` rather than `/faces/weblets/projsf-ch5/showOneDeck.js`. Using the `WebletsFilter` also reduces the overhead in processing the request because the JSF lifecycle is no longer invoked to service the weblet-managed resources via the `WebletsPhaseListener`.

Code Sample 5-9 maps the weblet container to filter URLs beginning with the `/projsf-ch5` prefix on the context root. Using this specific URL pattern for the `WebletsFilter` mapping prevents unnecessary overhead from being introduced by the weblet container for non-weblet requests. If a weblet services a particular pattern, such as `/projsf-ch5/*`, then it services all of `/projsf-ch5/*`, with no fallback to the context root.

Code Sample 5-9. *Weblet Container Configuration in the* `web.xml` *File*

```
<web-app>
  <filter>
    <filter-name>Weblet Container</filter-name>
    <filter-class>net.java.dev.weblets.WebletsFilter</filter-class>
  </filter>
  <filter-mapping>
    <filter-name>Weblet Container</filter-name>
    <url-pattern>/projsf-ch5/*</url-pattern>
```

```
  </filter-mapping>
  ...
</web-app>
```

The weblet container is responsible for parsing all weblet configuration files (weblet-config.xml). It locates them in the same way as JSF locates faces-config.xml files. The weblet container first searches for configuration files stored in the META-INF/ directory of each component library and then searches for /WEB-INF/weblets-config.xml in the web application root.

This design allows application developers to override the default URL mapping defined by the component writer in cases where the URL pattern is already used by a web application resource, such as a servlet or filter. For example, Code Sample 5-10 overrides the default <url-pattern> packaged with the component library and instead defines a custom mapping (for example, /projsf-chapter5-resources/*).

Code Sample 5-10. *Overriding Weblets Mapping*

```
<?xml version="1.0" encoding="UTF-8" ?>
<weblets-config xmlns="http://weblets.dev.java.net/config" >
  <weblet-mapping>
    <weblet-name>com.apress.projsf.ch5</weblet-name>
    <url-pattern>/projsf-chapter5-resources/*</url-pattern>
  </weblet-mapping>
</weblets-config>
```

The Renderers automatically consume this URL mapping change without the need for any code changes or recompilation.

Summary

As a new open source project, Weblets has tremendous potential to become a de facto standard that provides a generic and configurable resource-loading facility for web clients and the JSF component community. The key differentiators from the installables approach are the simplified packaging of JSF components and their resources and a minimal overhead of installing and setting up JSF component libraries for a particular web application project.

This chapter explored a new way of packaging resources with JSF components. You should now be able to leverage weblets in your own component library by including a suitable weblets-config.xml file and using the weblet:// protocol-style syntax to reference weblet-managed resources.

You should now understand how weblets integrate with JSF, understand the concepts used to package additional resources, and know how to set up and optimize an application to use these resources.

CHAPTER 6

Ajax Enabling the Deck Component

I, not events, have the power to make me happy or unhappy today. I can choose which it shall be. Yesterday is dead, tomorrow hasn't arrived yet. I have just one day, today, and I'm going to be happy in it.

—Julius Henry Marx, known as Groucho Marx

In this and Chapter 7, we will address the need for a smoother and richer user experience when interacting with your components in a JSF Web application. As they are currently designed, your components will work perfectly well in a traditional HTML Web application and will perform a traditional valid form `POST`. As you have probably noticed, an undesired side effect of this traditional way of building Web applications is that a form `POST` will cause the Web application to perform a full-page refresh when the response returns to the client browser. This extra flicker when the page reloads is not just annoying but also affects the performance of the application. Other side effects might be lost data, lost scroll position, and lost focus.

It is here that Ajax comes to the rescue, providing functionality to asynchronously communicate with underlying servers and any business services used by the Web application, without forcing a reload of the page and its resources. This, in turn, reduces flicker and allows the page to maintain scroll position and focus. By leveraging a communication channel in JavaScript called `XMLHttpRequest`, developers can go beyond tweaking the DOM representation in the browser to provide some dynamic rich features. Excellent examples of applications implementing Ajax technology are Google GMail, Oracle Collaboration Suite, and Google Suggest; these applications prove Ajax is a valid solution for delivering rich features for current Internet platforms.

With increasing consumer awareness about the possibilities of RIA solutions, the demand for a smoother and richer interaction is no longer optional.

Requirements for the Deck Component's Ajax Implementation

First, you need to ensure that your deck component's Ajax implementation can execute a complete JSF lifecycle on a postback (and therefore utilize all the benefits of JSF). You also need to figure out what has changed during the JSF lifecycle and update the client-side DOM representation with just those changes.

Second, you need to prevent client-side events from going back to the server unnecessarily, making sure that only events affecting business logic perform round-trips to the server. That means you need to short-circuit the user interface interactivity locally at the browser so that potential components such as splitters, table column reorders, date pickers, and color pop-ups are not round-tripping to the server.

Finally, and most important, you want to make it easy on the application developer by abstracting the presentation specifics (for example, HTML, JavaScript, XUL, and HTC).

The Ajax-Enabled Deck Component

In this chapter, you will examine how to "Ajax enable" your `ProShowOneDeck` component and therefore improve the user experience when interacting with this component. As mentioned in Chapter 2, you do not need to create new `UIComponents` if the behavior already exists. In this case, you have already implemented the behavioral aspects of your `ProShowOneDeck` component in the `UIShowOne` component, so you need only to create a new `Renderer` that contains your client-side DHTML/Ajax implementation and all the resources needed to Ajax enable it.

To do this, you will use Ajax and two open source frameworks—Delta DOM (D^2) and the Dojo toolkit:

Ajax: Ajax is a new name describing a Web development technique for creating richer and more user-friendly Web applications using an already established technology suite—the DOM, JavaScript, and `XMLHttpRequest`.

D^2: D^2 (pronounced *D-squared*) is an open source project hosted on Java.net (`http://d2.dev.java.net/`). Delta DOM is extremely useful in the context of merging DOM differences into a DOM tree.

Dojo toolkit: Dojo is an open source DHTML toolkit written in JavaScript by Alex Russel (`http://www.dojotoolkit.org`). The Dojo toolkit contains Ajax features supporting a back button, bookmarking, and file upload.

Ajax and the two open source frameworks are complementary, and in this chapter you will learn how you can use them to handle postback events for your `ProShowOneDeck` component. You will also provide a public API that can be used by all Ajax-enabled JSF components to turn "full" postback on and off.

After reading this chapter, you should understand what Ajax solves and what issues you might encounter when creating rich user interface components with this technology. You will learn about D^2 and how to use it to build your own *Rich Internet Components*. Finally, you will gain an understanding of the excellent Dojo toolkit and how to use it in the context of JSF and component design.

Figure 6-1 shows the 12 classes you will create in this chapter.

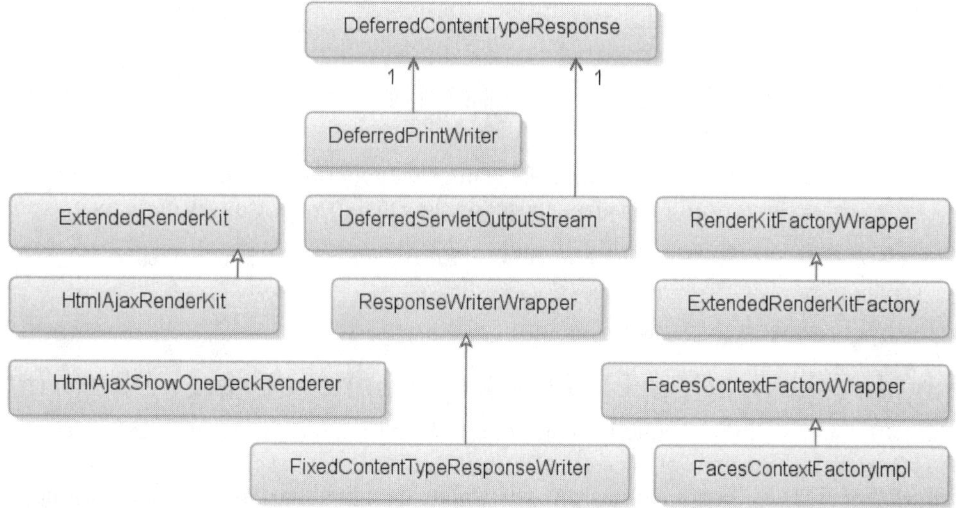

Figure 6-1. *Class diagram showing classes created in this chapter*

The classes are as follows:

- `ExtendedRenderKit` extends an existing `RenderKit` without needing to repeat the registration of common `Renderers` in `faces-config.xml`.
- `HtmlAjaxRenderKit` can dynamically pick either the default `ResponseWriter` or the custom `FixedContentTypeResponseWriter`.
- `HtmlAjaxShowOneDeckRenderer` is your new custom `Renderer`, which extends the `HtmlShowOneDeckRenderer` from Chapter 3 and adds JavaScript libraries to include Ajax support.
- `DeferredContentTypeResponse` is responsible for wrapping the `HttpServletResponse` object to detect whether the JSP page directive indicates that the `ResponseWriter` should define the `contentType`.
- `DeferredPrintWriter` sets the `contentType` header on the response just before streaming the first character of the payload.
- `DeferredServletOutputStream` sets the `contentType` header on the response just before streaming the first byte of the payload.
- The `ResponseWriterWrapper` class is only delegating, without decorating, to the standard `ResponseWriter`.
- `FixedContentTypeResponseWriter` is responsible for writing out a document (content type `text/plain`) on any subsequent postback performed by your Ajax-enabled components.

- `RenderKitFactoryWrapper` extends the JSF implementation's abstract `RenderKitFactory` class to provide a loose coupling to the underlying JSF implementation.
- `ExtendedRenderKitFactory` enhances the `RenderKitFactory` by adding support for creating `ExtendedRenderKits`.
- `FacesContextFactoryWrapper` is only delegating, without decorating, to the standard `FacesContextFactory` and provides a loose coupling to the underlying JSF implementation.
- `FacesContextFactoryImpl` class intercepts `HttpServletResponse` and creates a new servlet response—`DeferredContentTypeResponse`.

Designing the Ajax-Enabled Deck Component Using a Blueprint

The blueprint for creating a custom JSF component, from Chapter 3, contained seven steps. Those seven steps cover most of the common use cases for designing components. However, as you will see in Table 6-1, sometimes you will need to do more than what is covered by those seven steps.

Table 6-1. *Steps in the Blueprint for Creating a New JSF Component*

#	Step	Description
1	Creating a UI prototype	Create a prototype of the UI and intended behavior for your component using the appropriate markup.
2	Creating events and listeners	(Optional) Create custom events and listeners in the case your specific needs are not covered by the JSF specification.
3	Creating a behavioral superclass	(Optional) If the component behavior is not to be found, create a new behavioral superclass (for example, `UIShowOne`).
4	Creating a client-specific `Renderer`	Create the `Renderer` you need that will write out the client-side markup for your JSF component.
5	Creating a renderer-specific subclass	(Optional) Create a renderer-specific subclass. Although this is an optional step, it is good practice to implement it.
6	Registering a `UIComponent` and `Renderer`	Register your new `UIComponent` and `Renderer` in the `faces-config.xml` file.
7	Creating a JSP tag handler and TLD	This step is needed in the case you are using JSP as your default view handler. An alternative solution is to use Facelets (`http://facelets.dev.java.net/`).
8	**Creating a `RenderKit` and `ResponseWriter`**	(Optional) If you plan to support alternative markup such as Mozilla XUL, then you need to create a new `RenderKit` with an associating `ResponseWriter`. The default `RenderKit` is `HTML_BASIC` with the `contentType` set to `text/html`.

#	Step	Description
9	**Extending the JSF implementation**	(Optional) This step is needed in the case you have to provide extensions to the JSF implementation (for example, extending JSF factory classes or providing a custom JSF life-cycle implementation).
10	**Registering a `RenderKit` and JSF extension**	(Optional) Register your custom `RenderKit` and/or extensions to the JSF implementation.
11	**Registering resources with Weblets**	(Optional) Register your resources such as images, JavaScript libraries, and CSS files with Weblets so that they can be packaged and loaded directly out of the component library JAR file.

This chapter adds four more steps—creating a `RenderKit`, extending the JSF implementation, registering a RenderKit and JSF extension, and registering resources with Weblets—to the blueprint. Fortunately, JSF is sufficiently extensible to find a way to achieve your goal, even if not part of the standard implementation.

Before you get to steps 8, 9, 10, and 11, you need to go through the other steps to ensure you have not missed anything; again, according to the first step, you need to define the new component implementing it in the intended markup that will eventually be sent to the client, so let's look at what you want to achieve.

Step 1: Creating a UI Prototype

True to the blueprint, you first need to create a prototype of the intended markup. Remember that creating a prototype will help you find out what elements your `Renderer` has to generate, what renderer-specific attributes the application developer will need, and what resources (for example, JavaScript, images, and so on) are needed.

Figure 6-2 shows the end result of your deck component implemented in HTML.

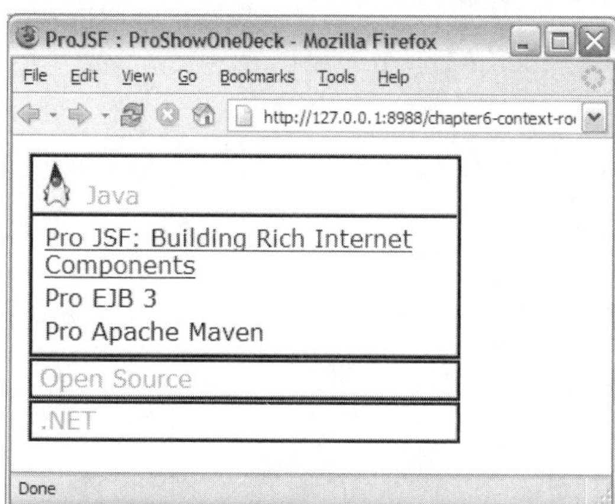

Figure 6-2. *Decks implemented in HTML*

Code Sample 6-1 shows the HTML needed to create the page shown in Figure 6-2 with your new DHTML/Ajax deck component.

Code Sample 6-1. *Deck HTML Implementation*

```
<html>
  <head>
    <title>Pro JSF : ProShowOneDeck Prototype</title>
    <style type="text/css" >
      .ProShowOne { ... }
      .ProShowItem { ... }
      .ProShowItemHeader { ... }
      .ProShowItemContent { ... }
    </style>
  </head>
  <body>
    <div style="width:200px;" >
      <div class="ProShowOne">
        <div class="ProShowItem">
          <div class="ProShowItemHeader"
               onclick="alert('first')" >
            <img src="resources/java_small.jpg"
                 alt="The Duke"
                 style="margin-right: 8px; vertical-align:bottom;" />
            Java
          </div>
          <div class="ProShowItemContent">
            <table>
              <tbody>
                <tr>
                  <td>
                    <a href="http://www.apress.com/...">
                      Pro JSF: Building Rich Internet Components
                    </a>
                  </td>
                </tr>
                <tr>
                  <td>Pro EJB 3</td>
                </tr>
                <tr>
                  <td>Pro Apache Maven</td>
                </tr>
              </tbody>
            </table>
          </div>
        </div>
        <div class="ProShowItem">
          <div class="ProShowItemHeader"
```

```
            onclick="alert('second')" >
          Open Source
        </div>
      </div>
      <div class="ProShowItem">
        <div class="ProShowItemHeader"
            onclick="alert('third')">
          .NET
        </div>
      </div>
    </div>
  </div>
 </body>
</html>
```

You are not changing the UI of your component, and as you can see, the HTML document is identical to the page you created in Chapter 3, which leverages your HTML version of the UIShowOne component Renderer—HtmlShowOneDeckRenderer.

The JSF page source shown in Code Sample 6-2 uses the finished implementation of your Ajax-enabled component, and as you can see, the page source does not contain any Ajax "code," which means no extra burden is placed on the application developer to Ajax enable elements in the page or the application. This is what you want to achieve—simplicity for application developers. Fortunately, with JSF, it is possible!

Code Sample 6-2. *JSF Page Source*

```
<?xml version = '1.0' encoding = 'windows-1252'?>
<jsp:root ...>
 <jsp:directive.page contentType="application/x-javaserver-faces"/>
 <f:view>
    ...
    <pro:showOneDeck showItemId="first"
                     showListener="#{showOneDeckBean.doShow}">
      <pro:showItem id="first" >
        <f:facet name="header">
          <h:panelGroup>
            <h:graphicImage url="/resources/java_small.jpg" alt="The Duke"
                            style="margin-right: 8px; vertical-align:bottom;" />
            <h:outputText value="Java"/>
          </h:panelGroup>
        </f:facet>
        <h:panelGrid columns="1">
          <h:outputLink value="http://apress.com/book/bookDisplay.html?bID=10044">
            <h:outputText value="Pro JSF: Building Rich Internet Components"/>
    ...
 </f:view>
</jsp:root>
```

As you can see, not much in the code is different from the initial JSF implementation (see Chapter 3), but when the user clicks one of the unexpanded nodes, you will send an `XMLHttpRequest` to the server, instead of a regular form postback.

Note the differences from a regular form submit. This implementation of your JSF component will prevent an unnecessary reload of page content that should not be affected by the user action expanding nodes in your deck component. It also removes any flickering of the page when expanding the new node with its content and collapsing the previously opened node.

The only step for the application developer to Ajax enable the application is to set the right `contentType`, which in this case is `application/x-javaserver-faces`. You needed to handle the initial request differently than subsequent postbacks with Ajax so that on the initial request you have `text/html` as the `contentType` and `text/plain` for subsequent requests. By specifying a custom `contentType` like in Code Sample 6-2, you can intercept it and allow JSF to decide what `contentType` is going to be set on the response. Rest assured, we will discuss the `contentType` and what impact it has on your component development. For now, this is all you need to know.

DOM MUTATION SUPPORT IN FIREFOX

If you are a user of Mozilla Firefox and are currently using a version older than Mozilla Firefox 1.5, you might experience some flickering when using the Ajax-enabled `ShowOneDeck` component. This is a bug in the Mozilla Firefox browser implementation. For more information, please see `https://bugzilla.mozilla.org/show_bug.cgi?id=238493`. You can download a more recent version of Mozilla Firefox from `http://www.mozilla.org/projects/firefox/`.

Step 4: Creating a Client-Specific Renderer

In your solution for the `UIShowOne` component, you have done most of the work already in Chapter 3, so you will need only to extend the `HtmlShowOneDeckRenderer`, and since this chapter does not introduce any new behavior, you can skip steps 2 and 3 in your blueprint and go straight to step 4—creating a client-specific renderer.

Ajax and JSF Architectures

Several architectural possibilities exist to provide Ajax support in a client-server environment (for example, in JSF). In all cases, one part of Ajax will impact the architectural decision, and that is how the Ajax solution manages updates to the DOM when processing the Ajax response.

Somewhere you have to apply changes between the current HTML document and what has been returned from the server based on user interaction, so that you can apply changes to the current HTML document without reloading the page. The following are two possible architectural solutions:

Partial-Page Rendering (PPR): This is the first successful implementation of Ajax in JSF and is currently used by a component library called ADF Faces. This type of architecture relies on a regular form submit. The response is in fragments that contain information of what is needed for the change. The PPR handler will then figure out where to slot in these changes. This approach puts a burden on the application developer to figure out what changed (for example, the application developer has to set partial targets to define what components are involved in this partial update). In this architecture, the unit of update is a `UIComponent` subtree, so the markup for each `UIComponent` subtree is replaced for each partial target. PPR is also relying on `iframes`, not `XMLHttpRequest`, to provide asynchronous communication, which has the benefit of supporting older versions of browsers.

Delta DOM Rendering (D^2R): This approach puts no extra burden on the application developer, and the unit of update is delta data (for example, attributes on the element nodes). D^2R simulates a regular form `POST` and sends a form data set to the server using the `XMLHttpRequest` object. The server will not notice any difference between this `POST` and a regular `POST` and will deliver with a full-page response. An Ajax handler will handle the response, compare it with the current HTML document, and then merge in any changes to the HTML document. You can implement D^2R in two ways—on the client or on the server side. In the client-side implementation, the Ajax handler will detect and apply DOM deltas on the client. In the server-side implementation, before the `ResponseWriter` writes out the markup to the client, the markup will be cached on the server. On subsequent postback, before the `ResponseWriter` writes out the new markup to the client, the server-side implementation will compare the cached version with the new page response and send the differences as delta data over to the client where the Ajax handler will merge it with the HTML document.

DOM Mutation

Using the DR^2 client-side implementation, Ajax-enabled components that rely on modifying the DOM will lose any changes made since the last form POST, but those DOM changes would be lost on a full-page refresh as well. At the Apply Request Values phase, any additional information not represented by the component hierarchy will be dropped, and when the page is rendered, the client-side Ajax handler will perform a DOM diff, replacing anything that does not match the DOM on the response. This has the benefit of providing additional security and preventing any malicious tampering with the application by modifying the DOM representation in the browser.

With the server-side implementation, the security is still applied at the JSF component level, but in this scenario the malicious script is not removed on the client as part of the response. This is because the server has a cached version of the page dating from before the attack, so the server is not aware of the tampering of the DOM. When the merge of the cached and new markup is done, you are sending only delta data back to the server and are not implicitly "removing" any malicious code on the client.

Selecting Ajax Architecture

Although PPR provides less work for the component author and some control for the application developer, we will focus on the D^2R approach for this book. Without getting into the details of comparing the client and server-side D^2R solutions, both implementations are similar. Basically, you need to calculate the difference between the initial HTML document and the targeted HTML document. Before the page is submitted, the start point is known only on the client; after submit, the end point is known only on the server. So, something needs to be transmitted to get the start point and end point both on the server or both on the client.

We have decided to use the client-side D^2R since it offers maximum flexibility. This solution applies the diff between the initial HTML document and the targeted HTML document on the client and also allows client-side JavaScript to perform any modifications at the client. If no modifications are permitted by other components, then the diff could be moved to the server by remembering what was previously rendered and be used as the start point on the next submit.

With the client-side D²R solution, you can leverage either the `responseXML` property or the `responseText` property of the `XMLHttpRequest` object (see Figure 6-3). The `responseText` property returns a string representing the document sent from the server. The `responseXML` property returns a proper XML DOM object representing the document. It is a completely accessible DOM that can be manipulated and traversed in the same way as you would do with an HTML document.

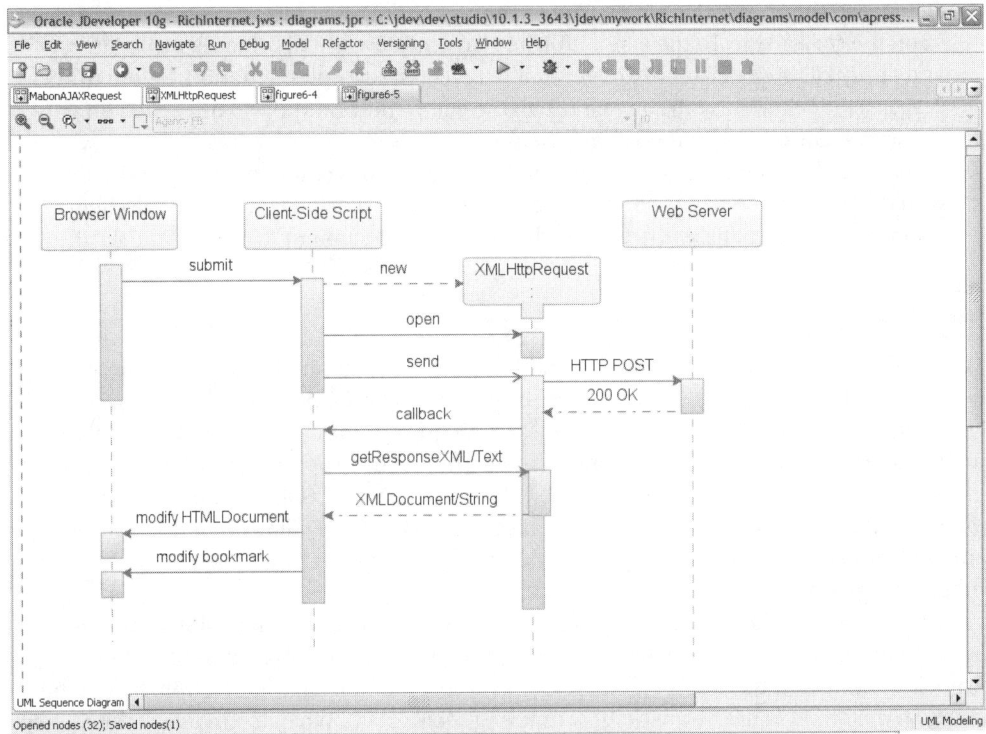

Figure 6-3. *Sequence diagram over your Ajax postback implementation*

When the user clicks a component (for example, a submit button) that has been designed to use Ajax, the regular form submit will be overridden, and a new instance of the `XMLHttpRequest` object will be created. You can then use this `XMLHttpRequest` object to open a channel to the server and send the encoded data as a `url-formencoded` stream back to the server (HTTP `POST`). Since the Web server will not detect the difference between your Ajax postback and a regular postback, this will not affect your server code.

Your implementation is to have interactive `UIComponents` that change their states always perform `XMLHttpRequests` and to have `UICommand` components perform form postbacks when a file upload is present on the page.

Providing File Upload Functionality

For security reasons, the only standard way a developer can provide an implementation that gives the user access to upload files from the client file system is to use a form element or `form.submit()`. This means that in Ajax a file upload requires using a `form.submit()` and a hidden `<iframe>`, instead of `XMLHttpRequest`. Normally, the JSF `ResponseWriter` will deliver a full-page (HTML) response, but a hidden `<iframe>` that receives HTML or XHTML will also receive `<script>` elements. These `<script>` elements will be executed immediately! It is also important to understand that these `<script>` elements will be executed in the context of the hidden `<iframe>`, not in the main page where they would normally be executed on a full-page response.

We have chosen to use the `responseText` property on the `XMLHttpRequest` object, whose payload contains the HTML document in plain-text format, which has the positive side effect that, in the presence of file upload, the returned document will not be executed as HTML or XHTML. This will also prevent any `<script>` elements from being executed in the wrong context. This, on the other hand, requires that you handle these `<script>` elements so the intended behavior of the script gets executed in the right context and not in the hidden `<iframe>`.

So, if you solve the previous issue with file upload and the response for the `<iframe>`, you still have one more thing to do. On the initial request, you are still expecting the content type to be `text/html`. With the solution just outlined, you need to support dynamic content types (for example, on the initial request or a regular form postback), serve up `text/html`, and (on any subsequent request performed by your Ajax-enabled components) serve up `text/plain`.

FILE UPLOAD WITH THE DOJO TOOLKIT

Unfortunately, too often the implementation provided just covers the basic usage, and the hard parts to implement have been left to the consuming application developer to work around. After some research, we found that the Dojo toolkit provides excellent solutions to most of the Ajax undesired side effects mentioned—back button support, bookmarking, and file upload—out of the box.

Ajax Resources

As you know by now, implementing Ajax in any Web application means writing JavaScript, which can be dreadful, especially when it comes to cross-browser support and accessibility. On the other hand, with Ajax, developers can build more appealing JavaScript applications such as Google Maps, but quite often it means more code on the client side to achieve this richness. As a component author, you are free to choose any direction by either providing your own client-side Ajax JavaScript or, as we recommend, searching for already available Ajax JavaScript libraries. Several open source and commercial JavaScript libraries can help you with the hard-core JavaScript/Ajax implementations and let you focus on the important part—designing your JSF component.

We have decided to go with the open source JavaScript toolkit called Dojo for the `XMLHttpRequest` transport mechanisms and the D^2 open source project for parsing and merging the source document with the target document.

Introducing the DOJO Toolkit

The Dojo open source project provides a modern, capable, "Webish," and easy-to-use DHTML toolkit. Part of that effort includes smoothing out many of the sharp edges of the DHTML programming and user experiences. On the back of high-profile success stories such as Google Maps and Google Suggest, Ajax and the `XMLHttpRequest` object have been getting a lot of attention. In spite of all the publicity, application developers have been on their own when it comes to solving the usability problems that come along with Ajax. The Dojo open source project provides a DHTML toolkit written in JavaScript and aims to solve some long-standing historical problems with DHTML, which have prevented the mass adoption of dynamic Web application development.

The Dojo toolkit allows you to build dynamic capabilities into Web applications and any other environment that supports JavaScript. With the Dojo toolkit, you can make Web applications more usable, responsive, and functional. Other benefits and features of the toolkit are the lower-level APIs and compatibility layers to write portable JavaScript and simplify complex scripts, event systems, I/O APIs, and generic language enhancements.

The Dojo toolkit provides all these features by layering capabilities onto a small core that provides the package system and little else. When you write scripts using the Dojo toolkit, you can include as little or as much of the available APIs as you want to suit your needs.

Introducing the D^2 Open Source Project

D^2 is an open source project hosted on `d2.dev.java.net`. The D^2 project provides an implementation from the Change Detection in Hierarchically Structured Information research project (see sidebar for more information about this project). The research project focuses on finding a minimum-cost edit script that transforms one data tree to another and includes efficient algorithms for computing such an edit script. The D^2 project contains two implementations—one client-side JavaScript implementation and one server-side Java implementation—that are built based on this research. This supports an incremental transformation of any JSF-rendered HTML DOM by executing the algorithm either on the client or on the server.

CHANGE DETECTION IN HIERARCHICALLY STRUCTURED INFORMATION[1]

Detecting and representing changes to data is important for active databases, data warehousing, view maintenance, and version and configuration management. Most previous work in change management has dealt with flat-file and relational data; we focus on hierarchically structured data. Since in many cases changes must be computed from old and new versions of the data, we define the hierarchical change detection problem as the problem of finding a "minimum-cost edit script" that transforms one data tree to another, and we present efficient algorithms for computing such an edit script. Our algorithms make use of some key domain characteristics to achieve substantially better performance than previous, general-purpose algorithms. We study the performance of our algorithms both analytically and empirically, and we describe the application of our techniques to hierarchically structured documents.

---

1. Source: "Change Detection in Hierarchically Structured Information" by Sudarshan S. Chawathe, Anand Rajaraman, Hector Garcia-Molina, and Jennifer Widom; Department of Computer Science, Stanford University.

The d2.js library also contains functions needed to pass information about the user selections, submit the form, and handle the response coming back from the server. The d2.js library is in turn utilizing the Dojo toolkit's built-in Ajax support to submit the form using the XMLHttpRequest object instead of the regular form POST, as shown in Code Sample 6-3.

Code Sample 6-3. *Excerpt from the* d2.js *Library*

```
var d2 = new Object();

d2.submit = function (form, content)
{
  var targetDocument = form.ownerDocument;
  var contentType = targetDocument.contentType;

  // IE does not support document.contentType
  if (contentType == null)
    contentType = 'text/html';

  dojo.io.bind(
  {
    formNode: form,
    headers: { 'X-D2-Content-Type': contentType },
    content: content,
    mimetype: "text/plain",
    load: d2._loadtext,
    error: d2._error
  });
}
```

Code Sample 6-3 is an excerpt from the d2.js library and shows the submit function you will use in the Ajax implementation. As you can see, the d2.js library is referencing the dojo.io package, which provides portable code for XMLHttpRequest and other transport mechanisms that are more complicated. Most of the magic of the dojo.io package is exposed through the bind() method. The dojo.io.bind() method is a generic asynchronous request API that wraps multiple transport layers (queues of iframes, XMLHttpRequest, mod_pubsub, LivePage, and so on). Dojo attempts to pick the best available transport for the request at hand, and by default, only XMLHttpRequest will ever be chosen since no other transports are rolled in.

The d2.submit() function calls the dojo.io.bind() method, passing information about what form to submit, the content (a map of name/value pairs that will be sent to the server as request parameters), the accepted request header, and the MIME type for this request.

The D^2 library also defines a callback function—d2._loadtext—that can get the response data from the server. The d2._loadtext function replaces the targeted document's inner HTML with the inner HTML from the document returned on the response.

■ **Note** The D^2 open source project also provides an excellent facility to compare and merge two DOM documents.

The HtmlAjaxShowOneDeckRenderer Class

With Ajax you could argue that you are implementing new behavior; however, it is only client-side behavior and not JSF server-side behavior, so you do not need to provide a new server-side behavioral superclass. For the application developer, there is no difference between the component events on the server using the `HtmlShowOneDeckRenderer` and your new Ajax-enabled `HtmlAjaxShowOneDeckRenderer`. Figure 6-4 shows the `HtmlAjaxShowOneDeckRenderer` extending the `HtmlShowOneDeckRenderer` created in Chapter 3.

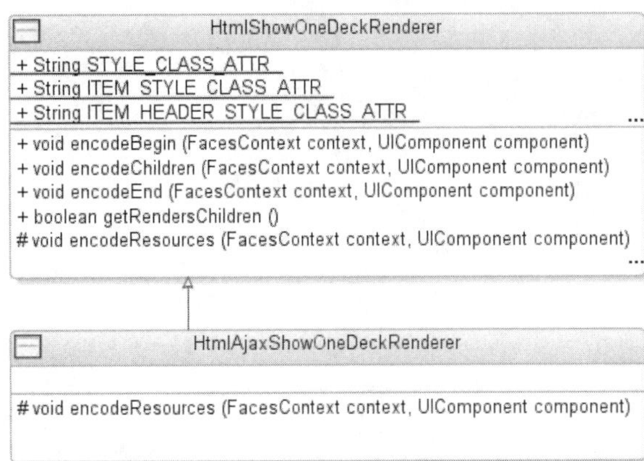

Figure 6-4. *Class diagram showing the* `HtmlAjaxShowOneDeckRenderer` *extending the* `HtmlShowOneDeckRenderer` *created in Chapter 3*

The only things you need to add to your new `HtmlAjaxShowOneDeckRenderer` are the JavaScript libraries needed to perform your Ajax postback, as shown in Code Sample 6-4.

Code Sample 6-4. *Extending the* `HtmlShowOneDeckRenderer`

```
package com.apress.projsf.ch6.render.html.ajax;

import java.io.IOException;

import javax.faces.component.UIComponent;
import javax.faces.context.FacesContext;

import com.apress.projsf.ch3.render.html.basic.HtmlShowOneDeckRenderer;

public class HtmlAjaxShowOneDeckRenderer extends HtmlShowOneDeckRenderer
{
  protected void encodeResources(
    FacesContext context,
    UIComponent  component) throws IOException
  {
```

```
    writeScriptResource(context, "weblet://org.dojotoolkit.browserio/dojo.js");
    writeScriptResource(context, "weblet://net.java.dev.d2/d2.js");
    writeScriptResource(context, "weblet://com.apress.projsf.ch6/showOneDeck.js");
  }
}
```

As you can see, you extend the `com.apress.projsf.ch3.render.html.HtmlShowOneDeckRenderer` and its `encodeResources()` method with three new calls to the `dojo.js` toolkit library, the `d2.js` library, and your own updated `showOneDeck.js` for this new `Renderer`. An application developer might add two or more `ProShowOneDeck` components to the page, but the semantics behind the `writeScriptResource()` method, provided by your `Renderer` implementation and described in Chapter 3, will make sure these resources are written only once.

The ShowOneDeck Ajax Implementation

The `showOneDeck.js` library was first introduced in Chapter 3, and this chapter will provide some modifications to this library to complete your client-side Ajax implementation. Code Sample 6-5 shows the HTML version, and Code Sample 6-6 shows the Ajax version of the library.

Code Sample 6-5. *The HTML Version of the* `ShowOneDeck.js` *Library*

```
function _showOneDeck_click(formClientId, clientId, itemId)
{
  var form = document.forms[formClientId];
  var input = form[clientId];
  if (!input)
  {
    input = document.createElement("input");
    input.name = clientId;
    form.appendChild(input);
  }
  input.value = itemId;
  form.submit();
}
```

Code Sample 6-6. *The Ajax Version of the* `ShowOneDeck.js` *Library*

```
function _showOneDeck_click(formClientId, clientId, itemId)
{
  var form = document.forms[formClientId];
  var content = new Object();
  content[clientId] = itemId;
  d2.submit(form, content);
}
```

As you can see, the `_showOneDeck_click()` function (Code Sample 6-5) is similar to the one used with the traditional HTML `Renderer` (Code Sample 6-6), with one exception. You are now calling the `d2.submit()` function instead of the traditional `form.submit()` function. In this case, you pass the activated form ID and the ID of the selected node to the `d2.submit()` function. The `d2.submit()` function calls the underlying `dojo.io.bind()` method, passing information about what form to submit, the content (that is, the ID of the selected component), the accepted request header (`'X-D2-Content-Type': 'text/html'`), and the MIME type (`text/plain`) for this request. This information will determine what item to expand and what `ResponseWriter` to use for this request.

Step 6: Registering a UIComponent and Renderer

This chapter does not contain any behavioral superclass, but you still have to register your client-specific `Renderer`. The `HtmlAjaxShowOneDeckRenderer` is registered in `faces-config.xml`, as shown in Code Sample 6-7.

Code Sample 6-7. *Register the Ajax-Enabled* `Renderer` *and* `RenderKit`

```
<?xml version="1.0" encoding="UTF-8" ?>
<!DOCTYPE faces-config
   PUBLIC "-//Sun Microsystems, Inc.//DTD JavaServer Faces Config 1.1//EN"
          "http://java.sun.com/dtd/web-facesconfig_1_1.dtd">

<faces-config xmlns="http://java.sun.com/JSF/Configuration" >
    ...

<render-kit>
  <render-kit-id> ... </render-kit-id>
  <render-kit-class> ... </render-kit-class>
    <renderer>
      <component-family>com.apress.projsf.ShowOne</component-family>
      <renderer-type>com.apress.projsf.Deck</renderer-type>
      <renderer-class>
        com.apress.projsf.ch6.render.html.ajax.HtmlAjaxShowOneDeckRenderer
      </renderer-class>
    </renderer>
  </render-kit>

</faces-config>
```

The component family and renderer type are the same as defined in Chapter 3 for the regular HTML version of the `ProShowOneDeck` component. This allows you to reuse the `ProShowOneDeckTag` handler and the TLD defined in Chapter 3.

Step 8: Creating a RenderKit and ResponseWriter

Developers who want to include Ajax support in JSF applications have more than one strategy to choose from, as discussed earlier. The strategy we decided to take in this chapter—D²R—requires more than just a new `Renderer` to provide Ajax functionality. As discussed in the "Providing File Upload Functionality" section, you need to control the output to the client so that on the initial request, or regular form postback, you write out the requested document with the `contentType` set to `text/html` and on any subsequent Ajax postback respond with the `contentType` set to `text/plain`.

What markup is written to the client is controlled by the `ResponseWriter`, which in turn is created by the `RenderKit`. The default `RenderKit` provided by a JSF implementation is the standard HTML `RenderKit`, which comes with a default `ResponseWriter` that supports only content of type `text/html`. To be able to support the content type `text/plain` as required by your Ajax `Renderer`, you have to decorate the default `ResponseWriter` with functionality to fix the `contentType` in the case of an Ajax request—`FixedContentTypeResponseWriter`. With this new `ResponseWriter`, you also have to provide a custom `RenderKit`—`HtmlAjaxRenderKit`—that can dynamically pick either the default `ResponseWriter` or the custom `FixedContentTypeResponseWriter`. Figure 6-5 shows how to create the right `ResponseWriter`.

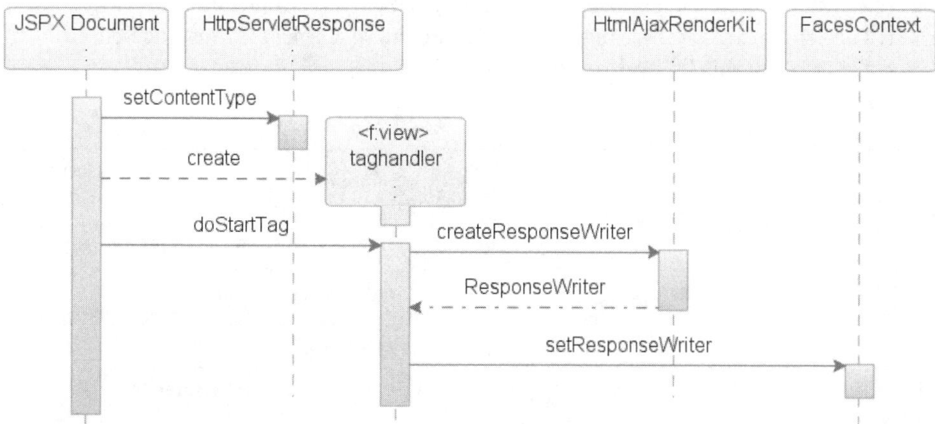

Figure 6-5. *Creating the right* `ResponseWriter`

Is this all? No, one issue when creating your own `RenderKit` is that application developers are allowed to set only one default `RenderKit` per Web application. So, unless you want to reimplement all the standard HTML `RenderKit` `Renderers` (or even worse, reimplement every component library the application developer might use), you have to figure out a way to provide access to `HTML_BASIC` renderers from your custom `RenderKit`. This is also one of the reasons most component authors avoid creating a new `RenderKit` and default to the standard HTML `RenderKit`. But, to implement this strategy, you need a new `ResponseWriter` that can handle `text/plain`, and thus you also need a new `RenderKit`.

What you need is a way to wrap your custom `RenderKit` around the standard HTML `RenderKit` to avoid having to implement all renderers an application developer might use.

Registering RenderKits to Wrap

Each JSF application has to have one default `RenderKit`, which means you need to come up with a way to register your `RenderKit` so you can identify what `RenderKit` is to be wrapped at application start-up.

Code Sample 6-8 provides an example of what the syntax looks like that you will use to register your `RenderKit` (`your.render.kit.id`) and the identifier for the `RenderKit` (`[wrapped.render.kit.id]`) you are about to wrap.

Code Sample 6-8. *Alternative* `RenderKit` *Registration*

```
<render-kit>
  <render-kit-id>your.render.kit.id[wrapped.render.kit.id]</render-kit-id>
  <render-kit-class>your.render.kit.Class</render-kit-class>
  <renderer>
    ...
  </renderer>
</render-kit>
```

Figure 6-6 shows how the `ExtendedRenderKitFactory` wraps the standard HTML `RenderKit`. The `RenderKitFactory` is responsible for returning a `RenderKit` instance based on the `RenderKit` ID for this JSF Web application.

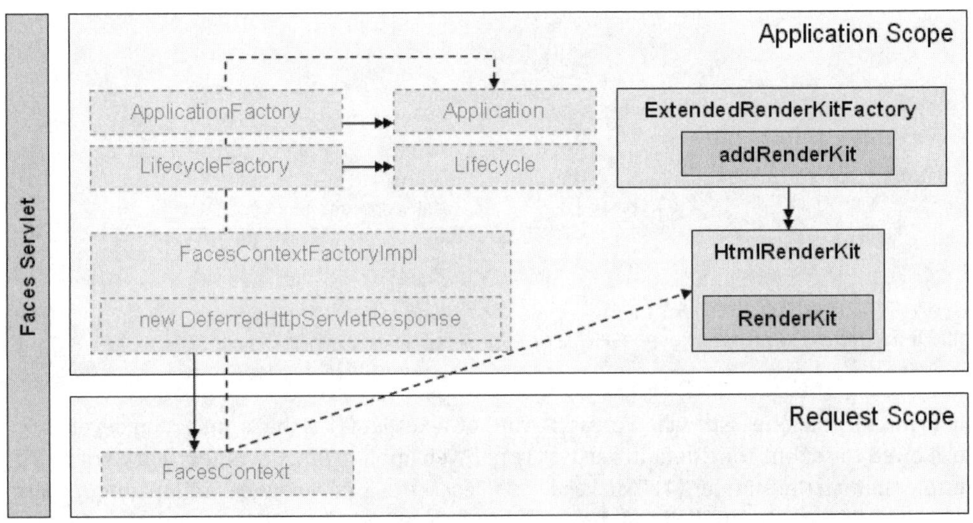

Figure 6-6. *Extending the* `RenderKitFactory` *and wrapping the standard HTML* `RenderKit`

Now when you have a way to identify what `RenderKits` are involved, you need to decorate the default `RenderKitFactory` class with filtering capabilities to process `RenderKit` IDs matching your syntax. Any `RenderKit` IDs defined in the `faces-config.xml` not matching your syntax will be delegated to the standard `RenderKitFactory`. If a `RenderKit` ID matches your syntax—`your.render.kit.id[wrapped.render.kit.id]`—you wrap the `RenderKit` defined by the first part of the implementation—`your.render.kit.id`—around the `RenderKit` defined between the square brackets—`[wrapped.render.kit.id]`.

The ExtendedRenderKitFactory Class

To make sure your solution is agnostic to the JSF implementation used by the application developer, you need to provide generic APIs to your application developers, as well as to component authors. To achieve this, we have decided to provide a `RenderKitFactoryWrapper` that extends the JSF implementation's abstract `RenderKitFactory` class to provide you with a loose coupling to the underlying JSF implementation.

In Figure 6-7, you can see the relationship between the default `RenderKitFactory` provided by the JSF implementation and your `RenderKitFactoryWrapper` and the decorating `ExtendedRenderKitFactory` class. The `RenderKitFactoryWrapper`'s sole purpose is to give you the loose coupling to the underlying implementation you need by delegating to the underlying `RenderKitFactory` implementation.

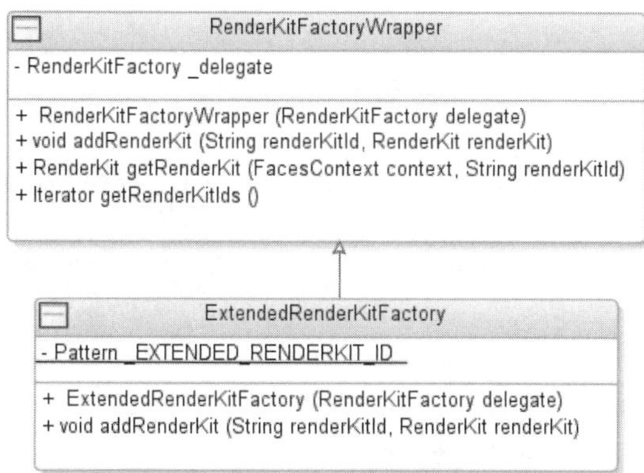

Figure 6-7. *Class diagram of the* `DecoratingRenderKitFactory`

The `ExtendedRenderKitFactory` is the class where you decorate the `RenderKitFactory` provided by the JSF implementation with functionality to wrap one `RenderKit` around another, if the RenderKit ID provided by the component author matches the syntax defined earlier—`your.render.kit.id[wrapped.render.kit.id]`, as shown in Code Sample 6-9.

Code Sample 6-9. *The* `ExtendedRenderKitFactory` *Class*

```
package com.apress.projsf.ch6.render;

import java.util.regex.Matcher;
import java.util.regex.Pattern;

import javax.faces.render.RenderKit;
import javax.faces.render.RenderKitFactory;

/**
 * The ExtendedRenderKitFactory supports dynamic extension of
 * RenderKits without needing to reregister all the renderers from the base
 * RenderKit.
```

```
 *
 * The following syntax must be used to register the extended RenderKit.
 *
 * <render-kit-id>extended-render-kit-id[base-render-kit-id]</render-kit-id>
 *
 * and the RenderKit implementation class must be of type ExtendedRenderKit.
 */
public class ExtendedRenderKitFactory extends RenderKitFactoryWrapper
{
  /**
   * Creates a new ExtendedRenderKitFactory.
   *
   * @param delegate  the RenderKitFactory delegate
   */
  public ExtendedRenderKitFactory (
    RenderKitFactory delegate)
  {
    super(delegate);
  }

  /**
   * Adds a new RenderKit to this RenderKitFactory.
   *
   * If the renderKitId syntax is of the form
   * extended-render-kit-id[base-render-kit-id] and the RenderKit is
   * and instance of ExtendedRenderKit, then the extended-render-kit-id
   * is used to register the RenderKit, and the base-render-kit-id is used
   * as the base RenderKit for the ExtendedRenderKit.
   *
   * @param renderKitId  the RenderKit identifier
   * @param renderKit    the RenderKit implementation
   */
  public void addRenderKit(
    String    renderKitId,
    RenderKit renderKit)
  {
    Matcher matcher = _EXTENDED_RENDERKIT_ID.matcher(renderKitId);
    if (matcher.matches() &&
        renderKit instanceof ExtendedRenderKit)
    {
      renderKitId = matcher.group(1);
      String baseRenderKitId = matcher.group(2);

      ExtendedRenderKit extension = (ExtendedRenderKit)renderKit;
      RenderKit base = getRenderKit(null, baseRenderKitId);
      extension.setRenderKit(base);
    }
```

```
    super.addRenderKit(renderKitId, renderKit);
  }

  static final private Pattern _EXTENDED_RENDERKIT_ID =
                          Pattern.compile("([^\\[]+)\\[([^\\]]+)\\]");
}
```

If the syntax provided by the component author matches the pattern you have defined to identify an extended RenderKit, then you divide the string representing the RenderKit ID into two groups. Group 1 represents the RenderKit ID you'll be using to register the RenderKit, and group 2 is the ID for the base RenderKit. If the RenderKit ID syntax does not match the pattern used to define an extended RenderKit, then the ID is not modified and is still passed to the wrapped RenderKitFactory to register the RenderKit—super.addRenderKit(renderKitId, renderKit).

■ **Note** We have implemented a solution to wrap only one RenderKit, but this decorating RenderKitFactory class could potentially support wrapping multiple RenderKits. For simplicity, we decided to wrap only one RenderKit (for example, HTML_BASIC).

The ExtendedRenderKit Class

The ExtendedRenderKit class provides the same benefits as the RenderKitFactoryWrapper class (that is, a loose coupling to the underlying JSF implementation's RenderKit class). As mentioned earlier, the RenderKit is responsible for providing a ResponseWriter when requested and also represents a collection of Renderer instances that, together, know how to render UIComponent instances for a specific client-user agent.

In Figure 6-8 you can see the relationship between the default RenderKit class and the ExtendedRenderKit and the custom HtmlAjaxRenderKit classes shown in Code Sample 6-10.

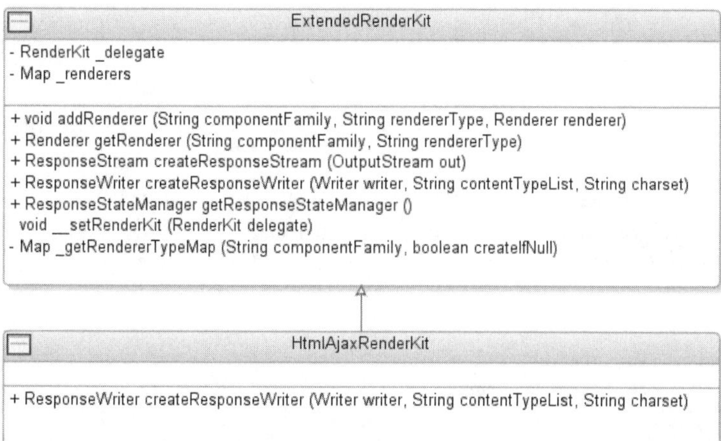

Figure 6-8. *Class diagram of the* HtmlAjaxRenderKit

Code Sample 6-10. *The* ExtendedRenderKit *Class*

```
package com.apress.projsf.ch6.render;

import java.io.OutputStream;
import java.io.Writer;
import java.util.Map;
import java.util.TreeMap;

import javax.faces.context.ResponseStream;
import javax.faces.context.ResponseWriter;
import javax.faces.render.RenderKit;
import javax.faces.render.Renderer;
import javax.faces.render.ResponseStateManager;

/**
 * ExtendedRenderKit supports dynamic extension of another RenderKit
 * without needing to reregister all the renderers from the base
 * RenderKit.
 */
public class ExtendedRenderKit extends RenderKit
{
  /**
   * Adds a Renderer to this RenderKit.
   *
   * @param componentFamily  the component family
   * @param rendererType     the renderer type
   * @param renderer         the renderer implementation
   */
  public void addRenderer(String  componentFamily,
                          String  rendererType,
                          Renderer  renderer)
  {
    Map map = _getRendererTypeMap(componentFamily, true);
    map.put(rendererType, renderer);
  }

  /**
   * Returns a Renderer for the specified component family and renderer type.
   * If a Renderer was registered directly on this ExtendedRenderKit, then
   * it is returned; otherwise, the Renderer lookup is delegated to the base
   * RenderKit.
   *
   * @param componentFamily  the component family
   * @param rendererType     the renderer type
   *
   * @return the previously registered renderer implementation
   */
```

```
  public Renderer getRenderer(
    String componentFamily,
    String rendererType)
  {
    Map map = _getRendererTypeMap(componentFamily, false);
    Renderer renderer = (map != null) ? (Renderer)map.get(rendererType) : null;

    if (renderer == null)
      renderer = _base.getRenderer(componentFamily, rendererType);

    return renderer;
  }

  private Map _getRendererTypeMap(
    String  componentFamily,
    boolean createIfNull)
  {
    Map componentFamilyMap = (Map)_renderers.get(componentFamily);
    if (componentFamilyMap == null && createIfNull)
    {
      componentFamilyMap = new TreeMap();
      _renderers.put(componentFamily, componentFamilyMap);
    }
    return componentFamilyMap;
  }

  ...

  /**
   * Sets the base RenderKit, since it is not available
   * when this instance is constructed.
   *
   * @param base  the base RenderKit
   */
  void setRenderKit(
    RenderKit base)
  {
    _base = base;
  }

  private RenderKit _base;
  private final Map _renderers = new TreeMap();
}
```

The ExtendedRenderKit is not only providing a loose coupling to the underlying implementation—the abstract RenderKit class—but it also is providing the means of looking up renderers in your HtmlAjaxRenderKit and, if the Renderer requested is not available in the

HtmlAjaxRenderKit, calling the getRenderer() method on the base RenderKit. The aforementioned ExtendedRenderKitFactory class uses the setRenderKit() method to set the base RenderKit (for example, the standard HTML_BASIC RenderKit) at application start-up.

The HtmlAjaxRenderKit Class

You're down to the last piece in the RenderKit puzzle, your custom RenderKit—the HtmlAjaxRenderKit class. The HtmlRenderKit class is responsible for providing the right ResponseWriter depending on the incoming request from the client, as shown in Code Sample 6-11.

Code Sample 6-11. *The* HtmlAjaxRenderKit *Class*

```
package com.apress.projsf.ch6.render.html.ajax;

import java.io.Writer;
import java.util.Map;

import javax.faces.context.ExternalContext;
import javax.faces.context.FacesContext;
import javax.faces.context.ResponseWriter;

import com.apress.projsf.ch6.render.ExtendedRenderKit;
import com.apress.projsf.ch6.render.FixedContentTypeResponseWriter;

/**
 * HtmlAjaxRenderKit is an extended RenderKit, using HTML_BASIC as the
 * base RenderKit.
 */
public class HtmlAjaxRenderKit extends ExtendedRenderKit
{
  /**
   * Creates the ResponseWriter, fixing the content type
   * to "text/plain" for d2 Ajax requests.
   *
   * @param writer           the writer
   * @param contentTypeList  the acceptable content types (q-values)
   * @param charset          the character encoding of the writer
   *
   * @return  the newly created ResponseWriter
   */
  public ResponseWriter createResponseWriter(
    Writer writer,
    String contentTypeList,
    String charset)
  {
    FacesContext context = FacesContext.getCurrentInstance();
    ExternalContext external = context.getExternalContext();
```

```
    Map requestHeaders = external.getRequestHeaderMap();

    if (contentTypeList == null)
    {
      contentTypeList = (String)requestHeaders.get("Accept");
      // IE sends a vague Accept header of "*/*"
      contentTypeList = contentTypeList.replaceFirst("(\\*/\\*)", "text/html");
    }

    ResponseWriter out =
      super.createResponseWriter(writer, contentTypeList, charset);

    // Detect D2 request
    String d2ContentType = (String)requestHeaders.get("X-D2-Content-Type");

    if ("text/html".equals(d2ContentType))
    {
      out = new FixedContentTypeResponseWriter(out, "text/plain");
    }

    return out;
  }
```

To be able to know what ResponseWriter to select, you need to know whether this is an initial request, a regular form postback, or an Ajax postback. If the user clicked the ProShowOneDeck component, you pass a custom header on the XMLHttpRequest—X-D2-Content-Type. In your custom createResponseWriter() method, you check for your custom request header; if set to true, you create a new instance of the FixedContentTypeResponseWriter. On the initial request or a regular form postback (for example, an h:commandButton was clicked), your custom request header will not be present; thus, you will delegate the responsibility to create a ResponseWriter to super (for example, the default RenderKit).

The FixedContentTypeResponseWriter Class

The FixedContentTypeResponseWriter is responsible for writing out a document (content type text/plain) on any subsequent postback performed by your Ajax-enabled components. This will allow you to leverage the XMLHttpRequest response facility to retrieve the document via the responseText property. To process the response and modify the DOM in the target document, you will use the D^2 open source project.

One of the benefits of writing out a plain-text string representing your document is that, in the presence of file upload functionality, the returned document's innerHTML will be properly inserted in the targeted <iframe>, but not executed as HTML; this prevents any <script> elements from being executed in the wrong context.

Figure 6-9 shows that the <f:view> tag will call the createResponseWriter() method on the custom HtmlAjaxRenderKit during the JSF lifecycle's Render Response phase and pass either the default ResponseWriter or the custom FixedContentTypeResponseWriter to the FacesContext based on the initial request or subsequent postback.

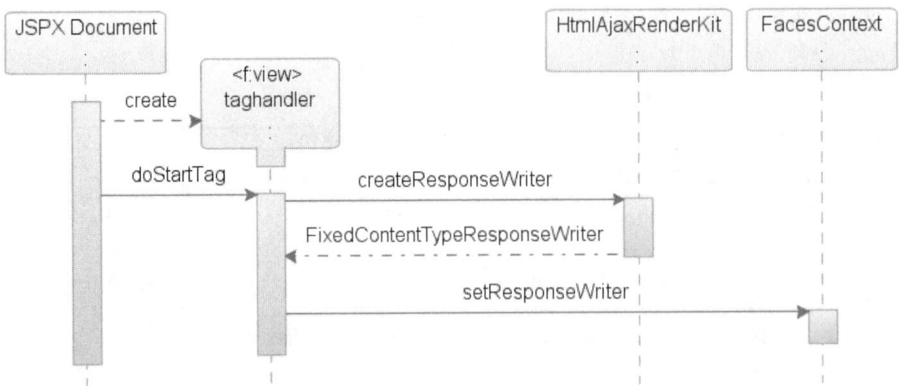

Figure 6-9. *Creating the* `FixedContentTypeResponseWriter` *during Ajax postback*

Figure 6-10 illustrates the structure and dependencies of the `FixedContentTypeResponseWriter` class. The `ResponseWriterWrapper` class is only delegating, without decorating, to the standard `ResponseWriter`, as shown in Code Sample 6-12.

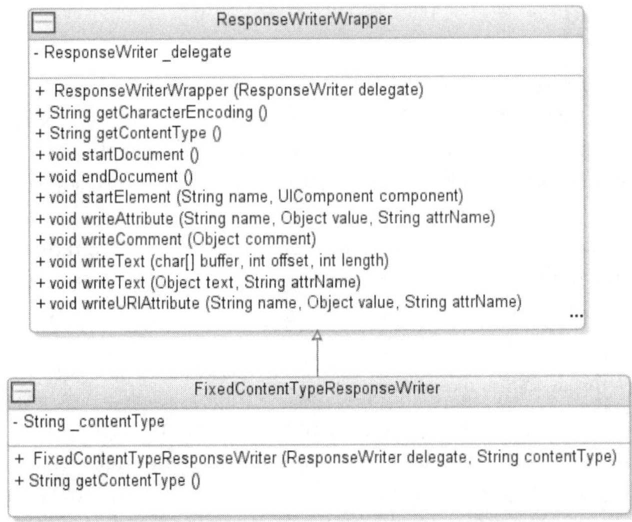

Figure 6-10. *Diagram of* `FixedContentTypeResponseWriter`

Code Sample 6-12. *The* `FixedContentTypeResponseWriter`

```
package com.apress.projsf.ch6.render;

import javax.faces.context.ResponseWriter;

/**
```

```
 * FixedContentTypeResponseWriter is used to override the content type
 * when delivering the response.
 */
public class FixedContentTypeResponseWriter extends ResponseWriterWrapper
{
  /**
   * Creates a new FixedContentTypeResponseWriter.
   *
   * @param delegate     the ResponseWriter delegate
   * @param contentType  the fixed content type to be used
   */
  public FixedContentTypeResponseWriter(
    ResponseWriter delegate,
    String         contentType)
  {
    super(delegate);
    _contentType = contentType;
  }

  /**
   * Returns the fixed content type for this ResponseWriter.
   *
   * @return  the fixed content type
   */
  public String getContentType()
  {
    return _contentType;
  }

  private final String _contentType;
}
```

The FixedContentTypeResponseWriter takes two arguments—the ResponseWriter that will be wrapped and the contentType for this request (for example, text/plain). Since you cannot set the contentType directly on the default ResponseWriter, overriding the getContentType() method of super (the delegated ResponseWriter), ensure that the content type you have defined will be used to produce the correct output to the client.

Step 9: Extending the JSF Implementation

Up until now, you have been focusing on how to wrap the existing RenderKit and how to provide the correct ResponseWriter for the request based on what type of postback was performed. This ensures that the ResponseWriter has the correct content type. Unfortunately, JSP typically ignores that, so you will need to take control of the contentType set on the HttpServletResponse object.

By default, the JSP engine will set the contentType on the HttpServletResponse object to whatever the application developer has defined in the JSP page directive (for example, <jsp:directive.page contentType="text/html" />) or to the JSP engine's default value, which is `text/html` for JSP classic and `text/xml` for JSP documents. This is acceptable for most traditional JSP applications, since they are targeted Web clients that support HTML; however, for a JSF application that might support multiple `contentTypes` (for example, HTML and XML), this is too restrictive.

■**Note** For more information about the `HttpServletResponse` object, please refer to the Servlet specification (`http://java.sun.com/products/servlet/2.1/servlet-2.1.pdf`).

The Content Type Situation

This is the situation you are facing: you don't know what `contentType` is needed—`text/html` or `text/plain`—until the `<f:view>` tag calls the `createResponseWriter()` method, but the `contentType` is by default already set on the `HttpServletResponse` object before the `ResponseWriter` is created by the `<f:view>` tag. Figure 6-11 shows the default processing of the JSP document.

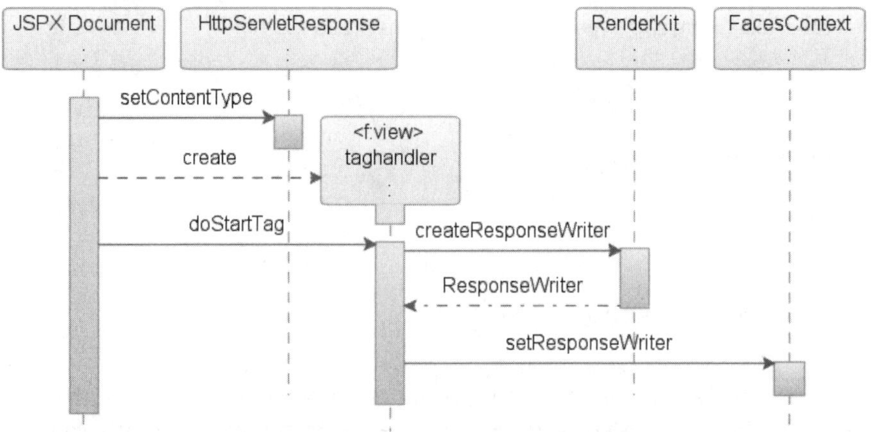

Figure 6-11. *Default processing of the JSP document*

On the initial request, you need to know whether the `ResponseWriter` should control the content type to be sent with the `HttpServletResponse` object to the client. You can do this by providing a custom content type via the JSP page directive—`<jsp:directive.page contentType="application/x-javaserver-faces" />`. If the application developer omits the special `contentType` in the JSP page directive, the implementation will work the traditional way of having the JSP engine default the `contentType`.

If the JSP page directive is set to `application/x-javaserver-faces`, you need to defer setting the `contentType` on the `HttpServletResponse` object until after the `ResponseWriter` has been created. This ensures that the `contentType` set on the `HttpServletResponse` matches the markup written by the `ResponseWriter` for this request. The way you can defer setting the `contentType` is to wrap the `HttpServletResponse` with your own deferred servlet response—`DeferredContentTypeResponse`.

Extending the FacesContextFactory

You need to pass the servlet response to the `FacesContext`, and the most convenient way is to wrap the `HttpServletResponse` object with your own response object just before the `FacesContext` gets created for the incoming request. This avoids the need for a servlet filter and can also work for portlets. Figure 6-12 shows the initial processing of the request.

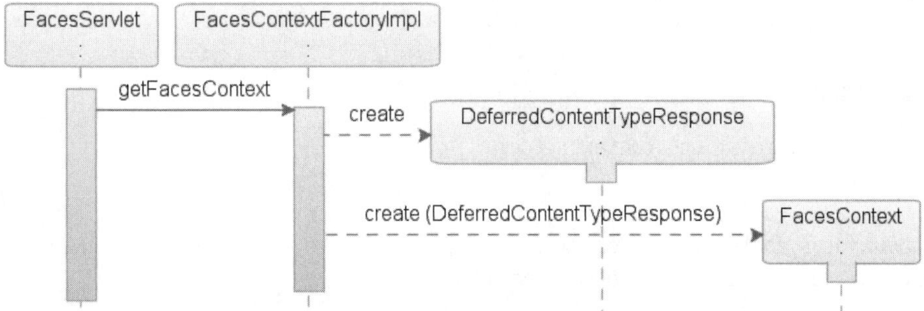

Figure 6-12. *Initial processing of the request*

First you need to extend the `FacesContextFactory` with a means to create a custom `ServletResponse` and wrap it around the `HttpServletResponse`, and then you pass the custom `ServletResponse` to the `FacesContext`. That way, you will have control over the `ServletResponse`, and you can intercept the `contentType` when it's being set by the JSP engine and, if needed, defer setting the `contentType` until you have access to the `contentType` used by the `ResponseWriter`.

Looking at the sequence of the initial process, the `FacesServlet` will first call the `getFacesContext` on your implementation of the `FacesContextFactory`—`FacesContextFactoryImpl`. The `FacesContextFactoryImpl` will first create a new servlet response, `DeferredContentTypeResponse`; this will wrap the standard `HttpServletResponse`. You then pass the `DeferredContentTypeResponse` to the `FacesContext`. Figure 6-13 shows the `FacesContextFactory` implementation in detail.

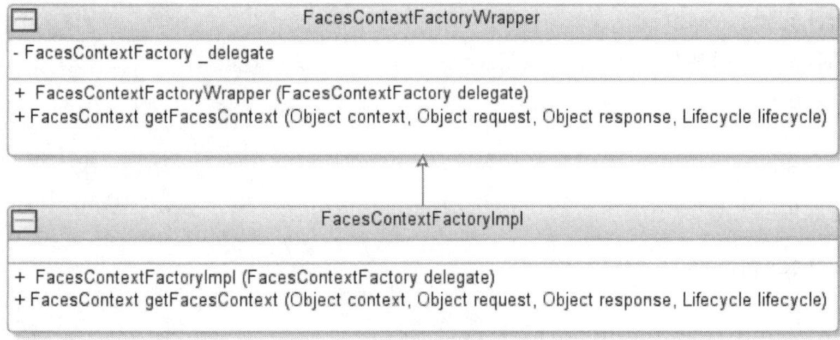

Figure 6-13. *Diagram over the* `FacesContext` *implementation*

First you create a FacesContextFactoryWrapper wrapper class that is only delegating, without decorating, to the standard FacesContextFactory, and that will provide you with a loose coupling to the JSF implementation used by the application developer. Then you extend your wrapper class with the FacesContextFactoryImpl class to add some decorations. This class intercepts the HttpServletResponse and creates a new servlet response, DeferredContentTypeResponse; this will defer setting the contentType, if needed, until the ResponseWriter is created.

The FacesContextFactoryImpl Class

The FacesContextFactoryImpl class, on the other hand, supports additional processing of the servlet response object, as shown in Code Sample 6-13.

Code Sample 6-13. *The* FacesContextFactoryImpl *Class*

```
package com.apress.projsf.ch6.context;

import javax.faces.FacesException;
import javax.faces.context.FacesContext;
import javax.faces.context.FacesContextFactory;
import javax.faces.lifecycle.Lifecycle;

import javax.servlet.http.HttpServletResponse;

import com.apress.projsf.ch6.external.servlet.DeferredContentTypeResponse;

/**
 * FacesContextFactoryImpl supports additional processing of the response.
 */
public class FacesContextFactoryImpl extends FacesContextFactoryWrapper
{
  /**
   * Creates a new FacesContextFactoryImpl.
   *
   * @param delegate  the FacesContextFactory delegate
   */
  public FacesContextFactoryImpl(
    FacesContextFactory delegate)
  {
    super(delegate);
  }

  /**
   * Returns the new FacesContext instance.
   *
   * @param context     the servlet or portlet context
```

```
   * @param request     the servlet or portlet request
   * @param response    the servlet or portlet response
   * @param lifecycle   the Faces lifecycle
   *
   * @return the new FacesContext instance
   *
   * @throws FacesException  if an error occurs
   */
  public FacesContext getFacesContext(Object context,
                                      Object request,
                                      Object response,
                                      Lifecycle lifecycle) throws FacesException
  {
    if (response instanceof HttpServletResponse)
    {
      response = new DeferredContentTypeResponse((HttpServletResponse)response);
    }

    return super.getFacesContext(context, request, response, lifecycle);
  }
}
```

If the response object is an instance of type `HttpServletResponse`, you will create a new instance of the `DeferredContentTypeResponse` and pass the `HttpServletResponse` as an argument. If the response does not match `HttpServletResponse`, then you just pass it through to `super` without further processing. (Note that you can support portlets using a similar technique, but we have omitted this in the example.)

Overriding the HttpServletResponse

The `DeferredContentTypeResponse` is not only responsible for wrapping the `HttpServletResponse` object, but it is also responsible for detecting whether the JSP page directive indicates that the `contentType` should be set by the `ResponseWriter` (*JSF major*). If the request is JSF major, you set the `contentType` after the `ResponseWriter` has been created and, most important, at the first time the response output stream is being written back to the browser over the network. Figure 6-14 shows the processing of the response object during the Render Response phase.

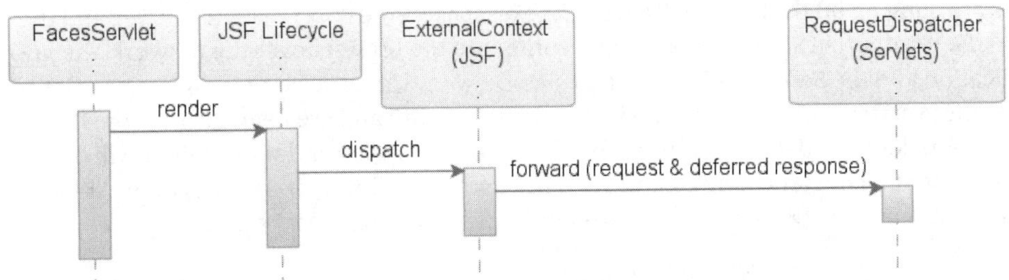

Figure 6-14. *Processing of the response object during the Render Response phase*

At the initial processing of the Render Response phase, your DeferredContentTypeResponse is being passed to the servlet RequestDispatcher. The RequestDispatcher forwards the JSF viewId (for example, /projsf.jspx) for this request to the JSP engine for processing, as shown in Figure 6-15.

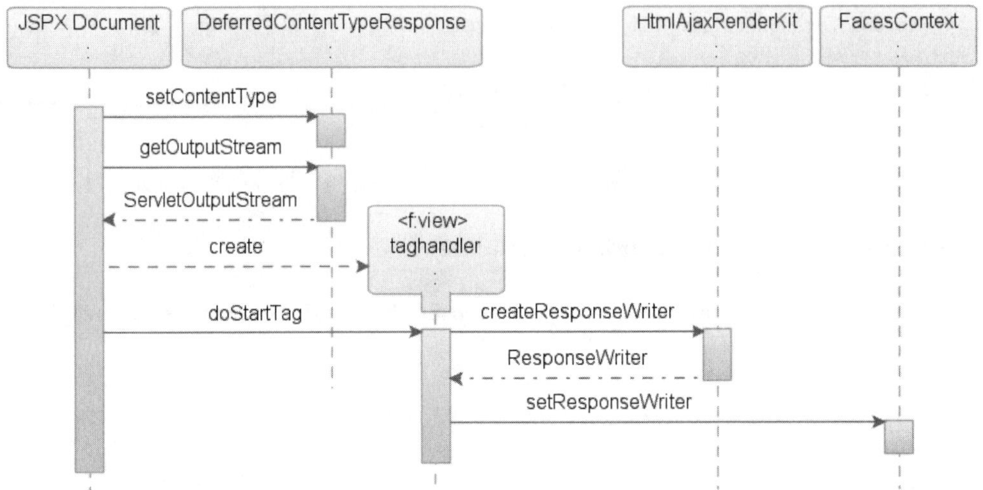

Figure 6-15. *Processing of JSP document*

Since you have wrapped the default HttpServletResponse with the deferred servlet response, you can now intercept the contentType to determine whether the ResponseWriter should dictate the contentType for this request (JSF major) or if you should let the JSP engine set the contentType immediately (*JSP major*).

When the JSP document is being processed, it will first try to set the content type on the ServletResponse and get the output stream. If this is a JSF major response, the DeferredContentTypeResponse object will defer setting the contentType until after the ResponseWriter is created. Next, the <f:view> tag handler is created, which will call createResponseWriter on the HtmlAjaxRenderKit and set the returned ResponseWriter on the FacesContext. The contentType will be set the first time the buffered JSP tag—<f:view>—is writing content out to the browser over the network.

Figure 6-16 illustrates the deferred content type implementation. As you can see, two classes are hanging off the DeferredContentTypeResponse—the DeferredPrintWriter and the DeferredServletOutputStream. To write any content to the browser over the network, the Java specification and the Servlet API define two classes—ServletOutputStream and PrintWriter. Both of these classes basically provide similar functionality and are needed since the JSP specification does not define whether the JSP Container or the Servlet Container will be used to convert characters to bytes and send the data to the browser over the network—character stream (PrintWriter) or byte stream (ServletOutputStream) output.

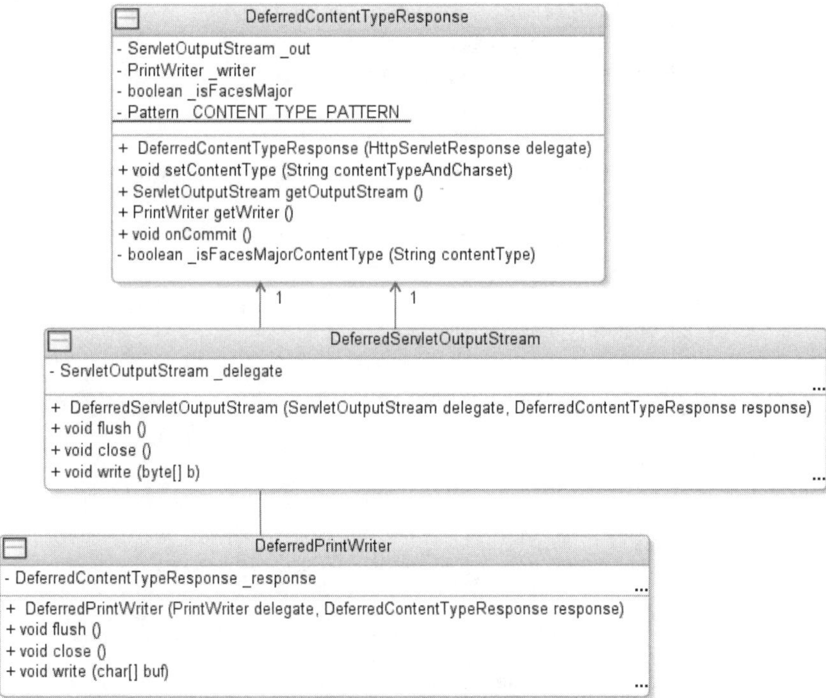

Figure 6-16. *Diagram over the* `DeferredContentType` *implementation*

On the first attempt to write to the browser, you need to set the `contentType` on the `ServletResponse`. To achieve this, you need to decorate the default `ServletOutputStream` (`DeferredServletOutputStream`) and `PrintWriter` (`DeferredPrintWriter`) with functionality to set the `contentType` on the first write and make sure it is done only once.

The DeferredContentTypeResponse Class

The `DeferredContentTypeResponse` decorates the JSP `HttpServletResponse` with functionality to support setting a JSF major content type. Code Sample 6-14 shows the deferred `HttpServletResponse`.

Code Sample 6-14. *The* `DeferredContentTypeResponse`

```
package com.apress.projsf.ch6.external.servlet;

import java.io.IOException;
import java.io.PrintWriter;
import java.util.regex.Matcher;
import java.util.regex.Pattern;

import javax.faces.context.FacesContext;
import javax.faces.context.ResponseWriter;
```

```
import javax.servlet.ServletOutputStream;
import javax.servlet.http.HttpServletResponse;
import javax.servlet.http.HttpServletResponseWrapper;

/**
 * DeferredContentTypeResponse manages setting the JSF major content type.
 */
public class DeferredContentTypeResponse extends HttpServletResponseWrapper
{
  /**
   * Creates a new DeferredContentTypeResponse.
   *
   * @param delegate  the HttpServletResponse delegate
   */
  public DeferredContentTypeResponse(
    HttpServletResponse delegate)
  {
    super(delegate);
  }

  /**
   * Attempt to set the content type as deferred.
   *
   * @param contentTypeAndCharset  the content type and character set
   *                               for this response
   */
  public void setContentType(
    String contentTypeAndCharset)
  {
    Matcher matcher = _CONTENT_TYPE_PATTERN.matcher(contentTypeAndCharset);
    if (matcher.matches())
    {
      String contentType = matcher.group(1);
      String charset = (matcher.groupCount() > 1) ? matcher.group(2) : null;

      // remember _isFacesMajor for later, during onCommit,
      // after Faces ResponseWriter has been created
      _isFacesMajor = isFacesMajorContentType(contentType);

      if (_isFacesMajor)
      {
        // although we'll set the content type on onCommit,
        // you need to set the charset now
        // <f:view> will need charset when creating the ResponseWriter
        super.setCharacterEncoding(charset);
      }
```

```
      else
      {
        // content type will not be set on onCommit,
        // so set both content type and charset now
        super.setContentType(contentTypeAndCharset);
      }
    }
  }

  /**
   * Returns true if the specified content type
   * matches "application/x-javaserver-faces".
   *
   * @param contentType  the response content type
   *
   * @return true if the content type is "application/x-javaserver-faces"
   */
  private boolean isFacesMajorContentType(
    String contentType)
  {
    return ("application/x-javaserver-faces".equals(contentType));
  }
```

When the JSP engine calls the setContentType() method on your JSP HttpServletResponseWrapper, it passes a string representing both the contentType and the character encoding defined by the application developer in the JSP page directive. The setContentType() method will check the string to see whether it matches the pattern defined by the Servlet specification. If it matches, you divide the string into two groups—one for the content type (contentType) and one for character encoding (charset). You can use the extracted contentType to test whether this is a JSF major request. The isFacesMajorContentType() method will return true or false depending on the contentType defined in the JSP page directive (for example, application/x-javaserver-faces). If it is a JSF major request, you still need to set the character set—charset—on the ServletResponse, since <f:view> needs the character set when creating the ResponseWriter. Code Sample 6-15 shows the DeferredContentTypeResponse class.

Code Sample 6-15. DeferredContentTypeResponse *Class*

```
  public ServletOutputStream getOutputStream() throws IOException
  {
    if (_out == null)
    {
      _out = new DeferredServletOutputStream(super.getOutputStream(), this);
    }
    return _out;
  }
```

```
  public PrintWriter getWriter() throws IOException
  {
    if (_writer == null)
    {
      _writer = new DeferredPrintWriter(super.getWriter(), this);
    }
    return _writer;
  }

  public void onCommit() throws IOException
  {
    if (_isFacesMajor)
    {
      FacesContext context = FacesContext.getCurrentInstance();
      ResponseWriter out = context.getResponseWriter();
      String contentType = out.getContentType();

      // set real content type via super.setContentType
      super.setContentType(contentType);
    }
  }

  private ServletOutputStream _out;
  private PrintWriter         _writer;
  private boolean             _isFacesMajor;

  static private final Pattern _CONTENT_TYPE_PATTERN =
                               Pattern.compile("([^;]+)(?:;charset=(.*))?");
}
```

In your DeferredContentTypeResponse class, you have two methods—getWriter() and getOutputStream()—that, depending on the J2EE container implementation, will be used to write out bytes, representing the markup, to the network. We will cover the deferred writers in the "The DeferredServletOutputStream Class" and "The DeferredPrintWriter Class" sections. The onCommit() method will be called the first time data is being written to the browser over the network by either the ServletOutputStream or the PrintWriter. If the request is a JSF major, the onCommit() method will get the contentType from the ResponseWriter and set it on the HttpServletResponse object.

The DeferredServletOutputStream Class

Eventually the buffered JSP tag will be full, and markup will be written to the client. If this is a JSF major request, the contentType has not yet been set, so you need to make sure that at the first call to the write() method on the ServletOutputStream object you set the content type on the HttpServletResponse. Figure 6-17 shows the initial processing of the request.

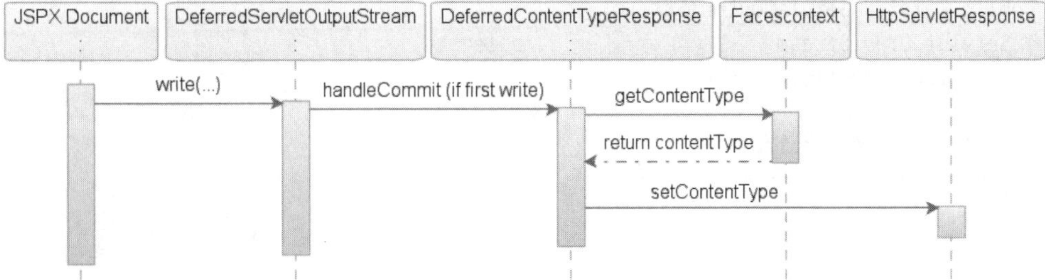

Figure 6-17. *Initial processing of request*

If this is a JSF major request, the `contentType` has been deferred and not yet set on the `ServletResponse`. It is important to ensure that the `contentType` is set on the response object before data gets written to the browser, since it needs the `contentType` to be able to parse the content sent with the output stream. You can do this by overriding the default `ServletOutputStream` and providing a way to call the aforementioned `onCommit()` method on the `DeferredContentTypeResponse` and by setting a flag indicating whether the `contentType` has been set on the `ServletResponse`.

The `DeferredServletOutputStream` decorates the ServletOutputStream with a method—`handleCommit()`—that sets a flag indicating that the `contentType` has been set, and it calls the `onCommit()` method on the `DeferredContentTypeResponse` (see Code Sample 6-16). This ensures that the content type written to the client by the `ResponseWriter` is now matching the `contentType` set on the response object.

Code Sample 6-16. *The* `DeferredServletOutputStream` *Class*

```
package com.apress.projsf.ch6.external.servlet;

import java.io.IOException;

import javax.servlet.ServletOutputStream;

/**
 * DeferredServletOutputStream provides a callback when the first bytes
 * are written to the output stream.
 */
public class DeferredServletOutputStream extends ServletOutputStream
{
  /**
   * Creates a new DeferredServletOutputStream.
   *
   * @param delegate  the ServletOutputStream delegate
   * @param response  the callback target
   */
```

```
  public DeferredServletOutputStream(
    ServletOutputStream                    delegate,
    DeferredContentTypeResponse response)
  {
    _delegate = delegate;
    _response = response;
  }

  ...

  public void write(
    byte[] b,
    int off,
    int len) throws IOException
  {
    if (!_committed)
      _handleCommit();
    _delegate.write(b, off, len);
  }

  ...

  /**
   * The _handleCommit() method is called only once, when
   * the first write(), print(), println(), flush(), or close() call
   * is made to this ServletOutputStream.
   */
  private void _handleCommit() throws IOException
  {
    _committed = true;
    _response.onCommit();
  }

  private final ServletOutputStream                    _delegate;
  private final DeferredContentTypeResponse _response;
  private       boolean                                _committed;
}
```

The extended `ServletOutputStream` class is an abstract class that the servlet container implements, and it provides an output stream for sending binary data to the client. Note that the `handleCommit()` method is called only once, when the first `write()` call is made to this `ServletOutputStream`.

The DeferredPrintWriter Class

The `DeferredPrintWriter` performs the same duty as the `DeferredServletOutputStream`—writing markup to the client except that this class provides a writer for sending character data (see Code Sample 6-17). The underlying servlet implementation performs the conversion of the character-based stream to bytes.

Code Sample 6-17. *The* `DeferredPrintWriter` *Class*

```
package com.apress.projsf.ch6.external.servlet;

import java.io.IOException;
import java.io.PrintWriter;

/**
 * DeferredPrintWriter provides a callback when the first characters
 * are written to the writer.
 */
public class DeferredPrintWriter extends PrintWriter
{
  /**
   * Creates a new DeferredPrintWriter.
   *
   * @param delegate  the PrintWriter delegate
   * @param response  the callback target
   */
  public DeferredPrintWriter(
    PrintWriter                            delegate,
    DeferredContentTypeResponse response)
  {
    super(delegate);
    _response = response;
  }

  ...

  public void write(
    char[] buf,
    int off,
    int len)
  {
    if (!_committed)
      _handleCommit();
    super.write(buf, off, len);
  }

  private void handleCommit()
```

```
  {
    try
    {
      _committed = true;
      _response.onCommit();
    }
    catch (IOException e)
    {
      setError();
    }
  }

  private boolean _committed;
  private final DeferredContentTypeResponse _response;
}
```

As you can see, this class is almost identical to the ServletOutputStream with two differences—the signature of the method calls are using char instead of byte, and the methods in this class never throw I/O exceptions. Since methods cannot throw I/O exceptions, you are forced to implement your handleCommit() method slightly differently than you implement the one in the DeferredServletOutputStream class. This ensures that you handle any IOException that might be thrown. Besides this, the handleCommit() method is called only once, when the first write() call is made to this PrintWriter.

Step 10: Registering the RenderKit and JSF Extension

As mentioned in Chapter 1, the Application instance will, at application start-up, store resources defined in the JSF configuration file, faces-config.xml. For your JSF Ajax implementation, you need to make sure you not only register your custom Renderers and their RenderKits but that you also register your JSF extensions (for example, the custom FacesContextFactory and RenderKitFactory), as shown in Code Sample 6-18.

Code Sample 6-18. *Register the Ajax-Enabled* Renderer *and* RenderKit

```
<?xml version="1.0" encoding="UTF-8" ?>
<!DOCTYPE faces-config
   PUBLIC "-//Sun Microsystems, Inc.//DTD JavaServer Faces Config 1.1//EN"
          "http://java.sun.com/dtd/web-facesconfig_1_1.dtd">

<faces-config xmlns="http://java.sun.com/JSF/Configuration" >
  <factory>
    <faces-context-factory>
      com.apress.projsf.ch6.context.FacesContextFactoryImpl
    </faces-context-factory>
    <render-kit-factory>
      com.apress.projsf.ch6.render.ExtendedRenderKitFactory
    </render-kit-factory>
  </factory>
```

```
  ...

  <render-kit>
    <render-kit-id>com.apress.projsf.html.ajax[HTML_BASIC]</render-kit-id>
    <render-kit-class>
      com.apress.projsf.ch6.render.html.ajax.HtmlAjaxRenderKit
    </render-kit-class>
    <renderer>
      <component-family>com.apress.projsf.ShowOne</component-family>
      <renderer-type>com.apress.projsf.Deck</renderer-type>
      <renderer-class>
        com.apress.projsf.ch6.render.html.ajax.HtmlAjaxShowOneDeckRenderer
      </renderer-class>
    </renderer>
  </render-kit>

</faces-config>
```

At the top of your faces-config.xml file, you register your FacesContextFactoryImpl class and the ExtendedRenderKitFactory class followed by your new RenderKit—HtmlAjaxRenderKit. As you can see, you use the new pattern (see the section "Registering RenderKits to Wrap") to wrap your new RenderKit around the standard HTML RenderKit (for example, com.apress.projsf.html.ajax[HTML_BASIC]).

Step 11: Registering Resources with Weblets

For the HtmlAjaxShowOneDeckRenderer, you need to register two additional JavaScript libraries—the Dojo toolkit and the D[2] library—as weblets; this will enable you to package these libraries as part of your custom JSF component library.

Note For more information about weblets, please see Chapter 5, or visit the Weblets project's Web site at http://weblets.dev.java.net.

Registering the Dojo Toolkit

Code Sample 6-19 shows the weblet configuration for the Dojo toolkit, after we repackaged the Dojo toolkit JavaScript into a Java package, org.dojotoolkit.browserio.

Code Sample 6-19. *Weblet Configuration for the Dojo Toolkit*

```
<?xml version="1.0" encoding="UTF-8" ?>
<weblets-config xmlns="http://weblets.dev.java.net/config" >

  <weblet>
    <weblet-name>org.dojotoolkit.browserio</weblet-name>
    <weblet-class>net.java.dev.weblets.packaged.PackagedWeblet</weblet-class>
```

```
    <weblet-version>0.1</weblet-version>
    <init-param>
      <param-name>package</param-name>
      <param-value>org.dojotoolkit.browserio</param-value>
    </init-param>
  </weblet>

  <weblet-mapping>
    <weblet-name>org.dojotoolkit.browserio</weblet-name>
    <url-pattern>/dojo/*</url-pattern>
  </weblet-mapping>

</weblets-config>
```

Registering the D² Library

Code Sample 6-20 shows the weblet configuration for the D² library. In future, the D² library will include this weblet configuration automatically.

Code Sample 6-20. *Weblet Configuration for the D² Library*

```
<?xml version="1.0" encoding="UTF-8" ?>
<weblets-config xmlns="http://weblets.dev.java.net/config" >

  <weblet>
    <weblet-name>net.java.dev.d2</weblet-name>
    <weblet-class>net.java.dev.weblets.packaged.PackagedWeblet</weblet-class>
    <init-param>
      <param-name>package</param-name>
      <param-value>net.java.dev.d2</param-value>
    </init-param>
  </weblet>

  <weblet-mapping>
    <weblet-name>net.java.dev.d2</weblet-name>
    <url-pattern>/d2/*</url-pattern>
  </weblet-mapping>

</weblets-config>
```

The `PackagedWeblet` is a built-in weblet implementation that can be read from a particular Java package using the `ClassLoader` and stream the result to the browser. The package initialization parameter tells the `PackagedWeblet` which Java package to use as a root when resolving weblet-managed resource requests.

Summary

In this chapter, we discussed how to use Ajax in general terms and as part of JSF, and we also talked about what pros and cons it brings to the plate. We also covered different architectural approaches implementing Ajax support in JSF—PPR and D^2R. In addition, we discussed potential pitfalls of Ajax, such as file upload support, and how to solve them in the context of JSF.

We explored how to use two open source projects—the Dojo toolkit and D^2 project—to Ajax enable your `ProShowOneDeck` component and prove that providing richer functionality in well-defined and easy-to-use JSF components is not hard. With the use of rich toolkits such as Dojo and D^2, the number of resource files is increasing, and weblet functionality provides an easy way to package your additional resources into the same library as your components.

From this chapter, you gained an understanding of how to Ajax enable JSF components using available resources and now have a deeper understanding of the `contentType` issue between JSP and JSF. You also gained knowledge about how you solve the `contentType` issue and allow JSF to control the `contentType`, which will give you the opportunity to support multiple content types when needed.

CHAPTER 7

Ajax Enabling the Date Field Component

When you innovate, you've got to be prepared for everyone telling you you're nuts.

—Larry Ellison, founder and CEO, Oracle

Chapter 6 introduced the concept of using Ajax and `XMLHttpRequest` to asynchronously communicate with the Web server without the Web server knowing the difference between a regular postback and an Ajax postback. The direct benefit is that it leaves the JSF lifecycle untouched, which allows the application developer to use Ajax-enabled components with regular JSF `Events` and `Listeners`.

This chapter will address the need to fetch data using Ajax. The most common use cases for fetching data using Ajax are to populate drop-down lists and add type-ahead functionality in text fields. In contrast to using Ajax postback for events, fetching data should not affect the surrounding components on the page. And if fetching data is not affecting other parts of the DOM tree, then you do not need to go through the full lifecycle of JSF just to get the data, right?

Plenty of examples are available on the Web today where fetching data is improving the usability of a Web application. The most prominent examples of asynchronous data transfer are Google Suggest's autosuggest feature and Google Gmail's file upload feature.

Requirements for the Date Component's Ajax Implementation

The requirement for the `ProInputDate` component is to provide a visual calendar that can be used to select a date. To support this visual calendar, you need to provide a pop-up window for the actual calendar and asynchronously fetch data representing dates that can be displayed. The visual calendar will allow the user to select only the available dates (for example, working days). All other days (for example, holidays and weekends) should be displayed but not be selectable. When a date is selected, it should be copied to the input field using the correct date format. When a value is submitted back to the server, it should successfully pass validation only if it is an available date (for example, a working day).

The Ajax-Enabled Date Component

In this chapter, you will enhance the `ProInputDate` component created in Chapter 2. Based on the new requirements, you have three goals to achieve in this chapter. First, you need to provide the `ProInputDate` component with a visual calendar. Second, you need to create a `Validator` that can be used by the application developer to provide a list of available dates. These dates can then be validated against user entries in the `ProInputDate` text field. Third, you want to be able to reuse the same managed bean defined for the `Validator` to fetch the list of available dates in the visual calendar, if the validator is attached to the `ProInputDate` component.

To do this, you will use Ajax, two open source frameworks (the Dojo toolkit and Mabon), and the JSON data-interchange format. You've worked with Ajax and the Dojo toolkit before, but the following are new:

JSON: JSON is a lightweight data-interchange format. It is based on a subset of the JavaScript programming language (Standard ECMA-262, Third Edition). JSON is a text format that is completely language independent but uses conventions that are familiar to programmers of the C family of languages, including C, C++, C#, Java, JavaScript, Perl, Python, and many others.

Mabon: Mabon is an open source project hosted on the Java.net Web site (`http://mabon.dev.java.net`), and it stands for Managed Bean Object Notation. Mabon allows the component author of Ajax-enabled components to access JSF managed beans outside the scope of the standard JSF lifecycle by using a JSON-syntax communication channel.

In this chapter, you will look at how you can leverage Ajax, Mabon, JSON, and the Dojo toolkit to provide a visual calendar and asynchronously fetch data for the `ProInputDate` component.

After reading this chapter, you should have an understanding of the difference between Ajax event and data fetch, as well as what issues you may run into while creating rich user interface components with this technology. You should also gain knowledge of an open source project called Mabon and how you can use it to build your own rich Internet components.

Figure 7-1 shows the three classes you will create in this chapter.

Figure 7-1. *Class diagram showing classes created in this chapter*

The classes are as follows:

- The `HtmlAjaxInputDateRenderer` is the new custom `Renderer`, which extends the `HtmlInputDateRenderer` from Chapter 2 and adds resources to include Ajax support.
- The `DateValidator` checks to see whether a `Date` value is available, according to some rules.
- The `ValidateDateTag` class represents the custom action that will be used by the application developer to register a `DateValidator` instance to a `ProInputDate` component.

Designing JSF Components Using a Blueprint

The blueprint for creating a custom JSF component, from Chapter 3, contained seven steps. Those seven steps cover most of the common use cases for designing components. However, as you can see in Table 7-1, this chapter adds one more step to the evolving blueprint from the previous chapter—creating converters and validators—making a total of twelve steps.

Table 7-1. *Steps in the Blueprint for Creating a New JSF Component*

#	Steps	Description
1	Creating a UI prototype	Create the prototype of the UI and intended behavior for your component using appropriate markup.
2	Creating events and listeners	(Optional) Create custom events and listeners in case your specific needs are not covered by the JSF specification.
3	Creating a behavioral superclass	(Optional) If the component behavior is not to be found, create a new behavioral superclass (for example, `UIShowOne`).
4	**Creating converters and validators**	(Optional) Create custom converters and validators in case your specific needs are not covered by the JSF specification.
5	Creating a client-specific renderer	Create the `Renderer` you need that will write out the client-side markup for your JSF component.
6	Creating a renderer-specific subclass	(Optional) Create a renderer-specific subclass. Although this is an optional step, it is good practice to implement it.
7	Registering a `UIComponent` and `Renderer`	Register your new `UIComponent` and `Renderer` in the `faces-config.xml` file.
8	Creating a JSP tag handler and TLD	This step is needed in the case you are using JSP as your default view handler. An alternative solution is to use Facelets (`http://facelets.dev.java.net/`).
9	Creating a `RenderKit` and `ResponseWriter`	(Optional) If you plan to support alternative markup such as Mozilla XUL, then you need to create a new `RenderKit` with an associating `ResponseWriter`. The default `RenderKit` is `HTML_BASIC` with the `contentType` set to `text/html`.

Continued

Table 7-1. *Continued*

#	Steps	Description
10	Extending the JSF implementation	(Optional) This step is needed in the case you have to provide extensions to the JSF implementation (for example, extending JSF factory classes or providing a custom JSF lifecycle implementation).
11	Registering the `RenderKit` and JSF extension	(Optional) Register your custom `RenderKit` and/or extensions to the JSF implementation.
12	Registering resources with weblets	(Optional) Register your resources such as images, JavaScript libraries, and CSS files with weblets so that they can be packaged and loaded directly out of the component library JAR file.

You have done most of the work in Chapter 2, so you only need to extend the `ProInputDate` component with DHTML/Ajax functionality, and since you don't need any new behavior, you can start with step 1, skip steps 2 and 3 in the blueprint, and then move on to steps 4, 5, 7, 8, and 12.

Step 1: Creating a UI Prototype

Back to the blueprint! Let's create the prototype that will help you find out what elements, renderer-specific attributes, and other resources (for example, images) are needed to create a UI for the date component.

Figure 7-2 shows the result of the prototype and displays a page with an input field, a button with a calendar icon, and a table representing the pop-up calendar.

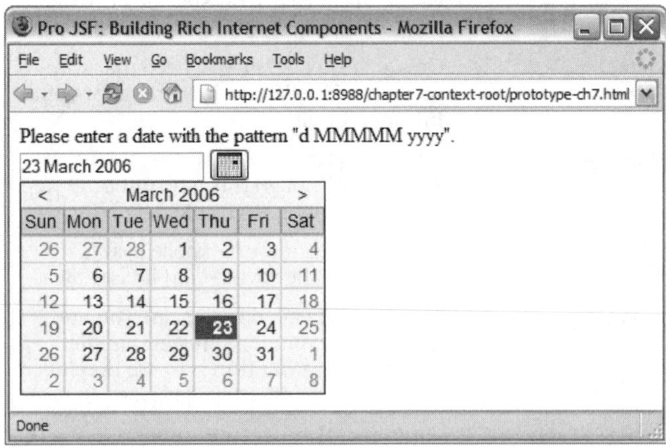

Figure 7-2. `ProInputDate` *implemented in DHTML/Ajax*

Figure 7-2 shows the end result of your prototype implementation. As you can see, we have done some work on the ProInputDate component (from Chapter 2) and added a pop-up calendar, which will appear when the button is clicked. Dates that are not selectable are marked red, and dates outside the scope of the current month are gray.

Code Sample 7-1 shows the markup needed to create the prototype DHTML/Ajax date component shown in Figure 7-2.

Code Sample 7-1. *Input and Button Markup for Calendar*

```
<html>
  <head>
    <meta http-equiv="Content-Type"
          content="text/html; charset=windows-1252" ></meta>
    <title>Pro JSF: Building Rich Internet Components</title>
    <style type="text/css" >@import url(projsf-ch7/inputDate.css);</style>
  </head>
  <body>
    <form name="form" method="post"
          enctype="application/x-www-form-urlencoded" >
      Please enter a date with the pattern "d MMMMM yyyy".
      <br>
      <div title="Date Field Component" >
      <input type="text" name="dateField" value="23 March 2006" />
      <button type="button" name="button" class="ProInputDateButton" >
      <img style="vertical-align: middle;" src="projsf-ch7/inputDateButton.gif" >
      </button>
      </div>
    </form>
    <table id="calendar" cellspacing="0" cellpadding="0"
           class="ProInputDateCalendar"
           style="position: absolute; visibility: visible; top: 53px; left: 8px;" >
      <thead>
        <tr class="toolbar" >
          <td>&lt;</td>
          <td colspan="5" >March 2006</td>
          <td>&gt;</td>
        </tr>
        <tr class="headings" >
          <td>Sun</td>
          <td>Mon</td>
          <td>Tue</td>
          <td>Wed</td>
          <td>Thu</td>
          <td>Fri</td>
          <td>Sat</td>
        </tr>
```

```
        </thead>
        <tbody>
          ...
          <tr>
            <td class="noselect">19</td>
            <td class="">20</td>
            <td class="">21</td>
            <td class="">22</td>
            <td class="selected">23</td>
            <td class="">24</td>
            <td class="noselect">25</td>
          </tr>
          ...
        </tbody>
      </table>
    </body>
  </html>
```

As you can see, it is a simple prototype containing an input field that will be used to enter a date and a regular button that will be used to launch the calendar pop-up. Finally, a table represents your calendar pop-up as it will look when implemented in your new Ajax `Renderer`. At the top of the code listing, you can see that we have referenced the `inputDate.css` file. This style sheet contains information that will be used to display the availability of each date presented by the calendar.

THE @IMPORT RULE

As you may have noticed, we used this rule in the prototype to import a style sheet. Like the `<link>` element, the `@import` rule links an external style sheet to a document. The difference is that the `<link>` element is defined in the head section of a page and specifies the name of the style sheet to import using its `href` attribute. In practice, you can use the `@import` rule in the document body, which allows you to encapsulate styles in a style sheet and import them inside any `<style>` element on the rendered page.

Before creating your input date component, look at the final result and how it will be used in a JSP page. Code Sample 7-2 uses the input date component with the Ajax `Renderer`.

Code Sample 7-2. *JSF Page Source*

```
<?xml version = '1.0' encoding = 'windows-1252'?>
<jsp:root xmlns:jsp="http://java.sun.com/JSP/Page" version="1.2"
          xmlns:pro="http://projsf.apress.com/tags"
```

```
          xmlns:f="http://java.sun.com/jsf/core"
          xmlns:h="http://java.sun.com/jsf/html" >
  <jsp:directive.page contentType="text/html"/>
  <f:view>
    ...
        <h:form id="form" >
          <pro:inputDate id="dateField"
                         title="Date Field Component"
                         value="#{backingBean.date}" >
            <f:convertDateTime pattern="d MMMMM yyyy" />
            <pro:validateDate availability="#{backingBean.getAvailability}" />
          </pro:inputDate>
          <br/>
          <h:message for="theDate" />
          <br/>
          <h:commandButton value="Submit" />
        </h:form>
    ...
  </f:view>
</jsp:root>
```

As you can see, the JSF page has no Ajax "code" in the page source, which means no extra burden is put on the application developer to Ajax enable elements in the page. We have said it before, and we will say it again—make it easy for the application developer!

The only thing that is different in this page from the page created in Chapter 2 is the addition of a Validator—<pro:validateDate .. />. The Validator will be used during regular postback to compare dates entered in the input field against information available in the backing bean. This backing bean will also be used to set dates that are selectable or not in the pop-up calendar. Remember the <f:convertDateTime pattern="d MMMMM yyyy" > Converter from Chapter 2? This converter makes sure that whatever the user enters follows a format you can convert to a Date object on the server.

Fetching Data with Ajax

In Chapter 6, you got familiar with the difference between a regular postback and an Ajax postback to handle events. Fetching data the conventional way versus using Ajax has similar differences, except that it should not have the side effect of changing the state of surrounding components.

The only difference between Figure 7-3 and the Ajax sequence diagram in Chapter 6 (Figure 6-3) is the HTTP method. The W3C recommends you use the HTTP GET method to fetch data when there are no side effects requested by the user (for example, Google Suggest).

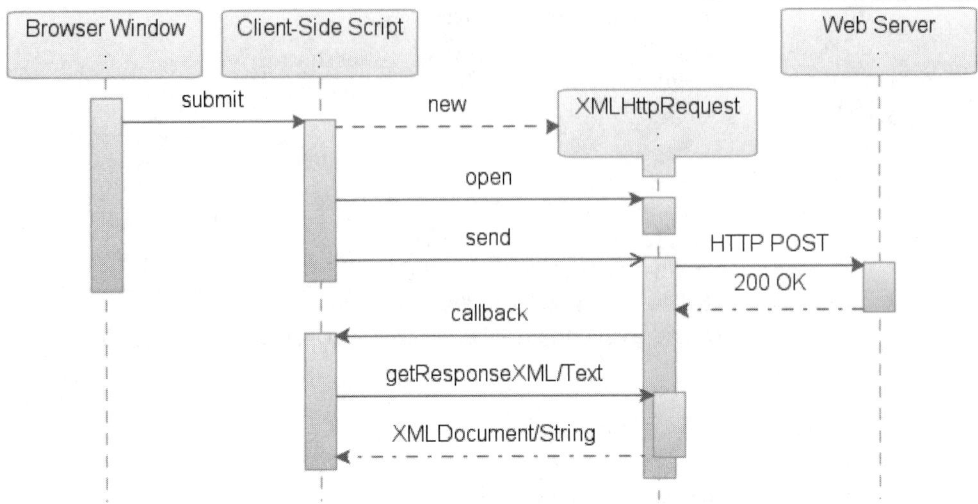

Figure 7-3. *Sequence diagram of an* `XMLHttpRequest` *using the HTTP* `GET` *method*

Different JSF Ajax Approaches

If you get no side effects, then there is no change to the JSF component hierarchy; thus, there is no need to go through the JSF lifecycle. But, if you want to reuse the managed bean referenced by the validator, the only way to get to it is via the JSF `MethodBinding` facility. Three solutions exist to support your requirements—adding functionality to the `Renderer`, using a `PhaseListener`, and providing a new JSF `Lifecycle`.

The Renderer Approach

This approach adds functionality to the `Renderer` to detect the Ajax request. The JSF default lifecycle first restores the component hierarchy during the Restore View phase, and the `Renderer` takes control during the Apply Request Values phase. After the Ajax request has been processed, the `Renderer` calls `responseComplete()` on the `FacesContext` to terminate processing of remaining phases in the `Lifecycle`. On the surface this may seem like the preferred approach, but it has some severe drawbacks.

A component hierarchy is required, which can incur additional overhead for each request, especially when client-side state saving is used. Calling the `responseComplete()` method will take effect only after this phase is done processing. The Apply Request Values phase calls the `decode()` method on all `Renderers` in the view, which can cause undesired side effects that are out of your control, such as a `commandButton` set to `immediate="true"` by the application developer. This causes application logic to be called before the Apply Request Values phase is complete.

Additionally, this approach typically requires HTTP `POST` to send the state string back to the server.

The PhaseListener Approach

This approach adds a PhaseListener (PhaseId.RESTORE_VIEW) that short-circuits the Lifecycle and does all the processing in the PhaseListener itself. When it is done, it calls responseComplete() on the FacesContext.

For this approach to work, it has to render a reference containing information about the managed bean used by the Validator in the initial request. The PhaseListener uses this information during postback to create a MethodBinding that can then be used to invoke logic behind the validator and return data to the client. Since there is no component hierarchy created, and thus no Renderers, there is no risk that command components with immediate set to true will cause any side effects.

But, this approach has one issue; there is no way to prevent application developers from attaching additional PhaseListeners at the same phase, which can cause undesired side effects. Also, you have no way of knowing in which order these PhaseListeners will be executed.

The Lifecycle Approach

This approach adds a new Lifecycle that is mapped to an Ajax request and contains only the lifecycle phases needed to process the request, invokes the application logic defined by a MethodBinding, and renders the response. This eliminates the overhead of creating and restoring the component tree, and thus no Renderers are required. You will also not encounter any issues with immediate="true".

Another positive side effect of using a custom Lifecycle is that any PhaseListener added by the application developer will have no impact on this solution; application developers can even add PhaseListeners to this custom Lifecycle. However, if a custom PhaseListener is used to place additional managed beans onto the request, you can run into issues, unless they are registered for the custom Lifecycle as well.

Selecting a JSF Ajax Approach

In this book, we have decided to go with the Lifecycle approach, since it has no application logic side effects and low overhead. It is here that the Mabon open source project can help you focus on the design of your Ajax calendar component.

Issue with Relative Variables

One valid approach of defining a MethodBinding is to use relative variables in the MethodBinding expression. This will have an unfortunate impact on both the PhaseListener approach and the Lifecycle approach. For a data fetch to work with these two approaches, you need absolute variables in the MethodBinding expression (for example, #{ backingBean.getValidDates}).

An example of a MethodBinding expression using relative variables would be a UIData component (for example <h:dataTable ...>) that is stamping out information about employees. Each stamped row represents an Employee object. For each Employee object, a list of available dates can be used to validate a selected date. Each stamped component has an EL expression starting with the relative variable defined by the parent <h:dataTable ...> (for example var="row"), as shown in Code Sample 7-3.

Code Sample 7-3. *Data-Bound Table Component*

```
<h:dataTable var="row" value="#{managedBean.employeeList}">
  <h:column>
    <pro:inputDate id="dateField"
                   title="Date Field Component"
                   value="#{row.date}" >
      <pro:validateDate availability="#{row.getValidDates}" />
    </pro:inputDate>
  </h:column>
```

The `var` attribute defines a relative variable `row`, which is used by each stamped component to retrieve the unique data for each row. This works fine as long as you have access to the component hierarchy during postback. On the client, each row's expression looks the same, so any client-side Ajax implementation depending on this expression to invoke an underlying managed bean method is out of luck. Any attached managed beans will work during regular postback, but an Ajax request using the `PhaseListener` or `Lifecycle` approach will not be able to locate the right row of data. Therefore, Ajax components relying on managed beans to provide them with data (for example, to fetch available dates for a specific employee) are not going to work properly when set up with a relative variable.

Possible Solutions to Relative Variables

You could try to solve this by implementing support for the `UIData` component, but you have no guarantee that the parent component is of type `UIData`, since it is perfectly legal for component authors to provide components that stamp out objects without subclassing the `UIData` component. Examples of such components are the Oracle's ADF Faces `table` and `treeTable` components.

The best solution would be if the JSF specification provided support for converting relative expressions to absolute expressions. Component writers could then convert relative variables to absolute during initial render. The rendered expression could take the form of `#{managedBean.employeeList[1].getValidDates}`, indicating this to be row one in the stamped collection.

Step 4: Creating Converters and Validators

As discussed in Chapter 1, the JSF implementation provides helper classes for any type of `UIComponent`. These helper classes are divided into converters, validators, and an event and listener model, each of them with its own area of expertise. In this section, you will build your own `Validator` to perform validation on the strongly typed `Date` object to make sure a selected date is actually available (for example, is not a weekend or a holiday).

Code Sample 7-4 uses the `Validator` you will design. Its purpose is to validate the entered value and compare it with a list of dates that are flagged as "not available." The contract for the application developer's backing bean provided is to return an array of booleans—`#{managedBean.getValidDates}`. The array indicates whether a date is available (`true`) or not (`false`). This array provided by the backing bean is also used at the browser to show which dates are available for selection.

Code Sample 7-4. `ProInputDate` *Component with Attached Date Validator*

```
<pro:inputDate id="dateField"
            title="Date Field Component"
            value="#{managedBean.date}" >
  <pro:validateDate availability="#{managedBean.getValidDates}" />
</pro:inputDate>
```

Figure 7-4 shows the `DateValidator` class.

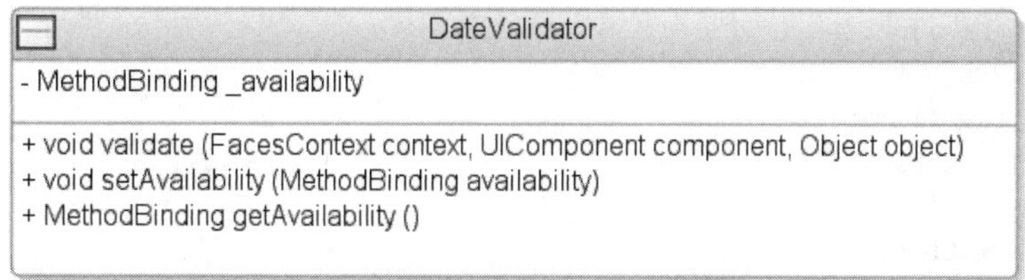

Figure 7-4. *Class diagram showing the* `DateValidator`

The DateValidator Class

The `DateValidator` class (see Code Sample 7-5) checks to see whether the `Date` value is available, according to some rules, in a backing bean defined by an application developer.

Code Sample 7-5. *The* `validate()` *Method*

```
package com.apress.projsf.ch7.validate;

import java.util.Date;

import javax.faces.application.FacesMessage;
import javax.faces.component.UIComponent;
import javax.faces.context.FacesContext;
import javax.faces.el.MethodBinding;
import javax.faces.validator.Validator;
import javax.faces.validator.ValidatorException;

/**
 * DateValidator checks to see whether a Date value is available, according
 * to a managed bean method binding.
 */
public class DateValidator implements Validator
{
  /**
   * Validates the object value to make sure it is a Date and available.
   *
   * @param context     the Faces context
```

```
   * @param component   the Faces component
   * @param object      the object to validate
   */
  public void validate(
    FacesContext context,
    UIComponent  component,
    Object       object)
  {
    if (_ availability != null)
    {

      Date date = (Date)object;
      long millis = date.getTime();
      long millisPerDay = 1000 * 60 * 60 * 24;
      Integer days = new Integer((int)(millis / millisPerDay));
      Object[] args = new Object[] {days, days};
      boolean[] result = (boolean[])_availability.invoke(context, args);
      if (!result[0])
      {
        FacesMessage message = new FacesMessage("Date is unavailable");
        throw new ValidatorException(message);
      }
    }
  }
```

The validate() method is called after the conversion of the entered string to Date is successful. The reason for passing a new Object[]{days, days} is to be able to reuse it later. The Validator has only one value, so the range is over a single day (from days to days, inclusive). It will then call the backing bean passing the arguments needed, context and args. The backing bean returns a boolean[] array, indicating availability for each day in the range (inclusive) since January 1, 1970.

Code Sample 7-6 shows the accessors for the method binding of the available days with the signature (int, int).

Code Sample 7-6. *The* setAvailability() *and* getAvailability() *Methods*

```
  public void setAvailability(
    MethodBinding availability)
  {
    _availability = availability;
  }
  public MethodBinding getAvailability()
  {
    return _availability;
  }

  private MethodBinding _availability;
}
```

Although you have designed this `Validator` with your Ajax-enabled component in mind, it is also fully functional with the basic HTML `RenderKit`.

Step 5: Creating a Client-Specific Renderer

You now know how to create your new Ajax-enabled `ProInputDate` component. Since you already have an `HtmlInputDateRenderer` for this component, it makes sense to extend it to add rich functionality. One of the benefits of extending a component's client-side functionality is that you need only to override the `encodeBegin()` method of the `Renderer`. Everything else stays the same.

In the previous chapter, you added *only* Ajax functionality to your `HtmlShowOneDeckRenderer`, since the markup was already there. In this case, you have to provide some additional markup to support the pop-up calendar.

You also need to determine the date format pattern that is used by the `DateTimeConverter` and the target URL for the validator managed bean, if any. One of the positive side effects of a component model is that a component author can extend the initial functionality of a component. For the application developer, there is no difference between using the "simple" `HtmlInputDateRenderer` and using the Ajax-enabled `HtmlAjaxInputDateRenderer`. Figure 7-5 shows a class diagram with the `HtmlAjaxInputDateRenderer`.

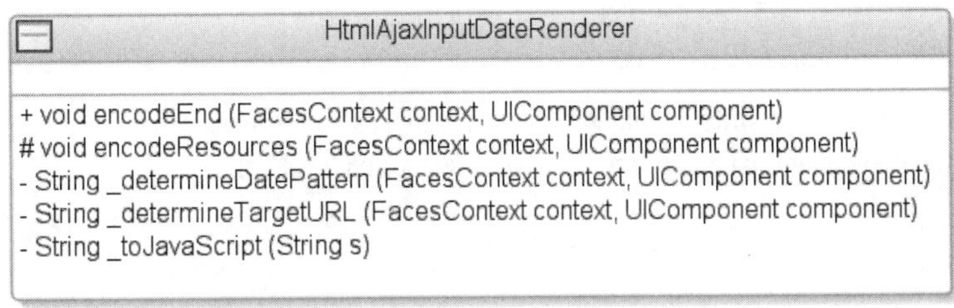

Figure 7-5. *Class diagram showing the* `HtmlAjaxInputDateRenderer`

Before you venture into the fun stuff, working on your new Ajax `Renderer`, you need to understand what Mabon is and what it can provide for component writers who are interested in Ajax data fetch.

What Is Mabon?

Mabon is an open source project hosted on the `http://mabon.dev.java.net` Web site. Mabon offers a convenient way to hook in a specially designed lifecycle that is ideal for Ajax-enabled components that need to fetch data directly from a backing bean, without the overhead of a full JSF lifecycle. It also provides a Mabon protocol—`mabon:/`—that is used to reference the backing bean and a JavaScript convenience function that is used to send the target URL and any arguments needed and then asynchronously receive data from the managed bean.

Mabon and JSON

As you know, the `XMLHttpRequest` provides two response types—`responseText` and `responseXML`—that can be used to fetch data. The question to ask is, when should I use each? Answers to this question can differ depending on whom you ask, but we can recommend one rule. Ask yourself whether you control the syntax of the response.

The `responseXML` type returns a complete DOM object (which gives you ample ways of walking the DOM tree), allowing you to find the information needed, and apply changes to the current document. This is useful when your component will impact surrounding elements, and you don't control the response (for example, when you are communicating with a Web Service).

For the date component, you do control the response, and you are looking at only fetching data for your component, not modifying the whole page's DOM structure.

The `responseText` type returns plain text, which allows you to leverage JSON syntax for the response. For components leveraging Ajax, JSON is an extremely useful data-interchange format, since it can be easily parsed with the `eval()` function.

The `eval()` function takes one argument, a string of JavaScript code, and parses and executes this string in one go rather than trying to process each part separately. This is significantly faster than any other type of parsing, such as XML DOM parsing.

This is the reason why Mabon implements JSON—you control the response, and JSON syntax is easy and fast to parse.

■ **Note** It is also important that component writers make it clear to the application developer that any managed beans attached to the component need to return data types supported by JSON.

VALID DATA TYPES IN JSON

JSON (`http://www.json.org`) has a simple data structure—objects and arrays. Objects are collections of name/value pairs, and arrays are ordered lists of values. In JSON, they take on these forms:

- An object is an unordered set of name/value pairs. An object begins with a left brace ({) and ends with a right brace (}). Each name is followed by a colon (:) and the name/value pairs are separated by a comma (,).
- An array is an ordered collection of values. An array begins with a left bracket ([) and ends with a right bracket (]). Commas (,) separate values.
- A value can be a string in double quotes, a number, `true` or `false` or `null`, or an object, or an array. These structures can be nested.

Structure of Mabon

Mabon consists of a custom JSF `Lifecycle` to process Ajax data fetch requests and a custom JSF `ViewHandler` used to write out the data fetch URLs (see Figure 7-6).

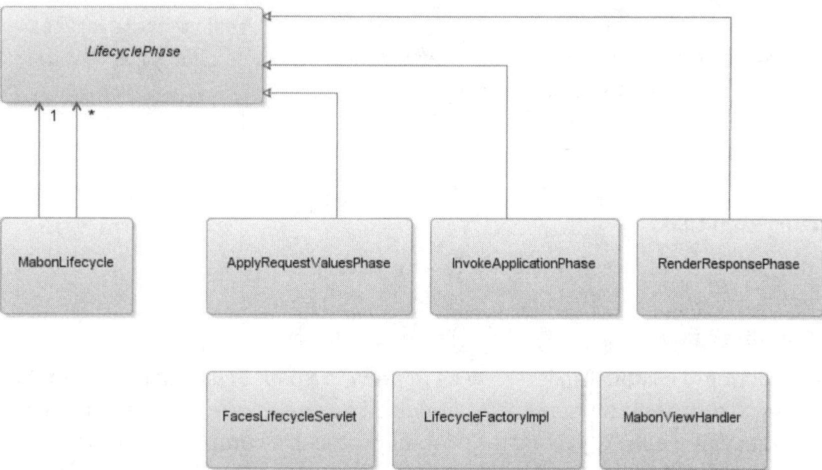

Figure 7-6. *Class diagram of Mabon*

The MabonLifecycle Class

The `MabonLifecycle` consists of three phases—`ApplyRequestValuesPhase`, `InvokeApplicationPhase`, and `RenderResponsePhase`. The `MabonLifecycle` is responsible for executing these three phases. Additionally, it is also responsible for handling any `PhaseListeners` attached to the `MabonLifecycle`.

The LifecyclePhase Class

The Mabon `LifecyclePhase` is the base class for all lifecycle phases.

The ApplyRequestValuesPhase, InvokeApplicationPhase, and RenderResponsePhase Classes

Since you are only fetching data and not modifying the component hierarchy or the underlying model in any way, you do not need to include the Restore View, Process Validations, and Update Model phases. The Mabon phases are performing similar operations to the default lifecycle equivalents, such as decoding an incoming request, invoking application logic, and rendering the response. We will cover these three in more detail shortly.

The FacesLifecycleServlet Class

This is a reusable servlet that will initialize the `FacesContextFactory` and look up the `MabonLifecycle` in its first request. It will create the `FacesContext` and then invoke the three lifecycle phases that are part of the `MabonLifecycle`. The servlet mapping defined by the Web application will direct Mabon requests to this `FacesLifecycleServlet`.

JSF 1.2 SPECIFICATION

After the release of the JSF 1.2 specification, the Mabon `FacesLifecycleServlet` will no longer be needed. A component developer using the Mabon project to serve data to Ajax-enabled components can change the servlet entry for Mabon to use the JSF 1.2 `javax.faces.webapp.FacesServlet` class instead of the `net.java.dev.mabon.webapp.FacesLifecycleServlet` class. The `FacesLifecycleServlet` provided by Mabon uses the same syntax as JSF 1.2 `FacesServlet` to customize the `Lifecycle`, simplifying the upgrade path to JSF 1.2 for the application developer.

The LifecycleFactoryImpl Class

This class's only purpose is to add a second lifecycle—the `MabonLifecycle`.

The MabonViewHandler Class

During the initial rendering, a custom `Renderer` needs to provide a path to the backing bean that can be intercepted by the `FacesLifecycleServlet` and used during `InvokeApplicationPhase` to call the referenced backing bean. By using the Mabon protocol, a component author can get a unique path from the `MabonViewHandler` that can be rendered to the client. If the component writer passes the string shown in Code Sample 7-7 with the path argument of the `ViewHandler.getResourceURL()` method, the `MabonViewHandler` will return the string shown in Code Sample 7-8 that can be written to the client.

Code Sample 7-7. *The Mabon Protocol*

```
mabon:/managedBean.getValidDates
```

Code Sample 7-8. *String Returned After Mabon Has Evaluated the Mabon Protocol*

```
/<context-root>/<mabon-servlet-mapping>/managedBean.getValidDates
```

During an Ajax request, this URL is sent on the request and intercepted by the `FacesLifecycleServlet`.

Mabon: Initial Request

The Mabon implementation is designed specifically for Ajax requests and implements a communication channel using JSON syntax. This solution allows Ajax components that use managed beans to fetch data and to communicate with the server without having to go through a full JSF lifecycle. So how does it work? At application start-up (see Figure 7-7), Mabon will add the `MabonLifecycle` as part of the JSF `LifecycleFactory` context.

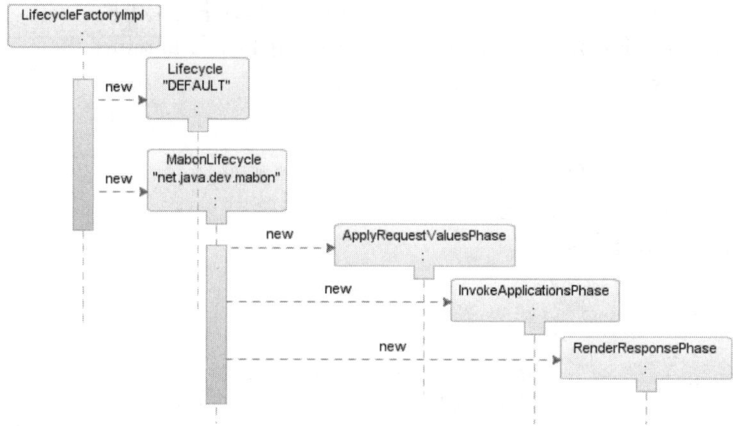

Figure 7-7. *Sequence diagram of Mabon at application start-up*

On the initial request (as shown in Figure 7-8), Mabon is just delegating through to the underlying JSF implementation and is active only during the Render Response phase, if needed.

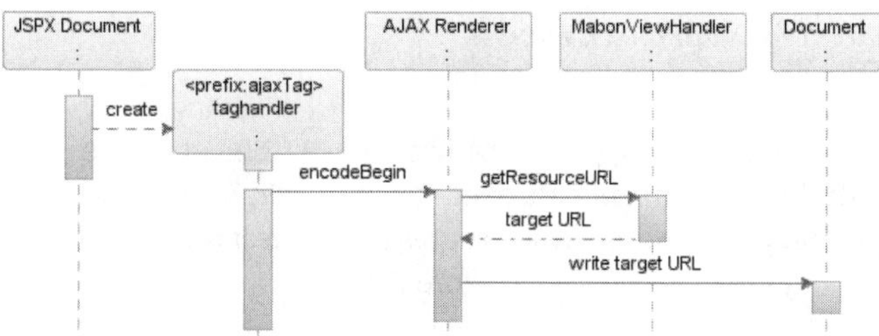

Figure 7-8. *Sequence diagram of Mabon initial request*

In the Figure 7-8 sequence diagram, a page that contains a custom Ajax component is executed. To work, the Ajax component needs to get data from an underlying backing bean. During `encodeBegin()`, the Ajax `Renderer` for that component will use the Mabon protocol—`mabon:/`—to write out a target URL that references the backing bean. To get this URL, the `Renderer` will call the `getResourceURL()` on the `MabonViewHandler`. It will pass a string matching the method binding expression for the backing bean (for example, `mabon:/managedBean.getValidDates`). The `getResourceURL()` method will return a full path—`/<context-root>/<mabon-servlet-mapping>/managedBean.getValidDates`—that can be written out to the document.

Mabon: Data Fetch Request

After the page has been rendered to the client, it contains a target URL to the backing bean that is needed by the Ajax component to fetch data (for example, `/<context-root>/<mabon` ➥

mapping>/managedBean.getValidDates). In subsequent Ajax requests, this string will be intercepted by the Mabon implementation and used to invoke the backing bean and return the result to the client (see Figure 7-9).

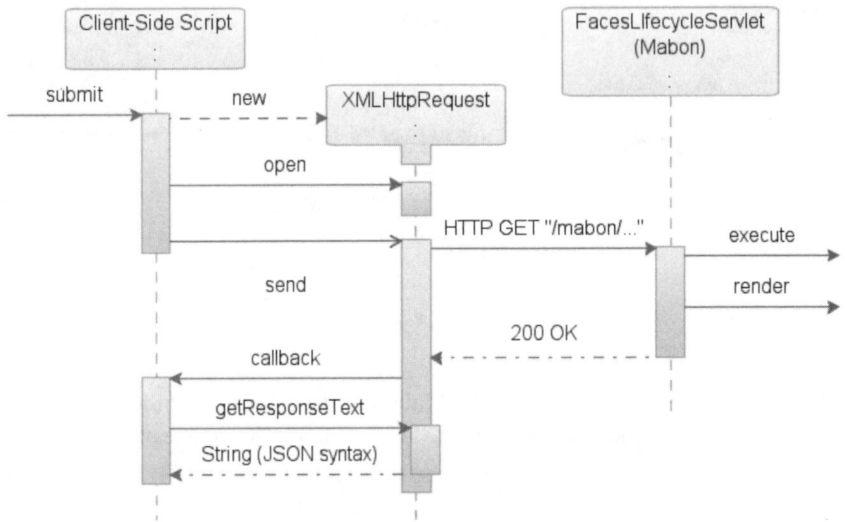

Figure 7-9. *Sequence diagram of Mabon/Ajax data fetch request*

On submit, an Ajax-enabled component creates a new `XMLHttpRequest` object, which asynchronously communicates with the server to get data from the managed bean. This request is intercepted by the `FacesLifecycleServlet`, which routes the request through the Mabon `Lifecycle` instead of the default JSF `Lifecycle` (see Figure 7-10).

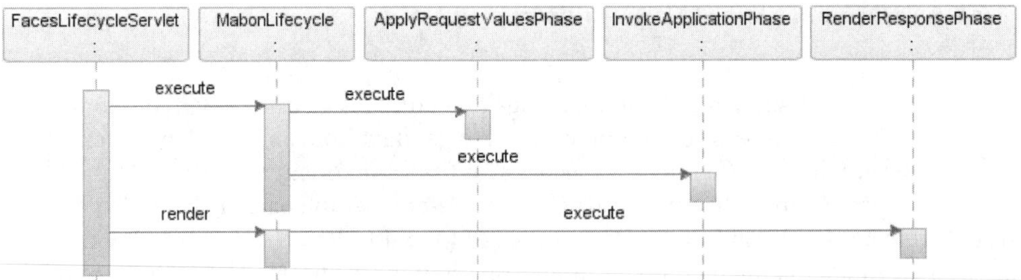

Figure 7-10. *Sequence diagram over Mabon lifecycle during postback*

When the `FacesLifecycleServlet` intercepts the request, the processing of the request starts by calling each Mabon lifecycle phase, in sequence. First, you execute the

ApplyRequestValuesPhase, which will decode the request and get the managed bean reference and method arguments needed for the managed bean off the request. Second, you execute the InvokeApplicationPhase that will create a MethodBinding based on the managed bean reference, invoke this MethodBinding passing any arguments, and return the result. Third, the RenderResponsePhase takes the result and writes it back to the client.

Mabon APIs

The following sections cover the available APIs and how to register Mabon with an application.

Mabon Servlet Configuration

If you are planning on using Mabon for your Ajax-enabled components, you should be aware that it adds an extra step for the application developer using your JSF component library. The application developer needs to add the entry shown in Code Sample 7-9 to the Web application configuration file—web.xml.

Code Sample 7-9. *Mabon Servlet Configuration*

```
<servlet>
  <servlet-name>Mabon Servlet</servlet-name>
  <servlet-class>net.java.dev.mabon.webapp.FacesLifecycleServlet</servlet-class>
  <init-param>
    <param-name>javax.faces.LIFECYCLE_ID</param-name>
    <param-value>net.java.dev.mabon</param-value>
  </init-param>
</servlet>
...
<servlet-mapping>
  <servlet-name>Mabon Servlet</servlet-name>
  <url-pattern>/mabon/*</url-pattern>
</servlet-mapping>
```

The servlet class—net.java.dev.mabon.webapp.FacesLifecycleServlet—and the initialization parameter (for example, net.java.dev.mabon) is part of the Mabon contract.

The application developer can decide to set the mapping to the same url-pattern(s) as defined by default (for example, /mabon/*) or override the default URL mapping in case it is colliding with resources used by the Web application. Mabon automatically consumes this URL mapping change without requiring any code changes.

Mabon JavaScript APIs

The Mabon project provides a convenience JavaScript library that you can use to send your request to the server. The Mabon send() function leverages the Dojo toolkit's bind() function to asynchronously communicate with the server. We discussed the Dojo toolkit in Chapter 6. Code Sample 7-10 shows the source of the Mabon JavaScript library.

Code Sample 7-10. *The* mabon.js *Library*

```
var mabon = new Object();

mabon.send = function (
  kvparams)
{
  var content = {args:'[' + kvparams.args.join(',') + ']'};

  dojo.io.bind(
  {
    url: kvparams.url,
    method: 'get',
    content: content,
    mimetype: "text/javascript",
    load: function(type, data, evt) { kvparams.callback(eval(data)); },
    error: function(type, data, evt)
             {
               alert('Oops! The server returned an error, please try again.');
             }
  });
}
```

The Mabon send() function takes one argument—a Map. To call the mabon.send() function from your Ajax implementation, you would have to construct the Map using JavaScript Map syntax, as shown in Code Sample 7-11.

Code Sample 7-11. *Passing Arguments to the Mabon* send() *Function*

```
mabon.send(
          { url: targetURL,
            args: [item1, item2],
            callback: callback_function }
        );
```

Mabon Protocol

Now that you know how to configure Mabon, it is time to look at how you can reference managed beans that are needed to fetch data.

The Mabon protocol-like syntax is convenient and easy to understand. The syntax starts with mabon:/ followed by the managed bean name and finally the method name, as shown in Code Sample 7-12.

Code Sample 7-12. *Using the* mabon:/ *Syntax*

```
ViewHandler.getResourceURL(context, "mabon:/<managed bean name>.<method>");
```

The syntax uses a prefix to indicate this is a Mabon-managed request, the managed bean name, and the method needed. This syntax—`<mabon prefix><managed bean><method>`—defined by the Mabon contract is used to return a target URL referencing the managed bean. The target URL will be intercepted by the `FacesLifecycleServlet` and deciphered by the Mabon Apply Request Values phase.

■ **Note** Although the Mabon project uses a protocol-like syntax to reference managed beans, this is not a real protocol handler, so the new `URL("mabon:/...").openStream()` would not work from Java code—but you don't need it to, since the client is not Java code.

The HtmlAjaxInputDateRenderer Class

The `HtmlAjaxInputDateRenderer` (see Code Sample 7-13) extends the `HtmlInputDateRenderer` to add a pop-up calendar and Ajax-based data fetch of available days.

Code Sample 7-13. *Determine Date Pattern and Launch Calendar Pop-Up*

```
package com.apress.projsf.ch7.render.html.ajax;

import java.io.IOException;import java.text.DateFormat;
import java.text.SimpleDateFormat;
import java.util.Map;

import javax.faces.application.Application;
import javax.faces.application.ViewHandler;
import javax.faces.component.UIComponent;
import javax.faces.component.UIInput;
import javax.faces.context.FacesContext;
import javax.faces.context.ResponseWriter;
import javax.faces.convert.Converter;
import javax.faces.convert.DateTimeConverter;
import javax.faces.el.MethodBinding;
import javax.faces.validator.Validator;

import com.apress.projsf.ch2.render.html.basic.HtmlInputDateRenderer;
import com.apress.projsf.ch7.validate.DateValidator;

/**
 * HtmlAjaxInputDateRenderer extends the HtmlInputDateRenderer
 * to add a pop-up calendar and Ajax-based data fetch of available days.
 */
public class HtmlAjaxInputDateRenderer extends HtmlInputDateRenderer
{
```

```
/**
 * Encodes the content of this component, including a button to
 * trigger the pop-up calendar.
 *
 * @param context    the Faces context
 * @param component  the Faces component
 *
 * @throws IOException  if an I/O exception occurs during rendering
 */
public void encodeBegin(
  FacesContext context,
  UIComponent  component) throws IOException
{
  String valueString = getValueAsString(context, component);
  String clientId = component.getClientId(context);
  String pattern = _determineDatePattern(context, component);
  String targetURL = _determineTargetURL(context, component);

  Map attrs = component.getAttributes();
  String title = (String)attrs.get(TITLE_ATTR);
  String onchange = (String)attrs.get(ONCHANGE_ATTR);

  ResponseWriter out = context.getResponseWriter();
  out.startElement("div", component);

  if (title != null)
    out.writeAttribute("title", title, TITLE_ATTR);

  // <input id="[clientId]" name="[clientId]"
  //        value="[converted-value]" onchange="[onchange]" />
  out.startElement("input", component);
  out.writeAttribute("style", "vertical-align:bottom;", null);
  out.writeAttribute("id", clientId, null);
  out.writeAttribute("name", clientId, null);
  if (valueString != null)
    out.writeAttribute("value", valueString, null);
  if (onchange != null)
    out.writeAttribute("onchange", onchange, ONCHANGE_ATTR);
  out.endElement("input");

  // <button type="button" >
  //   <img src="weblet://com.apress.projsf.ch7/inputDateButton.gif" >
  // </button>
  ViewHandler handler = context.getApplication().getViewHandler();
  String overlayURL = handler.getResourceURL(context,
                        "weblet://com.apress.projsf.ch7/inputDateButton.gif");
  out.startElement("button", null);
```

```
    out.writeAttribute("type", "button", null);
    out.writeAttribute("class", "ProInputDateButton", null);
    out.writeAttribute("onclick",
                       "new HtmlInputDate(" + _toJavaScript(clientId) + "," +
                                          _toJavaScript(pattern) + "," +
                                          _toJavaScript(targetURL) +
                                          ").showPopup()",
                       null);
    out.startElement("img", null);
    out.writeAttribute("style", "vertical-align:middle;", null);
    out.writeAttribute("src", overlayURL, null);
    out.endElement("img");
    out.endElement("button");
    out.endElement("div");
  }

  private String _toJavaScript(
    String s)
  {
    if (s == null)
      return "null";

    return "'" + s + "'";
  }
```

First, you call the encodeBegin() method on the HtmlAjaxInputDateRenderer to get the client ID of the ProInputDate component, which will later be used to determine where to return the selected date. Second, you call two methods—_determineDatePattern and _determineTargetURL. These methods get hold of the date format pattern and the target URL for the managed bean bound to the DateValidator. Then you write out the markup for the response. As you can see in Code Sample 7-14, you use weblets to load an image that will be used as an icon for the button. You then write out the button with the image and the onclick event handler that will be used to fetch data from the managed bean and to pop up the calendar.

Code Sample 7-14. *The* encodeResources() *Method*

```
protected void encodeResources(
  FacesContext context,
  UIComponent  component) throws IOException
{
  writeScriptResource(context, "weblet://org.dojotoolkit.browserio/dojo.js");
  writeScriptResource(context, "weblet://net.java.dev.mabon/mabon.js");
  writeScriptResource(context, "weblet://com.apress.projsf.ch7/inputDate.js");

  writeStyleResource(context, "weblet://com.apress.projsf.ch7/inputDate.css");
}
```

By overriding the HtmlRenderer base class encodeResources() method, you have extended the HtmlInputDateRenderer with three new calls to the dojo.js, the mabon.js, and your own inputDate.js library. An application developer might add two or more ProInputDate components to the page, but the semantics behind the writeScriptResource() method (provided by your Renderer implementation and described in Chapter 3), HtmlRenderer, will make sure these resources are written only once.

For your Ajax implementation to work, you need to know what date pattern has been set on the DateTimeConverter by the application developer. The _determineDatePattern() method shown in Code Sample 7-15 will return the date pattern set by the DateTimeConverter.

Code Sample 7-15. *The* _determineDatePattern() *Method*

```
private String _determineDatePattern(
  FacesContext context,
  UIComponent  component)
{
  UIInput input = (UIInput)component;
  Converter converter = getConverter(context, input);

  if (converter instanceof DateTimeConverter)
  {
    DateTimeConverter dateTime = (DateTimeConverter)converter;
    return dateTime.getPattern();
  }
  else
  {
    SimpleDateFormat dateFormat = (SimpleDateFormat)
                              DateFormat.getDateInstance(DateFormat.SHORT);
    return dateFormat.toPattern();
  }
}
```

This date pattern will be used in two places. First, it will parse the date entered by the user in the input element. This parsed date will then be used to set the selected date in the calendar. Second, it will make sure that the date selected in the calendar follows the correct date format when added to the input element.

The method shown in Code Sample 7-16 is crucial to your Ajax solution, since it provides you with the required binding reference to the backing bean. You first get all the validators attached to this input component. You then check to see whether any of these validators are instances of the DateValidator.

Code Sample 7-16. *The* _determineTargetURL() *Method*

```
private String _determineTargetURL(
  FacesContext context,
  UIComponent  component)
{
```

```
    UIInput input = (UIInput)component;
    Validator[] validators = input.getValidators();

    for (int i=0; i < validators.length; i++)
    {
      if (validators[i] instanceof DateValidator)
      {
        DateValidator validateDate = (DateValidator)validators[i];
        MethodBinding binding = validateDate.getAvailability();
        if (binding != null)
        {
          String expression = binding.getExpressionString();
          // #{backingBean.methodName} -> backingBean.methodName
          String bindingRef = expression.substring(2, expression.length()-1);

          Application application = context.getApplication();
          ViewHandler handler = application.getViewHandler();
          return handler.getResourceURL(context, "mabon:/" + bindingRef);
        }
      }
    }

    return null;
  }
}
```

If it is an instance of the `DateValidator`, you check to see whether you have a `MethodBinding`. If you have a `MethodBinding`, you get the expression (for example, `#{managedBean.methodName}`) and strip off the `#{}`. This leaves you with `managedBean.methodName`, which you concatenate with `mabon:/`. The `MabonViewHandler` will recognize the string and return a resource URL that will be written to the client (for example, `/context-root/mabon-servlet-mapping/managedBean.methodName`).

Ajax Resources

Since you have decided to use Mabon, you do not need to worry about fetching data from the backing bean. You can leave this to Mabon. What you do need to be concerned about, though, is how to handle the returned data on the `XMLHttpRequest` object, how to pop up the actual calendar, and how to handle user interactions (for example, the next and previous months).

Object-Oriented JavaScript

You can leverage several good Web resources and books to provide good JavaScript solutions. In the following sections, we will provide you with an overview of the `HtmlInputDate` Ajax solution.

You have created a custom `HtmlInputDate` JavaScript object, which uses the prototype feature of JavaScript to properly isolate all the internal state needed by your component at the browser.

■ **Note** Prototype-based programming is a style and subset of object-oriented programming in which classes are not present, and behavior reuse (known as *inheritance* in class-based languages) takes place by cloning existing objects, which serve as prototypes for new ones. It is also known as *classless*, *prototype-oriented*, or *instance-based* programming (`http://en.wikipedia.org`).

You have three main user interactions to consider for the visual specification of your component. You need to be able to pop up the calendar, navigate to the relevant month and year, and then select an available date.

The inputDate.css Resource

In your `ProInputDate` Ajax renderer, we have decided to leverage CSS to provide you with a very good-looking calendar and at the same time provide the ability to set and detect what dates are selectable. Code Sample 7-17 shows an excerpt from the `inputDate.css` file.

Code Sample 7-17. *The* `inputDate.css` *File*

```
.ProInputDateCalendar {…}
.ProInputDateCalendar tbody .other
{
  color: rgb(128,128,128);
}

.ProInputDateCalendar tbody .noselect
{
  color: rgb(208,64,64);
}

.ProInputDateCalendar tbody .selected
{
  background-color: rgb(32,80,255);
  color: white;
  font-weight: bold;
}

.ProInputDateCalendar tbody .today
{
  font-weight: bold;
}
```

These styles use *descendant selectors* relative to the element with the class `ProInputDateCalendar`. Descendant selectors are a way to apply styles to specific areas of a page to reduce the need to embed classes within elements. Composed of two or more selectors separated by whitespace, descendant selectors apply styles to elements that are contained within other elements. For the selectors defined in Code Sample 7-17, some style classes are defined (for example, `.other`, `.onselect`, `.selected`, and `.today`). These class names will set the style on cells in the calendar's tbody element, indicating whether a cell is selectable. Later in your Ajax implementation, you will see how you use these class names to determine whether the user clicked a valid date.

■ **Note** CSS 1 first introduced descendant selectors (then called *contextual selectors*) in 1996.

The HtmlInputDate.prototype.showPopup Method

The showPopup method is responsible for launching the calendar when the user clicks the button (see Figure 7-11). It will first create an instance of the HtmlInputDate JavaScript object that will store the calendar's internal state. Then, it will read the user-defined date string from the input field and parse that date string into a Date object. If the parsing is successful, use the Date object; otherwise, use today's Date. Next it ensures that there is no previous selection before calling the _scroll method and passing zero as an argument to ensure fully populated calendar day cells but staying on the current month (zero navigation). Finally, the showPopup method, as shown in Code Sample 7-18, will select an initial date (if possible), unless the calendar is dismissed.

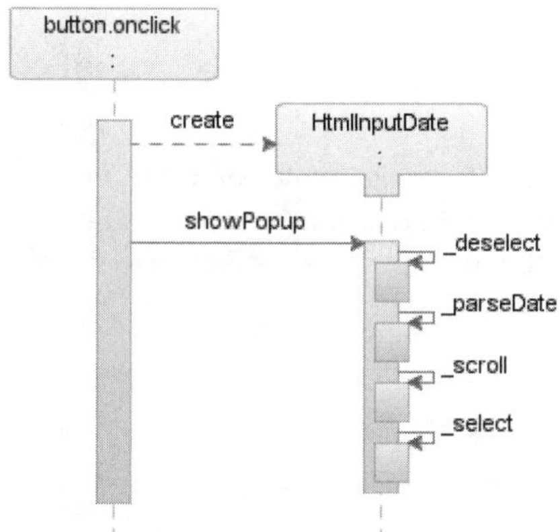

Figure 7-11. HtmlInputDate.prototype.showPopup *method*

Code Sample 7-18. *The* HtmlInputDate.prototype.showPopup *Method*

```
/**
 * Shows the pop-up calendar.
 */
HtmlInputDate.prototype.showPopup = function()
{
  var tableNode = this._tableNode;

  if (tableNode.style.visibility == 'hidden')
```

```
  {
    var dateString = this._input.value;
    var parsedDate = this._parseDate(dateString, this._pattern);
    var activeDate = (parsedDate != null) ? parsedDate : new Date();

    this._deselect();

    var month = activeDate.getMonth();
    var year = activeDate.getFullYear();
    this._currentMonth = month;
    this._currentYear = year;

    this._scroll(0);

    if (parsedDate)
      this._select(parsedDate.getDate());
  }
  else
  {
    this._hidePopup();
  }
}
```

The HtmlInputDate.prototype._scroll Method

This method, as shown in Code Sample 7-19, allows the user to navigate plus or minus one month using the arrow controls in the calendar (see Figure 7-12). It is also here that you use Mabon to determine the availability of dates defined by the managed bean attached to the ProInputDate component.

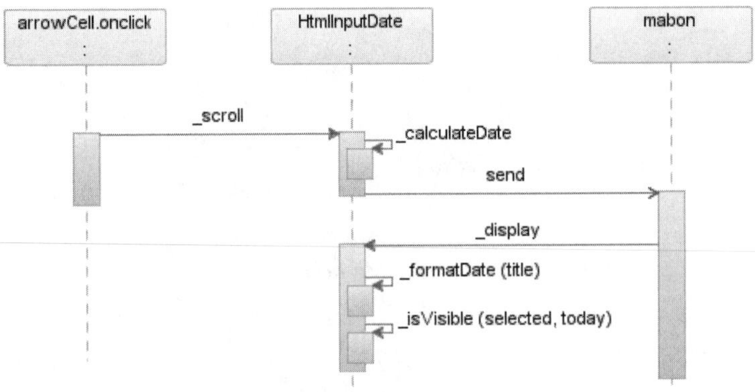

Figure 7-12. HtmlInputDate.prototype._scroll *method*

Code Sample 7-19. *The* `HtmlInputDate.prototype._scroll` *Method*

```
/**
 * Scrolls the visible month by +/- offset months.
 *
 * @param offset  the number of months to scroll
 * @private
 */
HtmlInputDate.prototype._scroll = function(offset)
{
  this._currentMonth = this._currentMonth + offset;
  this._currentYear += Math.floor(this._currentMonth / 12);
  this._currentMonth = (this._currentMonth + 12) % 12;

  if (this._targetURL)
  {
    var startDate = this._calculateDate(1);
    var endDate = this._calculateDate(31);

    var millisPerDay = 1000 * 60 * 60 * 24;
    var startDay = Math.floor(startDate.getTime() / millisPerDay);
    var endDay = Math.floor(endDate.getTime() / millisPerDay);

    var self = this;
    mabon.send(
      {
        url: this._targetURL,
        args: [startDay, endDay],
        callback: function(result) { self._display(result); }
      });
  }
  else
  {
    var available = [];
    for (var i=0; i < 32; i++)
    {
      available.push(true);
    }
    this._display(available);
  }
}
```

The HtmlInputDate.prototype._clickCell Method

This method, as shown in Code Sample 7-20, is called when the user clicks a cell representing a date in the calendar. The method (see Figure 7-13) will check to see whether the user clicked a cell that is outside the range of the displayed month and if so navigate to the month for that selected date—`this._scroll(1)` or `this._scroll(-1)`. If the selection is within the boundaries of the month, you need to see whether the date is actually available, and if it is, you can add the selected date to the input element.

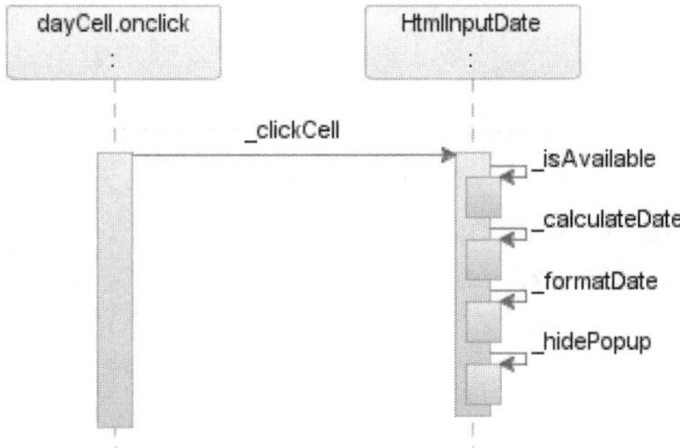

Figure 7-13. `HtmlInputDate.prototype._clickCell` *method*

Code Sample 7-20. *The* `HtmlInputDate.prototype._clickCell` *Method*

```
/**
 * Selects the cell when it is clicked.
 *
 * @param event  the click event
 * @private
 */
HtmlInputDate.prototype._clickCell = function(event)
{
  var cellNode = (event.target || event.srcElement);
  var rowNode = cellNode.parentNode;

  var row = rowNode.sectionRowIndex;
  var col = cellNode.cellIndex;
  var day = Number(cellNode.firstChild.nodeValue);

  if (row == 0 && day > 7)
  {
    this._scroll(-1);
  }
  else if (row > 3 && day < 15)
  {
    this._scroll(1);
  }
  else
  {
    if (this._isAvailable(day))
```

```
    {
      var selectedDate = this._calculateDate(day);
      this._input.value = this._formatDate(selectedDate, this._pattern);

      this._hidePopup();
    }
  }
}
```

You can get hold of the target node invoking the event by calling `event.target`, but Internet Explorer implements this slightly differently—`event.srcElement`. Thus, you have the `(event.target || event.srcElement)` syntax, which evaluates to either `event.target` or `event.srcElement`, whichever is defined.

Step 7: Registering a UIComponent and Renderer

For your JSF Ajax `ProInputDate` implementation, you need to make sure you register your custom `Renderer` with the Ajax `RenderKit` created in Chapter 6, as shown in Code Sample 7-21.

Code Sample 7-21. *Registering the* `HtmlAjaxInputDateRenderer`

```
<faces-config xmlns="http://java.sun.com/JSF/Configuration" >
  ...
  <render-kit>
    <render-kit-id>com.apress.projsf.ajax[HTML_BASIC]</render-kit-id>
    <render-kit-class>
      com.apress.projsf.ch6.render.html.ajax.HtmlAjaxRenderKit
    </render-kit-class>
    ...
    <renderer>
      <component-family>javax.faces.Input</component-family>
      <renderer-type>com.apress.projsf.Date</renderer-type>
      <renderer-class>
        com.apress.projsf.ch7.render.html.ajax.HtmlAjaxInputDateRenderer
      </renderer-class>
    </renderer>
  </render-kit>

</faces-config>
```

The new `HtmlAjaxInputDateRenderer` is still part of the same component family and has the same renderer type as the `HtmlInputDateRenderer` created in Chapter 2.

Step 8: Creating a JSP Tag Handler and TLD

You need a custom action for your validator so that an application developer can add it as a child to a `ProInputDate` component. The `ValidateDateTag` tag handler class represents the custom action `validateDate` that will be used by the application developer to register a `DateValidator` instance to a `ProInputDate` component.

The ValidateDateTag Class

Figure 7-14 shows a class diagram of your `ValidateDateTag`.

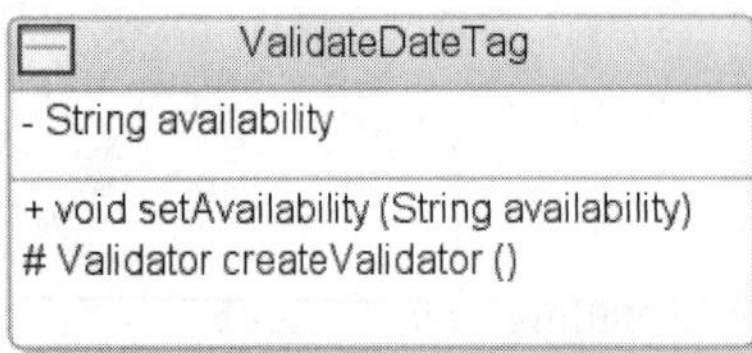

Figure 7-14. *Class diagram showing your three tag handlers*

Code Sample 7-22 shows the actual code behind this `ValidateDateTag` class.

Code Sample 7-22. *The* `ValidateDateTag` *Class*

```
package com.apress.projsf.ch7.taglib;

import javax.faces.application.Application;
import javax.faces.component.UIComponent;
import javax.faces.context.FacesContext;
import javax.faces.el.MethodBinding;
import javax.faces.validator.Validator;
import javax.faces.webapp.ValidatorTag;

import javax.servlet.jsp.JspException;

import com.apress.projsf.ch7.validate.DateValidator;

/**
 * ValidateDateTag listener tag handler.
 */
public class ValidateDateTag extends ValidatorTag
{
  /**
   * Sets the availability method binding with signature (int, int)
   * returns boolean[], indicating availablilty for each day in
   * range (inclusive) since January 1, 1970.
   *
   * @param availability  the availability method binding
   */
  public void setAvailability(
    String availability)
  {
    _availability = availability;
  }
```

```
  /**
   * Create and return a new {@link DateValidator} to be registered
   * on the surrounding {@link UIComponent}.
   *
   * @throws JspException  if a new validator instance cannot be created
   */
  protected Validator createValidator() throws JspException
  {
    DateValidator validator = new DateValidator();

    if (_availability != null)
    {
      FacesContext context = FacesContext.getCurrentInstance();
      Application application = context.getApplication();
      MethodBinding binding = application.createMethodBinding(_availability,
                                                              new Class[]
                                                              {
                                                                int.class,
                                                                int.class
                                                              });
      validator.setAvailability(binding);
    }

    return validator;
  }

  private String _availability;
}
```

The `setAvailability()` method sets the method binding, defined by the application developer, with the signature `(int, int)` and returns a `boolean[]` array, indicating the availability for each day in the range (inclusive) since January 1, 1970. Code Sample 7-23 shows an excerpt of a backing bean that could be bound to your date validator.

Code Sample 7-23. *Excerpt of Backing Bean Following the Contract of Your Validator*

```
public boolean[] getAvailability(
  int startDays,
  int endDays)
{
  ...
  boolean[] availability = new boolean[totalDays];
  ...
  return availability;
}
```

The Tag Library Descriptor

You have defined the behavior of your ValidateDateTag tag handler class. It is now time to register the name of the custom action and define some rules for how it can be used, as shown in Code Sample 7-24.

Code Sample 7-24. *Tag Library Descriptor*

```
<?xml version="1.0" encoding="UTF-8" ?>
<!DOCTYPE taglib
   PUBLIC "-//Sun Microsystems, Inc.//DTD JSP Tag Library 1.2//EN"
          "http://java.sun.com/dtd/web-jsptaglibrary_1_2.dtd" >
<taglib>

  <tlib-version>1.0</tlib-version>
  <jsp-version>1.2</jsp-version>
  <short-name>pro</short-name>
  <uri>http://projsf.apress.com/tags</uri>
  <description>
    This tag library contains JavaServer Faces tag handlers for the
    ProJSF component library.
  </description>

  ...
  <tag>
    <name>validateDate</name>
    <tag-class>com.apress.projsf.ch7.taglib.ValidateDateTag</tag-class>
    <body-content>JSP</body-content>
    <description>
    </description>

    <attribute>
      <name>availability</name>
      <required>false</required>
      <rtexprvalue>false</rtexprvalue>
      <description>
         The availability method binding with signature (Int, Int)
         returns boolean[], indicating availablilty for each day in
         range (inclusive)
      </description>
    </attribute>
  </tag>
</taglib>
```

As you can see, this tag has only one attribute—availability. To emphasize, any method binding defined has to follow the contract set up by the DateValidator.

Step 12: Registering Your Ajax Resources with Weblets

For the `HtmlAjaxInputDateRenderer`, you need to register two files—`inputDate.js` and `inputDate.css`—as weblets, which will enable you to package them as part of your custom JSF component library (see Code Sample 7-25).

Note For more information about weblets, please see Chapter 5, or visit the Weblets project's site at `http://weblets.dev.java.net`.

Code Sample 7-25. *Weblet Configuration for the* `HtmlAjaxInputDateRenderer` *Resources*

```
<?xml version="1.0" encoding="UTF-8" ?>
<weblets-config xmlns="http://weblets.dev.java.net/config" >
  ...
  <weblet>
    <weblet-name>com.apress.projsf.ch7</weblet-name>
    <weblet-class>net.java.dev.weblets.packaged.PackagedWeblet</weblet-class>
    <init-param>
      <param-name>package</param-name>
      <param-value>com.apress.projsf.ch7.render.html.ajax.resources</param-value>
    </init-param>
  </weblet>
  ...
  <weblet-mapping>
    <weblet-name>com.apress.projsf.ch7</weblet-name>
    <url-pattern>/projsf-ch7/*</url-pattern>
  </weblet-mapping>
</weblets-config>
```

The `PackagedWeblet` is a built-in weblet implementation that can read from a particular Java package using the `ClassLoader` and stream the result to the browser. The package initialization parameter tells the `PackagedWeblet` which Java package to use as a root when resolving weblet-managed resource requests.

Summary

This chapter discussed how you can use Ajax to fetch data and how you can leverage the JSF managed bean facility as a data source.

The chapter also covered the different `XMLHttpRequest` response types—`responseText` and `responseXML`—that you can use to return the result from the server. We also showed you how to use the `eval()` function to efficiently parse JSON-syntax responses.

We covered a new open source project called Mabon that extends JSF to provide a custom lifecycle that invokes a managed bean method remotely and then transfers the result to the client using JSON syntax.

From this chapter, we hope you have gained an understanding of how to Ajax-enable data fetch for your JSF components; in addition, you should now have a deeper understanding of object-oriented JavaScript programming techniques. You should now also be able to create your own custom validator.

CHAPTER 8

Providing Mozilla XUL Renderers

None of this was here. It was a giant space, and there were creatures, and they were growling, and I heard a voice say "zuul." It was right here!

—Dana Barrette, *Ghostbusters*

The more advanced Web applications become, the more they look and feel like desktop applications. With the speed at which Internet technologies are evolving, we will soon be facing a new type of Internet application—single-page interface (SPIF) applications. These are RIAs that behave like desktop applications, making the traditional page flow a thing of the past. An example of a traditional page flow application is a shopping cart. In a SPIF application, users don't need to navigate to new pages when stepping through the online store. Great examples of SPIF applications are the Mozilla Amazon Browser (`http://www.faser.net/mab/`) and OpenLaszlo's Amazon Store (`http://www.laszlosystems.com/lps/sample-apps/amazon/amazon2.lzx?lzt=html`). Both provide the user with a rich, intuitive user interface and are not forcing the user to navigate from page to page.

Unless you are a serious JavaScript or Ajax hacker, you should think twice before choosing Ajax to build a SPIF application. In context, a SPIF application built on top of a pure Ajax solution definitely means more client-side code. More client-side code means more work at the browser, which means that code-intensive SPIF applications will need powerful processors to give the user the responsiveness desired. Although computers have become faster, the processor problem with JavaScript functionality in the past has not completely disappeared—not to mention that maintaining all that JavaScript code is not a task for the faint of heart!

If you combined the asynchronous communication channel provided by Ajax with a feature-rich, client-side component model, you would be golden. As you learned in Chapter 4, RITs, Mozilla XUL, and Microsoft HTC provide developers with well-confined environments for building reusable components. With JSF, it is possible to provide a solution that combines Ajax and XUL or combines Ajax and HTC and therefore gives the component writer the best of both worlds and gives the application developer a lightweight and responsive framework.

This chapter will focus on using XUL and show how you can leverage XUL's extensibility and the declarative component model to enhance your JSF components. You will provide a new XUL `RenderKit` for the `ProInputDate` and `ProShowOneDeck` components.

Requirements for the Deck and Date Components' XUL Implementations

The requirements for the ProInputDate and ProShowOneDeck components in this chapter are simple—you need to leverage the declarative component model provided by Mozilla's GRE. To support this, you need to provide XUL-specific Renderer classes for the deck and date components. There should be no loss of functionality supporting this client-specific component model compared to what is provided by the deck and date components created in Chapters 6 and 7.

What Mozilla XUL Brings to JSF

Since XUL components are part of the Mozilla GRE, there is no need to "explode" the JSF page structure into the appropriate markup on the server before sending the markup to the client. This in turn will reduce the network payload since rendering is taken care of by the client and not by the actual server implementation.

Another great feature of XUL is its extensibility, providing a declarative way to create new components and extend existing XUL components. To enable this feature, XUL uses XBL. You attach these behavioral XBL components to markup using CSS selectors.

And, of course, XUL provides out-of-the-box rich client interactivity without forcing the component author to implement this in an alternative solution such as JavaScript.

We will show how you can combine the Ajax asynchronous communication channel—XMLHttpRequest—with the highly interactive components provided by XUL to design reusable and extremely interactive components based on the JSF standard.

What JSF Brings to XUL

One element that JSF brings to XUL is a common programming model—JSP and Java. You could argue that developers interested in XUL can use XUL directly, but the point we are making here is that not only does JSF provide a familiar programming model (at least for the majority of J2EE developers), it also provides a server-side component model that hides the XUL specifics without the application developer knowing or needing to know the implementation details.

Another element that JSF brings is the standard request lifecycle that includes automatic state saving and state restoring, validation, data model, and event handling.

The XUL Implementation of the Deck and Date Components

One noticeable benefit of using a component model such as XUL with standard JSF components is that it provides a set of UI widgets that are not available in HTML, such as menus, toolbars, pop-ups, and trees. This means component writers do not need to "create" these using traditional browser techniques, which is not a trivial task. These XUL widgets are available through the Mozilla GRE, and as such, they have the benefit of not needing to download components to draw an application in the browser. You can also design your own components with XUL; the browser will download these once on initial request and cache them in the browser.

The following are the main technologies in this chapter: XUL, XBL, Ajax, Dojo Toolkit, D[2], and Mabon. Although this list of technologies is pretty extensive, we have covered most of the technologies in previous chapters; also, in this chapter, they will play more of a supporting role, similar to weblets (which were introduced in Chapter 5). After this chapter, you should be able to create rich user interface components with the Mozilla XUL and XBL technologies. Figure 8-1 shows the nine classes you will create in this chapter.

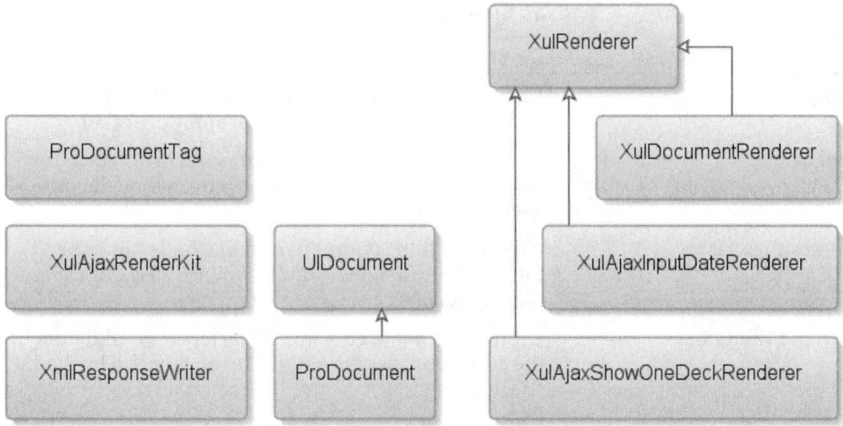

Figure 8-1. *Class diagram showing all classes created in this chapter*

The classes are as follows:

- `ProDocumentTag` is the tag handler class representing the `ProDocument` component.
- `XulAjaxRenderKit` is the new custom `RenderKit`, which is responsible for dynamically selecting the correct `ResponseWriter` on the incoming request.
- `XmlResponseWriter` extends the default `ResponseWriter` with support for XML documents.
- `UIDocument` is a behavioral superclass representing the document component.
- `ProDocument` is the renderer-specific subclass for the `UIDocument` class.
- `XulRenderer` is a port of the `HtmlRenderer` created in Chapter 2.
- `XulDocumentRenderer` is the `Renderer` in charge of writing the root elements in a XUL document.
- `XulAjaxInputDateRenderer` is a new custom `Renderer` for the date component, which extends the `XulRenderer` and adds resources to include XUL and Ajax support.
- And finally, `XulAjaxShowOneDeckRenderer` is a new custom `Renderer` for the deck component, which extends the `XulRenderer` and adds resources to include XUL and Ajax support.

Designing JSF XUL Components Using a Blueprint

The blueprint defined for the HTML-based JSF components applies to XUL-based JSF components as well. The XUL implementation is not introducing any new behavior, so you need to provide only a new set of XUL `Renderers`. Whenever you introduce a new `Renderer` that supports alternative markup to HTML, you have to provide a new `RenderKit` (that is, a XUL `RenderKit`). In this chapter, you will simply follow the blueprint (see Table 8-1) starting with step 1 and skipping steps 2, 4, and 10.

Table 8-1. *Steps in the Blueprint for Creating a New JSF Component*

#	Steps	Description
1	Creating a UI prototype	Create a prototype of the UI and intended behavior for your component using the appropriate markup.
2	Creating events and listeners	(Optional) Create custom events and listeners in the case your specific needs are not covered by the JSF specification.
3	Creating a behavioral superclass	(Optional) If the component behavior is not to be found, create a new behavioral superclass (for example, `UIShowOne`).
4	Creating converters and validators	(Optional) Create custom converters and validators in the case your specific needs are not covered by the JSF specification.
5	Creating a client-specific `Renderer`	Create the `Renderer` you need that will write out the client-side markup for your JSF component.
6	Creating a renderer-specific subclass	(Optional) Create a renderer-specific subclass; although this is an optional step, it is good practice to implement it.
7	Registering a `UIComponent` and `Renderer`	Register your new `UIComponent` and `Renderer` in the `faces-config.xml` file.
8	Creating a JSP tag handler and TLD	This step is needed in the case you are using JSP as your default view handler. An alternative solution is to use Facelets (`http://facelets.dev.java.net/`).
9	Creating a `RenderKit` and `ResponseWriter`	(Optional) If you plan to support alternative markup such as Mozilla XUL, then you need to create a new `RenderKit` with an associating `ResponseWriter`. The default `RenderKit` is `HTML_BASIC` with the `contentType` set to `text/html`.
10	Extending the JSF implementation	(Optional) This step is needed in the case you have to provide extensions to the JSF implementation (for example, extending JSF factory classes or providing a custom JSF lifecycle implementation).
11	Registering the `RenderKit` and JSF extension	(Optional) Register your custom `RenderKit` and/or extensions to the JSF implementation.
12	Registering resources with Weblets	(Optional) Register your resources such as images, JavaScript libraries, and CSS files with Weblets so that they can be packaged and loaded directly out of the component library JAR file.

It might seem like a lot of work to have to cover nine out of twelve steps just to provide a XUL implementation, but you have already done most of the work in previous chapters; as such, each step is fairly simple. Let's start with step 1 and look at the new components' markup.

Step 1: Creating a UI Prototype

To be able to prototype what you want to achieve in this chapter, you will have to use XUL to find out what XUL elements, renderer-specific attributes, and other resources (for example, JavaScript, images, and so on) you need. Since you are providing a XUL implementation for both the date and deck components, you also have to provide two prototypes, one for each component.

■ **Note** During our research for information about XUL and XBL, we found two really good resources on the Internet: Mozilla (`http://www.mozilla.org/projects/xul/`) and XULPlanet (`http://www.xulplanet.com/`).

The XUL Date Implementation Prototype

Figure 8-2 shows the end result of the `<pro:inputDate>` prototype implemented in XUL.

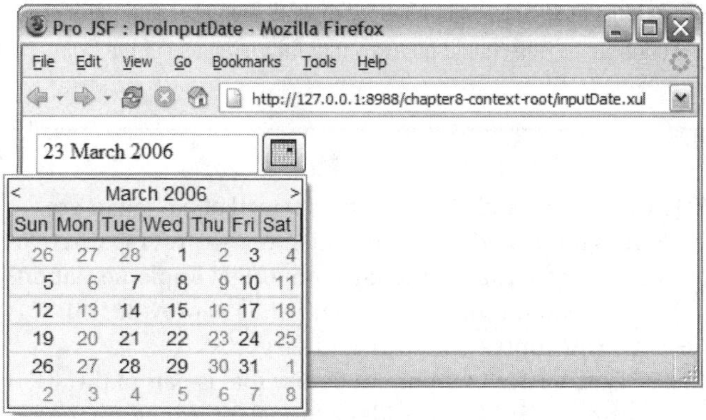

Figure 8-2. *The* `<pro:inputDate>` *component implemented in a XUL page*

Code Sample 8-1 shows the XUL markup for a page using the XUL `<pro:inputDate>` prototype shown in Figure 8-2.

Code Sample 8-1. *The Markup Needed to Create the XUL Prototype Page*

```
<?xml version="1.0" ?>
<?xml-stylesheet href="projsf-ch8/document.css" type="text/css"?>
<?xml-stylesheet href="projsf-ch8/pro.css" type="text/css"?>
<xul:window xmlns="http://www.w3.org/1999/xhtml"
        xmlns:xul="http://www.mozilla.org/keymaster/gatekeeper/there.is.only.xul"
```

```
            xmlns:pro="http://projsf.apress.com/tags"
            orient="horizontal" align="start"
            title="Pro JSF : ProInputDate">
  <xul:hbox align="center" flex="1">
    <xul:script type="text/javascript" src="/.../faces/weblets/mabon/mabon.js"/>
    <xul:script type="text/javascript">
      var djConfig={preventBackButtonFix: true,
                    libraryScriptUri:'/.../faces/weblets/dojo/dojo.js'};
    </xul:script>
    <xul:script type="text/javascript" src="/.../faces/weblets/dojo/dojo.js"/>
    <pro:inputDate id="dateField"
                   value="31 October 2005"
                   pattern="d MMMMM yyyy"
                   targetURL="projsf-ch8/sample-availability.json"/>
  </xul:hbox>
</xul:window>
```

A XUL document requires two elements to be valid: an XML processing instruction (`<?xml version="1.0"?>`) on the first line that identifies the file as XML and a `window` element (`<window xmlns="..." >`) that defines the XUL Web page, which is similar to `<html>` for HTML.

Caution At the time of writing, the Dojo toolkit needs to be configured to work with XUL, and therefore you need the `preventBackButtonFix` workaround. This should go away in a future release of the Dojo toolkit.

One of the benefits of using XUL over traditional HTML is that instead of having to provide all the markup in the `Renderer`, XUL is interested in only one element—`<pro:inputDate>`. You can also see that the prototype is similar in syntax to the JSF component implementation. From the source you can see that the XUL element that the `Renderer` has to provide is the `<pro:inputDate>` element with at least two attributes—`pattern` and `targetURL`.

One of the great features of XUL is its extensive component library that is part of the Mozilla GRE. As with many good frameworks, XUL also provides a model for extending the component set whenever a need for it arises. As discussed in Chapter 4, the language that developers can use to extend XUL is XBL. XBL allows developers to add "custom" components to the extensive set of existing XUL elements. In this case, the functionality you are looking for is not available out of the box, so you will have to create your own custom XUL component (for example, `<pro:inputDate ...>`) using XBL.

The XBL Date Component Prototype

Like XUL, XBL is an XML language, so it has similar syntax rules. The `<bindings>` element is the root element of an XBL file and contains one or more binding elements. Each binding element declares a single binding. You can use the `id` attribute to identify the binding. Code Sample 8-2 shows the XBL file (`bindings.xml`) and the first binding (`inputDate`).

Code Sample 8-2. *The* `bindings.xml` *File*

```
<?xml version="1.0"?>
<bindings xmlns="http://www.mozilla.org/xbl"
          xmlns:xbl="http://www.mozilla.org/xbl"
          xmlns:html="http://www.w3.org/1999/xhtml"
          xmlns:xul="http://www.mozilla.org/keymaster/gatekeeper/there.is.only.xul">
  <binding id="inputDate">
    <resources>
      <stylesheet src="styles.css" />
    </resources>
    <content>
      <xul:hbox>
        <xul:textbox id="input"
                     style="margin-left:0px;margin-right:0px;"
                     xbl:inherits="value"
                     onchange="this.parentNode.parentNode.flushChanges();" />
        <xul:button popup="calendar"
                    image="/.../projsf-ch8/inputDateButton.gif"
                    style="margin-left:0px;margin-right:0px;min-width:2em;"/>
      </xul:hbox>
```

The XBL component prototype in Code Sample 8-2 shows the root `<bindings>` element containing one `<binding>` element. The namespace in the `<bindings>` element defines what syntax will be used, and in the prototype in Code Sample 8-2 it is XBL—`xmlns=http://www.mozilla.org/xbl`. The `id` attribute on the `<binding>` element (that is, `inputDate`) identifies the binding. Using CSS, you can assign a binding to an element by setting the `-moz-binding` URI property to reference the binding inside the XBL document (for example, `-moz-binding: url('[filename].xml#inputDate')`).

The prototype also contains a set of XUL elements, as shown in Table 8-2.

Table 8-2. *XUL Elements Used in This Chapter**

XUL Element [`xul:`]	Description
`hbox`	A container element that can contain any number of child elements and that renders its children horizontally.
`vbox`	A container element that can contain any number of child elements and that renders its children vertically.
`textnode`	With the `<textnode>` element, the entire node is replaced with text corresponding to the result of the `value` attribute.
`label`	This element provides a label for a control element. If the user clicks the label, the focus moves to the associated control, specified with the `control` attribute.
`textbox`	A text input field in which the user can enter text. It is similar to the HTML `<input>` element. Only one line of text is displayed by default. You can specify the `multiline` attribute to display a field with multiple rows.

Continued

Table 8-2. *Continued*

XUL Element [xul:]	Description
button	A button that can be clicked by the user. You can use event handlers to trap mouse events, keyboard events, and other events. It is typically rendered as a gray outset rectangle. The popup attribute used in this chapter is a common attribute for all XUL elements.
popupset	A container for <popup> elements. You should declare all <popup> elements as children of a <popupset>. This element does not directly display on-screen. Child pop-ups will be displayed when asked to be displayed by other elements.
popup	A container that appears in a child window. The pop-up window does not have any special frame. Pop-ups can be displayed when an element is clicked by assigning the ID of the <popup> element to either the popup, context, or tooltip attribute of the element. A pop-up is a type of box that defaults to vertical orientation.
grid	A <grid> element contains both <rows> and <columns> elements. It is used to create a grid of elements. Both the rows and columns are displayed at once, although only one will typically contain content, while the other may provide size information. Whichever is last in the grid is displayed on top.
columns	Defines the columns of a grid. Each child of a <columns> element should be a <column> element.
column	A single column in a <columns> element. Each child of the <column> element is placed in each successive cell of the grid. The column with the most child elements determines the number of rows in each column.
rows	Defines the rows of a grid. Each child of a <rows> element should be a <row> element.
row	A single row in a <rows> element. Each child of the <row> element is placed in each successive cell of the grid. The row with the most child elements determines the number of columns in each row.

**Source: XULPlanet (*http://www.xulplanet.com*)*

Being able to combine XUL components (and HTML elements) is extremely useful to simplify development because you can create a single, complex, and reusable component. Another neat feature of using the XUL component model is the built-in pop-up support. Instead of having to write client-side script to support a pop-up window, you can simply create a set of pop-up windows in the XBL binding, as shown in Code Sample 8-3, and use the common XUL popup attribute to launch a pop-up window in the Mozilla browser. In your case, this pop-up functionality will be used for the <pro:inputDate> component's calendar.

The XUL popup element has a set of predefined event handlers (for example, onpopupshowing) that you can use to dynamically set the contents when the user requests to display the calendar. In this case, you are calling a method called popup().

You construct the pop-up calendar with a <vbox> element as the parent container and an <hbox> element to hold the toolbar, as shown in Code Sample 8-3. The toolbar contains two <text> elements that are used to navigate to the previous and next months.

Code Sample 8-3. *The* `bindings.xml` *File*

```
      <xul:popupset>
        <xul:popup id="calendar" position="after_end"
                onpopupshowing="document.popupNode.parentNode.parentNode.popup()">
          <xul:vbox class="calendar" >
            <xul:hbox class="toolbar" >
              <xul:text value="&lt;"
                   onclick="document.popupNode.parentNode.parentNode.scroll(-1)" />
              <xul:label id="title" flex="1"
                        style="text-align:center;padding: 1px;" />
              <xul:text value="&gt;"
                   onclick="document.popupNode.parentNode.parentNode.scroll(1)" />
            </xul:hbox>
        <xul:grid id="grid"
           onclick="document.popupNode.parentNode.parentNode.clickCell(event)" >
          <xul:columns>
            <xul:column/>
            <xul:column/>
            <xul:column/>
            <xul:column/>
            <xul:column/>
            <xul:column/>
            <xul:column/>
          </xul:columns>

          <xul:rows>
            <xul:row class="headings" >
              <xul:label value="Sun" />
              <xul:label value="Mon" />
              <xul:label value="Tue" />
              <xul:label value="Wed" />
              <xul:label value="Thu" />
              <xul:label value="Fri" />
              <xul:label value="Sat" />
            </xul:row>
            <xul:row class="cells" >
              <xul:label/>
              ... //Six empty rows with seven empty labels.
              <xul:label/>
            </xul:row>
          </xul:rows>
        </xul:grid>
      </xul:vbox>
    </xul:popup>
  </xul:popupset>
</content>
```

The calendar also contains a XUL `<grid>` element that is used to display all the days of the month when the calendar is displayed in the browser. This implementation also supports selecting a date by clicking in its cell (for example, `onclick="... clickCell(event)"`).

The prototype also contains a set of XBL elements, as shown in Table 8-3.

Table 8-3. *XBL Elements Used in the* `<pro:inputDate>` *Component**

XBL Element	Description
`children`	The `<children>` element selects certain child elements to be included at a predefined location in the XBL component markup, much like facets in JSF.
`implementation`	Within the `<implementation>` element, you define individual `<field>`, `<property>`, and `<method>` elements, one for each one that you want.
`field`	A `<field>` element is a simple holder for values.
`property`	The `<property>` element declares a JavaScript property that is added to the element's object. The `<property>` element may have a `<getter>` child element and a `<setter>` child element to get and set the value of the property, respectively.
`method`	This declares a JavaScript method that is added to the element's object. The method can take arguments, declared with the `<parameter>` element.
`constructor`	The code inside this element is called when the binding is attached to an element. You can use this to initialize the content the binding uses. The `<constructor>` element should be placed inside the `<implementation>` element.
`parameter`	This declares a parameter to a method. Each parameter has a `name` attribute, which becomes a variable that is declared in the method body and has the value that was passed in to the method.
`body`	The content of the `<body>` element should be the JavaScript code to execute when the method is called.

* *Source: XULPlanet (*`http://www.xulplanet.com`*)*

You define any component-specific logic, such as selection of dates and scrolling to the next and previous months, in the `<implementation>` element. The `<implementation>` element contains all the calendar logic including a field, a constructor, and the methods for the `inputDate` binding. A `<field>` is a simple container for values, and Code Sample 8-4 defines four fields: `currentMonth`, `currentYear`, `selectedMillis`, and `monthNames`.

Code Sample 8-4. *The* `<implementation>` *Element in the* `bindings.xml` *File*

```
<implementation>
  <field name="currentMonth"/>
  <field name="currentYear"/>
  <field name="selectedMillis"/>
  <field name="monthNames"/>
```

The script within the `<constructor>` element, as shown in Code Sample 8-5, is called when the binding is attached to an element. By using a `<constructor>` in the `<implementation>`

element, you can initialize the content the binding uses. In this case, you prepopulate the monthNames field with the names of the months.

Code Sample 8-5. *The Constructor of the* bindings.xml *File*

```
<constructor>
<![CDATA[
  this.monthNames = ['January','February', 'March', 'April', 'May',
                     'June', 'July', 'August', 'September',
                     'October', 'November', 'December'];

  var currentNode = this;
  while (currentNode != null)
  {
    if (currentNode.localName == 'form' &&
        currentNode.namespaceURI == 'http://www.w3.org/1999/xhtml')
    {
      var formNode = currentNode;
      var clientId = this.getAttribute('id');
      var inputNode = formNode.elements[clientId];
      if (inputNode == null)
      {
        inputNode = document.createElementNS('http://www.w3.org/1999/xhtml',
                                             'input');
        inputNode.type = 'hidden';
        inputNode.name = clientId;
        formNode.appendChild(inputNode);
      }
      this.inputNode = inputNode;
      break;
    }
    currentNode = currentNode.parentNode;
  }
]]>
</constructor>
```

XUL has no mechanism to submit forms, because XUL uses a different UI model in which form submission is rarely applicable. It is legal to mix XHTML elements with a XUL application, though, in this case, an application developer using JSF to build applications will not necessarily know the differences between a JSF HTML component (for example, a <h:commandButton>) and a JSF XUL component. To ensure that the JSF XUL component supports regular form submit, you have to add a hidden input field, as shown in Code Sample 8-5, that will contain data from the <pro:inputDate>.

Compared to the HTML Ajax solution, the popup method, as shown in Code Sample 8-6, is invoked when the calendar is launched and not by the button's onclick handler. Another difference is that you don't need to keep track of the calendar's state like you did in the HTML Ajax solution. Figure 8-3 shows a sequence diagram of the pop-up implementation.

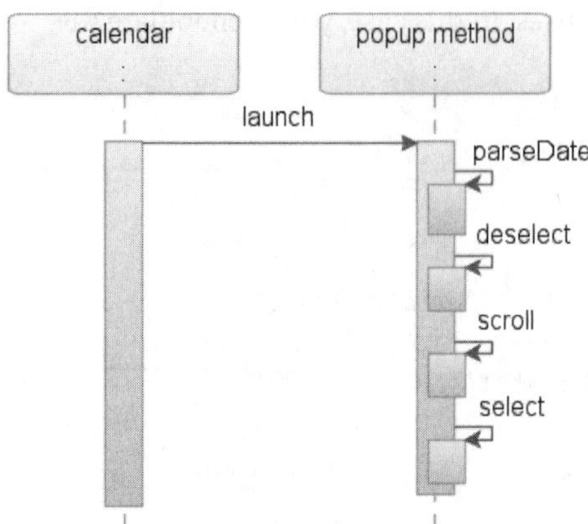

Figure 8-3. *Sequence diagram of the XBL* inputDate *binding* popup *method*

Code Sample 8-6. *The* popup *Method in the* bindings.xml *File*

```
<method name="popup">
  <body>
  <![CDATA[
    var dateString = document.getElementById('input').value;
    var parsedDate = this.parse(dateString, this.getAttribute('pattern'));
    var activeDate = (parsedDate != null) ? parsedDate : new Date();

    this.deselect();

    var month = activeDate.getMonth();
    var year = activeDate.getFullYear();
    this.currentMonth = month;
    this.currentYear = year;

    this.scroll(0);

    if (parsedDate != null)
      this.select(parsedDate.getDate());
  }
  ]]>
  </body>
</method>
```

The popup method will first read the user-defined date string from the input field and then parse that date string into a Date object. If parsing is successful, it uses the Date object; otherwise, it uses today's Date. Next it ensures there is no previous selection, before calling the scroll method, by passing zero as an argument to ensure fully populated calendar day cells but staying on the current month (zero navigation). Finally, the popup method will select an initial date (if possible).

The scroll method, as shown in Code Sample 8-7, allows the user to navigate plus or minus one month using arrow controls in the calendar. You can use Mabon to determine the availability of dates defined by the managed bean attached to the enhanced DateValidator.

Code Sample 8-7. *The* scroll *Method in the* bindings.xml *File*

```
<method name="scroll">
   <parameter name="offset"/>
  <body>
    <![CDATA[
    var gridNode = document.getElementById('grid');
    var month = this.currentMonth + offset;
    var year  = this.currentYear;
    year += Math.floor(month / 12);
    month = (month + 12) % 12;
    this.currentMonth = month;
    this.currentYear = year;

    var targetURL = this.getAttribute('targetURL');

    if (targetURL)
    {
      var startDate = new Date(year, month, 1);
      var endDate = new Date(year, month, 31);

      var millisPerDay = 1000 * 60 * 60 * 24;
      var startDay = Math.floor(startDate.getTime() / millisPerDay);
      var endDay = Math.floor(endDate.getTime() / millisPerDay);

      // use Mabon to determine availability
      var self = this;
      mabon.send(
        {
          url: targetURL,
          args: [startDay, endDay],
          result: function(result) { self.display(result); }
        });
    }
    else
    {
      var available = [];
      for (var i=0; i < 32; i++)
      {
        available.push(true);
      }
      this.display(available);
    }
  ]]>
  </body>
</method>
```

The clickCell method, as shown in Code Sample 8-8, is called when the user clicks a cell representing a date in the calendar. The method will check to see whether the user clicked a cell that is outside the range of the displayed month and, if so, navigate to the month for that selected date—this.scroll(1) or this.scroll(-1). If the selection is within the boundaries of the month, you need to see whether this date is available and, if it is, add the selected date to the <input> element.

Code Sample 8-8. *The* clickCell *Method in the* bindings.xml *File*

```
<method name="clickCell">
  <parameter name="event"/>
  <body>
  <![CDATA[
    var cellNode = event.target;
    var rowNode = cellNode.parentNode;

    var row = this.getChildIndex(rowNode) - 1;
    var col = this.getChildIndex(cellNode);
    var day = Number(cellNode.value);

    // detect other month cells
    if (row == -1)
    {
      // header cells
      return;
    }
    else if (row == 0 && day > 7)
    {
      this.scroll(-1);
    }
    else if (row > 3 && day < 15)
    {
      this.scroll(1);
    }
    else
    {
      if (this.isAvailable(day))
      {
        // transfer value to input field
        var input = document.getElementById('input');
        var selectedDate = this.calculateDate(day);
        input.value = this.format(selectedDate,
                                  this.getAttribute('pattern'));

        // hide the pop-up
        document.getElementById('calendar').hidePopup();
      }
    }
```

```
        ]]>
        </body>
      </method>
      ...
    </implementation>
  </binding>
</bindings>
```

The XUL Deck Implementation Prototype

The next prototype is the `<pro:showOneDeck>` XUL component, as shown in Figure 8-4.

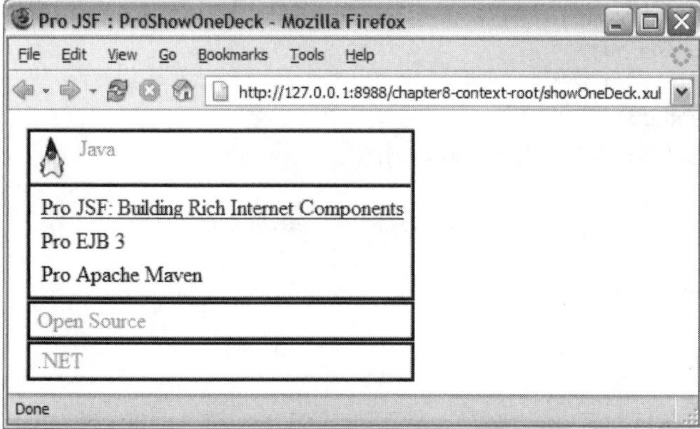

Figure 8-4. *The* `<pro:showOneDeck>` *component implemented in a XUL page*

To be able to asynchronously communicate with the server when a deck is activated, you have to download a set of JavaScript libraries—`dojo.js` and `d2.js`—to the page. These libraries need to be part of the component and should be downloaded automatically to the client on initial request. Apart from having less rendered markup and the usage of XUL elements, this XUL page, as shown in Code Sample 8-9, is similar to the page you created in Chapter 6, which leveraged the HTML version of the `ProShowOneDeck` `Renderer`, `HtmlAjaxShowOneDeckRenderer`.

Code Sample 8-9. *The Markup Needed to Create the XUL Prototype Page*

```
<?xml version="1.0" encoding="UTF-8" ?>
<?xml-stylesheet href="projsf-ch8/document.css" type="text/css"?>
<?xml-stylesheet href="projsf-ch8/pro.css" type="text/css"?>
<?xml-stylesheet href="resources/stylesheet.css" type="text/css"?>
<xul:window xmlns="http://www.w3.org/1999/xhtml"
          xmlns:xul="http://www.mozilla.org/keymaster/gatekeeper/there.is.only.xul"
           xmlns:pro="http://projsf.apress.com/tags"
           orient="horizontal"
           align="start"
           title="Pro JSF : ProShowOneDeck">
```

```
  <xul:hbox align="center" flex="1">
    <table width="300px">
      <tbody>
        <tr>
          <td>
            <xul:script type="application/x-javascript">
              var djConfig={preventBackButtonFix: true,
                            libraryScriptUri:'/faces/weblets/dojo$0.1/dojo.js'};
            </xul:script>
            <xul:script type="application/x-javascript"
                        src="/.../faces/weblets/dojo$0.1/dojo.js"/>
            <xul:script type="application/x-javascript"
                        src="/.../faces/weblets/d2/d2.js"/>
            <pro:showOneDeck showItemId="first">
              <pro:showItem itemId="first"
                            active="true">
                <pro:showItemHeader>
                  <img src="/.../resources/java_small.jpg"
                       alt="The Duke"
                       style="margin-right: 8px; vertical-align:bottom;"/>
                    Java
                </pro:showItemHeader>
                <table>
                  <tbody>
                    <tr>
                      <td>
                        <a href="http://apress.com/book/bookDisplay.html?bID=10044">
                          Pro JSF: Building Rich Internet Components
                        </a>
                      </td>
                    </tr>
     ...
  </xul:hbox>
</xul:window>
```

The XBL Deck Component Prototype

The structure of the <pro:showOneDeck> XUL component is slightly different from the <pro:inputDate>, since it is of a composite nature containing not one but four <binding> elements—showOneDeck, showItem, showItemActive, and showItemHeader.

The showOneDeck binding will be displayed as a XUL <vbox> element at runtime. The <children> element selects child elements to be included at a predefined location, much like facets in JSF. The prototype in Code Sample 8-10 adds the includes attribute. This attribute allows only certain elements to appear in the content of the <pro:showOneDeck> component (for example, <pro:showItem>).

Code Sample 8-10. *The* showOneDeck *Binding*

```
<binding id="showOneDeck" display="xul:vbox" >
  <resources>
    <stylesheet src="styles.css" />
  </resources>
  <content>
    <xul:vbox class="showOneDeck"
              xbl:inherits="className=styleClass" >
      <children includes="showItem" />
    </xul:vbox>
  </content>
</binding>
```

The <pro:showItem> component, as shown in Code Sample 8-11, is the part of the <pro:showOneDeck> implementation that will expand when the user interacts with it. This binding contains one method, expand, that is invoked when the header is clicked.

As you can see, you are using the d2.js library, passing the activated form id and the id of the selected node to the d2.submit() function. The d2.submit() function calls the dojo.io.bind() method, passing information about which form to submit, content (such as the ID of the selected component), the accepted request header ('X-D2-Content-Type': <contentType>), and the MIME type (text/xml) for this request. This information will determine which node to expand and which ResponseWriter to use for this request.

Code Sample 8-11. *The* showItem *Binding and the* expand *Method*

```
<binding id="showItem" display="xul:vbox" >
  <resources>
    <stylesheet src="styles.css" />
  </resources>
  <content>
    <xul:vbox class="showItem" flex="1" >
      <xul:hbox id="showItemHeader"
                onclick="this.parentNode.parentNode.expand()"
                class="showItemHeader"
                xbl:inherits="className=headerStyleClass" >
        <children includes="showItemHeader" />
      </xul:hbox>
      <xul:hbox style="display:none;" >
        <children/>
      </xul:hbox>
    </xul:vbox>
  </content>
  <implementation>
    <method name="expand" >
      <body>
      <![CDATA[
        var showOneNode = this.parentNode;
```

```
        var showOneClientId = showOneNode.getAttribute('id');
        var currentNode = this;
        while (currentNode != null)
        {
          if (currentNode.localName == 'form' &&
              currentNode.namespaceURI == 'http://www.w3.org/1999/xhtml')
          {
            var formNode = currentNode;
            var content = new Object();
            content[showOneClientId] = this.getAttribute('itemId');
            d2.submit(formNode, content);
            break;
          }
          currentNode = currentNode.parentNode;
        }
      ]]>
      </body>
    </method>
  </implementation>
</binding>
```

The D² library also defines a callback function—d2._loadxml—that gets the response data from the server. The d2._loadxml function will replace the target document's XML nodes with the XML nodes from the document returned on the response.

The <pro:showItemActive> component, as shown in Code Sample 8-12, is responsible for showing the header—<children includes="showItemHeader" />—and all the children—<children/>—that are part of the expanded showOneDeck node.

Code Sample 8-12. *The* showItemActive *Binding*

```
<binding id="showItemActive" display="xul:vbox" >
  <resources>
    <stylesheet src="styles.css" />
  </resources>
  <content>
    <xul:vbox class="showItem" flex="1" >
      <xul:hbox id="showItemHeader"
                class="showItemHeader"
                xbl:inherits="className=headerStyleClass" >
        <children includes="showItemHeader" />
      </xul:hbox>
      <xul:hbox class="showItemContent"
                xbl:inherits="className=contentStyleClass" >
        <children/>
      </xul:hbox>
    </xul:vbox>
  </content>
</binding>
```

The `<pro:showItemHeader>` component, as shown in Code Sample 8-13, is a container responsible for any children representing the header of the `showOneDeck` component.

Code Sample 8-13. *The* `showItemHeader` *Binding*

```
  <binding id="showItemHeader" display="xul:hbox" >
    <content>
      <children/>
    </content>
  </binding>
</bindings>
```

Figure 8-5 shows the complete structure of the `bindings.xml` file.

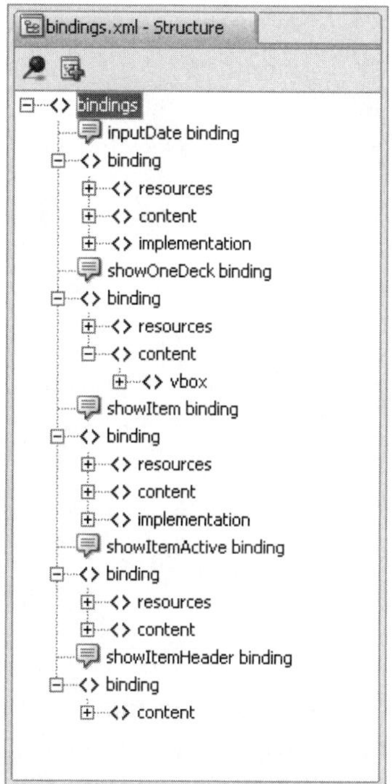

Figure 8-5. *Structure of* `bindings.xml` *as shown in the Oracle JDeveloper 10.1.3 structure window*

Defining the Binding Element Using a Style Sheet

The `id` attribute on the `binding` element (`#inpuDate`) identifies the binding. Using CSS, a developer can assign a binding to an element by setting the `-moz-binding` URI property to reference the `binding` inside the XBL document, as shown in Code Sample 8-14.

Code Sample 8-14. *The* pro.css *File*

```
@namespace pro url(http://projsf.apress.com/tags);

pro|inputDate
{
  -moz-binding: url('bindings.xml#inputDate');
}

pro|showOneDeck
{
  -moz-binding: url('bindings.xml#showOneDeck');
  display: -moz-box;
  -moz-box-orient: vertical;
}

pro|showItem
{
  -moz-binding: url('bindings.xml#showItem');
  display: -moz-box;
}

pro|showItem[active='true']
{
  -moz-binding: url('bindings.xml#showItemActive');
  display: -moz-box;
}

pro|showItemHeader
{
  -moz-binding: url('bindings.xml#showItemHeader');
  display: -moz-box;
}
```

In Code Sample 8-14, the CSS selector for the `<pro:inputDate>` element has the `-moz-binding` set to point to the XBL prototype file `bindings.xml` and refers to a specific binding with the ID `inputDate` in the XBL file. This is similar to how anchors are used in HTML files. You also have two `pro|showItem` selectors in the CSS. One of them has `[active='true']` attached to it, which means any `<pro:showItem>` element that has an `active` attribute set to `true` should use this XBL binding. This way, you can have one XUL element and provide multiple bindings.

Step 3: Creating a Behavioral Superclass

We need to cover one important fact before we show how to design the first JSF XUL component—XUL is not HTML. Although much of the functionality is shared between HTML and XUL, it is important to understand that they are different document objects. XUL is an XML language, and the XUL document is a subtype of the more generic XML document. This distinction between the two document objects is important.

A regular HTML document is usually structured as shown in Code Sample 8-15.

Code Sample 8-15. *HTML Document Structure*

```
<html>
<head>
  <title>Pro JSF : HTML Document</title>
</head>
<body>

</body>
</html>
```

A valid XUL document looks like Code Sample 8-16.

Code Sample 8-16. *XUL Document Structure*

```
<?xml version="1.0" encoding="ISO-8859-1" ?>
<xul:window
xmlns:xul="http://www.mozilla.org/keymaster/gatekeeper/there.is.only.xul"
          title="Pro JSF : XUL Document">

</xul:window>
```

Now, you have a document type that is different from HTML and requires another content type—`application/vnd.mozilla.xul+xml`—rather than the regular `text/html`. This inevitably brings you back to the problem of JSP owning the content type and the default JSF `ResponseWriter` supporting only HTML documents (see Chapter 6 for more information). What you need to support XUL is the following:

- A `ResponseWriter` that can handle XML
- A XUL `RenderKit` to create the `ResponseWriter` and pass the XUL `contentType`
- A document component that can write out the proper headers (for example, `window`) for a XUL page
- A custom content type in the JSP document that can be used to handle the initial request differently from subsequent postbacks with Ajax (for example, `application/x-javaserver-faces`)

The UIDocument Class

From the beginning we have emphasized that if you are not introducing a new behavior, you don't need to create a behavioral superclass; however, with so many rules, an exception must exist, right? Creating a document component that will represent the shell of the page is most likely client-side rendering and is not introducing a new server-side behavior. But, you cannot have a `Renderer` without attaching it to a behavioral superclass. So, for the XUL document `Renderer` to work properly, you have to introduce a `UIDocument` component, as shown in Figure 8-6.

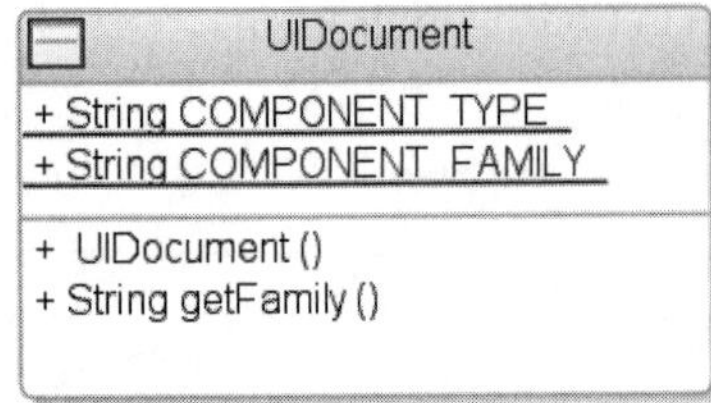

Figure 8-6. *Class diagram showing the* `UIDocument` *class*

Using a document component, an application developer can design JSF applications without knowing what document type will be delivered to the client. Since no behavior exists, this "special" behavioral superclass (see Code Sample 8-17) is acting only as a placeholder for the document `Renderer`. Potentially, you could add event support in the future, but for now, this is more than enough.

Code Sample 8-17. *The* `UIDocument` *Class*

```
package com.apress.projsf.ch8.component;

import javax.faces.component.UIComponentBase;

/**
 * The UIDocument component.
 */
public class UIDocument extends UIComponentBase
{
  public static final String COMPONENT_TYPE = "com.apress.projsf.Document";
  public static final String COMPONENT_FAMILY = "com.apress.projsf.Document";

  /**
   * Creates a new UIDocument.
   */
  public UIDocument()
  {
  }

  public String getFamily()
  {
    return COMPONENT_FAMILY;
  }
}
```

Step 5: Creating a Client-Specific Renderer

The XUL solution contains four `Renderer` classes—`XulRenderer`, `XulDocumentRenderer`, `XulAjaxInputDateRenderer`, and `XulAjaxShowOneDeckRenderer`—and the XUL resources. Figure 8-7 shows an overview of the `Renderer` classes you will create.

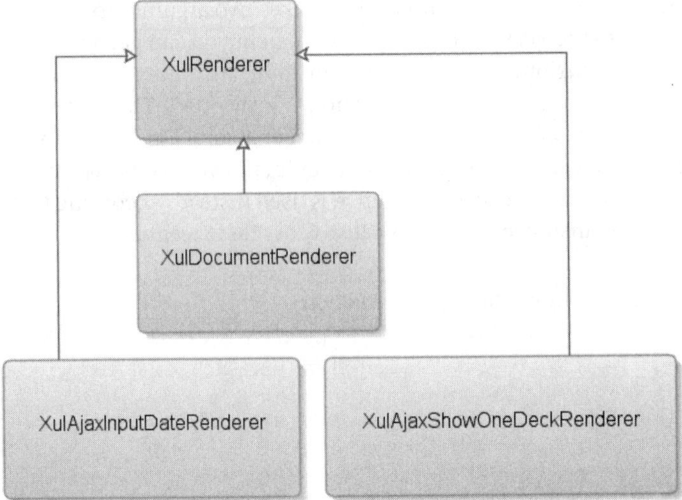

Figure 8-7. *Class diagram showing the XUL* `Renderers`

The `XulRenderer` is basically a port of the `HtmlRenderer` you created in Chapter 2. By porting the `HtmlRenderer` code to a XUL version, you now have "at-most-once" semantics for each script resource on the currently rendering XUL page.

The XulDocumentRenderer Class

A XUL document requires two entities to be valid: an XML processing instruction on the first line that identifies the file as XML and a `window` element that defines the XUL Web page. The `window` element is the root element in a XUL document and includes all other elements. The XML processing instruction belongs to the `ResponseWriter`, since it is not specific to XUL. The `window` element, on the other hand, is specific to XUL and belongs to a XUL `RenderKit` and its components. Figure 8-8 shows the `XulDocumentRenderer` class as displayed in a class diagram.

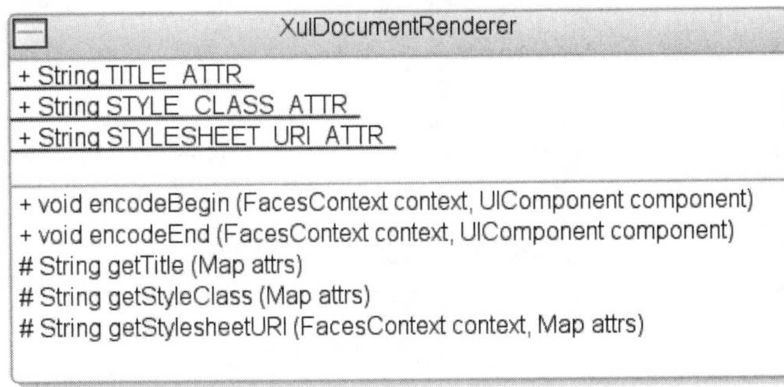

Figure 8-8. *Class diagram showing the* `XulDocumentRenderer` *class*

Code Sample 8-18 shows the encodeBegin() method, which takes two arguments—FacesContext context and UIComponent component. From the component you can get a hold of the Map containing all the available attributes. In this case, only three attributes exist on this UIDocument component—the window title, styleClass, and stylesheetURI. These are all renderer-specific attributes, as the UIDocument component has no behavioral attributes. The Map is necessary since Renderers cannot cast to the renderer-specific subclass, ProDocument, because this would fail when a behavioral UIDocument instance is used instead. According to the JSF specification, behavioral class instances must not cause ClassCastExceptions.

Code Sample 8-18. *The* XulDocumentRenderer encodeBegin() *Method*

```
package com.apress.projsf.ch8.render;

import java.io.IOException;
import java.util.Map;

import javax.faces.application.ViewHandler;
import javax.faces.component.UIComponent;
import javax.faces.context.FacesContext;
import javax.faces.context.ResponseWriter;

import com.apress.projsf.ch8.component.UIDocument;
import com.apress.projsf.ch8.render.xul.XulRenderer;

public class XulDocumentRenderer extends XulRenderer
{
  /**
   * The title attribute.
   */
  public static String TITLE_ATTR = "title";

  /**
   * The styleClass attribute.
   */
  public static String STYLE_CLASS_ATTR = "styleClass";

  /**
   * The stylesheetURI attribute.
   */
  public static String STYLESHEET_URI_ATTR = "stylesheetURI";

  public void encodeBegin(
    FacesContext context,
    UIComponent  component) throws IOException
  {
    ResponseWriter out = context.getResponseWriter();
    ViewHandler handler = context.getApplication().getViewHandler();
```

```
    Map attrs = component.getAttributes();
    String title = getTitle(attrs);
    String styleClass = getStyleClass(attrs);
    String stylesheetURI = getStylesheetURI(context, attrs);

    out.write("<?xml-stylesheet href=\"");
    out.writeText(handler.getResourceURL(context,
                       "weblet://com.apress.projsf.ch8/document.css"), null);
    out.write("\" type=\"text/css\"?>\n");

    out.write("<?xml-stylesheet href=\"");
    out.writeText(handler.getResourceURL(context,
                       "weblet://com.apress.projsf.ch8/pro.css"), null);
    out.write("\" type=\"text/css\"?>\n");

    if (stylesheetURI != null)
    {
      out.write("<?xml-stylesheet href=\"");
      out.writeText(handler.getResourceURL(context, stylesheetURI),
                    STYLESHEET_URI_ATTR);
      out.write("\" type=\"text/css\"?>");
    }
    out.startElement("xul:window", component);
    out.writeAttribute("xmlns", "http://www.w3.org/1999/xhtml", null);
    out.writeAttribute("xmlns:xul",
                   "http://www.mozilla.org/keymaster/gatekeeper/there.is.only.xul",
                    null);
    out.writeAttribute("xmlns:pro", "http://projsf.apress.com/tags", null);
    out.writeAttribute("orient", "horizontal", null);
    out.writeAttribute("align", "start", null);

    if (title != null)
      out.writeAttribute("title", title, TITLE_ATTR);

    super.encodeBegin(context, component);

    out.startElement("xul:hbox", null);
    if (styleClass != null)
      out.writeAttribute("class", styleClass, STYLE_CLASS_ATTR);
    out.writeAttribute("align", "center", null);
    out.writeAttribute("flex", "1", null);
  }
```

The `pro.css` file (see Code Sample 8-14) might look small; however, it is more important than might be realized at first. The `pro.css` file is actually the glue between the element in the XUL document and the actual custom XBL component. Another perk from XUL is that you can use this file to add more components, if needed. Thus, you avoid tampering with the actual `XulDocumentRenderer`.

The startElement() method takes the arguments name and component. The name argument is the name of the generated element (for example, xul:window), and the component argument is the UIComponent this element represents. In Code Sample 8-18, this is represented by the UIDocument component.

The XulDocumentRenderer encodeEnd() method (see Code Sample 8-19) is basically just closing the XUL "body" tag and the XUL window tag. The "body" tag—<xul:hbox>—is not required by XUL; it is something we have added to make the XUL base document similar to a regular HTML document.

Code Sample 8-19. *The* encodeEnd() *Method*

```
public void encodeEnd(
  FacesContext context,
  UIComponent  component) throws IOException
{
  ResponseWriter out = context.getResponseWriter();
  out.endElement("xul:hbox");
  out.endElement("xul:window");
}
```

The getTitle(), getStyleClass(), and getStylesheetURI() methods, as shown in Code Sample 8-20, return the values of the title, styleClass, and stylesheetURI attributes.

Code Sample 8-20. *The Getters for the* UIDocument *Attributes*

```
  protected String getTitle(
    Map attrs)
  {
    return (String)attrs.get(TITLE_ATTR);
  }

  protected String getStyleClass(
    Map attrs)
  {
    return (String)attrs.get(STYLE_CLASS_ATTR);
  }

  protected String getStylesheetURI(
    FacesContext context,
    Map          attrs)
  {
    String stylesheetURI = (String)attrs.get(STYLESHEET_URI_ATTR);

    if (stylesheetURI != null)
    {
      Application application = context.getApplication();
      ViewHandler handler = application.getViewHandler();
```

```
      stylesheetURI = handler.getResourceURL(context, stylesheetURI);
    }

    return stylesheetURI;
  }
}
```

The XulAjaxInputDateRenderer Class

How will XUL make your life easier? Although XUL/XBL reduces some of the work involved in building prototypes, you have some work to do. However, you still have to see the real gains of using a well-defined component model to design the JSF components. So, without further ado, Figure 8-9 shows the JSF XUL implementation.

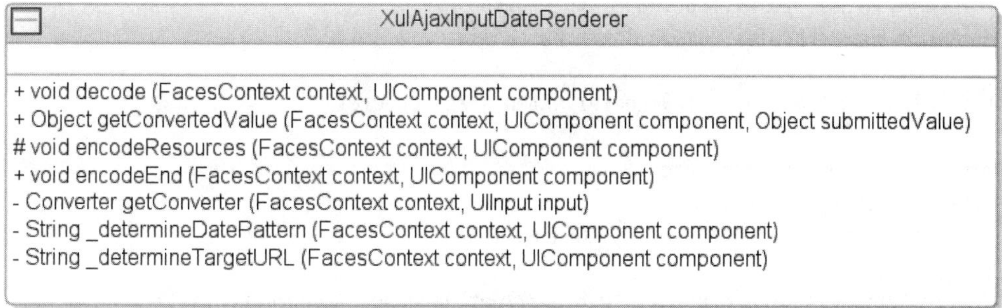

Figure 8-9. *Class diagram showing the* `XulAjaxInputDateRenderer` *class*

The `XulAjaxInputDateRenderer` really contains all the cool implementations. What is interesting about this `Renderer` is that you can recognize most of the code from previous chapters, while the actual output to the client is significantly smaller. XUL allows you to reuse the prototype by adding the functional `bindings.xml` and `pro.css` prototype files to the resources. The only element you need to write out to the client for this JSF XUL component is `<pro:inputDate ...>` and its attributes.

By overriding the `XulRenderer` base class's `encodeResources()` method (see Code Sample 8-21), you extend the `XulAjaxInputDateRenderer` with a new call to the `dojo.js` and `mabon.js` libraries. An application developer might add two or more `ProInputDate` components to the page, but the semantics behind the `writeScriptResource()` method provided by the `XulRenderer` implementation will make sure these resources are written only once.

Code Sample 8-21. *The* `XulAjaxInputDateRenderer`

```
package com.apress.projsf.ch8.render.xul.ajax;

import java.io.IOException;
import java.text.DateFormat;
import java.text.SimpleDateFormat;
```

```
import java.util.Map;
import java.util.TimeZone;

import javax.faces.application.Application;
import javax.faces.application.ViewHandler;
import javax.faces.component.UIComponent;
import javax.faces.component.UIInput;
import javax.faces.context.FacesContext;
import javax.faces.context.ResponseWriter;
import javax.faces.convert.Converter;
import javax.faces.convert.DateTimeConverter;
import javax.faces.el.MethodBinding;
import javax.faces.validator.Validator;

import com.apress.projsf.ch8.render.xul.XulRenderer;
import com.apress.projsf.ch7.validate.DateValidator;

public class XulAjaxInputDateRenderer extends XulRenderer
{
  protected void encodeResources(
    FacesContext context,
    UIComponent  component) throws IOException
  {
    writeScriptResource(context, "weblet://net.java.dev.mabon/mabon.js");
    writeScriptResource(context, "weblet://org.dojotoolkit.browserio/dojo.js");
  }
```

By design, the `<pro:inputDate>` component can have `Converters` added by a JSP tag. At initial render, during the creation of the component hierarchy, a custom JSP converter tag has not yet executed, so the `Converter` is not yet attached to the component, which means the `encodeBegin()` method cannot get a hold of the `Converter`. Instead, the `Renderer` is using the `encodeEnd()` method (see Code Sample 8-22) to write out the markup and get a hold of the `Converter` (see Chapter 2 for more information about the `getConverter()` method).

Code Sample 8-22. *The* `encodeEnd()` *Method*

```
public void encodeEnd(
  FacesContext context,
  UIComponent  component) throws IOException
{
  String pattern = _determineDatePattern(context, component);
  String targetURL = _determineTargetURL(context, component);

  UIInput input = (UIInput)component;
  String valueString = (String)input.getSubmittedValue();

  if (valueString == null)
```

```
  {
    Object value = input.getValue();
    if (value != null)
    {
      Converter converter = getConverter(context, input);
      valueString = converter.getAsString(context, component, value);
    }
  }
  String clientId = input.getClientId(context);

  ResponseWriter out = context.getResponseWriter();
  out.startElement("pro:inputDate", component);
  out.writeAttribute("id", clientId, null);
  out.writeAttribute("value", valueString, null);
  out.writeAttribute("pattern", pattern, null);
  out.writeAttribute("targetURL", targetURL, null);
  out.endElement("pro:inputDate");
}
```

In `encodeEnd()` you call two methods—`_determinePattern()` and `_determineTargetURL()`. These methods retrieve the date format pattern and the target URL for the managed bean bound to the `Validator`. Finally, you write out the `<pro:inputDate>` element, including attributes, to the client. That's it!

By adding the `decode()` method (see Code Sample 8-23) to the `XulAjaxInputDateRenderer`, you can control the decode processing of the `ProInputDate` component.

Code Sample 8-23. *The* `decode()` *Method*

```
public void decode(
  FacesContext context,
  UIComponent  component)
{
  UIInput input = (UIInput)component;
  String clientId = input.getClientId(context);

  ExternalContext external = context.getExternalContext();
  Map requestParams = external.getRequestParameterMap();
  String submittedValue = (String)requestParams.get(clientId);

  input.setSubmittedValue(submittedValue);
}
```

You get the client ID from the `UIComponent`—`getClientId(context)`—and use that client ID to get the submitted request parameter value for this component. To get the request parameters, you need to look up the external context. From the external context, you can look up the `Map` that contains the parameters passed on the request. This parameter value is then stored on the `UIComponent` via `setSubmittedValue()` to be processed further in subsequent phases of the lifecycle.

The getConvertedValue() method, as shown in Code Sample 8-24, converts the submitted value to a strongly typed object (for example, Date). This is similar to what you did in the HtmlInputDateRenderer (see Chapter 2).

Code Sample 8-24. *The* getConvertedValue() *Method*

```
public Object getConvertedValue(
  FacesContext context,
  UIComponent  component,
  Object       submittedValue) throws ConverterException
{
  UIInput input = (UIInput)component;
  Converter converter = getConverter(context, input);
  String valueString = (String)submittedValue;
  return converter.getAsObject(context, component, valueString);
}
```

You first get the Converter for the UIComponent in question and convert the submitted value to an Object using the getAsObject() method on the Converter. The new object returned by the getConvertedValue() method is set as a local value on the component, clearing the submitted value. The new strongly typed object is then validated. If no errors exist, the next step is to queue a ValueChangeEvent that will be delivered at the end of the Process Validations phase. When a conversion error occurs, the getConvertedValue() method throws a ConverterException.

The getConverter() method, shown in Code Sample 8-25, always returns a Converter. If the application developer has attached a Converter, it will be used; otherwise, the getConverter() method will use a default DateTimeConverter.

Code Sample 8-25. *The* getConverter() *Method*

```
private final Converter getConverter(
  FacesContext context,
  UIInput      input)
{
  Converter converter = input.getConverter();
  if (converter == null)
  {
    DateTimeConverter datetime = new DateTimeConverter();
    datetime.setLocale(context.getViewRoot().getLocale());
    datetime.setTimeZone(TimeZone.getDefault());
    converter = datetime;
  }
  return converter;
}
```

Code Sample 8-26 shows the _determineDatePattern() method. This method is identical to the one you used in the Ajax solution, and from a Java purist's point of view, we should probably have created a base class, or a utility class, for any custom Renderer that might need this method. But, for educational purposes, we decided that it is easier for you to understand if explained this way.

Code Sample 8-26. *The* `_determineDatePattern()` *Method*

```
private String _determineDatePattern(
  FacesContext context,
  UIComponent  component)
{
  UIInput input = (UIInput)component;
  Converter converter = getConverter(context, input);

  if (converter instanceof DateTimeConverter)
  {
    DateTimeConverter dateTime = (DateTimeConverter)converter;
    return dateTime.getPattern();
  }
  else
  {
    SimpleDateFormat dateFormat = (SimpleDateFormat)
                              DateFormat.getDateInstance(DateFormat.SHORT);
    return dateFormat.toPattern();
  }
}
```

For the XUL implementation to work, you need to know what date pattern has been set on the `DateTimeConverter` by the application developer. This date pattern will be used in two places—first to parse the date entered by the user in the `<input>` element. This parsed date will then set the selected date in the calendar. Second, it will make sure the date selected in the calendar follows the correct date format when added to the `<input>` element.

Code Sample 8-27 shows the `_determineTargetURL()`, which you saw in the previous chapter, but we will cover it again since it is equally crucial to the XUL solution. It provides you with the binding reference to the managed bean.

Code Sample 8-27. *The* `_determineTargetURL()` *Method*

```
  private String _determineTargetURL(
    FacesContext context,
    UIComponent  component)
  {
    UIInput input = (UIInput)component;
    Validator[] validators = input.getValidators();

    for (int i=0; i < validators.length; i++)
    {
      if (validators[i] instanceof DateValidator)
      {
        DateValidator validateDate = (DateValidator)validators[i];
        MethodBinding binding = validateDate.getAvailability();
        if (binding != null)
        {
```

```
            String expression = binding.getExpressionString();
            // #{backingBean.methodName} -> backingBean.methodName
            String bindingRef = expression.substring(2, expression.length() - 1);

            Application application = context.getApplication();
            ViewHandler handler = application.getViewHandler();
            return handler.getResourceURL(context, "mabon:/" + bindingRef);
          }
        }
      }

      return null;
    }
  }
```

You first get all the validators attached to this input component. You then check to see whether one or many of these validators are instances of the DateValidator. (The DateValidator was created in Chapter 7.)

If it is an instance of the DateValidator, you check to see if you have a MethodBinding. If you have a MethodBinding, you get the expression #{managedBean.methodName} and strip off the #{}. This leaves you with managedBean.methodName, which you concatenate with mabon:/. The MabonViewHandler will recognize the string and return a resource URL that will be written to the client (for example, /context-root/mabon-servlet-mapping/managedBean.methodName).

The XulAjaxShowOneDeckRenderer Class

Since the UIShowOne component is a container component, it needs to render its children; as such, you have to implement encodeBegin(), encodeChildren(), and encodeEnd() in the new Renderer—XulAjaxShowOneDeckRenderer. Figure 8-10 shows the XulAjaxShowOneDeckRenderer in a class diagram.

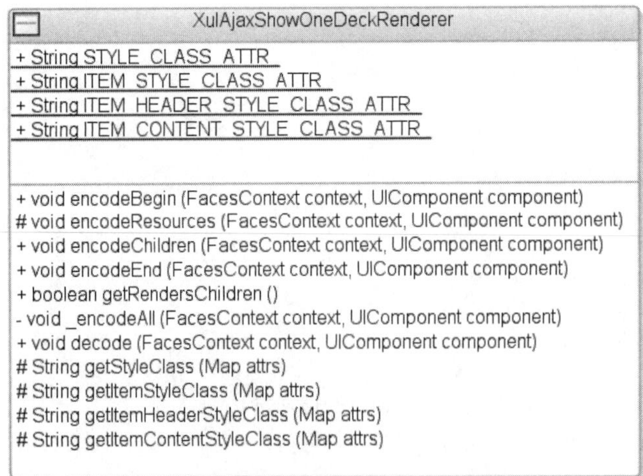

Figure 8-10. *Class diagram showing the* XulAjaxShowOneDeckRenderer *class*

Let's start with the XulAjaxShowOneDeckRenderer class's encodeBegin() method, as shown in Code Sample 8-28.

Code Sample 8-28. *The* XulAjaxShowOneDeckRenderer encodeBegin() *Method*

```
package com.apress.projsf.ch8.render.xul.ajax;

import java.io.IOException;
import java.util.Iterator;
import java.util.List;
import java.util.Map;

import javax.faces.component.UIComponent;
import javax.faces.context.ExternalContext;
import javax.faces.context.FacesContext;
import javax.faces.context.ResponseWriter;

import com.apress.projsf.ch3.component.UIShowItem;
import com.apress.projsf.ch3.component.UIShowOne;
import com.apress.projsf.ch3.event.ShowEvent;
import com.apress.projsf.ch8.render.xul.XulRenderer;

public class XulAjaxShowOneDeckRenderer extends XulRenderer
{
  /**
   * The styleClass attribute.
   */
  public static String STYLE_CLASS_ATTR = "styleClass";

  /**
   * The itemStyleClass attribute.
   */
  public static String ITEM_STYLE_CLASS_ATTR = "itemStyleClass";

  /**
   * The itemHeaderStyleClass attribute.
   */
  public static String ITEM_HEADER_STYLE_CLASS_ATTR = "itemHeaderStyleClass";

  /**
   * The itemContentStyleClass attribute.
   */
  public static String ITEM_CONTENT_STYLE_CLASS_ATTR = "itemContentStyleClass";

  public void encodeBegin(
    FacesContext context,
    UIComponent  component) throws IOException
```

```
{
  UIShowOne showOne = (UIShowOne)component;
  String clientId = showOne.getClientId(context);
  String showItemId = showOne.getShowItemId();

  ResponseWriter out = context.getResponseWriter();
  out.startElement("pro:showOneDeck", component);
  out.writeAttribute("id", clientId, null);
  out.writeAttribute("showItemId", showItemId, "showItemId");

  Map attrs = component.getAttributes();
  String styleClass = (String)attrs.get(STYLE_CLASS_ATTR);
  if (styleClass != null)
    out.writeAttribute("class", styleClass, STYLE_CLASS_ATTR);

  super.encodeBegin(context, component);
}
```

The `encodeBegin()` method takes two arguments—`FacesContext context` and `UIComponent component`. The Render Response phase will call the `encodeBegin()` method on the `UIShowOne` component, which in turn will delegate to the `encodeBegin()` method on the `XulAjaxShowOneDeckRenderer`, passing the `FacesContext` and the `UIShowOne` component instance.

Before you continue to write anything to the client, you also need to get hold of the component's unique identifier—`clientId`. You do this by calling the `getClientId()` method on the `UIShowOne` instance passed as an argument to the `Renderer`. You then include this unique identifier in the generated markup to ensure that you will be able to decode the request and apply any values or events to the right component on postback. For more information about `clientId`, see Chapter 2. The `showItemId` is the attribute for the node that is by default expanded on initial request.

You get the `ResponseWriter` and write out the first XUL element—`<pro:showOneDeck>`—that represents the component.

The `<pro:showOneDeck>` component relies on the Dojo toolkit and D[2] project to be able to asynchronously communicate with the server. To ensure that these resources are written only once, you will use the semantics behind the `writeScriptResource()` method (see Code Sample 8-29).

Code Sample 8-29. *The* `XulAjaxShowOneDeckRenderer encodeResources()` *Method*

```
protected void encodeResources(
  FacesContext context,
  UIComponent  component) throws IOException
{
  writeScriptResource(context, "weblet://org.dojotoolkit.browserio/dojo.js");
  writeScriptResource(context, "weblet://net.java.dev.d2/d2.js");
}
```

Code Sample 8-30 shows the encodeChildren() method. In the encodeChildren() method, you check whether the UIShowOne component has any children.

Code Sample 8-30. *The* encodeChildren() *Method*

```
public void encodeChildren(
  FacesContext context,
  UIComponent  component) throws IOException
{
  if (component.getChildCount() > 0)
  {
    UIShowOne showOne = (UIShowOne)component;
    String showItemId = showOne.getShowItemId();

    Map attrs = showOne.getAttributes();
    String styleClass = getItemStyleClass(attrs);
    String headerStyleClass = getItemHeaderStyleClass(attrs);
    String contentStyleClass = getItemContentStyleClass(attrs);
```

If the application developer has not added any children, you do not need to render this instance of the UIShowOne component to the client.

If the application developer has added children to the UIShowOne component, you check whether each child is an instance of UIShowItem (see Code Sample 8-31). If not, the child will not be rendered.

Code Sample 8-31. *The* encodeChildren() *Method*

```
List children = component.getChildren();
for (Iterator iter = children.iterator(); iter.hasNext();)
{
  UIComponent child = (UIComponent) iter.next();
  if (child instanceof UIShowItem)
  {
     UIShowItem showItem = (UIShowItem)child;
    String id = showItem.getId();
     boolean active = (id.equals(showItemId));

     ResponseWriter out = context.getResponseWriter();
     out.startElement("pro:showItem", showItem);
     out.writeAttribute("itemId", id, null);
     if (styleClass != null)
       out.writeAttribute("styleClass", styleClass, ITEM_STYLE_CLASS_ATTR);
     if (headerStyleClass != null)
       out.writeAttribute("headerStyleClass", headerStyleClass,
                          ITEM_HEADER_STYLE_CLASS_ATTR);
```

```
      if (contentStyleClass != null)
        out.writeAttribute("contentStyleClass", contentStyleClass,
                           ITEM_CONTENT_STYLE_CLASS_ATTR);
      if (active)
        out.writeAttribute("active", Boolean.toString(active), null);
```

If the child is a UIShowItem component instance, you gather the clientId and all attributes available on the UIShowItem component. The showItemId is then compared with the ID of the current UIShowItem component, and based on the outcome of this comparison, the active variable is set to true or false. The active variable is used to set the active attribute on the <pro:showItem> element and indicate whether this UIShowItem component should render its children.

After this, you write out the start element <pro:showItem>, as shown in Code Sample 8-32, and any attributes defined by the application developer.

Code Sample 8-32. *The* encodeChildren() *Method*

```
        // the header facet
        UIComponent header = showItem.getHeader();
        if (header != null)
        {
          out.startElement("pro:showItemHeader", null);
          processEncodes(context, header);
          out.endElement("pro:showItemHeader");
        }        // the expanded item contents
        if (active)
        {
          _encodeAll(context, showItem);
        }

        out.endElement("pro:showItem");
      }
    }
  }
}
```

You then get the header facet from the UIShowItem component by calling the getFacet() method. This convenience method returns the named facet (for example, header) if it exists; otherwise, it will return null. If the getFacet() method returned a facet, you call the _encodeAll() method to process any children of this facet. You use the active flag to determine whether this is the "active" UIShowItem component. If it is, you call the _encodeAll() method to start the encode process of any children to the UIShowItem component.

If you take a close look at the actual output required by the deck component, you will see that any children that are added are located at the end of the generated markup. So, the UIShowOne component's Renderer does not need much to close the generated markup (see Code Sample 8-33).

Code Sample 8-33. *The* `encodeEnd()` *Method*

```
public void encodeEnd(
  FacesContext context,
  UIComponent  component) throws IOException
{
  ResponseWriter out = context.getResponseWriter();
  out.endElement("pro:showOneDeck");
}
```

Code Sample 8-34 shows the `getRendersChildren()` method. For the `UIShowOne` component, the `Renderer` is responsible for rendering its children, so this flag needs to be set to `true`.

Code Sample 8-34. *The* `getRendersChildren()` *Method*

```
public boolean getRendersChildren()
{
  return true;
}
```

Code Sample 8-35 shows the `_encodeAll()` method. The requirement has not changed since we first introduced the deck component. It has to be flexible enough to handle any type of child component added to the `UIShowItem` component by the application developer. The `UIShowItem` component itself is not responsible for rendering its children, but sometimes an application developer has added a child container component in charge of rendering its children (for example, an `HtmlPanelGroup` component).

Code Sample 8-35. *The* `_encodeAll()` *Method*

```
private void _encodeAll(
  FacesContext context,
  UIComponent  component) throws IOException
{
  component.encodeBegin(context);
  if (component.getRendersChildren())
  {
    component.encodeChildren(context);
  }
  else
  {
    List kids = component.getChildren();
    Iterator it = kids.iterator();
    while (it.hasNext())
    {
      UIComponent kid = (UIComponent)it.next();
      _encodeAll(context, kid);
    }
  }
  component.encodeEnd(context);
}
```

To be able to achieve this, you first render the beginning of the current state of this UIComponent to the response contained in the specified FacesContext. You then check whether the component is responsible for rendering its children. If it is, you call encodeChildren() on the component to start rendering its children. If the component is not responsible for rendering its children, you call getChildren() on the component. The getChildren() method returns a List over all children of this UIComponent. If this component has no children, an empty List is returned, and you close the generated markup by calling the encodeEnd() method on the component. If it has children, you recursively call the _encodeAll() until all children have been rendered.

■ **Note** A new method, UIComponent.encodeAll(FacesContext), has been added to the JSF 1.2 release and implements equivalent functionality to the _encodeAll(FacesContext, UIComponent) method shown in Code Sample 8-35.

Code Sample 8-36 is identical to the decode() method in the first HtmlShowOneDeckRenderer introduced in Chapter 3. During the Apply Request Values phase, the method—processDecodes()—will be called on the UIViewRoot at the top of the component tree. The processDecodes() method on the UIViewRoot will recursively call processDecodes() for each UIComponent in the component tree. If a Renderer is present for any of these components, the UIComponent will delegate the responsibility of decoding to the Renderer. For more information about processDecodes(), please refer to Chapter 2.

Code Sample 8-36. *The* decode() *Method*

```
public void decode(
  FacesContext context,
  UIComponent  component)
{
  ExternalContext external = context.getExternalContext();
  Map requestParams = external.getRequestParameterMap();
  String clientId = component.getClientId(context);
  String newShowItemId = (String)requestParams.get(clientId);
  if (newShowItemId != null && newShowItemId.length() > 0)
  {
    UIShowOne showOne = (UIShowOne)component;
    String oldShowItemId = showOne.getShowItemId();
    if (!newShowItemId.equals(oldShowItemId))
    {
      showOne.setShowItemId(newShowItemId);
      ShowEvent event = new ShowEvent(showOne, oldShowItemId, newShowItemId);
      event.queue();
    }
  }
}
```

Code Sample 8-37 shows all the getters for the different style classes supported by the XulAjaxShowOneDeckRenderer.

Code Sample 8-37. *Getters for the* `XulAjaxShowOneDeckRenderer` *Attributes*

```
  protected String getStyleClass(
    Map attrs)
  {
    return (String)attrs.get(STYLE_CLASS_ATTR);
  }

  protected String getItemStyleClass(
    Map attrs)
  {
    return (String)attrs.get(ITEM_STYLE_CLASS_ATTR);
  }

  protected String getItemHeaderStyleClass(
    Map attrs)
  {
    return (String)attrs.get(ITEM_HEADER_STYLE_CLASS_ATTR);
  }

  protected String getItemContentStyleClass(
    Map attrs)
  {
    return (String)attrs.get(ITEM_CONTENT_STYLE_CLASS_ATTR);
  }
}
```

Step 6: Creating a Renderer-Specific Subclass

To follow best practices, you will create a renderer-specific subclass for the document component—`com.apress.projsf.ch8.component.pro.ProDocument`. This class provides getters and setters for three renderer-specific attributes on the JSF component—`stylesheetURI`, `styleClass`, and `title`. Figure 8-11 shows a class diagram with the `ProDocument` class.

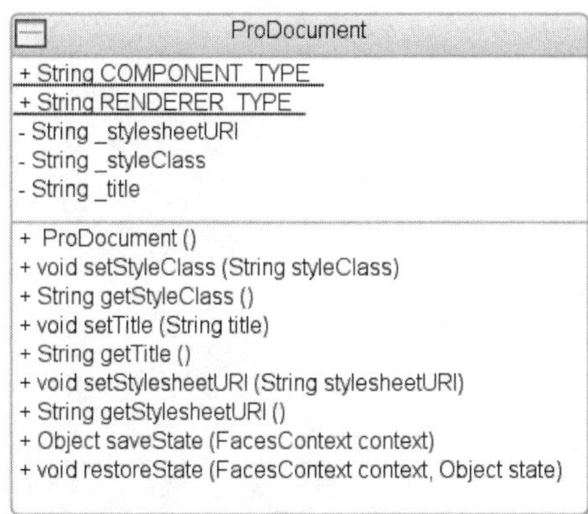

Figure 8-11. *Class diagram showing the* `ProDocument` *class*

As you can see, you are using the same pattern to build this component; for example, Code Sample 8-38 follows the same design as the ProInputDate subclass you created in Chapter 2.

Code Sample 8-38. *The* ProDocument *Class*

```
package com.apress.projsf.ch8.component.pro;

import javax.faces.context.FacesContext;
import javax.faces.el.ValueBinding;

import com.apress.projsf.ch8.component.UIDocument;

public class ProDocument extends UIDocument
{
  /**
   * The component type for this component.
   */
  public static final String COMPONENT_TYPE = "com.apress.projsf.ProDocument";

  /**
   * The renderer type for this component.
   */
  public static final String RENDERER_TYPE = "com.apress.projsf.Document";

  public ProDocument()
  {
    setRendererType(RENDERER_TYPE);
  }

  public void setStyleClass(
    String styleClass)
  {
    _styleClass = styleClass;
  }

  public String getStyleClass()
  {
    if (_styleClass != null)
      return _styleClass;

    ValueBinding binding = getValueBinding("styleClass");
    if (binding != null)
    {
      FacesContext context = FacesContext.getCurrentInstance();
      return (String)binding.getValue(context);
```

```
    }

    return null;
  }

  public void setTitle(
    String title)
  {
    _title = title;
  }

  public String getTitle()
  {
    if (_title != null)
      return _title;

    ValueBinding binding = getValueBinding("title");
    if (binding != null)
    {
      FacesContext context = FacesContext.getCurrentInstance();
      return (String)binding.getValue(context);
    }

    return null;
  }

  public void setStylesheetURI(
    String stylesheetURI)
  {
    _stylesheetURI = stylesheetURI;
  }

  public String getStylesheetURI()
  {
    if (_stylesheetURI != null)
      return _stylesheetURI;

    ValueBinding binding = getValueBinding("stylesheetURI");
    if (binding != null)
    {
      FacesContext context = FacesContext.getCurrentInstance();
      return (String)binding.getValue(context);
    }

    return null;
  }
```

```
  /**
   * Returns the saved state for this component.
   *
   * @param context the Faces context
   */
  public Object saveState(
    FacesContext context)
  {
    Object values[] = new Object[4];
    values[0] = super.saveState(context);
    values[1] = _title;
    values[2] = _styleClass;
    values[3] = _stylesheetURI;
    return values;
  }

  /**
   * Restores the state of this component.
   *
   * @param context the Faces context
   * @param state   the saved state
   */
  public void restoreState(
    FacesContext context,
    Object       state)
  {
    Object values[] = (Object[])state;
    super.restoreState(context, values[0]);
    _title = (String)values[1];
    _styleClass = (String)values[2];
    _stylesheetURI = (String)values[3];
  }

  private String _stylesheetURI;
  private String _styleClass;
  private String _title;
}
```

The first thing you do is make sure you extend the right component superclass, which is `UIDocument`. You then define constants for the component type and renderer type so that the correct renderer is associated with the component when it is created. This convenience subclass provides getters and setters and provides state saving for the three renderer-specific attributes—`styleSheetURI`, `styleClass`, and `title`.

Step 7: Registering a UIComponent and Renderer

You need to make sure you register your renderer-specific subclass `ProDocument`, the `XulDocumentRenderer` class, the `XulAjaxInputDateRenderer` class, and the `XulAjaxShowOneDeckRenderer` class in the `faces-config.xml` file, as shown in Code Sample 8-39.

Code Sample 8-39. *Registering the JSF XUL Implementation in* `faces-config.xml`

```
<?xml version="1.0" encoding="UTF-8" ?>
<!DOCTYPE faces-config
   PUBLIC "-//Sun Microsystems, Inc.//DTD JavaServer Faces Config 1.1//EN"
          "http://java.sun.com/dtd/web-facesconfig_1_1.dtd">

<faces-config xmlns="http://java.sun.com/JSF/Configuration" >

  <component>
    <component-type>
      com.apress.projsf.ProDocument
    </component-type>
    <component-class>
      com.apress.projsf.ch8.component.pro.ProDocument
    </component-class>

    <!-- UIComponent attributes -->
    <attribute>
      <description>
        The component identifier for this component.  This value must be
        unique within the closest parent component that is a naming
        container.
      </description>
      <attribute-name>id</attribute-name>
      <attribute-class>java.lang.String</attribute-class>
    </attribute>
    <attribute>
      <description>
        Flag indicating whether or not this component should be rendered
        (during Render Response Phase), or processed on any subsequent
        form submit.
      </description>
      <attribute-name>rendered</attribute-name>
      <attribute-class>boolean</attribute-class>
      <default-value>true</default-value>
    </attribute>
```

```
    <attribute>
      <description>
        The value binding expression linking this component to a
        property in a backing bean.
      </description>
      <attribute-name>binding</attribute-name>
      <attribute-class>javax.faces.el.ValueBinding</attribute-class>
    </attribute>

    <!-- ProDocument attributes -->
    <attribute>
      <attribute-name>title</attribute-name>
      <attribute-class>java.lang.String</attribute-class>
    </attribute>

    <attribute>
      <attribute-name>stylesheetURI</attribute-name>
      <attribute-class>java.lang.String</attribute-class>
    </attribute>
  </component>

  ...
    <renderer>
      <component-family>com.apress.projsf.Document</component-family>
      <renderer-type>com.apress.projsf.Document</renderer-type>
      <renderer-class>
        com.apress.projsf.ch8.render.xul.basic.XulDocumentRenderer
      </renderer-class>
    </renderer>
    <renderer>
      <component-family>javax.faces.Input</component-family>
      <renderer-type>com.apress.projsf.Date</renderer-type>
      <renderer-class>
        com.apress.projsf.ch8.render.xul.ajax.XulAjaxInputDateRenderer
      </renderer-class>
    </renderer>
    <renderer>
      <component-family>com.apress.projsf.ShowOne</component-family>
      <renderer-type>com.apress.projsf.Deck</renderer-type>
      <renderer-class>
        com.apress.projsf.ch8.render.xul.ajax.XulAjaxShowOneDeckRenderer
      </renderer-class>
    </renderer>
  </render-kit>
</faces-config>
```

Step 8: Creating a JSP Tag Handler and TLD

The UIDocument component needs a new custom action, <pro:document>, with a corresponding tag handler class, ProDocumentTag. On initial render, the ProDocumentTag is responsible for transferring all JSP custom action attributes from the tag handler to the component instance.

The ProDocumentTag Class

The ProDocumentTag, as shown in Code Sample 8-40, creates the component using the defined component type, com.apress.projsf.Document, which will create a ProDocument instance with a default renderer type of com.apress.projsf.Document. However, it is possible for the Web application faces-config.xml to override the component class that should be created for this component type. Therefore, the tag handler must explicitly set the renderer type on the newly created component instance. This will guarantee that the XulDocumentRenderer is used for the component instance created by the ProDocumentTag. Figure 8-12 shows the ProDocumentTag as viewed in a class diagram.

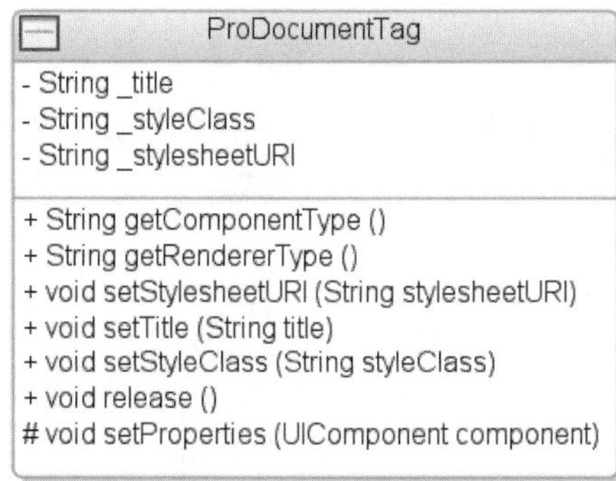

Figure 8-12. *Class diagram showing the* ProDocumentTag *class*

Code Sample 8-40. *The JSP Tag Handler*

```
package com.apress.projsf.ch8.taglib.pro

import javax.faces.component.UIComponent;

import com.apress.projsf.ch8.component.pro.ProDocument;
import com.apress.projsf.ch2.taglib.UIComponentTagSupport;

/**
 * ProDocumentTag component tag handler.
 */
public class ProDocumentTag extends UIComponentTagSupport
{
```

```
/**
 * Returns the component type.
 *
 * @return  the component type
 */
public String getComponentType()
{
  return ProDocument.COMPONENT_TYPE;
}

/**
 * Returns the renderer type.
 *
 * @return  the renderer type
 */
public String getRendererType()
{
  return ProDocument.RENDERER_TYPE;
}

public void setStylesheetURI(String stylesheetURI)
{
  _stylesheetURI = stylesheetURI;
}

public void setTitle(String title)
{
  _title = title;
}

public void setStyleClass(String styleClass)
{
  _styleClass = styleClass;
}

public void release()
{
  _title = null;
  _styleClass = null;
  _stylesheetURI = null;
}

protected void setProperties(
  UIComponent component)
{
  super.setProperties(component);
```

```
    // Renderer-specific attributes
    setStringProperty(component, "title", _title);
    setStringProperty(component, "styleClass", _styleClass);
    setStringProperty(component, "stylesheetURI", _stylesheetURI);
  }

  private String _title;
  private String _styleClass;
  private String _stylesheetURI;
}
```

The ProDocumentTag provides tag attribute setters and internal field storage for the renderer-specific XulDocumentRenderer attributes (title, styleClass, and stylesheetsURI). The setProperties() method transfers properties and attributes from this tag to the specified component if the corresponding properties of this tag handler instance are explicitly set.

Tag Library Descriptor

You have now defined the behavior of the ProDocumentTag handler. It is time to register the name of the custom action and set some rules for how it can be used. When creating a tag library for JSF custom components, the TLD file defines one custom action per Renderer. In this chapter, you need to define only one custom action—document—as shown in Code Sample 8-41.

Code Sample 8-41. *The TLD*

```
<?xml version="1.0" encoding="UTF-8" ?>
<!DOCTYPE taglib
   PUBLIC "-//Sun Microsystems, Inc.//DTD JSP Tag Library 1.2//EN"
          "http://java.sun.com/dtd/web-jsptaglibrary_1_2.dtd" >

<taglib>
  ...
  <uri>http://projsf.apress.com/tags</uri>
  ...
  <tag>
    <name>document</name>
    <tag-class>com.apress.projsf.ch8.taglib.pro.ProDocumentTag</tag-class>
    <body-content>JSP</body-content>
    <description>
      The document tag handler represents a ProDocument component that is used
      as the top component in the hierarchy, directly under the UIViewRoot.
    </description>

    <!-- UIComponent attributes -->
    <attribute>
      <name>id</name>
      <required>false</required>
      <rtexprvalue>false</rtexprvalue>
```

```
      <description>
        The component identifier for this component.  This value must be
        unique within the closest parent component that is a naming
        container.
      </description>
    </attribute>
    ...

    <!-- ProDocument attributes -->
    <attribute>
      <name>title</name>
      <required>false</required>
      <rtexprvalue>false</rtexprvalue>
      <description>
        Advisory title information about markup elements generated
        for this component.
      </description>
    </attribute>
    <attribute>
      <name>stylesheetURI</name>
      <required>false</required>
      <rtexprvalue>false</rtexprvalue>
      <description>
        User-defined stylesheet.
      </description>
    </attribute>
  </tag>
  ...
</taglib>
```

For each custom action in the TLD, you need a <tag> element. The name of the custom action element is defined in the nested <name> element (for example, <name>document</name>), and the tag handler class is defined in the <tag-class> element. The <body-content> element describes how this tag should be processed. If the custom action has attributes, they have to be defined with the <attribute> element. For each attribute in the TLD, the <rtexprvalue> element must be set to false, and the attribute class must be left unspecified, allowing it to default to String. For more information about the <rtexprvalue> element, see Chapter 2.

Step 9: Creating a RenderKit and ResponseWriter

For the solution to work, you need to control the output to the client so that you write out the requested XML document with the contentType set to application/vnd.mozilla.xul+xml on initial request and on regular form postback; on any subsequent Ajax postback, you respond with the contentType set to application/xml.

To be able to support the content type application/vnd.mozilla.xul+xml as required by the XUL Renderer classes, you have to extend the default ResponseWriter—XMLResponseWriter—with support for XML documents. This XMLResponseWriter will be used during the initial request and regular form postback.

The XulAjaxRenderKit Class

With the XUL Ajax postback, you face the same `contentType` issues discussed in Chapter 6. The good thing is that you took care of the problem in Chapter 6 by providing the `FixedContentTypeResponseWriter`, and since there is nothing special about using Ajax in XUL, you can reuse this `FixedContentTypeResponseWriter` for the XUL Ajax solution. The only requirement is that the application developer needs to set the correct content type, so that the `ResponseWriter` gets a chance to define the content type for the response.

With the new `XMLResponseWriter`, you also have to provide a custom `RenderKit`—`XulAjaxRenderKit`—that can dynamically pick either the `XMLResponseWriter` or the custom `FixedContentTypeResponseWriter` (see Figure 8-13).

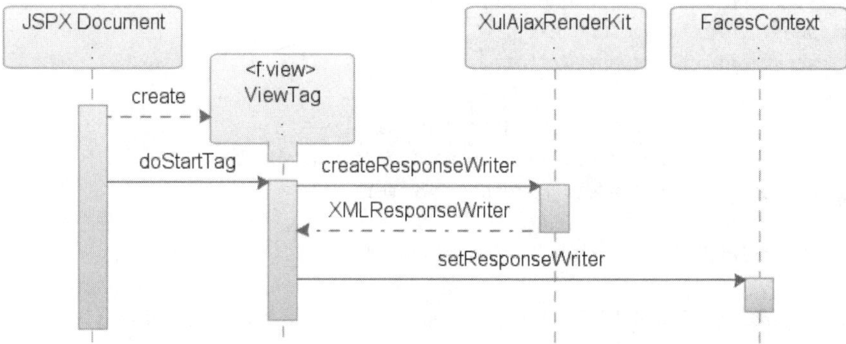

Figure 8-13. *Sequence diagram of creating the right* `ResponseWriter` *for the response*

You are probably asking yourself, do I have to reimplement every component library that an application developer might use? The answer is no! You use the strategy you used in Chapter 6, wrapping the `XulAjaxRenderKit` around the standard HTML `RenderKit` to avoid all that extra work.

Figure 8-14 shows the `XulAjaxRenderKit` in a class diagram.

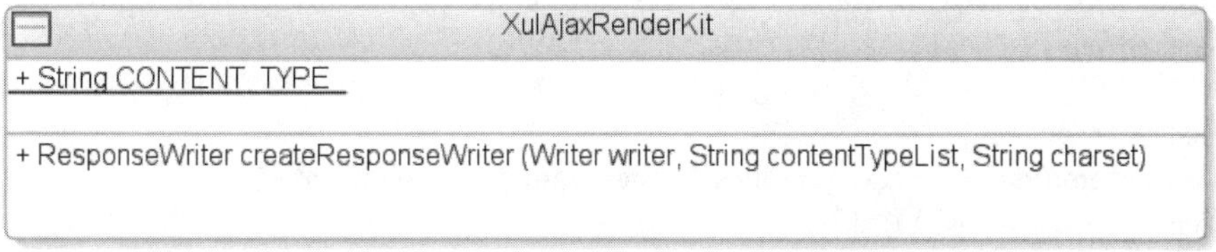

XulAjaxRenderKit

+ String CONTENT_TYPE

+ ResponseWriter createResponseWriter (Writer writer, String contentTypeList, String charset)

Figure 8-14. *Class diagram showing the* `XulAjaxRenderKit` *class*

In the `XulAjaxRenderKit` class, as shown in Code Sample 8-42, you set the `CONTENT_TYPE` variable to the accepted XUL `contentType`—`application/vnd.mozilla.xul+xml`. To find out which `ResponseWriter` to select, you need to know whether this is an initial request, a regular form postback, or an Ajax postback. If the user clicks the `pro:showOneDeck` component, the d2.submit function passes a custom header to the `XMLHttpRequest`—`X-D2-Content-Type`.

You check for the custom request header, and if it is set, you create a new instance of the `FixedContentTypeResponseWriter`. On initial request or a regular form postback (for example, an `h:commandButton` is clicked), the custom request header will not be present, and you will return the `XMLResponseWriter`.

Code Sample 8-42. *The* `XulAjaxRenderKit`

```
package com.apress.projsf.ch8.render.xul.ajax;

import java.io.Writer;
import java.util.Map;

import javax.faces.context.ExternalContext;
import javax.faces.context.FacesContext;
import javax.faces.context.ResponseWriter;

import com.apress.projsf.ch6.render.ExtendedRenderKit;
import com.apress.projsf.ch6.render.FixedContentTypeResponseWriter;
import com.apress.projsf.ch8.render.XmlResponseWriter;

public class XulAjaxRenderKit extends ExtendedRenderKit
{
  public static final String CONTENT_TYPE = "application/vnd.mozilla.xul+xml";

  public ResponseWriter createResponseWriter(
    Writer writer,
    String contentTypeList,
    String charset)
  {

    ResponseWriter out = new XmlResponseWriter(writer, charset, CONTENT_TYPE);

    FacesContext context = FacesContext.getCurrentInstance();
    ExternalContext external = context.getExternalContext();
    Map requestHeaders = external.getRequestHeaderMap();

    // Detect D2 request
    String d2ContentType = (String)requestHeaders.get("X-D2-Content-Type");
    if (d2ContentType != null)
    {
      out = new FixedContentTypeResponseWriter(out, "application/xml");
    }

    return out;
  }
}
```

The XMLResponseWriter Class

The `XMLResponseWriter` is the piece in the puzzle that writes the required XML markup to the requesting client (see Figure 8-15). If you did not create a new `ResponseWriter` for the XUL solution, it would produce the wrong output, because it would be HTML, not XML (XUL) syntax.

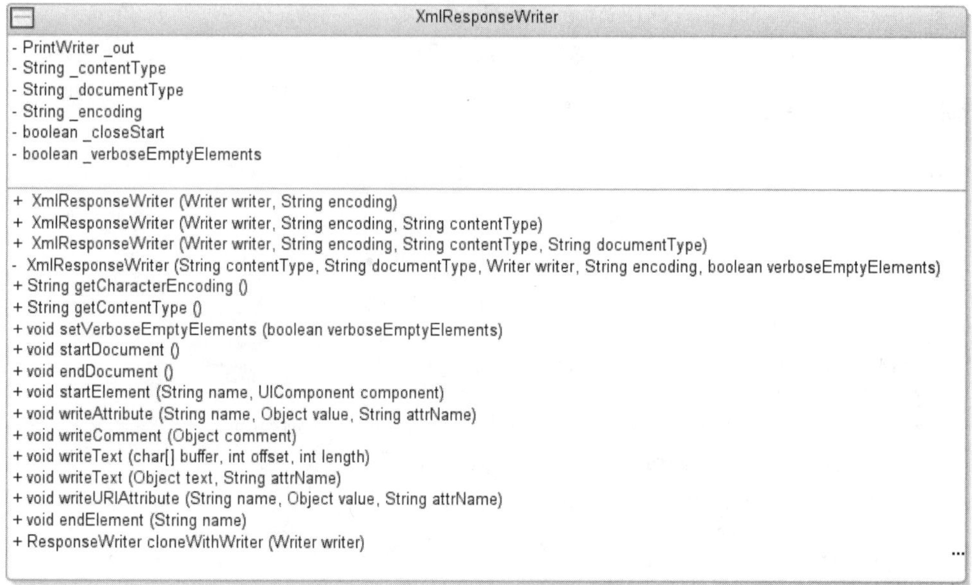

Figure 8-15. *Class diagram showing the* `XMLResponseWriter` *class*

The only real difference between this `XMLResponseWriter`, as shown in Code Sample 8-43, and the default HTML `ResponseWriter` is that the `ResponseWriter` writes out proper XML processing instructions and always makes sure to close elements with a close tag (for example, `<br></br>`). The `ResponseWriter` is not specific to XUL and can also be used to support other XML languages.

Code Sample 8-43. *The* `XMLResponseWriter`

```
package com.apress.projsf.ch8.render;

import java.io.IOException;
import java.io.PrintWriter;
import java.io.Writer;

import javax.faces.component.UIComponent;
import javax.faces.context.ResponseWriter;

public class XmlResponseWriter extends ResponseWriter
```

```
{
  public XmlResponseWriter(
    Writer writer,
    String encoding,
    String contentType)
  {
    this(writer, encoding, contentType, null);
  }
  ...
  public String getCharacterEncoding()
  {
    return _encoding;
  }

  public void startDocument() throws IOException
  {
    ...
      String charset = this.getCharacterEncoding();
      if (charset != null)
      {
        _out.write("<?xml version=\"1.0\" ");
        _out.write("encoding=\"");
        _out.write(charset);
        _out.write("\" ?>\n");
      }
      else
      {
        _out.write("<?xml version=\"1.0\" ?>\n");
      }
    }
...
}
```

Step 11: Registering a RenderKit

For the XUL Ajax implementation, you need to make sure you register the custom Renderers with the XulAjaxRenderKit, as shown in Code Sample 8-44.

Code Sample 8-44. *The XUL Registration in* faces-config.xml

```
<?xml version="1.0" encoding="UTF-8" ?>
<!DOCTYPE faces-config
   PUBLIC "-//Sun Microsystems, Inc.//DTD JavaServer Faces Config 1.1//EN"
          "http://java.sun.com/dtd/web-facesconfig_1_1.dtd">
<faces-config xmlns="http://java.sun.com/JSF/Configuration" >
...
```

```
  <render-kit>
    <render-kit-id>com.apress.projsf.xul.ajax[HTML_BASIC]</render-kit-id>
    <render-kit-class>
      com.apress.projsf.ch8.render.xul.ajax.XulAjaxRenderKit
    </render-kit-class>
    <renderer>
      <component-family>com.apress.projsf.Document</component-family>
      <renderer-type>com.apress.projsf.Document</renderer-type>
      <renderer-class>
        com.apress.projsf.ch8.render.xul.basic.XulDocumentRenderer
      </renderer-class>
    </renderer>
    <renderer>
      <component-family>javax.faces.Input</component-family>
      <renderer-type>com.apress.projsf.Date</renderer-type>
      <renderer-class>
        com.apress.projsf.ch8.render.xul.ajax.XulAjaxInputDateRenderer
      </renderer-class>
    </renderer>
    <renderer>
      <component-family>com.apress.projsf.ShowOne</component-family>
      <renderer-type>com.apress.projsf.Deck</renderer-type>
      <renderer-class>
        com.apress.projsf.ch8.render.xul.ajax.XulAjaxShowOneDeckRenderer
      </renderer-class>
    </renderer>
  </render-kit>
</faces-config>
```

Step 12: Registering Resources with Weblets

First, you need to register the XUL resources (`pro.css`, `bindings.xml`, `styles.css`) as weblets, which will enable you to package these resources as part of the custom JSF component library (see Code Sample 8-45). Second, you need to make sure you use weblets to load the image for the `ProInputDate` component's button (see Code Sample 8-46).

Note For more information about weblets, please see Chapter 5, or visit the Weblets project's site at `http://weblets.dev.java.net`.

Code Sample 8-45. *The Weblets Configuration File*

```
<?xml version="1.0" encoding="UTF-8" ?>
<weblets-config xmlns="http://weblets.dev.java.net/config" >
  ...
```

```
  <weblet>
    <weblet-name>com.apress.projsf.ch8</weblet-name>
    <weblet-class>net.java.dev.weblets.packaged.PackagedWeblet</weblet-class>
    <init-param>
      <param-name>package</param-name>
      <param-value>com.apress.projsf.ch8.render.xul.ajax.resources</param-value>
    </init-param>
  </weblet>
  ...
  <weblet-mapping>
    <weblet-name>com.apress.projsf.ch8</weblet-name>
    <url-pattern>/projsf-ch8/*</url-pattern>
  </weblet-mapping>

</weblets-config>
```

In Code Sample 8-46, you use weblets to serve resources from the JAR file. Note the difference between the `style.css` file and the `inputDateButton.gif` file. The `styles.css` file is automatically processed relative to the `bindings.xml` file by the XBL runtime, but the XUL button's image URL is processed relative to the main document. This will cause the image URL to not render, since the image is stored relative to the `bindings.xml` file and not to the main document. To solve this, you use the `weblet:/` relative protocol syntax to make it absolute at runtime but relative during design time.

Code Sample 8-46. *Using Relative* `weblet:/` *Protocol Syntax*

```
<?xml version="1.0"?>
<bindings xmlns="http://www.mozilla.org/xbl"
          xmlns:xbl="http://www.mozilla.org/xbl"
          xmlns:html="http://www.w3.org/1999/xhtml"
          xmlns:xul="http://www.mozilla.org/keymaster/gatekeeper/there.is.only.xul">
  <binding id="inputDate">
    <resources>
      <stylesheet src="styles.css" />
    </resources>
    <content>
      <xul:hbox>
        <xul:textbox id="input"
                     style="margin-left:0px;margin-right:0px;"
                     xbl:inherits="value"
                     onchange="this.parentNode.parentNode.flushChanges();" />
        <xul:button pop-up="calendar"
                    image="weblet:/inputDateButton.gif"
                    style="margin-left:0px;margin-right:0px;min-width:2em;"/>
      </xul:hbox>
```

Building Applications with JSF XUL Components

Figure 8-16 shows the final result of the JSF XUL implementation and how it will be used in JSP pages. The first page contains the `<pro:inputDate>` component tag and looks the same as the one you created previously (see Chapter 7), except this page uses a XUL `RenderKit`. This XUL implementation provides the same functionality as the Ajax implementation where dates that are not selectable are marked red and dates outside the scope of the current month are disabled. When the user enters a date and clicks a submit button, a full postback will occur, and the attached validator, if any, will be invoked. Code Sample 8-47 uses the input date component with the XUL `Renderer`.

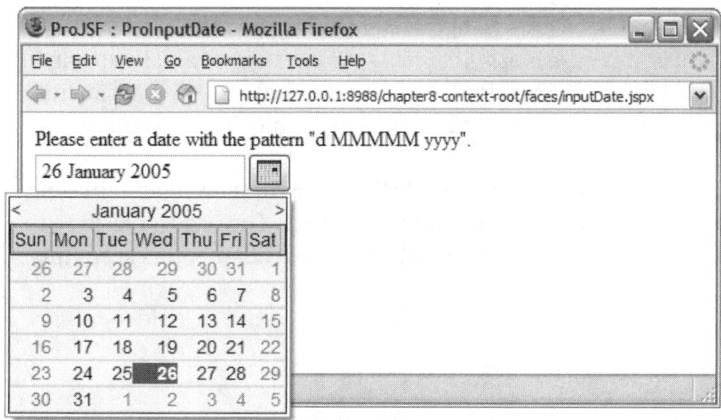

Figure 8-16. *JSF page rendered using the XUL* `RenderKit` *and the* `ProInputDate` *component*

Code Sample 8-47. *JSF Page Source for XUL Implementation*

```
<?xml version="1.0" encoding="UTF-8" ?>
<jsp:root xmlns:jsp="http://java.sun.com/JSP/Page" version="1.2"
          xmlns:bobh="http://www.bob.org/jsf/html"
          xmlns:f="http://java.sun.com/jsf/core"
          xmlns:h="http://java.sun.com/jsf/html" >
  <jsp:directive.page contentType="application/x-javaserver-faces"/>
  <f:view>
    <pro:document title="Pro JSF : ProInputDate" >
      <h:form id="form" >
        <pro:inputDate id="dateField"
                       title="Date Field Component"
                       value="#{inputDateBean.date}" >
          <f:convertDateTime pattern="d MMMMM yyyy" />
          <pro:validateDate availability="#{inputDateBean.getAvailability}" />
        </pro:inputDate>
        <br/>
```

```
        <h:message for="dateField" />
        <br/>
        <h:commandButton value="Submit" />
        <br/>
        <h:outputText value="#{inputDateBean.date}" >
          <f:convertDateTime pattern="d MMMMM yyyy" />
        </h:outputText>
      </h:form>
    </pro:document>
  </f:view>
</jsp:root>
```

The only step for the application developer to Ajax enable the application is to ensure to set the right contentType, which in this case is application/x-javaserver-faces. By specifying a custom contentType like the one in Code Sample 8-47 and Code Sample 8-48, you can intercept it and allow the ResponseWriter to decide what contentType is going to be set on the response.

Figure 8-17 shows the result of the second page. Code Sample 8-48 shows the source of the second page, which contains the showOneDeck component source. The page looks the same as the previous implementations of the showOneDeck component (see Chapter 6), except this page uses a XUL RenderKit.

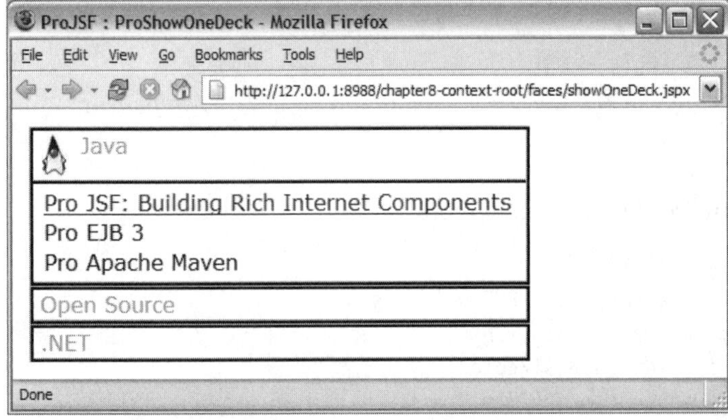

Figure 8-17. *JSF page rendered using the XUL* RenderKit *and the* ProShowOneDeck *component*

Code Sample 8-48. *JSF Page Source for XUL Implementation*

```
<?xml version="1.0" encoding="UTF-8" ?>
<jsp:root ...>
  <jsp:directive.page contentType="application/x-javaserver-faces"/>
  <f:view>
    ...
```

```
      <pro:showOneDeck showItemId="first"
                       showListener="#{showOneDeckBean.doShow}">
        <pro:showItem id="first" styleClass="showItem" >
          <f:facet name="header">
            <h:panelGroup>
              <h:graphicImage url="/resources/java_small.jpg" alt="The Duke"
                              style="margin-right: 8px; vertical-align:bottom;" />
              <h:outputText value="Java"/>
            </h:panelGroup>
          </f:facet>
          <h:panelGrid columns="1">
            <h:outputLink value="http://apress.com/book/bookDisplay.html?bID=10044">
              <h:outputText value="Pro JSF: Building Rich Internet Components"/>
      ...
  </f:view>
</jsp:root>
```

You might be asking yourself, "What's so cool about this? I have seen the exact same page sources in two other solutions." You are right, and that's the beauty of JSF! Without impacting the application developer, you can change a RenderKit ID to use other Renderers that support client-specific markup (XUL in this case) for optimized performance and responsiveness in the Mozilla browser.

Summary

The Mozilla Web site says it best: XUL is cool! We definitely recommend that component developers look at XUL as an alternative rendering technology for rich Web clients. Although initially it may seem overwhelming to create JSF components using XUL, it is actually pretty straightforward as long as you follow a well-defined blueprint.

A direct benefit of using XUL is the declarative component model you have at your disposal. XUL also enhances performance and reduces the amount of JavaScript you have to create and maintain.

We hope this chapter gave you a clear understanding that HTML is not the end of the road and that the limits of what we can do with the J2EE framework are sometimes in our own heads!

CHAPTER 9

■ ■ ■

Providing Microsoft HTC Renderers

If we value the pursuit of knowledge, we must be free to follow wherever that search may lead us. The free mind is not a barking dog to be tethered on a ten-foot chain.

—Adlai E. Stevenson Jr. (1900–1965)

In the previous chapter, we introduced the concept of SPIF applications and how component writers can leverage XUL to quickly and easily build standard JSF components for any browser supporting the Mozilla GRE (such as Firefox and Netscape). This provides an excellent solution; however, Firefox makes up less than 20 percent[1] of the browser market, which is dominated by Microsoft Internet Explorer.

Microsoft has often been seen as the evil empire among non-Microsoft developers, but you should recognize that Microsoft has contributed several bright ideas to standards organizations such as the W3C. Microsoft also introduced the now widely known `XMLHttpRequest` object. All of the pieces of Ajax—DHTML, JavaScript, and `XMLHttpRequest`—are available in Microsoft Internet Explorer, and the Microsoft Outlook Web Access solution has used these technologies to deliver a richer browser solution since 1998.

To be able to give application developers the freedom to deploy to both browser platforms (Microsoft's and Mozilla's), you have to include support for Microsoft Internet Explorer as well.

You could, of course, argue that you have already provided support for Internet Explorer with the HTML Ajax solution you created earlier, but that solution is still not leveraging Internet Explorer's full potential as a client platform.

In this chapter, you will leverage Microsoft's component model, which is similar to the one provided by Mozilla XUL. Microsoft's component model is called DHTML *behaviors* and allows developers to encapsulate regular DHTML in a separate file type: an HTC file. This file type allows developers to create reusable components that encapsulate dynamic behaviors, much the same way as XBL works for XUL. You should note that HTC defines only one element behavior per HTC file.

---

1. This is an approximate percentage of browser market at the time this book was written.

Requirements for the Deck and Date Components' HTC Implementations

The requirements for the `ProInputDate` and `ProShowOneDeck` components in this chapter are simple—you need to leverage the declarative component model provided by Microsoft Internet Explorer. To support this, you need to provide HTC-specific `Renderer` classes for the deck and date components. There should be no loss of functionality supporting this client-specific component model compared to what is provided by the deck and date components created in Chapters 6 and 7.

After this chapter, you should understand the difference between DHTML behaviors and HTC, what benefits you will gain, and what issues you can run into when creating rich user interface components with these technologies.

What HTC Brings to JSF

HTC provides similar benefits to component writers as XUL does. However, Internet Explorer is not providing any built-in HTC visual components. The HTC component model is part of the Internet Explorer runtime engine, so there is no need to "explode" the JSF page structure into the appropriate markup on the server before sending it to the client. This in turn will reduce the network payload, since rendering is taken care of by the client and not the actual server implementation.

And, of course, HTC also provides out-of-the-box rich client interactivity, such as pop-up functionality, eliminating the need for the component writer to implement this in an alternative solution such as Ajax.

In this chapter, you will learn how to combine the Ajax asynchronous communication channel—`XMLHttpRequest`—with the component model provided by HTC to design reusable and extremely interactive standard JSF components.

What JSF Brings to HTC

JSF brings the same benefit to HTC as it does to XUL: the common application programming model of JSP and Java. And, you can apply the same arguments about XUL to HTC; developers interested in HTC could use HTC directly, but the point is that JSF provides a familiar programming model and a standard request lifecycle that includes automatic state saving and restoring of state, validation, data model, and event handling.

The HTC Implementation of the Deck and Date Components

For JSF component writers, the fact that Microsoft is leveraging HTML markup in its HTC component model provides them with a simple encapsulation technique—a regular HTML file with the `.htc` extension. Therefore, the main player in this chapter is HTC.

Introduced in Microsoft Internet Explorer 5, HTC provides a mechanism to implement components in script as DHTML behaviors. Saved with an `.htc` extension, an HTC file is an HTML file that contains scripts and a set of HTC-specific elements that publish the HTML document as a component.

After this chapter, you should be able to create rich user interface components with Microsoft's DHTML behavior technology.

Figure 9-1 shows the three classes you will create in this chapter.

Figure 9-1. *Class diagram showing all classes created in this chapter*

The classes are as follows:

- `HtmlDocumentRenderer` is the `Renderer` in charge of writing the root elements in an HTML document.
- `HtcAjaxInputDateRenderer` is a new custom `Renderer` for the date component that extends the `HtmlInputDateRenderer` created in Chapter 2 and adds resources to include HTC and Ajax support.
- `HtcAjaxShowOneDeckRenderer` is a new custom `Renderer` for the deck component that extends the `HtmlRenderer` superclass created in Chapter 2 and adds resources to include HTC and Ajax support.

Designing JSF HTC Components Using a Blueprint

Blueprint, blueprint, blueprint! The blueprint for creating JSF components is created in such a way that it works for any markup. Because HTC is leveraging HTML markup, it can use the default HTML `RenderKit` provided by the JSF implementation. Alternatively, you can leverage the `HtmlAjaxRenderKit` you created in Chapter 6. The reason for using the `HtmlAjaxRenderKit` is that it is already designed for HTML and supports Ajax postback. In this chapter, you will simply follow the same blueprint finalized in Chapter 7, specifically steps 1, 5, 7, 11, and 12.

We'll show how to define the new component by implementing it in the intended markup that will eventually be sent to the client.

Step 1: Creating a UI Prototype

To be able to prototype what you want to achieve in this chapter, you have to use HTML, DHTML behaviors, and HTC file types to find out what elements, renderer-specific attributes, and other resources (for example, JavaScript, images, and so on) are needed.

■ **Note** For more information about DHTML behaviors and HTC, please visit Microsoft's MSDN Web site at `http://msdn.microsoft.com`.

The HTML Date Implementation Prototype

Figure 9-2 shows the page that includes the `<pro:inputDate>` prototype implemented in HTC.

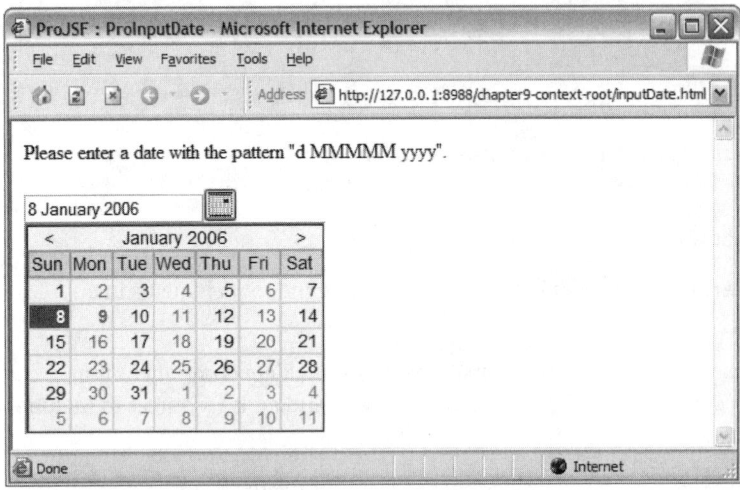

Figure 9-2. *The* `<pro:inputDate>` *component implemented in HTML and HTC*

Code Sample 9-1 shows the markup needed to create a page using the HTC `<pro:inputDate>` prototype shown in Figure 9-2.

Code Sample 9-1. *HTML Markup Needed for the* `<pro:inputDate>` *HTC Implementation*

```
<html xmlns:pro="http://projsf.apress.com/tags" >
  <head>
    <title>Pro JSF : ProInputDate</title>
  </head>
  <body>
    <form method="post">
      Please enter a date with the pattern "d MMMMM yyyy".
      <br></br>
      <script type="text/javascript"
              src="/.../faces/weblets/mabon/mabon.js" >
      </script>
```

```
      <script type="text/javascript"
              src="/.../faces/weblets/dojo/dojo.js" >
      </script>
      <?import namespace="pro"
               implementation="/.../projsf-ch9/inputDate.htc" ?>
      <pro:inputDate id="dateField"
                     value="26 January 2006"
                     pattern="d MMMMM yyyy"
                     targetURL="/.../projsf-ch9/sample-availability.json">
      </pro:inputDate>
    </form>
  </body>
</html>
```

The first noticeable change from XUL is that HTC uses HTML as the delivery vehicle instead of XML. You are also defining the namespace prefix `pro` in the `<html>` element. You can then import and bind the HTC component, or *element behavior* as it is called, to a specific tag name in the `pro` namespace. You define the tag name inside the HTC component, and once you import the HTC component, you can use the element behavior in the page with the prefix `pro` (for example, `<pro:inputDate>`).

You can also see the benefits of using HTC over traditional HTML when HTC needs only one element: `<pro:inputDate>`. HTML would have been a lot more verbose. This means the `Renderer` has to provide only the `<pro:inputDate>` HTC element with the accompanying attributes: `id`, `value`, `pattern`, and `targetURL`.

■ **Note** In Code Sample 9-1, the `<pro:inputDate>` element represents an HTC component, not a JSF component.

To be able to asynchronously communicate with the server when the `<pro:inputDate>` element is activated, you have to download two JavaScript libraries—`dojo.js` and `mabon.js`—to the page.

The HTC Date Element Behavior

Similar to XBL, developers can encapsulate a document hierarchy within the HTC component, or they can decide to explode the content into the HTML page and as such expose internal implementations.

Apart from encapsulation, another obvious benefit of using HTC is the familiarity with the syntax, since Internet Explorer parses the file as an HTML document. Deploying Microsoft DHTML applications has no specific requirements, except for the dependency on Microsoft Internet Explorer 5.0 and newer. You should also remember that with HTC you define one element behavior per HTC file.

A typical HTC file is usually structured as an HTML document with `<html>`, `<head>`, and `<body>` elements. It also contains scripts and HTC-specific elements (see Table 9-1) that define the component.

Table 9-1. *HTC-Specific Elements**

Name	Description
`document`	Represents the HTML document in a given browser window
`element`	Returns a reference to the tag in the primary document to which the element behavior is attached
`public:component`	Identifies the content of the file as an HTC component
`public:property`	Defines a property of the HTC component to be exposed to the containing document
`public:default`	Sets the default properties for an HTC component
`public:attach`	Binds a function to an event so that the function is called whenever the event fires on the specified object
`public:method`	Defines an HTC component method to be exposed to the containing document
`public:event`	Defines an HTC component event to be exposed to the containing document

* *Source:* `http://msdn.microsoft.com/workshop/author/behaviors/behaviors_node_entry.asp`

When you create an element behavior, it usually contains an enclosing `<public:component>` element and scripts in the `<head>` element and contains a `<body>` element that defines the actual markup for the element behavior. The file itself is saved with an `.htc` extension. Code Sample 9-2 shows the `<body>` section of the HTC file, `inputDate.htc`, since that will give you an understanding of how this component is constructed.

Code Sample 9-2. *The* `<body>` *Element of the* `<pro:inputDate>` *HTC Component*

```
<html>
   ...
<body>
  <input id="input" type="text" style="margin:0px"
         onchange="_flushChanges()" >
  <button type="button" style="margin:0px;width:2em;"
          onclick="_popup()" >
    <img src="/.../projsf-ch9/inputDateButton.gif" >
  </button>
```

The `<body>` element defines two form elements: `<input>` and `<button>`. Since Internet Explorer parses the HTC file as an encapsulated HTML document, any input fields in the HTC document will not participate in the parent document's form submit. This means you need to provide a way to transfer the value of the input field to a placeholder on the parent document (for example, `_flushChanges()`). The button is responsible for launching the actual pop-up calendar.

Caution It is illegal to have nested `<form>` elements in an HTML document, and since you cannot control where this component is going to end up, it is wise to not add any `<form>` elements to the element behavior.

A useful feature in Internet Explorer is XML *data islands*. You access an XML data island through an id attribute, and you can use them to embed "islands" of data inside HTML pages or, as in this case, inside an HTC file. More precisely, you will use this technique to embed markup for the pop-up calendar, as shown in Code Sample 9-3, so that you don't have to dynamically create the calendar using scripts.

Code Sample 9-3. *The XML Data Island for the* `<pro:inputDate>` *Calendar*

```
<!-- IE XML Data Island -->
<xml id="inputDatePopup" >
  <style type="text/css" >
    @import url("/.../projsf-ch9/inputDate.css");
  </style>
  <table id="tableNode"
         class="inputDate"
         cellspacing="0px"
         cellpadding="0px" >
   <thead>
     <tr class="toolbar">
       <td id="prevNode" >&lt;</td>
       <td id="titleNode" colspan="5" ></td>
       <td id="nextNode" >&gt;</td>
     </tr>
     <tr class="headings" >
       <td>Sun</td>
       <td>Mon</td>
       <td>Tue</td>
       <td>Wed</td>
       <td>Thu</td>
       <td>Fri</td>
       <td>Sat</td>
     </tr>
   </thead>
   <tbody>
    <tr><td></td><td></td><td></td><td></td><td></td><td></td><td></td></tr>
    <tr><td></td><td></td><td></td><td></td><td></td><td></td><td></td></tr>
    <tr><td></td><td></td><td></td><td></td><td></td><td></td><td></td></tr>
    <tr><td></td><td></td><td></td><td></td><td></td><td></td><td></td></tr>
    <tr><td></td><td></td><td></td><td></td><td></td><td></td><td></td></tr>
    <tr><td></td><td></td><td></td><td></td><td></td><td></td><td></td></tr>
   </tbody>
```

```
    </table>
  </xml>
</body>
```

The XML data island created in Code Sample 9-3 contains markup defining the inner HTML of the calendar component. The calendar is an ordinary HTML `<table>` element with a header for the title, a row for the navigation controls, and several rows and cells making up the actual calendar month.

In the `<head>` section of the HTC file, as shown in Code Sample 9-4, you define the element behavior prototype using the HTC-specific `<public:component>` element.

Code Sample 9-4. *The* `<head>` *Element in the* `<pro:inputDate>` *HTC Component*

```
<head>
  <public:component tagName="inputDate" >
    <public:defaults viewlinkcontent="true" />

    <public:property name="value" />
    <public:property name="pattern" />
    <public:property name="targetURL" />

    <public:attach event="ondocumentready" handler="_constuctor" />
  </public:component>
```

The enclosing `<public:component>` element has the `name` and `tagName` attributes set to `inputDate`. The `name` attribute identifies the element behavior, and the `tagName` attribute specifies the name of the custom tag. The code also has the `<public:default>` element's `viewlinkcontent` attribute set to `true`. This means the content of the element behavior is not exploded into the HTML document. Also, three public attributes (`value`, `pattern`, and `targetURL`)—or *properties* as they are called in HTC—are defined on the element behavior.

Although no `<constructor>` element exists like you had in XUL, other facilities initialize content that the element behavior uses. In Code Sample 9-4, you are using the `<public:attach>` element to bind an event handler (`_constructor`) to an HTC-specific event (`oncontentready` or `ondocumentready`). In this case we chose `ondocumentready` to work around a bug in Internet Explorer. Table 9-2 lists the HTC-specific events.

■ **Caution** Usually we prefer to use `oncontentready` to initialize the HTC component as soon as the browser has parsed its definition. In some cases, we must use `ondocumentready` instead, causing the HTC component to delay initialization until the main HTML document has been completely parsed by the browser. If the main HTML DOM is manipulated before the main document has finished loading, then Internet Explorer will produce a blank page with an Operation Aborted error dialog box. We found that having more than one HTC component on the same page, where one of the HTC components manipulates the private HTC `viewLink` DOM in response to `oncontentready`, produces the same Operation Aborted error dialog box. Changing the HTC behavior to use `ondocumentready` provides a workaround for this problem.

Table 9-2. *HTC-Specific Events**

Name	Description
oncontentready	Fires when the content of the element, to which the behavior is attached, has been completely parsed
oncontentsave	Fires just before the content of an element that is attached to an element behavior is saved or copied
ondetach	Fires before a behavior is detached from an element
ondocumentready	Fires when the behavior's containing document has been completely parsed

* *Source: MSDN* (http://msdn.microsoft.com/library/default.asp?url=/workshop/components/htc/reference/htcref.asp)

Local Variables and the _constructor() Function

In the <script> element, as shown in Code Sample 9-5, you first declare some local variables for this instance of <pro:inputDate> to hold information of the day names of a week and the month names of a year. You are also declaring a variable, internalState, to hold the inner state of this pop-up calendar, such as the current day and table title.

The _constructor() function is called as soon as the content has been delivered (for example, when the <pro:inputDate> element has been written to the client browser). In this case, the _constructor() function initializes the content of the pop-up calendar and sets the event handlers for the click event on the previous and next nodes; in addition, the actual table cells contain the currently selected month's dates.

Code Sample 9-5. *The* _constructor() *Function*

```
<script>
  var _DAY_NAMES = ['Sun', 'Mon', 'Tue',
                    'Wed', 'Thu', 'Fri', 'Sat'];
  var _MONTH_NAMES = ['January', 'February', 'March',
                      'April', 'May', 'June',
                      'July', 'August', 'September',
                      'October', 'November', 'December'];

  var internalState = [];
  var popup = window.createPopup();

  function _constuctor()
  {
    popup.document.open();
    popup.document.writeln('<html>');
    // eliminate scrollbars and spaces around the edges
    popup.document.writeln('<body style="margin:0px;padding:0px;overflow:auto;" >');
    popup.document.writeln(inputDatePopup.innerHTML);
    popup.document.writeln('</body>');
```

```
    popup.document.writeln('</html>');
    popup.document.close();

    var prevNode = popup.document.getElementById('prevNode');
    var nextNode = popup.document.getElementById('nextNode');
    var tableNode = popup.document.getElementById('tableNode');
    var titleNode = popup.document.getElementById('titleNode');

    prevNode.onclick = _scollPrev;
    nextNode.onclick = _scrollNext;
    tableNode.tBodies[0].onclick = _clickCell;

    internalState.tableNode = tableNode;
    internalState.titleNode = titleNode;

    if (element.value)
      input.value = element.value;

    if (element.id)
    {
      input.name = element.id;

      var currentNode = this;
      while (currentNode != null)
      {
        if (currentNode.tagName.toLowerCase() == 'form' &&
            currentNode.scopeName == 'HTML')
        {
          var formNode = currentNode;
          var clientId = element.id;
          var inputNode = formNode.elements[clientId];
          if (inputNode == null)
          {
            inputNode = document.createElement('input');
            inputNode.type = 'hidden';
            inputNode.name = clientId;
            formNode.appendChild(inputNode);
          }
          internalState.inputNode = inputNode;
          break;
        }
        currentNode = currentNode.parentNode;
      }
    }
  }
```

The _popup() Function

This _popup() function is more or less the same as the one used in the HTML Ajax solution with one minor difference—with HTC you do not need to handle the closing of the pop-up (see Figure 9-3). The Internet Explorer implementation handles this.

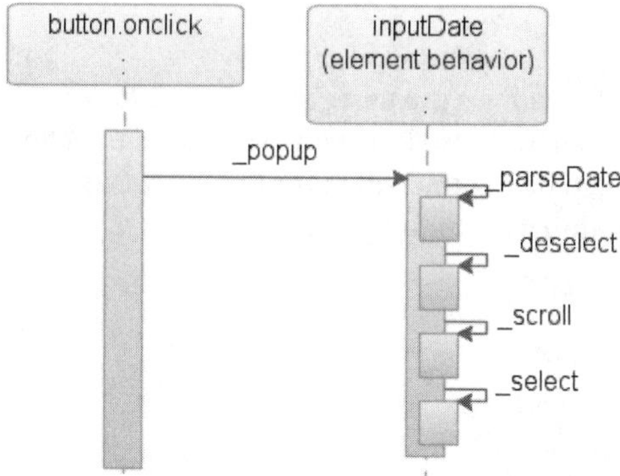

Figure 9-3. *HTC* `<pro:inputDate>` `_popup` *function*

The _popup() function, as shown in Code Sample 9-6, is responsible for launching the calendar when the user clicks the button. It will first read the user-defined date string from the input field and then parse that date string into a Date object. If parse was successful, you will use the Date object; otherwise, you will use today's Date.

Next you ensure that no previous selection is calling the _deselect() function. From the Date object, you get the active month and year, which you store on the internal state of this <pro:inputDate> instance. Finally, you call the _scroll() function, passing zero as an argument to ensure the fully populated calendar day cells but staying on the current month (zero navigation).

Code Sample 9-6. *The* `_popup` *Function in the HTC File*

```
function _popup()
{
  var dateString = input.value;
  var parsedDate = _parseDate(dateString, element.pattern);
  var activeDate = (parsedDate != null) ? parsedDate : new Date();

  _deselect();

  var month = activeDate.getMonth();
  var year = activeDate.getFullYear();
  internalState._currentMonth = month;
  internalState._currentYear = year;
```

```
  _scroll(0);

  if (parsedDate != null)
    _select(parsedDate.getDate());
}
```

The _scroll() Function

The `_scroll()` function, as shown in Code Sample 9-7, allows the users to navigate plus or minus one month using arrow controls in the calendar. It is also here you use Mabon to determine the availability of dates defined by the managed bean attached to the `HtcAjaxInputDate` component. Figure 9-4 shows the sequence of function calls in the `_scroll()` function.

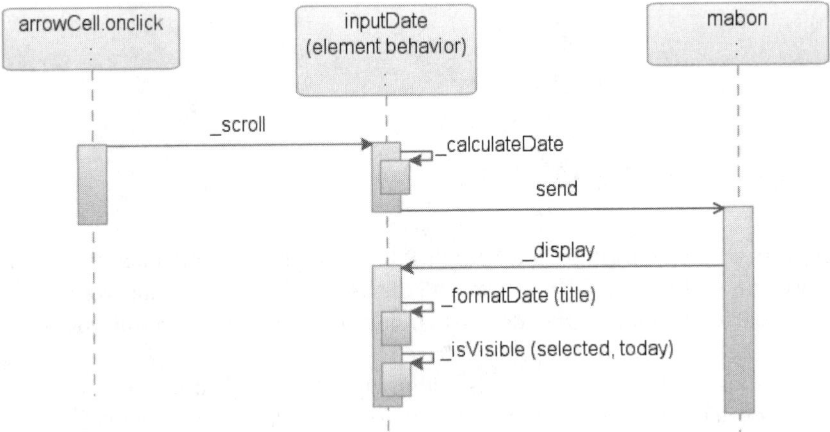

Figure 9-4. *HTC* `<pro:inputDate>` `_scroll()` *function*

Code Sample 9-7. *The* `_scroll` *Function in the HTC File*

```
function _scroll(offset)
{
  // scroll months, updating year as necessary
  internalState._currentMonth = internalState._currentMonth + offset;
  internalState._currentYear += Math.floor(internalState._currentMonth / 12);
  internalState._currentMonth = (internalState._currentMonth + 12) % 12;

  // use Mabon to retrieve availability
  if (element.targetURL)
  {
    var startDate = _calculateDate(1);
    var endDate = _calculateDate(31);
```

```
      var millisPerDay = 1000 * 60 * 60 * 24;
      var startDay = Math.floor(startDate.getTime() / millisPerDay);
      var endDay = Math.floor(endDate.getTime() / millisPerDay);

      // use Mabon to determine availability
      mabon.send(
        {
          url: element.targetURL,
          args: [startDay, endDay],
          callback: function(result) { _display(result); }
        });
    }
    else
    {
      var available = [];
      for (var i=0; i < 32; i++)
      {
        available.push(true);
      }
      _display(available);
    }
  }
```

The _clickCell() Function

The `_clickCell()` function, as shown in Code Sample 9-8, is called when the user clicks a cell representing a date in the calendar. Figure 9-5 shows the sequence of function calls in the `_clickCell()` function.

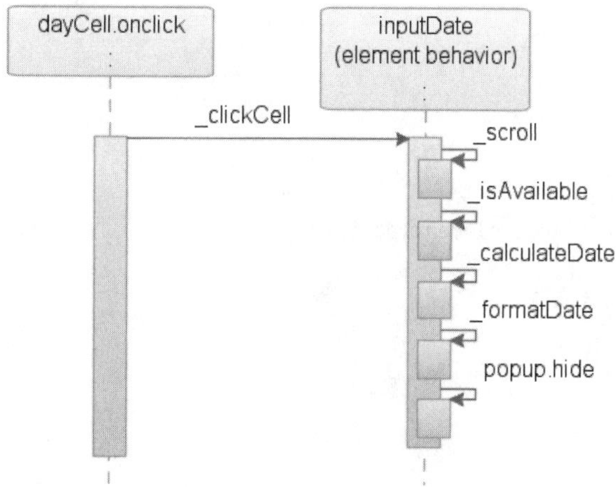

Figure 9-5. *HTC* `<pro:inputDate>` `_clickCell` *function*

You can obtain the target node invoking the event by calling `event.srcElement` (see Code Sample 9-8). When you have the target node, you can check to see whether the user clicked a cell that is outside the range of the displayed month and, if so, navigate to the month for that selected date: `_scrollNext()` or `_scrollPrev()`. If the selection is within the boundaries of the month, you need to see whether this date is available; if it is, add the selected date to the input element.

Code Sample 9-8. *The* `_clickCell()` *Function*

```
function _clickCell()
{
  var event = popup.document.parentWindow.event
  var cellNode = event.srcElement;
  var rowNode = cellNode.parentNode;

  var row = rowNode.sectionRowIndex;
  var col = cellNode.cellIndex;
  var day = Number(cellNode.innerText);

  if (row == -1)
  {
    return;
  }
  else if (row == 0 && day > 7)
  {
    _scrollPrev();
  }
  else if (row > 3 && day < 15)
  {
    _scrollNext();
  }
  else
  {
    if (_isAvailable(day))
    {
      var selectedDate = _calculateDate(day);
      input.value = _formatDate(selectedDate, element.pattern);

      // flush the changes for next postback
      _flushChanges();

      popup.hide();
    }
  }
}
```

The HTML Deck Implementation Prototype

Figure 9-6 shows a page that includes the `<pro:showOneDeck>` prototype implemented in HTC.

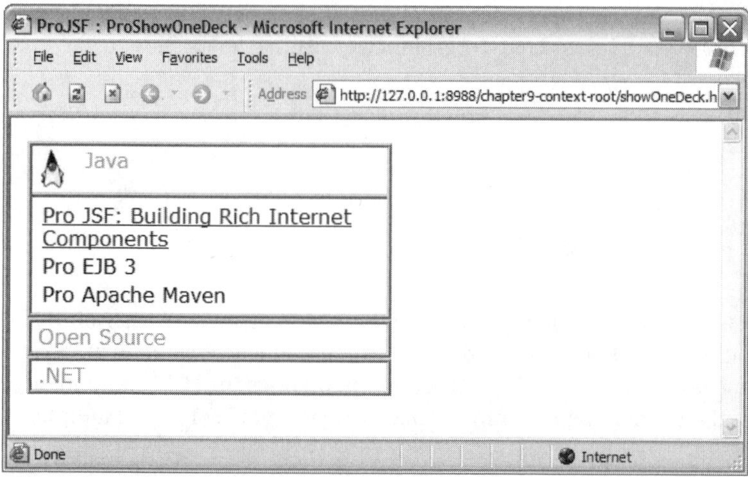

Figure 9-6. *The* `<pro:showOneDeck>` *component implemented in HTML and HTC*

Code Sample 9-9 shows the markup needed to create a page using the HTC `<pro:showOneDeck>` prototype shown in Figure 9-6.

Code Sample 9-9. *Markup to Create a Page Using the* `<pro:showOneDeck>` *HTC Prototype*

```
<html xmlns:pro="http://projsf.apress.com/tags" >
  <head>
    <title>ProJSF : ProShowOneDeck</title>
    <link rel="stylesheet" href="/.../resources/stylesheet.css"/>  </head>
  <body>
    <form id="form" method="post" >
      ...
        <?import namespace="pro"
                 implementation="/.../projsf-ch9/showItem.htc" ?>
        <pro:showOneDeck id="form:showOneDeck" style="display:block;">
          <pro:showItem itemId="first"
                        active="true"
                        style="display:block;">
            <pro:headerFacet>
              <img src="/.../resources/java_small.jpg"
                   alt="The Duke"
                   style="margin-right: 8px; vertical-align:bottom;" />
              Java
            </pro:headerFacet>
```

```
          <table>
            <tbody>
              <tr>
                <td>
                  <a href="http://apress.com/book/bookDisplay.html?bID=10044">
                  Pro JSF: Building Rich Internet Components
                  </a>
                </td>
              </tr>
      ...
    </form>
  </body>
</html>
```

First you need to define the namespace prefix pro in the <html> element, which allows you to import and bind the element behavior (showItem.htc) to a specific tag name in the pro namespace. The tag name is defined inside the HTC component; once the HTC component is imported, you can use the element behavior in the page with the prefix pro (for example, <pro:showItem>).

The HTC Deck Element Behavior

The structure of the <pro:showOneDeck> component is slightly different from the <pro:inputDate> component, since it is of a composite nature. If you look at what is needed to create the deck component in a JSP page, you need three JSP tag handlers: <pro:showOneDeck>, <pro:showItem>, and <f:facet name="header">. <pro:showOneDeck> is a container for <pro:showItem> and defines which <pro:showItem> should be expanded by default. <pro:showItem> is also a container and defines what should be displayed when interacted with. <f:facet name="header"> defines the clickable header of <pro:showItem>.

The problem you are facing is that HTC does not recognize JSF facets, and therefore you will have to come up with a way to define facets using HTC syntax. Also, HTC components are treated as encapsulated documents; for example, an HTC file is basically an HTML file parsed by Internet Explorer.

The first obvious approach is to define one HTC element behavior for each JSF tag (that is, showOneDeck.htc, showItem.htc, and headerFacet.htc), but from an HTC view only one will include actual behavior—showItem. The <pro:showItem> component is the one expanding and collapsing, not the <pro:showOneDeck> or the <pro:headerFacet>; thus, you should create only one HTC element behavior: showItem.htc.

Code Sample 9-10 shows the <body> section of the HTC file, showItem.htc, since that will give you an understanding of how this component is constructed.

Code Sample 9-10. *The* <body> *of the* <pro:showItem> *Component*

```
<html>
  ...
  <body style="display:block" class="showItem" >
    <div id="header" ></div>
    <div id="content" style="display:none;" ></div>
```

```
  </body>
</html>
```

This is a simple component in its structure. It contains only two <div> elements: one for the header of the <pro:showItem> and one for the actual content of the <pro:showItem>. You leverage CSS to make sure that elements outside the <pro:showItem> will wrap properly by setting the style attribute on the <body> element to display:block; in other words, other <pro:showItem> components will be stacked either above or below. You also set the content <div> element's style to display:none by default. This value causes the <div> element to take no space at all in the browser.

■ **Note** For more information about visual formatting using block boxes, please visit the W3C Web site at http://www.w3.org/TR/REC-CSS2/visuren.html#initial-containing-block.

In the <head> section of the HTC file, as shown in Code Sample 9-11, you define the element behavior prototype using the HTC-specific <public:component> element.

Code Sample 9-11. *The* <head> *Element in the* <pro:showItem> *HTC Component*

```
<head>
  <public:component tagName="showItem" >
    <public:property name="itemId" />
    <public:property name="styleClass" />
    <public:property name="headerStyleClass" />
    <public:property name="contentStyleClass" />
    <public:property name="active" />

    <public:attach event="oncontentready" handler="_constructor" />
  </public:component>
```

The enclosing <public:component> element has the tagName attribute set to showItem. The tagName attribute specifies the name of the custom tag.

Also, five public properties (itemId, styleClass, headerStyleClass, contentStyleClass, and active) are defined on the element behavior. The previous code sample uses the <public:attach> element to bind an event handler, _constructor, to the HTC-specific event oncontentready. The _constructor() function will initialize the internal state of the element behavior.

The _constructor() Function

The _constructor() function, as shown in Code Sample 9-12, is the core piece of the HTC element behavior. The oncontentready event will fire when the content of the <pro:showItem> element, to which the behavior is attached, has been parsed completely. This will invoke the _constructor() function, which will set the internal state of the <pro:showItem> tag based on the content written to the browser.

Code Sample 9-12. *The* `_constructor()` *Function*

```
<script type="text/javascript" >
    function _constructor()
    {
      header.className = (element.headerStyleClass || 'showItemHeader');
      header.onclick = _expand;

      for (var i=0; i < childNodes.length; i++)
      {
        var childNode = childNodes[i];
        if (childNode.scopeName == 'pro' &&
            childNode.nodeName == 'headerFacet')
        {
          // set header on showItem
          header.innerHTML = childNode.innerHTML;
        }
        else
        {
          // set content inside showItem
          switch (childNode.nodeType)
          {
            case 1: // Element
              content.insertAdjacentHTML("beforeEnd", childNode.outerHTML);
              break;
            case 3: // Text
              content.insertAdjacentHTML("beforeEnd", childNode.nodeValue);
              break;
          }
        }
      }

      // show the contents if active
      if (element.active == 'true')
      {
        content.className = (element.contentStyleClass || 'showItemContent');
        content.style.display = 'block';
      }

      defaults.viewLink = document;
    }
```

The source of the `_constructor()` function is simple. You first set the `onclick` event handler on the HTC component's header to use the `_expand` function so that this function will be invoked whenever the header is clicked. You then loop over all children of the `<pro:showItem>` tag listed in the parent document. If a child node is a `<pro:headerFacet>`, you then add its `innerHTML` to the header element in the HTC component body; otherwise, you add it to the content element. If the child node is being added to the content element, you have to check to see whether it is another element or just plain text.

If the `active` attribute on the `<pro:showItem>` tag is set to `true`, the content of the `<pro:showItem>` element behavior will be displayed. Before the `_constructor()` is done executing and the content of the HTC element behavior is displayed in the browser, you have to create a `viewLink` between the root element of the document fragment in the HTC file to the master element, `<pro:showItem>`, in the primary document. You can define a `viewLink` using a script shown previously or by inserting the appropriate declaration in the component section of the HTC file (see Code Sample 9-4).

■ **Note** The `insertAdjacentHTML` method is specific to Internet Explorer and appends the given HTML to the HTML content of the DOM element. The first argument on the `insertAdjacentHTML` method takes one of four string values: `beforeBegin`, `afterBegin`, `beforeEnd`, and `afterEnd`. The `beforeEnd` string tells the method to insert the HTML markup immediately before the end of the DOM element, after all the other content in the DOM element.

The _expand() Function

As shown in Figure 9-7, when the element behavior is bound to the `pro` namespace and attached to the `<pro:showItem ...>` tag, an `_expand()` function, as shown in Code Sample 9-13, is added as the event handler and will be invoked when the header is clicked.

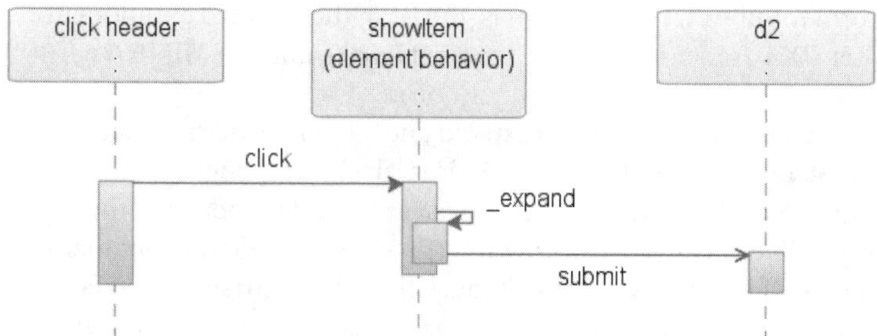

Figure 9-7. *HTC* `<pro:showItem>` `_expand` *function*

Code Sample 9-13. *The* `_expand()` *Function*

```
function _expand()
{
  var showOneNode = element.parentNode;
  var showOneClientId = showOneNode.id;

  var currentNode = element;
  while (currentNode != null)
```

```
    {
      var method = currentNode.method;

      if (method != null &&
          (method.toLowerCase() == 'get' ||
           method.toLowerCase() == 'post'))
      {

        //The following function call to d2 is needed to perform
        //an Ajax postback when implemented in the JSF HTC
        //ProShowOneDeck component.
        var formNode = currentNode;
        var content = new Object();
        content[showOneClientId] = element.itemId;
        d2.submit(formNode, content);
        break;
      }

      currentNode = currentNode.parentNode;
    }
  }
</script>
```

In the prototype you are constructing only the UI, but for Code Sample 9-13 the `d2.submit()` function has been added, passing the activated form `id` and the `id` of the selected node to the `d2.submit()` function. The `d2.submit()` function calls the `dojo.io.bind()` method, passing information about what form to submit, content (that is, the ID of the selected component), the accepted request header (`'X-D2-Content-Type': <contentType>`), and the MIME type (`text/plain`) for this request.

This information will determine which node to expand and which `ResponseWriter` to use for this request in your JSF implementation of the JSF HTC deck component.

The D^2 library also defines a callback function, `d2._loadtext`, that is used to get the response data from the server. The `d2._loadtext` function will replace the target document with the document returned on the response. This will cause the HTC `<pro:showItem>` component to invoke the `_constructor()` again and cause the `<pro:showItem>` to be updated with new content sent from the server.

To be able to asynchronously communicate with the server when a deck is activated, you also have to download a set of JavaScript libraries (`dojo.js` and `d2.js`) to the page. These libraries need to be part of your component and should be downloaded automatically to the client on initial request.

Step 5: Creating a Client-Specific Renderer

Your HTC solution contains three new `Renderer` classes: `HtmlDocumentRenderer`, `HtcAjaxInputDateRenderer`, and `HtcAjaxShowOneDeckRenderer`. Let's start by looking at the `HtmlDocumentRenderer` class.

The HtmlDocumentRenderer Class

The HtmlDocumentRenderer class (see Figure 9-8) is basically a port of the XulDocumentRenderer you created in Chapter 8. By porting the XulDocumentRenderer code to an HTML version, you can now provide application developers with one complete solution, allowing the component writer to switch the RenderKit without any changes to the actual application page description.

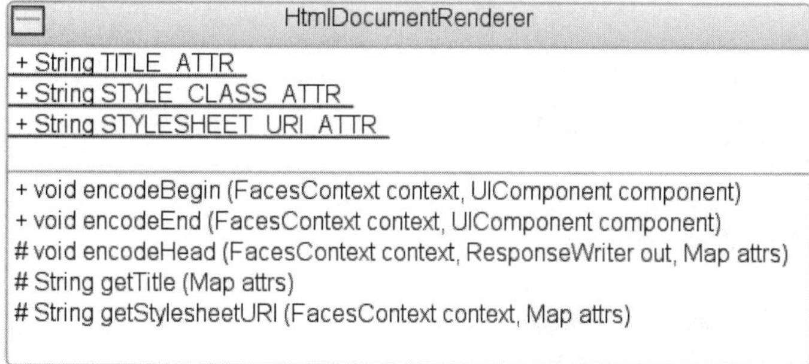

Figure 9-8. *Class diagram showing the* HtmlDocumentRenderer *class*

Another freebie is the "at-most-once" semantics for script resources you get when extending the HtmlRenderer.

The only requirement that the HTML document Renderer has is to support running applications on different clients, without forcing application developers to provide different solutions for each client. The HtmlDocumentRenderer, a top-level component that controls the root element rendered to the client, provides enormous possibilities and provides total control over the markup for the component writer.

You can use HtmlDocumentRenderer as the root component by any Renderer (for example, HtmlInputDateRenderer, HtmlAjaxInputDateRenderer, and HtcAjaxInputDateRenderer) that is targeting HTML as the default markup. Code Sample 9-14 shows the encodeBegin() method of the HtmlDocumentRenderer.

Code Sample 9-14. *The* HtmlDocumentRenderer encodeBegin() *Method*

```
package com.apress.projsf.ch9.render.html.basic;

import java.io.IOException;
import java.util.Map;

import javax.faces.application.Application;
import javax.faces.application.ViewHandler;
import javax.faces.component.UIComponent;
import javax.faces.context.FacesContext;
import javax.faces.context.ResponseWriter;

import com.apress.projsf.ch2.render.html.HtmlRenderer;
```

```
public class HtmlDocumentRenderer extends HtmlRenderer
{
  /**
   * The title attribute.
   /
  public static String TITLE_ATTR = "title";

  /*
   * The styleClass attribute.
   /
  public static String STYLE_CLASS_ATTR = "styleClass";

  /*
   * The stylesheetURI attribute.
   */
  public static String STYLESHEET_URI_ATTR = "stylesheetURI";

  public void encodeBegin(
    FacesContext context,
    UIComponent  component) throws IOException
  {
    ResponseWriter out = context.getResponseWriter();
    Map attrs = component.getAttributes();
    String styleClass = getStyleClass(attrs);

    out.startElement("html", component);
    out.startElement("head", null);
    encodeHead(context, out, attrs);
    out.endElement("head");
    out.startElement("body", null);
    if (styleClass != null)
      out.writeAttribute("class", styleClass, STYLE_CLASS_ATTR);
  }
```

The encodeBegin() method takes two arguments: FacesContext context and UIComponent component. From the component, you can obtain a Map containing all the available attributes. In this case, the application developer can set three attributes in his JSP document or backing bean (the title, the styleClass and the stylesheetURI), and the attribute map is passed as an argument to the encodeHead() method.

The startElement() method takes the following arguments: name and component. The name argument is the name of the element generated (for example, html), and the component argument is the UIComponent that this element represents. In Code Sample 9-14, this is represented with the component UIDocument.

The encodeEnd() method, as shown in Code Sample 9-15, is basically just closing the HTML <body> and <html> tags.

Code Sample 9-15. *The* encodeEnd() *Method*

```
public void encodeEnd(
  FacesContext context,
  UIComponent  component) throws IOException
{
  ResponseWriter out = context.getResponseWriter();
  out.endElement("body");
  out.endElement("html");
}
```

The encodeHead() method, as shown in Code Sample 9-16, is responsible for writing out the <head> element. The <head> element contains information about the document, and in this case it is the title and style sheet.

Code Sample 9-16. *The* encodeHead() *Method*

```
protected void encodeHead(
  FacesContext   context,
  ResponseWriter out,
  Map            attrs) throws IOException
{
  String title = getTitle(attrs);
  String stylesheetURI = getStylesheetURI(context, attrs);

  if (title != null)
  {
    out.startElement("title", null);
    out.writeText(title, TITLE_ATTR);
    out.endElement("title");
  }
  if (stylesheetURI != null)
  {
    out.startElement("link", null);
    out.writeAttribute("rel", "stylesheet", null);
    out.writeAttribute("href", stylesheetURI, STYLESHEET_URI_ATTR);
    out.endElement("link");
  }
}
```

The getTitle() and getStylesheetURI() methods, as shown in Code Sample 9-17, return the values of the title and stylesheetURI attributes.

Code Sample 9-17. *The Getters for the* UIDocument *Attributes*

```
  protected String getTitle(
    Map attrs)
```

```
  {
    return (String)attrs.get(TITLE_ATTR);
  }

  protected String getStyleClass(
    Map attrs)
  {
    return (String)attrs.get(STYLE_CLASS_ATTR);
  }

  protected String getStylesheetURI(
    FacesContext context,
    Map          attrs)
  {
    String stylesheetURI = (String)attrs.get(STYLESHEET_URI_ATTR);

    if (stylesheetURI != null)
    {
      Application application = context.getApplication();
      ViewHandler handler = application.getViewHandler();
      stylesheetURI = handler.getResourceURL(context, stylesheetURI);
    }

    return stylesheetURI;
  }
}
```

The HtcAjaxInputDateRenderer Class

You already know that XUL can make a JSF component writer's life easier, but how about HTC? Microsoft's HTC components provide a similar level of abstraction as Mozilla's XUL/XBL. So, without further ado, let's look at the JSF HTC implementation (see Figure 9-9).

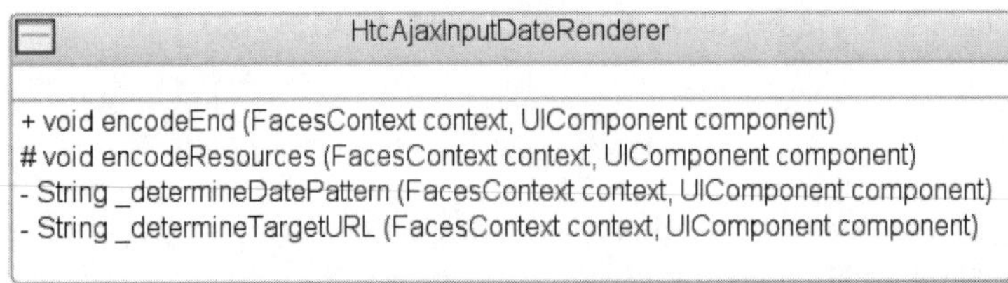

Figure 9-9. *Class diagram showing the* `HtcAjaxInputDateRenderer` *class*

Even in the HtcAjaxInputDateRenderer, you will recognize most of the code from previous chapters, except that the actual output to the client is a mix of regular HTML and HTC. As with XUL, HTC allows you to reuse the UI prototype. By adding the element behavior—the inputDate.htc prototype file—to your resources, the only element you need to write out for this JSF HTC component is <pro:inputDate ...> and its attributes.

By extending the HtmlInputDateRenderer, you get access to the writeScriptInline() method, as shown in Code Sample 9-18. The writeScriptInline() method provides the same "at-most-once" semantics for inline scripts as the writeScriptResource() method does for external resources. An application developer might add two or more ProInputDate components to the page, but the semantics behind the writeScriptInline() method, provided by the Renderer implementation, will make sure this inline script is written only once.

The writeScriptInline() method writes out a script that will add a namespace (http://projsf.apress.com/tags) and will set the namespace prefix to pro. When the namespace is added, you can import the element behavior (inputDate.htc) and attach it to the namespace prefix.

Code Sample 9-18. *The* HtcAjaxInputDateRenderer

```
package com.apress.projsf.ch9.render.htc.ajax;

import java.io.IOException;

import java.text.DateFormat;
import java.text.SimpleDateFormat;

import javax.faces.application.Application;
import javax.faces.application.ViewHandler;
import javax.faces.component.UIComponent;
import javax.faces.component.UIInput;
import javax.faces.context.FacesContext;
import javax.faces.context.ResponseWriter;
import javax.faces.convert.Converter;
import javax.faces.convert.DateTimeConverter;
import javax.faces.el.MethodBinding;
import javax.faces.validator.Validator;

import com.apress.projsf.ch5.render.html.basic.HtmlInputDateRenderer;
import com.apress.projsf.ch7.validate.DateValidator;

public class HtcAjaxInputDateRenderer extends HtmlInputDateRenderer
{
  protected void encodeResources(FacesContext context,
                                 UIComponent component) throws IOException
  {
    super.encodeResources(context, component);
```

```
    ViewHandler handler = context.getApplication().getViewHandler();
    String behaviorURL = handler.getResourceURL(context,
                              "weblet://com.apress.projsf.ch9/inputDate.htc");
    writeScriptInline(context,
                      "document.namespaces
                                .add('pro','http://projsf.apress.com/tags');\n" +
                      "document.namespaces
                                .item('pro').doImport('" + behaviorURL + "');
                      ");
  }
```

By design, the <pro:inputDate> component can have a Converter added by a JSP tag. At initial render, during the creation of the component hierarchy, a custom JSP converter tag has not yet been executed, so the Converter is not yet attached to the component inside the encodeBegin() method. Instead, the Renderer is using the encodeEnd() method, as shown in Code Sample 9-19, to write out the markup and to obtain the Converter.

Code Sample 9-19. *The* encodeEnd() *Method*

```
public void encodeEnd(
  FacesContext context,
  UIComponent  component) throws IOException
{
  String pattern = _determineDatePattern(context, component);
  String targetURL = _determineTargetURL(context, component);

  UIInput input = (UIInput)component;
  String valueString = (String)input.getSubmittedValue();

  if (valueString == null)
  {
    Object value = input.getValue();
    if (value != null)
    {
      Converter converter = getConverter(context, input);
      valueString = converter.getAsString(context, component, value);
    }
  }

  String clientId = input.getClientId(context);

  ResponseWriter out = context.getResponseWriter();
  out.startElement("pro:inputDate", component);
  out.writeAttribute("id", clientId, null);
  if (valueString != null)
    out.writeAttribute("value", valueString, null);
  if (pattern != null)
```

```
    out.writeAttribute("pattern", pattern, null);
  if (targetURL != null)
    out.writeAttribute("targetURL", targetURL, null);
  out.endElement("pro:inputDate");
}
```

In `encodeEnd()`, you call two methods—`_determineDatePattern()` and `_determineTargetURL()`. These methods obtain the date format pattern, and the target URL for the managed bean is bound to the `Validator`. Finally, you write out the `<pro:inputDate>` component with its attribute to the client.

The `_determineDatePattern()` method, as shown in Code Sample 9-20, is identical to the one you used in both the XUL Ajax and HTML Ajax solutions, and you could have created a base class, or utility class, for any custom `Renderer` that might need this method. But for educational purposes we decided that it is easier to understand when it is explained this way.

For the HTC implementation to work, you need to know what date pattern has been set on the `DateTimeConverter` by the application developer. This date pattern will be used in two places. First, it parses the date entered by the user in the `<input>` element. This parsed date will then be used to set the selected date in the calendar. Second, it makes sure the date selected in the calendar follows the correct date format when added to the `<input>` element.

Code Sample 9-20. *The `_determineDatePattern()` Method*

```
private String _determineDatePattern(
  FacesContext context,
  UIComponent  component)
{
  UIInput input = (UIInput)component;
  Converter converter = getConverter(context, input);

  if (converter instanceof DateTimeConverter)
  {
    DateTimeConverter dateTime = (DateTimeConverter)converter;
    return dateTime.getPattern();
  }
  else
  {
    SimpleDateFormat dateFormat = (SimpleDateFormat)
                                 DateFormat.getDateInstance(DateFormat.SHORT);
    return dateFormat.toPattern();
  }
}
```

You may have seen the `_determineTargetURL()` method, as shown in Code Sample 9-21, in previous chapters. It provides you with the needed binding reference to the managed bean. You first get all the validators attached to this input component. You then check to see whether one or many of these validators are an instance of the `DateValidator`. (The `DateValidator` was created in Chapter 7.)

Code Sample 9-21. *The* `_determineTargetURL()` *Method*

```
  private String _determineTargetURL(
    FacesContext context,
    UIComponent  component)
  {
    UIInput input = (UIInput)component;
    Validator[] validators = input.getValidators();

    for (int i=0; i < validators.length; i++)
    {
      if (validators[i] instanceof DateValidator)
      {
        DateValidator validateDate = (DateValidator)validators[i];
        MethodBinding binding = validateDate.getAvailability();
        if (binding != null)
        {
          String expression = binding.getExpressionString();
          // #{backingBean.methodName} -> backingBean.methodName
          String bindingRef = expression.substring(2, expression.length(): 1);

          Application application = context.getApplication();
          ViewHandler handler = application.getViewHandler();
          return handler.getResourceURL(context, "mabon:/" + bindingRef);
        }
      }
    }

    return null;
  }
}
```

If it is an instance of the `DateValidator`, you check to see whether you have a `MethodBinding`. If a `MethodBinding` exists, you get the expression (for example, `#{managedBean.methodName}`) and strip off the `#{}`. This leaves you with `managedBean.methodName`, which you concatenate with `mabon:/`. The `MabonViewHandler` will recognize the string and return a resource URL that will be written to the client (for example, `/context-root/mabon-servlet-mapping/managedBean.methodName`).

The HtcAjaxShowOneDeckRenderer Class

You are getting close! Since the `UIShowOne` component is a container component, it needs to render its children, and as such you have to implement `encodeBegin()`, `encodeChildren()`, and `encodeEnd()` in the new renderer (see Figure 9-10).

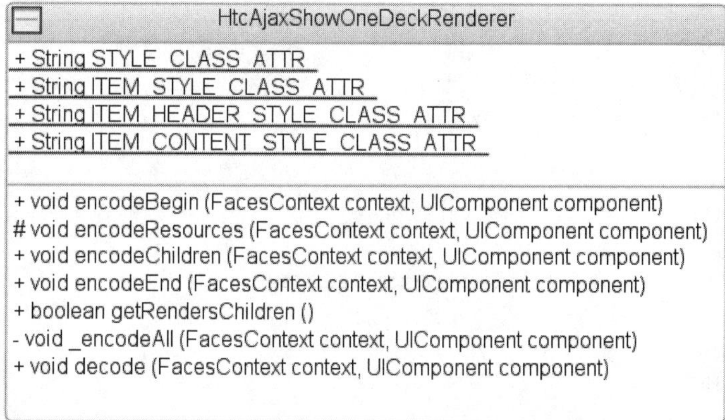

Figure 9-10. *Class diagram showing the* `HtcAjaxShowOneDeckRenderer` *class*

We'll first cover the `encodeBegin()` method for the `HtcAjaxShowOneDeckRenderer`, as shown in Code Sample 9-22. The `encodeBegin()` method takes two arguments: `FacesContext` and `UIComponent`. The Render Response phase will call `encodeBegin()` on the `UIShowOne` component, which in turn will delegate to the `encodeBegin()` method on the `HtcAjaxShowOneDeckRenderer`, passing the `FacesContext` and the `UIShowOne` component instance.

Code Sample 9-22. *The* `HtcAjaxShowOneDeckRenderer encodeBegin()` *Method*

```
package com.apress.projsf.ch9.render.htc.ajax;

import java.io.IOException;
import java.util.Iterator;
import java.util.List;
import java.util.Map;

import javax.faces.application.ViewHandler;
import javax.faces.component.UIComponent;
import javax.faces.context.ExternalContext;
import javax.faces.context.FacesContext;
import javax.faces.context.ResponseWriter;

import com.apress.projsf.ch2.render.html.HtmlRenderer;
import com.apress.projsf.ch3.component.UIShowItem;
import com.apress.projsf.ch3.component.UIShowOne;
import com.apress.projsf.ch3.event.ShowEvent;

public class HtcAjaxShowOneDeckRenderer extends HtmlRenderer
{
```

```
/**
 * The styleClass attribute.
 */
public static String STYLE_CLASS_ATTR = "styleClass";

/**
 * The itemStyleClass attribute.
 */
public static String ITEM_STYLE_CLASS_ATTR = "itemStyleClass";

/**
 * The itemHeaderStyleClass attribute.
 */
public static String ITEM_HEADER_STYLE_CLASS_ATTR = "itemHeaderStyleClass";

/**
 * The itemContentStyleClass attribute.
 */
public static String ITEM_CONTENT_STYLE_CLASS_ATTR = "itemContentStyleClass";

public void encodeBegin(
  FacesContext context,
  UIComponent component) throws IOException
{
  super.encodeBegin(context, component);

  UIShowOne showOne = (UIShowOne)component;
  String clientId = showOne.getClientId(context);

  ViewHandler handler = context.getApplication().getViewHandler();
  String showItemURL = handler.getResourceURL(context,
                        "weblet://com.apress.projsf.ch9/showItem.htc");

  ResponseWriter out = context.getResponseWriter();
  writeScriptInline(context, "document.namespaces.add('pro',
                               'http://projsf.apress.com/tags');");
  out.write("<?import namespace=\"pro\"
                   implementation=\"" + showItemURL + "\" ?>");

  out.startElement("pro:showOneDeck", component);
  out.writeAttribute("id", clientId, null);
  out.writeAttribute("style", "display:block;", null);
}
```

Before you write anything to the client, you need to obtain the component's unique identifier: clientId. You do this by calling the getClientId() method on the UIShowOne instance passed as an argument to the Renderer. You include this unique identifier in the generated markup to ensure that you will be able to decode the request and apply any values or events to the right component on postback. For more information about the clientId, see Chapter 2.

You then use weblets to obtain the resource URL of the <pro:showItem> HTC component that will be used to set the implementation attribute on the <?import> processing instruction. This is an alternative solution to the doImport() method used in the HtcAjaxInputDateRenderer (see Code Sample 9-18) to import an element behavior.

You get the ResponseWriter and write out the first element (<pro:showOneDeck>) representing the component.

The <pro:showOneDeck> component relies on the Dojo toolkit and D^2 project to be able to asynchronously communicate with the server. To ensure that these resources are loaded to the client and written only once, you will use the semantics behind the writeScriptResource() method, as shown in Code Sample 9-23.

Code Sample 9-23. *The* HtcAjaxShowOneDeckRenderer encodeResources() *Method*

```
protected void encodeResources(
  FacesContext context,
  UIComponent  component) throws IOException
{
  super.encodeResources(context, component);

  writeScriptResource(context, "weblet://org.dojotoolkit.browserio/dojo.js");
  writeScriptResource(context, "weblet://net.java.dev.d2/d2.js");
}
```

In the encodeChildren() method, as shown in Code Sample 9-24, you check to see whether this UIShowOne component has any children at all. If the application developer has not added any children, you do not need to render this instance of the UIShowOne component to the client. You then collect information about which default UIShowItem id to display and which style classes to use for the child items.

Code Sample 9-24. *The* encodeChildren() *Method*

```
public void encodeChildren(
  FacesContext context,
  UIComponent  component) throws IOException
{
  if (component.getChildCount() > 0)
  {
    UIShowOne showOne = (UIShowOne)component;
    String showItemId = showOne.getShowItemId();

    Map attrs = showOne.getAttributes();
    String styleClass = getItemStyleClass(attrs);
    String headerStyleClass = getItemHeaderStyleClass(attrs);
    String contentStyleClass = getItemContentStyleClass(attrs);
```

After that, you collect all children of the UIShowOne component, iterate over the list of children, and check whether each child is an instance of UIShowItem, as shown in Code Sample 9-25. If not, the child will not be rendered. If the child is a UIShowItem component instance, you gather the clientId and all attributes available on the UIShowItem component. The showItemId is then compared with the id of the current UIShowItem component, and based on the result, the active variable will be used as a true or false flag. This flag will later be used to set the active attribute on the <pro:showItem> tag to indicate whether this UIShowItem component should render its children.

Code Sample 9-25. *The* encodeChildren() *Method*

```
List children = component.getChildren();
for (Iterator iter = children.iterator(); iter.hasNext();)
{
  UIComponent child = (UIComponent) iter.next();
  if (child instanceof UIShowItem)
  {
    UIShowItem showItem = (UIShowItem)child;
    Map attrs = showItem.getAttributes();

    String id = showItem.getId();
    boolean active = (id.equals(showItemId));

    ResponseWriter out = context.getResponseWriter();
    out.startElement("pro:showItem", showItem);
    out.writeAttribute("itemId", id, null);
     if (styleClass != null)
       out.writeAttribute("styleClass", styleClass, ITEM_STYLE_CLASS_ATTR);
     if (headerStyleClass != null)
       out.writeAttribute("headerStyleClass", headerStyleClass,
                          ITEM_HEADER_STYLE_CLASS_ATTR);
     if (contentStyleClass != null)
       out.writeAttribute("contentStyleClass", contentStyleClass,
                          ITEM_CONTENT_STYLE_CLASS_ATTR);
    if (active)
      out.writeAttribute("active", Boolean.toString(active), null);
    out.writeAttribute("style", "display:block;", null);
```

In Code Sample 9-26, you then get the header facet from the UIShowItem component by calling the getHeader() method. This convenience method returns the named facet, header, if it exists; otherwise, it returns null. If the getHeader() method returns a facet, you call the _encodeAll() method to process any children of this facet. After the facet control, you use the active flag to determine whether this is the "active" UIShowItem component. If it is, you call the _encodeAll() method to start the encode process of any children to the UIShowItem component.

Code Sample 9-26. *The* `encodeChildren()` *Method*

```
        // the header facet
        UIComponent header = showItem.getHeader();
        if (header != null)
        {
          out.startElement("pro:headerFacet", null);
          _encodeAll(context, header);
          out.endElement("pro:headerFacet");
        }

        // the expanded item contents
        if (active)
        {
          _encodeAll(context, showItem);
        }

        out.endElement("pro:showItem");
      }
    }
  }
}
```

If you take a close look at the actual output required by the deck component, any children added will be at the end of the generated markup. This way, the `UIShowOne` component's renderer can quickly close the generated markup, as shown in Code Sample 9-27.

Code Sample 9-27. *The* `encodeEnd()` *Method*

```
public void encodeEnd(
  FacesContext context,
  UIComponent  component) throws IOException
{
  ResponseWriter out = context.getResponseWriter();
  out.endElement("pro:showOneDeck");
}
```

For the `UIShowOne` component, the `Renderer` is responsible for rendering its children, and thus this flag needs to be set to `true`, as shown in Code Sample 9-28.

Code Sample 9-28. *The* `getRendersChildren()` *Method*

```
public boolean getRendersChildren()
{
  return true;
}
```

The requirement has not changed since we first introduced the deck component. It has to be flexible enough to handle any type of child component that the application developer adds to the UIShowItem component. The UIShowItem component itself is not responsible for rendering its children, but an application developer may add a child container component in charge of rendering its children (for example, an HtmlPanelGroup component).

To be able to achieve this, you first render the beginning of the current state of this UIComponent to the ResponseWriter attached to the specified FacesContext. You then check whether the component is responsible for rendering its children. If it is, you call encodeChildren() on the component to start rendering its children. If the component is not responsible for rendering its children, you call getChildren() on the component. The getChildren() method returns a List of all children of the UIComponent. If this component has no children, an empty List is returned, and you close the generated markup by calling the encodeEnd() method on the component. If it has children, you recursively call the _encodeAll(), as shown in Code Sample 9-29, until all children have been rendered, and then you close the generated markup by calling the encodeEnd() method on the component.

Code Sample 9-29. *The* _encodeAll() *Method*

```
private void _encodeAll(
  FacesContext context,
  UIComponent  component) throws IOException
{
  component.encodeBegin(context);
  if (component.getRendersChildren())
  {
    component.encodeChildren(context);
  }
  else
  {
    List kids = component.getChildren();
    Iterator it = kids.iterator();
    while (it.hasNext())
    {
      UIComponent kid = (UIComponent)it.next();
      _encodeAll(context, kid);
    }
  }
  component.encodeEnd(context);
}
```

Remember, during the Apply Request Values phase, a method, processDecodes(), will be called on the UIViewRoot at the top of the component hierarchy. This processDecodes() method on the UIViewRoot will recursively call processDecodes() of each UIComponent in the component hierarchy. If a Renderer is present for any of these components, the UIComponent will delegate the responsibility of decoding to the Renderer. Code Sample 9-30 is identical to the encode() method in the first HtmlShowOneDeckRenderer introduced in Chapter 3. For more information about processDecodes(), please refer to Chapter 2.

Code Sample 9-30. *The* decode() *Method*

```
public void decode(
  FacesContext context,
  UIComponent component)
{
  ExternalContext external = context.getExternalContext();
  Map requestParams = external.getRequestParameterMap();
  String clientId = component.getClientId(context);
  String newShowItemId = (String)requestParams.get(clientId);
  if (newShowItemId != null && newShowItemId.length() > 0)
  {
    UIShowOne showOne = (UIShowOne)component;
    String oldShowItemId = showOne.getShowItemId();
    if (!newShowItemId.equals(oldShowItemId))
    {
      showOne.setShowItemId(newShowItemId);
      ShowEvent event = new ShowEvent(showOne, oldShowItemId, newShowItemId);
      event.queue();
    }
  }
}
```

Code Sample 9-31 shows all the getters for the different style classes supported by the HtcAjaxShowOneDeckRenderer.

Code Sample 9-31. *Getters for the* HtcAjaxShowOneDeckRenderer *Attributes*

```
  protected String getStyleClass(
    Map attrs)
  {
    return (String)attrs.get(STYLE_CLASS_ATTR);
  }

  protected String getItemStyleClass(
    Map attrs)
  {
    return (String)attrs.get(ITEM_STYLE_CLASS_ATTR);
  }

  protected String getItemHeaderStyleClass(
    Map attrs)
  {
    return (String)attrs.get(ITEM_HEADER_STYLE_CLASS_ATTR);
  }

  protected String getItemContentStyleClass(
    Map attrs)
  {
```

```
    return (String)attrs.get(ITEM_CONTENT_STYLE_CLASS_ATTR);
  }
}
```

Step 7: Registering a UIComponent and Renderer

For the HTC-Ajax implementation to work, you need to register the custom Renderers, as shown in Code Sample 9-32.

Code Sample 9-32. *The HTC Registration in the* faces-config.xml *File*

```
<?xml version="1.0" encoding="UTF-8" ?>
<!DOCTYPE faces-config
   PUBLIC "-//Sun Microsystems, Inc.//DTD JavaServer Faces Config 1.1//EN"
          "http://java.sun.com/dtd/web-facesconfig_1_1.dtd">
<faces-config xmlns="http://java.sun.com/JSF/Configuration" >
  <render-kit>
    <renderer>
      <component-family>com.apress.projsf.Document</component-family>
      <renderer-type>com.apress.projsf.Document</renderer-type>
      <renderer-class>
        com.apress.projsf.ch9.render.html.basic.HtmlDocumentRenderer
      </renderer-class>
  </renderer>
</render-kit>

<render-kit>
  ...
  <renderer>
      <component-family>javax.faces.Input</component-family>
      <renderer-type>com.apress.projsf.Date</renderer-type>
      <renderer-class>
        com.apress.projsf.ch9.render.htc.ajax.HtcAjaxInputDateRenderer
      </renderer-class>
    </renderer>
    <renderer>
      <component-family>com.apress.projsf.ShowOne</component-family>
      <renderer-type>com.apress.projsf.Deck</renderer-type>
      <renderer-class>
        com.apress.projsf.ch9.render.htc.ajax.HtcAjaxShowOneDeckRenderer
      </renderer-class>
    </renderer>
  </render-kit>
</faces-config>
```

Step 11: Registering a RenderKit and JSF Extension

Although you did not need to create a new RenderKit for the HTC solution, you still need to register a RenderKit with a unique RenderKit ID, as shown in Code Sample 9-33. You need this to ensure that you don't mix the HTC components with regular HTML components that work across multiple browsers.

Code Sample 9-33. *The HTC Registration in the* `faces-config.xml` *File*

```
<?xml version="1.0" encoding="UTF-8" ?>
<!DOCTYPE faces-config
   PUBLIC "-//Sun Microsystems, Inc.//DTD JavaServer Faces Config 1.1//EN"
          "http://java.sun.com/dtd/web-facesconfig_1_1.dtd">
<faces-config xmlns="http://java.sun.com/JSF/Configuration" >

  <render-kit>
    <!-- no renderkit-id, so these renderers are added to
         the default renderkit -->
    <renderer>
      <component-family>com.apress.projsf.Document</component-family>
      <renderer-type>com.apress.projsf.Document</renderer-type>
      <renderer-class>
        com.apress.projsf.ch9.render.html.basic.HtmlDocumentRenderer
      </renderer-class>
    </renderer>
  </render-kit>

  <render-kit>
    <render-kit-id>com.apress.projsf.htc.ajax[HTML_BASIC]</render-kit-id>
    <render-kit-class>
      com.apress.projsf.ch6.render.html.ajax.HtmlAjaxRenderKit
    </render-kit-class>
    <renderer>
      <component-family>javax.faces.Input</component-family>
      <renderer-type>com.apress.projsf.Date</renderer-type>
      <renderer-class>
        com.apress.projsf.ch9.render.htc.ajax.HtcAjaxInputDateRenderer
      </renderer-class>
    </renderer>
    <renderer>
      <component-family>com.apress.projsf.ShowOne</component-family>
      <renderer-type>com.apress.projsf.Deck</renderer-type>
      <renderer-class>
        com.apress.projsf.ch9.render.htc.ajax.HtcAjaxShowOneDeckRenderer
      </renderer-class>
    </renderer>
  </render-kit>
</faces-config>
```

As you can see, the `HtmlDocumentRenderer` is defaulted to use the basic HTML `RenderKit` since it is a basic HTML `Renderer`, whereas the `HtcAjaxInputDateRenderer` and `HtcAjaxShowOneDeckRenderer` are added to the `HtmlAjaxRenderKit`. Notice that you are reusing the `HtmlAjaxRenderKit` created in Chapter 6 but assigning it a new `RenderKit` ID (that is, `com.apress.projsf.htc.ajax[HTML_BASIC]`) to ensure that you are not mixing HTC-specific renderers with plain HTML renderers.

Step 12: Registering Resources with Weblets

You need to register the HTC resources (`inputDate.css`, `inputDate.htc`, `showOneDeck.css`, and `showOneDeck.htc`) as weblets, as shown in Code Sample 9-34, which will enable you to package these resources as part of the custom JSF component library.

Code Sample 9-34. *The Weblets Configuration File*

```
<?xml version="1.0" encoding="UTF-8" ?>
<weblets-config xmlns="http://weblets.dev.java.net/config" >

  <weblet>
    <weblet-name>com.apress.projsf.ch9</weblet-name>
    <weblet-class>net.java.dev.weblets.packaged.PackagedWeblet</weblet-class>
    <init-param>
      <param-name>package</param-name>
      <param-value>com.apress.projsf.ch9.render.htc.ajax.resources</param-value>
    </init-param>
    <mime-mapping>
      <extension>htc</extension>
      <mime-type>text/x-component</mime-type>
    </mime-mapping>
  </weblet>

  <weblet-mapping>
    <weblet-name>com.apress.projsf.ch9</weblet-name>
    <url-pattern>/projsf-ch9/*</url-pattern>
  </weblet-mapping>

</weblets-config>
```

Building Applications with JSF HTC Components

Figure 9-11 shows the end result of the JSF HTC `ProInputDate` implementation. As you can see, the page looks the same as the one you created in previous chapters, except that this page uses an HTC `Renderer`. This HTC Ajax implementation provides the same functionality as both the HTML Ajax and XUL Ajax implementations, where dates that are not selectable are marked red and dates outside the scope of the current month are gray. When the user enters a date and clicks a submit button, a full postback will occur, and the attached validator, if any, will be invoked.

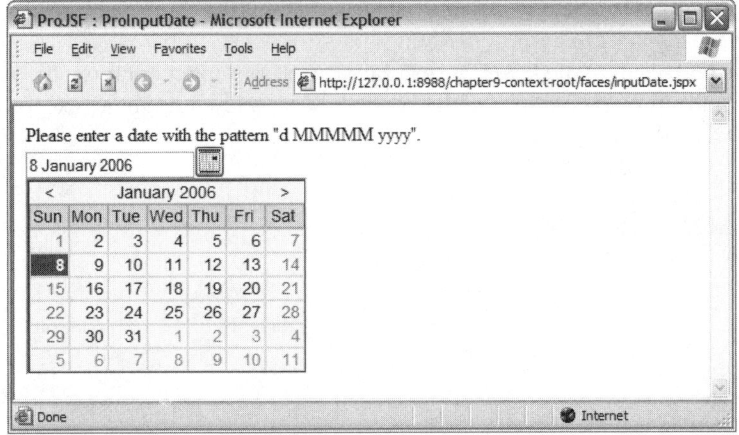

Figure 9-11. *The* `<pro:inputDate>` *component implemented in HTC*

Code Sample 9-35 shows the actual code behind this JSF page.

Code Sample 9-35. *JSF Page Source for HTC Implementation*

```
<?xml version="1.0" encoding="UTF-8" ?>
<jsp:root xmlns:jsp="http://java.sun.com/JSP/Page" version="1.2"
          xmlns:pro="http://projsf.apress.com/tags"
          xmlns:f="http://java.sun.com/jsf/core"
          xmlns:h="http://java.sun.com/jsf/html" >
  <jsp:directive.page contentType="application/x-javaserver-faces"/>
  <f:view>
    <pro:document title="Pro JSF : ProInputDate" >
      <h:form>
        <pro:inputDate id="dateField"
                       title="Date Field Component"
                       value="#{inputDateBean.date}" >
          <f:convertDateTime pattern="d MMMMM yyyy" />
          <pro:validateDate availability="#{inputDateBean.getAvailability}" />
        </pro:inputDate>
        <br/>
        <h:message for="dateField" />
        <br/>
        <h:commandButton value="Submit" />
        <br/>
        <h:outputText value="#{inputDateBean.date}" >
          <f:convertDateTime pattern="d MMMMM yyyy" />
        </h:outputText>
      </h:form>
    </pro:document>
  </f:view>
</jsp:root>
```

No changes to the application logic are required whatsoever! This is the same page you used for the XUL solution.

Figure 9-12 shows the end result of the JSF HTC `<pro:showOneDeck>` implementation. It looks the same as the previous implementations of the `<pro:showOneDeck>` component, except that this page uses an HTC `Renderer`.

Figure 9-12. `<pro:showOneDeck>` *implemented in HTC*

Code Sample 9-36 shows the actual code behind this JSF page.

Code Sample 9-36. *JSF Page Source for HTC Implementation*

```
<?xml version="1.0" encoding="UTF-8" ?>
<jsp:root ...>
  <jsp:directive.page contentType="application/x-javaserver-faces"/>
  <f:view>
      ...
      <pro:showOneDeck showItemId="first"
                       showListener="#{backingBean.doShow}">
        <pro:showItem id="first" >
          <f:facet name="header">
            <h:panelGroup>
              <h:graphicImage url="/resources/java_small.jpg" alt="The Duke"
                              style="margin-right: 8px; vertical-align:bottom;" />
              <h:outputText value="Java"/>
            </h:panelGroup>
          </f:facet>
          <h:panelGrid columns="1">
            <h:outputLink value="http://apress.com/book/bookDisplay.html?bID=10044">
              <h:outputText value="Pro JSF: Building Rich Internet Components"/>
      ...
  </f:view>
</jsp:root>
```

You are probably now telling yourself, "This is way cool! I have the same page source in three other solutions!" You are right, and that's the beauty of JSF! As we have said on multiple occasions, without impacting the application developer, you can create Rich Internet Components that support client-specific markup for optimized performance and responsiveness.

Summary

You have now completed four different solutions for the `ProInputDate` and `ProShowOneDeck` components. You used traditional HTML `Renderers`, HTML Ajax `Renderers`, XUL Ajax `Renderers`, and HTC Ajax `Renderers`. Who said JSF is not a rich client development platform?

With the experience you have gained so far, it is important to keep in mind that an application developer might be using your component in combination with other technologies that you did not even consider. You need to keep the abstraction for the application developer, and although tempting, you should not design your component with a dependency on the client-side rendered markup, since you do not have control over other components' generated markup.

One of things you want you to take from this chapter is that you should stay open to new and controversial suggestions; do not get locked into one technology stack because it is what you know or is what others tell you is the latest and greatest. Always ask yourself, "How can this solve my problems?"

After reading this chapter, you should have a clear understanding of what HTC is and how you can leverage it in your component design.

CHAPTER 10

■ ■ ■

Switching RenderKits Dynamically

Get used to working in components and only components, and you're future-proofed. Stick to JSF plus HTML hybrids, and someone is going to hate you in five years' time . . . .

—Duncan Mills, Java Evangelist, Oracle

Welcome to the last chapter of *Pro JSF and Ajax: Building Rich Internet Components*. This book has covered how JSF lets component writers mix and match technologies to streamline packaging and increase richness and user interactivity for their components. We have proven that JSF's component model can provide an abstraction layer on top of the underlying client-specific markup, which increases an application developer's productivity. We have also shown you that component writers can *manually* switch `RenderKits` without impacting the application developer or the actual application logic.

Now that you have a set of rich Internet components that support multiple client technologies at your disposal, only one question is left: how can you automatically select a `RenderKit` to deliver the proper markup to any user agent?

The main technology covered in this chapter is Oracle ADF Faces, which is a rich set of standard JSF components introduced in the fall of 2004. The Oracle ADF Faces component library provides various user interface components with built-in functionality, such as data tables, hierarchical tables, and color and date pickers. ADF Faces also includes many of the framework features most needed by JSF developers today.

After reading this chapter, you should be able to dynamically switch `RenderKits` and know how to set them up to detect different user agents, such as Mozilla GRE and Microsoft Internet Explorer.

Note At the time of writing this chapter, Oracle has completed the first step of donating the ADF Faces source code to the Apache Software Foundation. By the time this book hits the shelves, the Apache MyFaces community should be actively evolving the Oracle ADF Faces source code donation. For more information about the Apache MyFaces open source project, please visit `http://myfaces.apache.org`.

Requirements for Dynamically Switching RenderKits

The requirement is clear—the application developer wants to be able to dynamically change RenderKits, at runtime, based on the user agent. For example, if it is the Firefox browser requesting the page, the solution should serve XUL markup to the client.

A RenderKit's function is to help out with the delegation of Renderer to the UIComponent. A RenderKit groups instances of renderers of similar markup types, and in this book, you created RenderKits for HTML Ajax, Microsoft's DHTML/HTC, and Mozilla's XUL/XBL technologies. Each RenderKit is associated with a view (component hierarchy) as a UIViewRoot property at runtime. If an application developer wants to add a RenderKit with custom Renderers to the application, a RenderKit ID must be added to the application's JSF configuration file, as shown in Code Sample 10-1.

Code Sample 10-1. *Setting the Default* RenderKit *ID*

```
<?xml version="1.0" encoding="utf-8"?>
<!DOCTYPE faces-config PUBLIC
  "-//Sun Microsystems, Inc.//DTD JavaServer Faces Config 1.1//EN"
  "http://java.sun.com/dtd/web-facesconfig_1_1.dtd">
<faces-config xmlns="http://java.sun.com/JSF/Configuration">

  <application>
    <default-render-kit-id>com.apress.projsf.xul.ajax</default-render-kit-id>
  </application>
...
</faces-config>
```

This code sample shows the faces-config.xml file with the <default-render-kit-id> set to your custom XUL RenderKit. The faces-config.xml file is read once when the Web application is created and stored in the Application instance. The ViewHandler is responsible for returning the renderKitId for the current and subsequent requests from the client. It is important to understand that there can be only one default RenderKit per Web application, which is identified by a string (for example, com.apress.projsf.xul.ajax).

To solve the requirement of enabling access to the application with any browser and to provide a different RenderKit implementation for each browser, you have three tasks to complete in this chapter. First, you need to define the default RenderKit ID in the faces-config.xml file in such a way that you can dynamically set it at runtime. Second, you need to detect the user agent requesting the application. Third, you need to set the RenderKit ID using a ViewHandler. The custom ViewHandler is required if you want to have multiple RenderKit instances for the same application.

Note JSF 1.1 applications require a custom javax.faces.application.ViewHandler instance to dynamically select a RenderKit. However, JSF 1.2 adds support for directly specifying the RenderKit ID on the <f:view> tag of individual pages in a Web application.

The Dynamic RenderKit Implementation

Figure 10-1 shows the dynamic `RenderKit` solution.

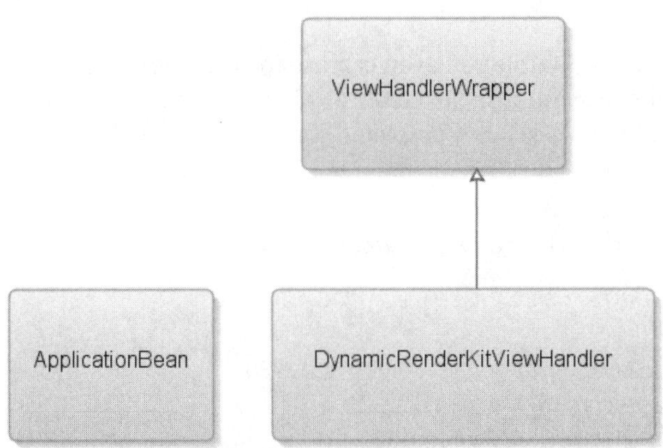

Figure 10-1. *Structure of dynamic* `RenderKit` *implementation*

The dynamic `RenderKit` solution contains three classes:

- `ViewHandlerWrapper` is a wrapper class that provides a loose coupling between the solution and the JSF implementation.
- `ApplicationBean` is a managed bean that contains logic to detect what agent has been used to request the application and contains information about what `renderKitId` to use.
- `DynamicRenderKitViewHandler` overrides the default `ViewHandler`'s `calculateRenderKitId()` method in order to get the correct ID from the `ApplicationBean`.

Syntax for Dynamic RenderKit ID

A feature in JSF that is often underutilized is the managed bean facility. This facility is not only useful for providing application logic, but you can also use it to initialize settings before launching the actual application. In this case, you will use the JSF EL syntax in the `faces-config.xml` file to set a pointer to the managed bean (for example, the `ApplicationBean`), which will be invoked and will return the correct `renderKitId` to the `ViewHandler` (see Code Sample 10-2).

Code Sample 10-2. *Setting the Default* `RenderKit` *ID*

```
<?xml version="1.0" encoding="utf-8"?>
<!DOCTYPE faces-config PUBLIC
  "-//Sun Microsystems, Inc.//DTD JavaServer Faces Config 1.1//EN"
  "http://java.sun.com/dtd/web-facesconfig_1_1.dtd">
<faces-config xmlns="http://java.sun.com/JSF/Configuration">
```

```
  <application>
    <default-render-kit-id>#{[managedBean].[property]}</default-render-kit-id>
  </application>
   ...
</faces-config>
```

With an explicit syntax shown in Code Sample 10-2, you can use the ViewHandler to first check the pattern of the string and then use the string to create a ValueBinding for the managed bean defined by the expression. In this case, the completed configuration would look something like Code Sample 10-3.

Code Sample 10-3. *Setting the Default* RenderKit *ID Using a Managed Bean*

```
<?xml version="1.0" encoding="utf-8"?>
<!DOCTYPE faces-config PUBLIC
  "-//Sun Microsystems, Inc.//DTD JavaServer Faces Config 1.1//EN"
  "http://java.sun.com/dtd/web-facesconfig_1_1.dtd">
<faces-config xmlns="http://java.sun.com/JSF/Configuration">

  <application>
    <default-render-kit-id>#{projsf.renderKitId}</default-render-kit-id>
  </application>
...
</faces-config>
```

In this case, the renderKitId is a JavaBean property of the ApplicationBean that returns the correct RenderKit identifier for the requesting user agent.

The Dynamic RenderKit Managed Bean

Let's look at the actual ApplicationBean class. Figure 10-2 shows the ApplicationBean in a class diagram, and in Code Sample 10-4, you can observe the User-Agent request header for choosing an appropriate RenderKit.

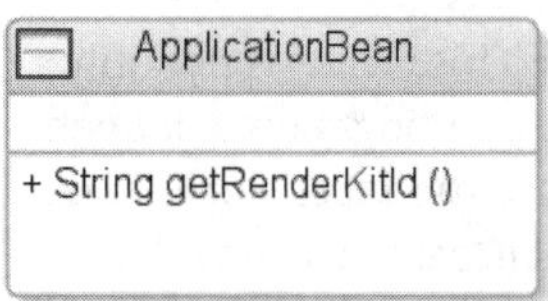

Figure 10-2. *Class diagram showing the* ApplicationBean *class*

Code Sample 10-4. *The* getRenderKitId() *Method with* User-Agent *Request Header*

```
package com.apress.projsf.ch10.application;

import java.util.Map;
```

```
import javax.faces.render.RenderKitFactory;
import javax.faces.context.FacesContext;
import javax.faces.context.ExternalContext;

/**
 * The ApplicationBean returns a dynamic RenderKit identifier, based on
 * the value of the User-Agent request header.
 */
public class ApplicationBean
{
  public String getRenderKitId()
  {
    FacesContext context = FacesContext.getCurrentInstance();
    ExternalContext external = context.getExternalContext();
    Map requestHeaders = getRequestHeaderMap();
    String userAgent = (String) requestHeaders.get("User-Agent");

    // Mozilla Firefox 1.0.7
    // Mozilla/5.0 (Windows; U; Windows NT 5.0; en-US; rv:1.7.12)
    // Gecko/20050915 Firefox/1.0.7
    if (userAgent.indexOf("Gecko/") != -1)
    {
      return "com.apress.projsf.xul.ajax";
    }
    // MS Internet Explorer 6.0
    // Mozilla/4.0 (compatible; MSIE 6.0; Windows NT 5.0)
    else if (userAgent.startsWith("Mozilla") &&
             userAgent.indexOf("MSIE") != -1)
    {
      return "com.apress.projsf.htc.ajax";
    }
    // Safari
    // Mozilla/5.0 (Macintosh; U; PPC Mac OS X; en-us)
    //             AppleWebKit/XX (KHTML, like Gecko) Safari/YY
    else if ((userAgent.indexOf("AppleWebKit") != -1) ||
             (userAgent.indexOf("Safari") != -1))
    {
      return "com.apress.projsf.html.ajax";
    }
    else
    {
      // default to standard HTML Basic for PDAs, etc.
      return RenderKitFactory.HTML_BASIC_RENDER_KIT;
    }
  }
}
```

In Code Sample 10-4, you are testing the User-Agent request header directly against known user agent identifiers to decide which RenderKit is appropriate to use in the response. Notice that some of the syntax for user agents can overlap, such as Mozilla appearing in the user agent header for Firefox, Internet Explorer, and Safari. Given the complexity of accurately parsing the wide range of possible User-Agent headers, it is best to reuse a common implementation rather than repeating the agent detection code each time it is needed.

Oracle ADF Faces provides a User-Agent abstraction to handle this case, and in Code Sample 10-5 we have simplified the ApplicationBean by leveraging some of the Oracle ADF Faces public APIs to obtain the user agent.

Code Sample 10-5. *The* getRenderKitId() *Method*

```
package com.apress.projsf.ch10.application;

import javax.faces.render.RenderKitFactory;

import oracle.adf.view.faces.context.AdfFacesContext;
import oracle.adf.view.faces.context.Agent;

/**
 * The ApplicationBean returns a dynamic RenderKit identifier, based on
 * the ADF Faces Agent name.
 */
public class ApplicationBean
{
  public String getRenderKitId()
  {
    AdfFacesContext afc = AdfFacesContext.getCurrentInstance();
    Agent agent = afc.getAgent();

    if (Agent.AGENT_GECKO.equals(agent.getAgentName()))
    {
      return "com.apress.projsf.xul.ajax";
    }
    else if (Agent.AGENT_IE.equals(agent.getAgentName()) &&
             Agent.TYPE_DESKTOP.equals(agent.getType()))
    {
      return "com.apress.projsf.htc.ajax";
    }
    else if (Agent.AGENT_WEBKIT.equals(agent.getAgentName()))
    {
      return "com.apress.projsf.html.ajax";
    }
    else
    {
      // default to standard HTML Basic for PDAs, etc.
```

```
      return RenderKitFactory.HTML_BASIC_RENDER_KIT;
    }
  }
}
```

From the `AdfFacesContext`, you can obtain the user agent by calling the `getAgent()` method. ADF Faces also comes with a set of predefined keys for each available Web client (for example, Microsoft Internet Explorer, Mozilla GRE, and so on). By comparing the agent name to these keys, you can determine which `renderKitId` to return.

The DynamicRenderKitViewHandler Class

Let's now look at the `DynamicRenderKitViewHandler` class. Figure 10-3 shows the `DynamicRenderKitViewHandler` in a class diagram, and in Code Sample 10-6, you can see how it uses the default `RenderKit` identifier as a base to locate agent-specific `RenderKits` for the incoming request.

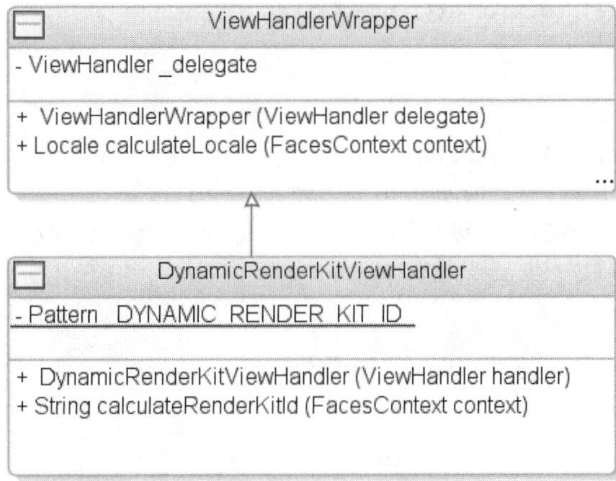

Figure 10-3. *Class diagram showing the* `DynamicRenderKitViewHandler` *implementation*

Code Sample 10-6. *The* `DynamicRenderKitViewHandler` *Class*

```
package com.apress.projsf.ch10.application;

import java.util.regex.Matcher;
import java.util.regex.Pattern;

import javax.faces.application.Application;
import javax.faces.application.ViewHandler;
import javax.faces.context.FacesContext;
import javax.faces.el.ValueBinding;
```

```
/**
 * The DynamicRenderKitViewHandler provides EL support
 * for the <default-render-kit-id> element in faces-config.xml.
 */
public class DynamicRenderKitViewHandler extends ViewHandlerWrapper
{
  public DynamicRenderKitViewHandler(
    ViewHandler handler)
  {
    super(handler);
  }

  public String calculateRenderKitId(
    FacesContext context)
  {
    String renderKitId = super.calculateRenderKitId(context);

    Matcher matcher = _DYNAMIC_RENDER_KIT_ID.matcher(renderKitId);
    if (matcher.matches())
    {
      String expression = matcher.group(1);
      Application application = context.getApplication();
      ValueBinding binding = application.createValueBinding(expression);
      if (binding.getType(context) == String.class)
        renderKitId = (String)binding.getValue(context);
    }

    // return either the calculated or dynamic RenderKit ID
    return renderKitId;
  }

  // Matches RenderKit identifier of the form "#{...}"
  static private final Pattern _DYNAMIC_RENDER_KIT_ID =
                              Pattern.compile("(\\Q#{\\E[^\\}]+\\Q}\\E)");
}
```

The DynamicRenderKitViewHandler overrides only one method, calculateRenderKitId(), which is used to calculate the RenderKit identifier to use for this request. You first calculate the RenderKit identifier by calling super. Then you detect whether the identifier is an expression that can be used to evaluate the dynamic RenderKit identifier. If it matches the EL-like syntax, you use the expression to create a ValueBinding that returns the value representing the renderKitId for this request. In practice, this will pick the right RenderKit for the browser accessing the application by following the dynamic RenderKit selection logic in your ApplicationBean.

Registering the Dynamic RenderKit Solution

You need to register the DynamicRenderKitViewHandler and the managed bean ApplicationBean with the component library in order for the dynamic switching to work (see Code Sample 10-7).

Code Sample 10-7. *Registering the Dynamic* RenderKit *Implementation*

```
<?xml version="1.0" encoding="UTF-8" ?>
<!DOCTYPE faces-config
   PUBLIC "-//Sun Microsystems, Inc.//DTD JavaServer Faces Config 1.1//EN"
          "http://java.sun.com/dtd/web-facesconfig_1_1.dtd">

<faces-config xmlns="http://java.sun.com/JSF/Configuration" >
  <factory>
    ...
  </factory>

  <application>
    <view-handler>
      com.apress.projsf.ch10.application.DynamicRenderKitViewHandler
    </view-handler>
  </application>

  <managed-bean>
    <managed-bean-name>projsf</managed-bean-name>
    <managed-bean-class>
       com.apress.projsf.ch10.application.ApplicationBean
    </managed-bean-class>
    <managed-bean-scope>application</managed-bean-scope>
  </managed-bean>
  ...
<faces-config>
```

First you set the <view-handler> to point to the custom ViewHandler—DynamicRenderKitViewHandler. Then you define the ApplicationBean in the same way most application developers would define their own managed beans. Notice that you set the managed bean on the application scope so that there will be only one instance for all Web applications.

You have now reached the end of this chapter—and the end of the book. You should now be able to dynamically switch RenderKits at runtime. This solution to switch RenderKits is not specific to the components created in this book; any component library can use the same technique with multiple RenderKits. Figure 10-4 shows how the deck component created in this book would look in three different devices.

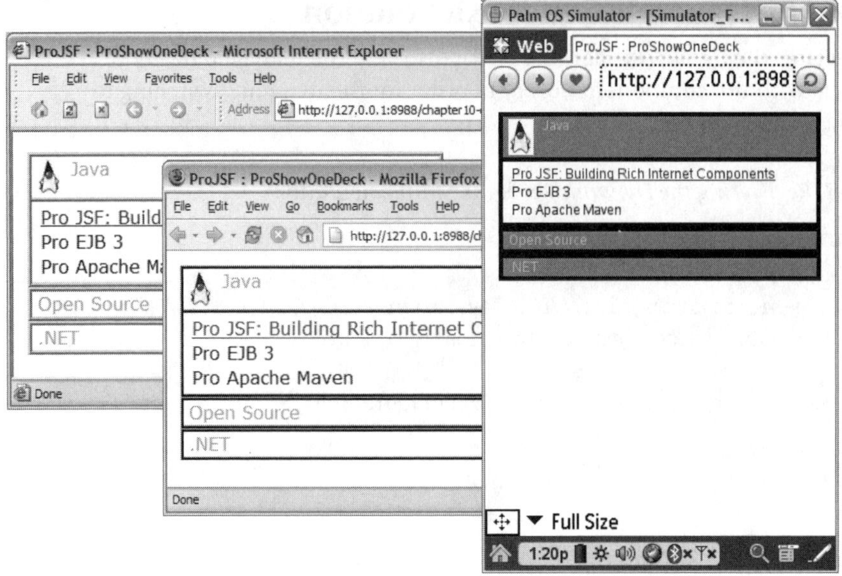

Figure 10-4. `ProShowOneDeck` *running in multiple clients using client-specific markup*

Summary

In this chapter, we showed you how easy it is to provide dynamic `RenderKit` switching with JSF. By using a component-driven design, application developers can build applications for any type of user agent without being impacted by the underlying client markup.

In the previous chapters, we demonstrated how you can write `Renderers` that support regular HTML, Ajax, XUL, and HTC. Some component writers are already looking at even more client technologies to provide application developers with a common programming model regardless of the user agent. A good example of this is the Oracle ADF Faces component library. It has built-in support for HTML, RIAs, character-based solutions, instant messenger clients such as Gaim and Yahoo, PDAs, and so on. The MyFaces open source project also provides an alternative `RenderKit` to HTML—the WML `RenderKit`.

Now that you know how to create reusable rich Internet components with JSF and how to use multiple `RenderKits`, we hope you will apply the techniques you have learned in this book to create your own custom components and build RIAs with JSF.

Index

C

D

E

F

H

L

M

N

O

P

Q–R

S

T

U